UNCORKED

The Life and Times of
Champagne Tony Lema

DAVID
CONGRATS
ON WINNING
" WHAT HOLE IS IT?"
ENJOY THE BOOK
YOUR NEIGHBOR,
Larry Baush

Larry Baush

ACES
PUBLISHING

9 Aces Publishing
Seattle, WA
info@9acespublishing.com

DEDICATION

For mom who loved the game of golf with a passion and passed that passion on to me. To dad who introduced me the game and to my loving wife who encouraged this project from the start.

CONTENTS

ACKNOWLEDGMENTS

My heartfelt thanks to Tony's family especially brother Harry and his wife Judi. Tony's other brother Walter and sister Bernice were also gracious with their time and stories. Ken Venturi, Jack Fry, Doc Giffin, Bobby Nichols, and Cliff Whittle were very generous with their time and provided great insights during interviews. Frederick Burger shared his research materials and interview notes for an article that he authored in the USGA publication *Golf Journal*, and these were a big help. Max Winters provided the insight that only a caddy and a friend could, and I thank him for his time. Thank you for the additional assistance via email from Jack Nicklaus and Peter Alliss.

PROLOGUE

Arnold Palmer was not going to be in the field at the 1964 British Open, played on the ancient links at the St. Andrews Old Course, but he would still be a factor in the outcome. He was exhausted, both mentally and physically, and felt that the trip across the Atlantic would take too much out of him.

Palmer would factor into the outcome, though, as he gave his friend Tony Lema, playing in his first British Open Championship, some advice on the finer points of negotiating links style golf. He also arranged for Lema to use Tip Anderson, the caddy employed by Palmer when he played in his first British Open in 1960, also held at the Old Course at St. Andrews.

Palmer gave Lema one other gift that would come in handy at St. Andrews—a Macgregor IMG Ironmaster—a blade putter similar to a George Low or Wilson 8802 model. Tony needed a new putter because he had smashed his previous putter a few months earlier at the Oklahoma City Open. He often fought to control his temper and in Oklahoma City; the temper won and the putter lost.

Armed with Palmer's caddy and putter, Tony arrived in St. Andrews for his first appearance in a British Open. He was one of only seven Americans to make the trip. At the time, the cost of traveling to the UK, along with archaic qualifying rules and a relatively low purse, kept most American players away. He arrived late in Scotland and was only able to make a perfunctory study of the intriguing links during two abbreviated practice rounds.

Jack Nicklaus also made the trip to St. Andrews for the Open. He was riding the crest of a wave that saw him challenge, and eventually overtake Palmer as the best golfer in the world. Nicklaus had been on a tear since coming out on the tour as a rookie in 1962, having won eight PGA

1

tournaments, including three majors: the U.S. Open in 1962, the Masters in 1963 and the PGA Championship in 1963.

The British bookmakers made Nicklaus the favorite and put him on the tote board at 7-to-2 odds in the British Open. Tony, listed next at 7-to-1, was in the midst of a torrid hot streak of his own during the past five weeks as he captured the Thunderbird Classic, the Buick Open, and the Cleveland Open—the last in a playoff against Palmer. In between, he finished 20th in the U.S. Open and 6th in the Whitemarsh Open the week before the British Open. Nicklaus won the Whitemarsh and in the process took the lead atop the PGA official money earnings list while Tony sat in the third spot.

Tony started playing very good golf beginning in the fall of 1962, continuing on through 1963 and the first half of 1964. He attributed his fine play to falling in love, and marrying in 1963, the former Betty Cline, whom he met when she was working as an airline flight attendant. Before falling in love with Betty, Tony lived the life of a playboy on tour.

In the months leading up to the 1964 British Open, he waffled between making the long trip to Scotland or not. Palmer, a close friend, encouraged him to make the trip, as did his business manager Fred Corcoran, an avid supporter of international golf. "I just want to see how they operate things over there," Tony finally said at the Whitemarsh Open announcing he would make the trip.

As he boarded the plane for his departure to Scotland, he told reporters, "I've won tournaments, and I've won money, now I want to win a major championship. It is on my schedule of things to do, and I am going to do it." Brimming with confidence, Tony knew that a major championship solidifies a golfer's place in history.

He fought off a spirited challenge by Nicklaus to arrive at the 18th tee of the final round with a comfortable lead. As he skillfully played a classic bump and run approach shot to the green the crowd rushed forward surrounding him. He fought through the crowd and emerged feeling exuberant and proud. He tapped in his short putt for a birdie and then threw the ball into the crowd as a major champion. He had capped off a true rags-to-riches saga and sat poised to assume the role of one of golf's superstars.

It is difficult to find a more popular champion than Tony Lema. His engaging style, sense of humor, generosity and champagne parties with the press after each of his victories made him one of golf's most endearing superstars. He was confident without being cocky, funny in a self-deprecating way, fashionable devoid of flamboyancy and charitable without trumpeting his kindness.

Inspired by Walter Hagen, he

emulated the style and countenance that Sir Walter exemplified. Tony took Hagen's maxim: to take time to smell the flowers along the way, to heart.

Part One
Growin' Up

1 COMING TO AMERICA
1898 - 1934

Antoine Harry Lima was born in Hamilton, Bermuda Island on July 24, 1898, to parents who emigrated from Portugal in search of a better life. When Antoine, who went by the name of Tony, was just shy of his 18th birthday, he too, set off to find a better life and his destination was America. He set sail on the vessel *Bermudian* for New York, and entered the country through Ellis Island on May 15, 1916. Like many immigrants before him, Antoine's name was butchered by officials who processed the paperwork. He entered his new homeland under the name of Toney Harry Lema. Tone, as family and friends knew him, was a laborer who would make his living with the strength of his body and the sweat of his brow.

Shortly, the lure of a better life drew him westward to California, viewed widely as a land of opportunity by many new immigrants to America, especially those of Portuguese descent. In California, they found work in the fields or in industry. Tone's destination was the central part of California.

After spending time with relatives in Byron, in Northern California, he was soon drawn by the lure of the city. He could earn better wages in the city and set off for Oakland.

Tone carved out a new life in Oakland and started to make a little money, although he was not rich by any means. He was doing well enough to pose for a portrait, a sign of the times of an up-and-coming man. In the photograph, he stands in a familiar pose next to a carved wooden pedestal against a painted country scene. Tone is dressed in a handsome suit and tie with a pair of polished, lace-up dress jodhpurs. He was not a tall man standing maybe 5'7" or 5'8", and his handsome broad face smiles at the camera under a full, thick mane of black hair. His body is slim, yet athletic and powerful.

Clotilda Silva was born in Waipahu, Oahu in the Hawaiian Islands, at that time a territory, on February 3, 1910. Her parents, Manuel and Probata, arranged for their passage to the Hawaiian Islands by entering into an agreement with an agent whereby they became indentured servants on a plantation. Many Canary Island immigrants utilized this route as a means of getting to America.

Once the term of indenture was complete, they continued to work in Hawaii. They had a master plan: they would save their money so they could move to the mainland of America. Soon enough, they met their goal and set sail for Oakland, California.

Upon arrival, the family set stakes down in Oakland, and Manuel went about finding work. He worked a number of jobs as a laborer around Oakland, as Cleo continued to grow into a young woman. The family saved their money and soon purchased land with a large main house and another much smaller house. Manuel eventually landed a job with the C&H sugar factory under the Carquinez Bridge that spanned the Carquinez Strait, north of Oakland. He became acquainted with another laborer at the factory, a young man also of Portuguese descent, and Tone Lema and Manuel soon became friends.

Manuel liked Tone. It dawned on him that Tone might make a good match for his daughter. Manuel, not the least bit disturbed by the seven-year difference in the ages between Tone and his daughter, decided he would get the ball rolling by bringing Tone home for dinner. Manuel informed Cleo, that he found a man for her, to which she replied, "I can find my own man, thank-you very much." Despite this inauspicious start, a romance blossomed between the two.

It was love at first sight. A courtship soon followed, and the two wed on December 17, 1927 in St. Joseph's Portuguese Church in a Catholic service conducted by the Reverend Joseph Galli.

Tone was 25-years-old, and Cleo just eighteen when the two married. Their wedding photograph shows a stocky, yet handsome Tone, dressed in a suit. Next to him, standing at least as tall as the short groom was his new bride. Cleo wore a lace wedding dress with matching headpiece and held a bouquet of flowers.

The newlyweds began their new life together in the small house located on the Silva property at 2203 92nd Avenue.

Cleo gave birth to the couple's first child, a daughter they christened Bernice Marie, on August 21, 1928. Tone continued to work various manual labor jobs and although not rich, the young couple managed to get by. As the economy took a drastic turn for the worse when the stock market crashed in 1929, the young family struggled to make due on Tone's wages. It was around this time that Tone and Cleo conceived their second child.

On July 17, 1930, the couple added a son and gave him his father's middle name Harry. Tone reveled in his role as a father rushing home from a hard day's work to dote on his children.

Two years later the family budget stretched even further with another mouth to feed. A son, Walter was born on October 28, 1931. Despite the tough times, Cleo and Tone took great pride and felt excitement about their growing family.

On February 25, 1934, in the midst of the depression, Cleo gave birth to the couple's fourth child. Anthony David Lema, known as Tony, was a bright faced, cute baby with a quick smile. The family's home could hardly contain the family with any sense of comfort as the four children shared one room.

2 TOUGH TIMES
1934 - 1947

Jobs across the country were very scarce during the depression. As a result, many out-of-work Americans and displaced farmers looked to California for hope. Although some work in agriculture or industry in the state remained, wages plummeted to a fraction of their pre-depression levels.

Despite the economic turmoil that surrounded him, Antoine continued to work various jobs and managed to keep the house on 92nd Avenue in the family's hands. Cleo and Tone managed to keep their children fed and clothed so that they lived like children, at least for the times.

In 1937, Tone found himself in need of work and found he qualified for a project administered by the WPA. The WPA paid hourly wages that were equivalent to the prevailing wages paid in the area of the project, so the pay was good, for the times, and the money helped at home to feed his four children. His assignment, a project digging trenches for a new sewer line, was backbreaking work where he toiled in all kinds of weather.

One day, Tone came home from work feeling ill and went straight to bed. He had the typical symptoms of pneumonia - a cough, chest pain, fever and difficulty breathing. Cleo and her mother cared for the bed-ridden Tone. When Tone became ill, antibiotics were not widely available.

Without antibiotics, Tone's condition continued to worsen. Over the next couple days, as Tone fought a losing battle against the infection, the family grew more and more concerned.

"We need to get him to a doctor," Probata told Cleo.

However before he could get medical attention, his condition turned critical. During the night, he lost his battle against the infection, lost consciousness, and passed away.

The loss was devastating to the family. Cleo lost a husband and a lover. The children lost a caring and loving father. The family lost the head of the household and the main wage earner.

Cleo now faced the daunting task of raising four small children alone during the hardest economic times this country has ever faced. She worked hard to provide for her children. She possessed incredible strength, faith and guile needed to raise a family under the most terribly trying conditions. The challenge must have been overwhelming, but she faced the situation and was resolute that she would prevail. Drawing on her Catholic faith, a strong work ethic, and help from her family, she persevered.

It was never easy for Cleo, however. She immediately set out to find work to support her family and she soon landed a job selling women's clothing in a store in downtown Oakland. Each day, after putting in a full shift at the store, she returned home to feed and raise her children. Her parents, mostly her mother Probata, helped keep an eye on the growing children while Cleo worked. Harry, the eldest son recalled years later that the four children spent time with the grandparents while Cleo worked, but "we never felt like we were at a babysitters or anything like that."

Growing up, the boys did the typical things of boys that age. They played athletic games like football, baseball and kick-the-can with the other kids in the neighborhood. During these games, Tony began to show a natural athletic ability and grace. He also exhibited a great deal of stamina. He began to grow into a tall lanky frame and developed great hand-eye coordination. Although adept in the games of sandlot football and baseball, he excelled at basketball.

A short time after Tone's death, Cleo moved the family from the small house on 92nd Avenue to a house on 105th Avenue located at the foot of the Oakland Hills. The new home provided a little more room while remaining a short distance away from her parents.

The 1930s was especially hard for the Lema family. While still struggling to scratch out an existence for her family, Cleo lost her mother in 1939 and her father in April of 1940.

Cleo was now truly alone, save for the help she received from her brothers, to raise four young children. Harry, the eldest son, decided he wanted to be a priest when he was in his early teens and entered seminary school across the bay from Oakland. Although saddened to see her son leave home to study, Cleo had one less mouth to feed.

The remaining two boys, Walter and Tony, were closest in age of the four siblings and spent a great deal of time together. Tony always had to be moving, involved in some activity. Cleo worried about her child's hyperactivity and consulted the family doctor who advised Cleo to wear him out physically. After work, and before fixing the evening meal, she would play catch with him in the driveway.

Walter and Tony began their schooling at St. Bernard's School, a Catholic school on 62nd Street in Oakland. Each day, Cleo found time to cook oatmeal-raisin cookies and laid them out on the counter for the boys to snack on after school. Walter and Tony rushed home from school, ate the cookies, and joined their friends at a local church with an upstairs gym. There, they would spend the rest of the afternoon playing basketball. Tony had a natural, athletic grace that he got from his mother's side of the family.

At times, Tony's restlessness presented a challenge to the nuns at St. Bernard's. Tony found it extremely difficult to remain in his assigned seat. Finally, the nuns called Cleo to explain the problem. Cleo sat her youngest child down and tried to explain to him that he had to stay in the seat assigned to him.

"But, I don't like that seat," the young boy complained. "It's in the front row—I don't like the front row."

"Just stay at the desk the Sisters assign to you," Cleo pleaded.

Cleo tried very hard to provide activities for her children, especially the fidgety Tony. Unable to afford bicycles for the children, she gave them roller skates every Christmas. She also bought herself a pair and joined her children, out in the street, where they skated up and down the block.

The American economy recovered with the outbreak of World War II as American factories supplied the allied fighting forces with the weapons, ammunition, and supplies needed to fight Germany, Japan, and Italy. The Lema family made it through the war years on the strength and shrewdness of Cleo.

"I don't know how she did it," Harry marveled. "She was incredibly strong and somehow kept our family together. We all grew very close because of it."

When Walter and Tony were in their early teens, they made their way up the hill to Lake Chabot Golf Course, a municipal course built in 1923. They heard a boy could make some good money by working as a caddy. In the days before golf carts, many players paid a caddy to carry their clubs around the course. A caddy could make between one and two dollars for their work which was a lot of money for a young teenage boy.

Exposed to golf for the first time as a caddy, Tony became interested in the game. With his athletic ability and hand-eye-coordination, he quickly picked up the game. He played the game whenever caddies were allowed on the course. In the late afternoons, the caddies would form one big gang to play a few holes. Tony was a natural.

Walter picked up a regular job as a caddy for Dan McCaffery. On the days he played, McCaffery would pick Walter up at home and Tony rode along to the course. McCaffery noticed Tony's interest in the game and cobbled together a set of clubs for him. He made the set up from his old, unused clubs. The head pro at Lake Chabot, Dick Fry, gave him the occasional pointer and Tony developed strategy on how to play by watching the better players while he caddied. Fry's son, Johnny helped his father run the pro shop and often played with Tony providing a competitive environment that spurred him.

Tony loved the game and developed a hunger to get better. What appealed to him about the game was the individuality of the sport; there were no teammates to blame when things went bad—or to share the glory when things went well. Fry encouraged Tony's enthusiasm by allowing him to play without charge. Soon, Fry put young Tony to work doing odd jobs around the pro shop and driving range.

As he reached his teens, he had no trouble making friends. He was fun to be around, extremely friendly, good at sports and liked to have a good time laughing at jokes or pranks. His two best friends were Bill Craig and Chet Smith. The three boys began spending all their free time together, to the point that Tony's sister Bernice referred to the boys as the "Three Musketeers."

3 HIGH SCHOOL
1947 - 1952

Cleo often worked two jobs including one clerking in a drug store. Cleo was too proud to accept welfare. She had to keep a roof over her children's heads and to put food on the table. However, holding down two jobs left her children with unsupervised time on their hands, time in which they could find trouble, especially the baby of the family, Tony.

In the years just prior to entering high school, as well as during his high school years, Tony was a handful for Cleo. The only thing that could keep him out of trouble was golf. When he spent his time at Lake Chabot caddying and working for Dick Fry around the pro shop, or on the driving range, he avoided trouble. Unless, he skipped school to play golf.

Cleo revealed years later, "There were times that Tony took my last dollar for greens fees and then would play hooky to go play golf." Cleo felt he should be spending more time studying and less time chasing a little white ball around a golf course.

Even so, Tony grew more serious about the game and soon started to play in local tournaments. He played in the few junior tournaments held in the area, as well as tournaments that featured grown men in the field. When he was a 14-year-old, he entered the Oakland City Championship, for the first time, qualifying to compete in the fifth flight. He lost to Wilbur Davis in an early round.

He enrolled at St. Joseph's High School, a Catholic parish high school located on Chestnut Street in Alameda. His brother, Walter was a standout student. St. Joe's, affiliated with the Notre Dame High School for girls, was billed as a co-educational high school; however, the sexes were segregated in the classroom and in activities.

Walter was a quiet and very bright student, and earned high grades in all his classes at St. Joe's. Meanwhile, Tony earned mediocre grades as he could not focus on schoolwork. Today, he most likely would be diagnosed as having ADHD. Some aspects of high school life, mostly the social facets, agreed with Tony, but he had conflicts with authority.

He continued to excel at sports, especially basketball. Tony played basketball for the boys club and the CYO team, and once enrolled at St. Joe's, he went out for the freshman basketball team. He excelled due mainly to his great shooting skills. Near the end of his freshman year, however, Tony was summarily kicked out of St. Joe's. What happened?

"Oh, I don't know," recalled John Fry who went to St. Joe's at the same time. "He either mouthed off to the principal, or he got in a fight during basketball, something like that. Tony had a bit of an attitude, you know."

Lacking the stabilizing force of a father figure, Tony was adrift and well down the path towards juvenile delinquency. After expulsions from more than one other high school, he ended up at St. Elizabeth High School, a Catholic diocesan institution located in the Fruitvale district of Oakland. The Franciscan fathers who ran the high school sat him down and explained that expulsion out of St. Elizabeth was not an option. They were prepared to do whatever it took to get him to graduation, which included tough love, discipline, and hard work.

Near St. Elizabeth High School, Tony stumbled upon the Poor Clares, an order of Franciscan nuns. The Poor Clares were a cloistered order, never showing their faces to anyone outside the order. A thick, large drape concealed them from parishioners who came to worship. Tony, who enjoyed a good scare, found the church, with the cloistered nuns, spooky, and often visited. He spoke with the nuns about spiritual matters and prayed with them.

Although he had a spiritual side, Tony succumbed to pressure from his peers, which landed him on the fringes of trouble. His mischief was never too serious, but there were a few close run-ins with the law. His partners in crime were Bill Craig and Chet Smith.

"We would booze it up quite a bit, and that is the worst thing kids can do," recalled Tony in a 1963 *Sports Illustrated* profile written by Gwilym S. Brown. "It gave us a lot of false courage, and we always wound up in a batch of trouble. I was fortunate never to get caught. It was part of my life I'd like to do all over again."

The three boys scraped together enough cash to buy a car. Because of the war, it was difficult to find gas and the boys found it increasingly challenging to keep fuel in the car. Bill Craig lived next door to an officer of the California Highway Patrol. The boys found the patrol car parked in front of the neighbor's house, always with a full tank of gasoline, a tempting source of fuel. They regularly siphoned off enough gas to fuel their exploits in the old car. On more than one occasion, the officer caught the boys and chased them off.

Other incidents could have been serious for Tony and his friends. One time, the three boys attempted to force a younger girl into a car. The girl diffused the situation by explaining to police that the boys were simply pulling a prank. Yet, another time, the three discovered an unattended beer delivery truck parked in front of a store, with the back door wide-open. One of them crept to the back of the truck, snatched a case of beer from it, and hustled back to their car.

Unfortunately, they pulled their caper off in full view of one of Oakland's finest who subsequently followed the boys. Rather than enjoying a beer party, the boys received a stern lecture. The cop seized their stolen property and left to return it to its rightful owner. If not for the benevolence of the cop, Tony could have found himself in serious trouble.

Other than those small incidents, he largely kept himself out of serious trouble by spending most of his time on the golf course. He played at Lake Chabot, often with John Fry, and dreaming of bigger things.

"I remember one time we were walking from the eighth green at Chabot to the ninth tee and we talked about which of us would be the first one with our name on a set of golf clubs," John Fry remembers. "Of course, we both thought we would be the first."

Tony was starting to get some tournament experience and it fired up his competitive nature. He wanted to improve and play well under tournament conditions where it takes much more than just a good golf swing to succeed. To play tournament golf and win, a player must be both in control of his emotions and have the right positive mindset to win.

Tony learned some of the finer points on the emotional side of the game from Lucius Bateman, an African-American who worked at the Airways Fairways Driving Range near the Oakland airport. Bateman was instrumental in the development of many young golfers in the Oakland area.

Bateman, introduced to golf as an 11-year-old caddy at the Edgewater Hotel and Golf Club near his home in Biloxi, Mississippi, taught himself the game. He worked hard and made his way up the ranks to head caddy, which provided him with playing privileges at the course. He threw himself into the game playing whenever he could and held the course record at Edgewater with a 69.

At Airways, Bateman allowed kids to hit balls, free of charge, at the driving range in the late afternoon as long as they helped him pick up balls on the range. He was very adept at teaching kids the finer points of the golf swing.

Rig Ballard, the owner of Airways, said that Bateman "had a knack of being able to spot flaws in a youngster's play without disturbing him."

Nevertheless, Bateman was discriminating when it came to choosing students.

"If they don't learn to be sportsmen as well as golfers, Lucius won't bother with them." Ballard said. "He holds that in highest esteem. Being a gentleman is most important."

Bateman had no time for kids who "mess around and get in trouble."

He arrived early in the morning to open the range and he worked until the early afternoon. He would then fit in a round of golf at the Alameda municipal course before returning to the range to work with kids in the late afternoon and early evening.

He never charged for the advice and expertise he provided. He could not charge for lessons without jeopardizing his amateur status. Becoming a professional golfer was not an option because of the Caucasian-only clause in the PGA by-laws at the time. He pursued his amateur career by playing in a number of amateur events with some success. His greatest success as a player, though, came in money games on the municipal courses around the Bay Area. What he learned in these fierce competitions, with real cash on the line, he passed on to the young players that came to learn the game at Airways Fairways.

"Lucius had street smarts," recalled John Fry. "He had a twinkle in his eye that told you he knew something that you didn't and he taught the kids course management and how to think their way around the course. He had some great players like John McMullen who played on the tour and damn near won the first tournament he played in out there."

Ken Venturi described Bateman saying, "That man knew a lot about the golf swing."

Bateman met Tony while playing in the Oakland City Champions event where Tony caddied. Tony knew of Bateman because of his work with Don Whitt, a very good Bay Area player who later played on the PGA Tour. Tony approached Bateman about helping him, and soon they started working together, as well.

"He didn't come right out and ask me," Bateman recalled years later when explaining how he came to work with Tony, "but he was a bright looking kid and we just kind of liked each other from the start. I started working with him along with a lot of kids I helped."

Bateman usually avoided kids with a propensity for trouble, but he saw something special in Tony.

"Tony would jump school a lot," Bateman later explained, "but he was a wide awake kid growing up in the war years and just after, restless without a father."

The two made a unique pair in the segregated days of the mid-1950s; a black man teaching a poor white kid a rich white man's game.

Even though the Bay Area did not suffer from the same degree of racial segregation as some other parts of the country, it was still rare for a black man to take a white child under his wing. "There's a kinship that goes beyond what color you are," Bateman explained.

The two would meet at the Alameda municipal course, which had a big practice field where Bateman began refining Tony's swing and game.

"Tony was a scraggly little kid who loved golf," Bateman remembered. "At first I didn't think he was going to be a very good golfer. He didn't seem to have much talent, but he was a fighter."

Tony began to improve dramatically, a typical result for a Bateman protégé, and tested himself whenever possible by playing both tournament golf and in money games. He developed a short game with a deft touch around the greens. Still quite skinny, he did not have the length off the tee that most of his competitors exhibited, but made up for his lack of distance with a stellar short game.

Eventually, Bateman started to take Tony to the toughest East Bay courses and the two challenged all comers to a best-ball match. To many unsuspecting souls, the black man and the skinny white kid appeared to be pushovers. It was not difficult finding opponents for a money game. "Tony was impressive in those money matches," Bateman said. "He would always come through in the clutch on key holes to help us win."

Bateman would tell Tony before these matches that he should be confident in the talent he had, play up to it, and, most importantly, "don't choke." Tony, who seldom choked, began to build a mental toughness as his confidence grew.

Bateman also impressed upon him the need to study good golfers to learn from their games. To this end, Tony and a friend decided to drive down to Monterey to watch the stars of the PGA Tour in the last round of the Crosby tournament. Both boys were about 16-years-old, and neither one had money to purchase a ticket into the event. They did what almost any teenage boy would do, they snuck onto the grounds. As they were wandering the course, a marshal came up and asked to see their tickets.

"Uh, we lost them," was the best reply they could muster.

Apparently, the marshal bought the story and allowed the two boys to stay. Another marshal soon approached the pair and requested to see their tickets. This time the lost tickets story did not fly and the marshal escorted the two boys off the premises. "That's okay," Tony told his friend, "one day I'll return and win this tournament."

By the time Tony was old enough to drive, he began looking for summer employment that would leave his days free for golf. Bateman provided a job at the driving range; however, the pay was not nearly enough for him to help with the financial needs at home.

"It was tough on my mother with four kids to raise," said Tony in the *Sports Illustrated* feature, "but we hung together. I've worked in shipyards, drugstores, car factories, canneries, gas stations and grocery stores; any possible way I could to make a buck. I took the swing shift at the shipyard just so I could play golf during the day."

Tony took to cars and driving with enthusiasm and he always liked to drive fast. He would later say that if he were not a professional golfer, then he would have been a drag race car driver.

One evening Tony left the house on his way to his job at a Heinz cannery. Around the same time, his brother, Harry, left the house to pick up a date across town. Tony sped away and was out of Harry's sight quickly, but when Harry turned a corner, he noticed that a police car had pulled another car over on the shoulder of the street. As Harry pulled past the two cars, he looked over and noticed that the cop had pulled Tony over. Harry tapped the horn, chuckled, waved and continued on to pick up his date. Despite his trouble with the cop, Tony had a chuckle, too.

Another time, the police chief of San Leandro had Tony in his office for speeding through the working-class suburb of Oakland. He ended his stern lecture saying, "Get the hell out of town and back to Oakland where you belong."

Tony never had too much money, only what he could earn working the odd jobs he landed. He always seemed to be broke, looking for a way to get his hands on some money. He attempted to augment his income by gambling for small amounts with other teenage boys at Lake Chabot.

"I remember we would park our cars up around the eighteenth green at Chabot," John Fry recalls. "We would park the cars so that our headlights were focused on the green and then in the dark we would chip and pitch to the green for quarters."

One of the other contestants in those chipping contests was a young man and accomplished amateur named Jerry Kroeckel. Kroeckel and Tony spent a great deal of time practicing together on the driving range at Lake Chabot.

One contemporary, quoted anonymously in the 1963 *Sports Illustrated* column said, "Tony hustled more than a few bucks on the golf course, but he was always poor. When he lost a $5 bet the money was slow coming. When he won, he wanted it quick."

Tony's lack of funds was apparent in the rag-tag collection of clubs that made up his set and in the threadbare quality of his clothes. When he showed up to play in tournaments, it was obvious that he was a player from a "muni," not a country club.

Tony arrived for a tournament at Harding Park, where Ken Venturi's parents, Fredrico and Ethyl, ran the pro shop. When Ethyl Venturi caught a glimpse of the beat-up, worn-out shoes, complete with the sole flapping loose, that Tony was wearing, she grabbed a box of new shoes off the shelf and gave them to the boy. Some versions of the story depict Tony wearing old tennis shoes instead of golf shoes. Either way, the generosity of Mrs. Venturi provided Tony with the new pair of golf shoes he obviously needed.

Tony and John Fry traveled around the Bay Area playing in as many tournaments as they could find. Sometimes one of them would drive or Fry's sister would chauffer them. In other instances, they were able to share a ride with another competitor. As a last resort, they would hitchhike.

"I remember one time we were playing in the National Juniors at the Stanford course in Palo Alto. Tony drove us to the course. He and I met in the quarterfinals of the event and I made a miraculous par on the last hole to send the match into a playoff. I hit a terrible drive, and had to chip out to the fairway. Tony hit a beautiful drive then hit his approach over the green. I hit a good shot up to the green and he chipped on and three-putted. I made the putt to win the match and he was so angry he almost left me there," John Fry recalled years later with a laugh.

Tony's temper cost him strokes on the course when it flared. Though he was quick to anger, it passed quickly. His temper manifested itself in the form of thrown and slammed down clubs, as well as some colorful language. He struggled with his temper throughout much his career.

"I remember playing with Tony at Chabot one time," John Fry reminisced. "We were playing the thirteenth hole which is a short par 4 up the hill. We both hit good drives, but Tony hit his wedge approach too hard and it landed on the maintenance road behind the green and then bounced over the fence out-of-bounds. Tony slammed down his club in anger. At that time out-of-bounds was only a one-stroke penalty, not stroke and distance, the way it is today. Tony dropped a ball by the fence and then knocked his next shot into the hole for a four." Even years later, Fry's jaw still dropped in astonishment when recalling Tony's fantastic recovery shot.

Fry went to his father, Dick, who often lectured John about getting angry on the golf course because it would only hurt his game. The younger Fry related Tony's angry outburst, and his recovery shot, to his father who explained it away as "that's Tony being Tony."

Tony learned that he could use his charming personality to get what he wanted. At home, he convinced his mother that his hands were too valuable to his golf game to put them at risk washing dishes. That chore fell to Walt and Bernice. At school, Tony sweet-talked the administrator in charge of recording attendance to mark him down as present when he intended to skip school.

Whenever he was not playing hooky to play golf, usually at Lake Chabot, he struggled through his course work. The faculty worked hard with him, but his frequent absences put his graduation at risk. Cleo did not learn the magnitude of the problem until she prepared for Tony's graduation. It was only then that she learned that summer school was required for Tony to graduate. He completed the required work and graduated in 1952.

Although his schoolwork suffered from his frequent absences, his golf game flourished. It was about this time that he started to show the kind of game capable of winning tournaments, and he knew it. His confidence continued to grow. Soon the local sports fans would learn how good Tony Lema was.

4 A BOY AMONGST MEN
1952 - 1953

Tony developed from a lanky boy into a tall and lanky young man. At this time, he resembled a cross between a very young Anthony Perkins and Tony Dow (Wally on *Leave it to Beaver*). He carried only one wood in his golf bag; an ancient driver given to him by Dick Fry. He hit it off the tee as well as the fairway instead of the more commonly used 3-wood or 4-wood.

Tony entered as many tournaments as he could, sometimes against men much older and more experienced. The competition excited and inspired him to improve. Amateurs usually competed in these tournaments under a match play format with qualifying rounds to weed out weaker players. Qualifying scores resulted in players seeded into flights and brackets and matched up for heads-up play. The winners of each match face off against each other, as the field reduces until there are just two remaining players, who then play for the championship.

Tony first made news when he qualified for the championship flight of the Regional Park Championship in August of 1950 at the tender age of 16 by shooting a 74 in the qualifying round. The Bay Area featured a tough group of competitive amateur players who had regular jobs during the week and played tournament golf on the weekends.

Ken Venturi described the amateurs of the Bay Area of this era as very formidable and that he would "put our fields up against any amateur field anywhere."

Tony's first round match would be a tough one against the defending champion, Bob Kicherer. Tilden Park golf course, one of the municipally owned courses in the Bay Area, hosted the tournament. Tony surprised many of those who followed the amateur golf scene by dispatching the defending champion in the first round. The press soon started to take note of the lanky teen from St. Elizabeth High School.

Aldo Galletti, a tough veteran of the Bay Area amateur circuit, beat Tony in the second round match. Tony found himself six holes down after only nine holes of the match. Galletti finished him off by the score of eight holes up with seven holes to play. Although sent packing, Tony gained valuable tournament experience and confidence.

He next made headlines when he entered the Olympic Club Invitational, a junior's tournament held in December of 1952. His first round 70 in the stroke play competition was good for the lead in the 16-17 year-old division. The historic Olympic Club golf course, founded by the San Francisco Athletic Club, has hosted the U.S. Open many times. His 70, a phenomenal round on this tough course bettered the round of Ken Venturi who led the 18-21 year old division with a score of 72.

Two days later, the sports page of the *Oakland Tribune* featured the headline: LEMA WINS GOLF TOURNAMENT after the second and final round. He shot a final round 83 in nasty weather conditions while battling the pressure of leading the tournament. Fortunately, his score was good enough to win, beating John Fry, who finished second. His family began to take notice of his golfing prowess. With his first taste of golfing success, he was eager for more glory.

Tony worked on his game and entered tournaments throughout 1952. He also began to read books on golf and became enamored with the exploits of Walter Hagen. Dubbed Sir Walter, Hagen was famous for his carousing lifestyle, which never seemed to impede on his golfing ability. Hagen would show up at the first tee for a tournament still dressed in his evening clothes from the night before.

After high school, Tony bounced from one job to the next usually working the night shift keeping his days free to play golf. Decades later, he explained why he had changed jobs so often. He recalled the time, just out of high school, he was working with three other young men packing pre-fabricated Quonset huts.

"It was a real knock-around kind of thing," he explained. "Well, the foreman came around and he puts us on the quota system. We were four young, healthy guys, and we tripled that quota in three weeks and he was back with a bonus, a great big, beautiful bonus. They laid us off.

"So that was it. I went from job to job and I made a point to let them know that I was my own boss and the jobs didn't last long because I always had trouble with the foreman after that. If it hadn't been for golf, I'd be sitting on my tail somewhere on a case of canned goods and copping an extra five-minute smoke break."

His golf game really started to come around as he gained confidence in his game. In March of 1953, he entered the San Francisco City Golf Tournament, one of the most prestigious amateur events on the west coast. Harding Park Golf Course, one of the crown jewels of the many Bay Area municipal golf courses hosted "The City."

Tony shot a 77 in the qualifying round and drew a first round match against Lloyd Del Nore. He quickly dispatched with Del Nore advancing to the next round to play Floyd Sisk. Because the amateurs playing in the tournament had day jobs, they played the matches on the weekend. The winners had to wait through the workweek before playing their next matches.

Tony could hardly wait for the next Saturday to play Sisk. The day dawned very cold and windy and the conditions did not let up as the matches played out. Tony handled the conditions well on his way to victory over Sisk.

During the San Francisco City Golf Tournament, *The Oakland Tribune* described Tony's game saying, "he plays trouble shots like an expert and chips and putts as if he intended to hole-out every shot. Like most youngsters, he can be very good one day and very bad the next."

The next match for Tony in "The City" was against Art Schroeder, a member of the Stanford golf team. The tournament was down to 16 remaining players.

Because Schroeder forged his game through competition on the collegiate level, Tony had his work cut out for him. After playing Schroeder even on the front nine, Tony began to putt poorly on the back nine as he left a series of putts short of the hole. He lost the match, three down with two holes to play.

He then entered the Oakland City Championship in the spring of 1953 held at his home course, Lake Chabot. With the home course advantage, Tony easily qualified and made it through the first round of match play. In the second match, he drew another Lake Chabot member, Tony Perry, owner of a hotel in Oakland.

The match was nip-and-tuck leading to a decisive moment on the 325-yard sixteenth hole. Perry pulled out his driver, aimed over the out-of-bounds stakes, and carried his ball over the trouble to six-feet short of the green. Tony followed a more conservative route playing his tee shot around the out-of-bounds leaving himself a nine-iron into the green. He stuffed his approach shot to ten-feet and drained the putt. Meanwhile Perry took three strokes from the front of the green.

Tony won the hole and the match three-up. His score was two-under-par when the match concluded. Next, he met Joe Padauana in the quarter finals scheduled the next weekend. Before he could play his next match, Tony had an appointment with Uncle Sam to take his Army physical. He was prime draft material since he could not afford to go to college and was single, the two most widely used deferral options.

He reported for his Army physical before turning his attention back to golf. He and Padauana teed off in their quarterfinals match on Saturday morning. Padauana, an East Oakland barber, played mostly for fun, and usually had a very good time on the golf course. He was one of those golfers who always enjoyed himself whether he was playing well or not, and on this day, he played well. But so did Tony.

Once again, the sixteenth hole proved to be the pivotal point of the match. Padauana aimed for the green, a solid 325-yards distance, and actually drove the ball 50-feet over the green. On his chip shot, he had about 25-feet of fairway and apron to negotiate and 25-feet of green. He dubbed his chip shot and the ball barely made it to the green. From there Padauana two putted for a par.

Tony again played the hole conservatively and halved the hole with a routine par retaining his one-up lead as the pair headed to the seventeenth hole. Tony closed out the match on the seventeenth advancing to the semifinals. He had never gone this deep in a major match play tournament before. He experienced the excitement and tension that accompanies being in contention.

In the semifinal match, Tony met Elmer Clites, an accomplished veteran of Bay Area amateur events. Clites, considered the favorite because of his experience, proved he was a solid competitor as he and Tony fought back and forth throughout the round. However, in the end, Clites began to putt poorly with five three-putts in the match. Tony took advantage of his opponent's misfortunes on the greens to emerge victorious and advance into the finals for the championship.

His opponent in the finals was none other than his friend John Fry. Fry defeated Henry Lowell in the quarter final round due, in large part, to a hot putter. Even so, the determined Lowell gave Fry a difficult match.

In his semifinal match, Fry met Jerry Kroeckel, a deputy sheriff, and practice partner of Tony's. The two battled to sudden death before Fry beat the cop on the twenty-first hole.

After the amazing performances of both Tony and Fry, the stage was set for the two teenage friends to battle for the title of Oakland City Champion. This would be the first time in the tournament's history that two teenagers met in the final match.

During the week between the semi-final matches and the final match, Tony injured his back at his job operating a stamping machine at the Heinz food cannery in Oakland. Tournament organizers offered a postponement of the final grueling 36-hole match in order to give his back a chance to heal, but Tony refused, insisting on playing the match as scheduled.

The first round teed off early on Sunday, May 24, 1953 at 8:00 a.m. The final eighteen holes would tee off at 12:30 p.m. that same day. Dick Fry, John's father and the Head Pro at Chabot, encouraged the two boys to avoid slow play. Around the club, the consensus was the match was a toss-up. Regulars at the club conceded Fry held the advantage when it came to distance while Tony held the advantage around the greens. The largest gallery in tournament history, estimated at around 1,000 spectators, including Bateman, followed the players as they headed out for the morning round.

Tony quickly fell two down before he fought back with an eagle on the par 5 fourth hole and squared the match with a birdie on the following hole. The tone was set as the two battled back-and-forth exchanging the lead through the morning round. Tony birdied the unique par 6 finishing hole to take a one up lead into the afternoon round.

The two teens took Dick Fry's lecture about not playing slow to heart as they finished the morning round in a little more than three hours. Because of the feverish pace of the morning round, the two combatants had to sit around the clubhouse cooling their heels before the scheduled start of the afternoon round.

The afternoon started much the same as the morning round as Tony again took a bogey on the first hole. Just like that, his one-up lead evaporated and the two were all-square once again. Fry fell one hole behind with a bogey on the par 5 third hole and Tony extended his lead to two holes when he birdied the fourth hole. However, Fry was not going away. He got one hole back after Tony bogeyed the fifth hole. Tony then held a one-hole lead in the back-and-forth match as the two teens stood on the sixth tee. Tony bogeyed the next three holes while Fry was able to secure two pars and a bogie. The match now stood, once again, all even. The pair headed into the final nine holes tied. Tony shot a 39 on the front nine in the afternoon round while Fry shot a 38.

Both boys could feel the pressure mounting as neither one could gain a meaningful lead.

Tony regained the lead with a birdie on the tenth hole, but Fry evened the match with a birdie on the twelfth hole. The large crowd was witnessing an exciting match, and had there been an admission fee, it would have been well worth the price. The two halved the next four holes leading to the seventeenth. Both players missed the green and Tony lived up to his short game reputation by getting up-and-down for his par to win the hole. He could feel the nervous excitement welling up inside him as he struggled to stay in the moment and concentrate on the shot at hand.

Tony held a one-hole lead on the eighteenth tee, the unusual par 6. Tony reached the green with three good shots while Fry faced a wedge shot for his third shot. He gambled in an effort to get close to the pin near the front of the green. His only chance to win the hole and send the match into overtime was if he could get an eagle four and Tony two-putted for a birdie five. Fry came up short of the green with his delicate pitch. He then chipped up and two-putted for par. To win the match, Tony needed only to three putt and halve the hole. He easily two-putted for a birdie and captured the title. On that historic day, he became the youngest winner in the tournament's history. The achievement filled him with pride and exhilaration.

He shot a 71 in the morning round and a 73 in the afternoon round while Fry scored 72 in the morning and came back with a 73 in the afternoon. One stroke separated the two long-time playing companions. Some in attendance called it the best match they had ever witnessed. They saw eight birdies and one eagle offset by 13 bogies—a fine display of golf by the two teenagers. The tournament, and Tony's victory, received a great deal of press.

Mark Weiss Jewelers, the sponsor of the Oakland City Championship, put up the prize for first place, a 12-piece silver service in a beautiful mahogany box. Tony had never seen such a beautiful set of silverware and could hardly contain his excitement when presented the prize. Finally, the game he loved and spent so much time pursuing provided something he could take home to his mother, something tangible.

"He loved his mother," John Fry said. "He knew how hard she worked. To him that was a huge thing to go home and say, 'Here, mom. This is for you.'"

His mother used the silver service for decades when hosting holiday meals and special events.

He played in a few more tournaments that summer including the U.S. Public Links Amateur, a major U.S.G.A tournament in Seattle, Washington at the West Seattle Golf Course. After losing in an early match, his family had to wire him money in order to make the return trip home. At the end of the summer, his golf career would have to take a backseat in order to serve Uncle Sam.

5 SIEMPER FI
1953 - 1955

Tony decided that instead of waiting for the vagaries of the draft, he would enlist in the Marines.

"It was a spur of the moment thing. I was just batting around doing nothing," Tony explained regarding his enlistment in a March 25, 1963 *Sports Illustrated* profile.

Years later, he explained his reasoning for enlisting more fully to sportswriter Jerry Izenberg.

"One day the chief of police told us to get out of town and not come back," Tony explained. "He said the trouble was getting bigger each time he saw us and the next time he was going to throw us in the can. So, I joined the service."

Both he and Bill Craig enlisted, at the same time, assured that they would spend boot camp together. They reported for duty at the Navy base in Alameda on October 6, 1953, before reporting to Camp Pendleton, in San Diego, for basic training. In February of 1954, while on leave from Camp Pendleton, Tony returned to Lake Chabot for a casual round of golf and, despite the fact he was playing infrequently, shot a 68.

He went through basic training building up his body while learning the skills to become a topographical surveyor in the artillery. He shipped out from Camp Pendleton in March of 1953, en route to Korea.

By the time Tony arrived in Korea, the war had evolved into a stalemate while negotiations for an armistice took place first at Kaesong and later at Panmunjon.

Tony, fortunately, never came close to battle. The only thing resembling physical combat for him came when he had a dispute with a sergeant inside a mess tent. One of them suggested they step outside to settle their dispute. Once outside, Tony took a swing at the sergeant, who ducked. The roundhouse punch that Tony flailed succeeded in only making contact with a tent pole resulting in a broken arm.

While his arm was mending, the brass at headquarters in Tokyo discovered he was a very good golfer. Soon, he received transfer papers to report to Tokyo. There, he finished out his tour of duty playing golf with officers, and for the circumstances, lived the easy life.

During his time in the service, he kept a promise to his mother and attended Mass regularly. He was always trying to balance his wild nature with his Catholic faith. In Tokyo, he met Reverend John Durkin, an Air Force Chaplain, while playing golf. The Father took a liking to Tony and began to provide spiritual guidance as the two became close friends. Like Dick Fry and Lucius Bateman before him, Father Durkin became one of Tony's surrogate father figures.

While in the service, Tony began a life-long custom of regular letter writing. He sent a constant stream of letters to Cleo, his brothers, and sister.

He did not climb up the ranks with promotions. His discharge papers show his rank as a Private First Class and he received the Korean Service Medal, National Defense Service Medal, and the United Nations Service Medal; all medals that are awarded for service rather than any sort of gallantry. He gained 20 pounds during his time in the Marines filling out and adding muscle to his lanky frame. More importantly, the Marines provided him with maturity and discipline that he sorely needed.

He returned to the States to await his discharge, delayed for three months in late 1954 due to some sort of paper shuffle. While he waited, he worked on his golf game. He also competed in the All-Marine Championship at Parris Island and in the All-Service Championship at Langley Air Force Base in Virginia. Finally discharged on February 3, 1956, it was time to head back home to the Bay Area.

6 RETURN TO THE BAY AREA
1955 - 1956

In early 1955 Tony, discharged from the Marines but still in uniform, drove his new-used car towards his mother's house and civilian life. Music blared from the radio as he sailed along Foothill Boulevard, near 167th Avenue, through Hayward, California his mind occupied with what he would do as a civilian. Suddenly, he snapped to attention as a siren wail drowned out the music from the radio. He glanced in his rearview mirror, saw a cop, red light flashing, and closing in on him quickly.

"I was probably thinking more about my future than how fast I was going, when a cop flagged me down," Tony admitted years later.

Tony always liked to drive fast. On this day, in his haste to return to his family, he drove along doing 70 in a 55 mile per hour zone. Actually, his mind was so completely occupied he sped right past the cop in an adjacent lane unaware. With the siren wailing behind him, Tony eased the car over to the shoulder. He thought to himself that this was one hell of a way to get back into civilian life.

"Say, you're going a little fast," the officer said as he approached the car. Once at the rolled down window he saw who was behind the wheel. "Oh, hi Tony," he calmly said.

Tony recognized the cop, Jerry Kroeckel of Oakland, his old practice partner and competitor from Lake Chabot. The two men were both Oakland City Amateur Champions and knew each other well.

Tony and Kroeckel lit up cigarettes and caught up with each other on the shoulder of the road. Kroeckel, glancing at Tony's uniform, asked him what his plans were. Tony admitted he really did not have any. He said he might return to his job on the stamping machine at the Heinz cannery, or a similar job at the Gerber Food cannery in Oakland.

"You were always a pretty good golfer, Tony," Kroeckel said. "They are looking for an assistant pro at the San Francisco Golf Club. Why don't you give it a try?" A few days earlier, Kroeckel played in a pro-am at Silverado Golf Resort with John Geersten, the pro at San Francisco Golf Club. Geertsen mentioned to Kroeckel that he was looking for an assistant pro.

The idea of being an assistant pro appealed to Tony. He went straight over to the venerable and exclusive San Francisco Country Club. He spoke with Geersten, and according to Tony, Geersten "liked the cut of my jib," and he hired Tony on the spot. He was now a professional golfer. Without quite realizing it, he changed his life from a dead-end path of toiling in one factory or another to one of limitless possibilities.

Even so, the life of an assistant pro is not a particularly glamorous job. The hours are long and the work tedious. Assistant pros spend their time providing services to the members of the club. As the new hire, Tony found himself at the bottom of the pecking order with the least desirable hours and the dirtiest jobs. Nevertheless, he loved the work. The thought of a stuffy office job, or a backbreaking factory job, filled him with dread.

One of the dirtiest jobs at the club was picking up balls on the practice range. The range sloped downhill and balls would roll down into the woods at the bottom of the hill. Geersten, who ran a tight shop, would show up for work in the morning and check the baskets of balls that Tony filled the night before. He counted the balls to make sure Tony found and picked up all the balls. To pass the pro's inspection, Tony had to root around in the trees and brush in a daily Easter egg hunt to find all the stray balls.

During breaks in his workday, Tony would fit in practice whenever he could. He also played the course with Venturi and Harvie Ward, both talented amateurs. The practice and competition kept his game sharp.

Although Tony's job was not glamorous, the golf club was. Designed by A.W. Tillinghast, who also designed such other famous courses as Bethpage Black, Wing Foot and Baltusrol, the course presented a challenge to players. Many of the holes featured doglegs requiring a player to shape his shot. SFGC is located near the ocean, Lake Merced, and San Francisco State University and is the centerpiece of a small area of fine golf courses. In addition to SFGC, Harding Park Golf Course and The Olympic Club with its two 18-hole layouts are in the same neighborhood.

The membership at SFGC are very conservative and there is a definite air of old money on the grounds. To become a member, one must be not only wealthy, but has to have pedigree as well to gain the approval of the membership committee. A prospective member needs no fewer than seven current members to nominate them.

While Tony worked at SFGC in 1952, Ken Venturi played in the U.S. Amateur at Seattle Golf Club. Arnold Blom birdied the eighteenth hole to defeat him in the first round. Ken's disappointment in losing was soon forgotten when Eddie Lowery, approached him.

Lowery caddied for Francis Ouimet in the 1913 U.S. Open where Ouimet defeated Harry Varden and Ted Ray in an 18-hole playoff.

Ouimet's fantastic and surprising win, as a teen, helped feed a golf boon in the country. Ouimet credited his short, young caddy as a vital cog in the victory.

"I'd like you to meet Byron Nelson," Lowery said to Venturi.

Nelson was one of Venturi's heroes and he was stunned to learn that the great golfer had been in his gallery that day.

"This is quite an honor Mr. Nelson." Venturi said. "I wish that I could have played better today."

"You played very well today, Ken," Nelson replied. "How would you like to work with me? Eddie and I are going back to San Francisco and wondered if you might like to join us for a round of golf tomorrow."

Ken quickly accepted the offer. The only problem was that he had to drive back to San Francisco while Nelson and Lowery flew down. Venturi drove all day and despite a flat tire, made it back to San Francisco in time for the round at SFGC. Although Venturi shot a very good round of 66, Nelson kept his comments to "nice shot, Ken," or "good putt, Ken." After the round, the three men sat in the clubhouse sipping on soft drinks while Venturi patiently waited for praise on his fine round—none came.

Unable to contain himself any longer, Venturi inquired "Mr. Nelson, what did you think of my round today?"

"Ken that was a good round." Nelson replied. "I'll be here three or four days and there are about seven or eight things we've got to work on to make you a good player. I'll meet you out here tomorrow at 9:00 a.m."

Venturi was flabbergasted. He had just shot a six-under par 66 and Nelson had spotted *seven or eight* things to work on in his swing? Despite this, Venturi met Nelson the next morning and thus began a long teacher-student relationship between the two great golfers.

Nelson often traveled out West, from his ranch in Texas, to San Francisco Golf Club to work with Venturi while Tony was the assistant pro. After his sessions with Nelson, Venturi would grab Tony and the two would go to the range. Venturi would repeat what Nelson told him, word for word.

"I did this mostly to ingrain the ideas in my own head and it helped me to pass them on to Tony," Venturi recently reminisced.

As he worked on his own game, Tony melded these tips from Nelson, by way of Venturi, together with what he had learned from Lucius Bateman and Dick Fry. He spent every spare moment on the range and the hard work began to pay dividends. His game improved to the point that he was able to qualify for the 1956 U.S. Open at Oak Hill Country Club in Rochester, New York. Tony played in the qualifier at the urging of Eddie Lowery. Lowery, a United States Golf Association board member encouraged all the head pros and their assistants in the Bay Area to try to qualify for the Open. He felt padding the field would ensure additional spots for the region in the Open.

Tony knew that Lowery did not give him much chance to qualify because he did not have any experience at this level of tournament golf. In addition, Tony did not delude himself about his chances. Yet he surprised himself, Lowery, and many others, by qualifying for the national open along with about a half dozen other local golfers.

Because he was still new to his job, when the papers listed him as a qualifier, many members of SFGC did not recognize his name. The papers received numerous phone calls from members of SFGC saying there must be a mistake because, "The club did not employ anybody by that name." Once the membership realized their mistake, and after he made it through the regional qualifying stage, they generously raised $600 to help pay his expenses for the long trip to Rochester.

Tony's 1956 U.S. Open debut at Oak Hill was a part of his ongoing education as a professional golfer. It was his first exposure to major professional golf. To say the experience overwhelmed him would be an understatement. Intimidated by the big name players, he snuck off to an adjoining 18 holes at the 36-hole Oak Hill complex to practice. He was unaware of the existence of a 36-hole cut with the field reduced down to the lowest fifty scores and ties after the first two rounds. Tony stood at 148 after two rounds and did not learn about the cut until he was in his hotel lobby reading a newspaper after dinner. He overheard spectators discussing the score needed to make the cut.

"What's this?" He asked one of the fans. "Doesn't everyone play tomorrow?"

To his surprise, the answer was "No. There's a cutoff and 149 will probably make it."

He had birdied the last hole for his 148. As he went up to his room he thought about the embarrassment he would have felt if he had bogeyed the hole for a 150 and shown up the next day.

The U.S. Open featured a 36-hole final round on Saturday until 1965. Tony arrived at the first tee, to begin his final 36 holes, greeted by a throng of about ten thousand fans. Even though he realized the fans were there to see the leaders tee off much later, their presence made him extremely nervous. He almost missed his drive completely. He did make contact, but he finished the day with a 79 and an 81 for a 308. This score was only good enough to beat one other player in the field, an amateur by the name of John Garrett. Nevertheless, he did win $200 for his efforts.

While the experience was exciting, Tony was discouraged. He felt that his game was nowhere near the level needed to play major tournament golf. A few months later, at the Western Open conducted at the Presidio Golf Club in San Francisco, he again felt this inadequacy. PGA Tour tournaments allowed players to qualify for a small number of spots in the field on the Monday prior to the tournament. Because it was local, Tony decided to enter the event through the Monday qualifying, earning a spot in the tournament.

At tour events, the unknown pros tee off very early, or very late. Tony was able to fit in a full workday at SFGC, before his late first round and after his early second round. He did play well enough to make the cut.

In the final round, he played with Dow Finsterwald and Bob Rosburg, both seasoned and well-known pros. Tony felt out of his element paired with these two stars.

Finsterwald put on a clinic that day driving the ball perfectly and knocking down the pins with his iron shots. He shot a 66 on the par-72 Presidio course and as Tony watched the display of golf he thought to himself, "If this is the way I have to play golf before I can make it on tour, then the tour is no place for me." Finsterwald fashioned a 66 that climbed him up the leader board to fifth place. Tony's final round of 72 gave him a 291 and placed him in a tie for 22nd place and a check for $185.

Humbled, he wanted nothing more than to return to his job and happily clean clubs for the members. He did not think he possessed the skills necessary to make it on tour. He did feel that the tournament experience was valuable as he learned how to navigate his way around the complexities surrounding a tournament. On the positive side, he made the cut in both of the PGA Tour events he played in.

Still, he felt the world of a professional touring golf pro was out of his league. An astonishing tournament three months later in El Centro, a small border town in Southern California, caused him to reconsider.

7 VICTORY VACATION
1957

Jay Hebert, hitting shots on the practice tee on the Saturday of the Caliente Open in Tijuana, Mexico, took notice of a young pro he did not know. He listened while the young player complained loudly about the fact that he had missed the cut. Hebert strolled over and stood behind the stranger watching him hit balls before stepping forward to introduce himself. This is how Tony met Jay Hebert, winner of the recently concluded Bing Crosby tournament.

Tony had landed a new job, and he was on a four-week break, playing in a few PGA winter tour events, before reporting for his new position. He was the new head pro at Ruby View Golf Course, a nine-hole municipal track in Elko, Nevada. After missing the cut at the Caliente, he was on the range, working on his game.

He and Hebert started to chat. Hebert asked Tony how he did at the Crosby. Tony informed him that he made a check for $66.

Hebert's win at the Crosby, was his first victory on tour in his seven-year career. Tony's highlight—or rather, lowlight—at the Crosby was falling off a cliff on the ninth hole when he swung too hard trying to extricate his ball from an ice plant. He fell and landed on his knee bruising his kneecap, but was otherwise unhurt.

"How long have you been out on the tour? " Hebert asked.

"Four weeks," Tony stammered out sheepishly.

"Four weeks!?" asked Hebert incredulously. "You shouldn't be discouraged."

Hebert went on to explain to Tony that missing the cut was a common occurrence on tour, even to the most experienced and talented touring pro. He gave Tony some more encouragement and went back to hitting balls.

Tony discovered the human side of the men who played on tour thanks to his exchange with Hebert. He always remembered Hebert's generosity and the fact he took the time to lend encouraging words to an unknown player.

Tony received funding for his short excursion on tour from Eddie

Lowery who lent him $500. Wanting to test his game, once again against the finest PGA Tour pros, Tony entered the Crosby, the Caliente Open, the Imperial Valley Open, and the Phoenix Open. While both the Crosby and the Phoenix stops were premier events with strong fields, the Caliente and the Imperial Valley tournaments were second-tier events.

After lingering in Tijuana to work on his game and sightsee, he drove to the Barbara Worth Country Club, in El Centro, a small farming community in Southern California. He arrived late Monday and checked in for the Imperial Valley tournament. After checking in, he only had time for a nine-hole practice round.

He was unable to get in additional practice on the course as there was a two-day pro-am preceding the tournament proper. Because he was unknown, he did not qualify for the pro-am. He and the other nameless pros not in the pro-am unhappily cooled their heels in the clubhouse bar while they waited for the tournament to start on Thursday.

He admitted in *Golfer's Gold* that, "I had spells in those days where I could really lush it up."

His time in the bar contributed to mediocre scores in the first two rounds. In the third round, he found something that clicked and carded a 67. His round shot him up the leader board to fifth place, six shots back of the leader, Paul Harney. At this point, his thoughts were not on winning. Instead, he focused on cashing a nice check that would help him pay back the loan from Lowery.

To make enough prize money to pay Lowery back, he would have to shoot a low score in the fourth round. Tall old trees on the Barbara Worth course put a premium on straight driving. In the early part of the fourth round, Tony found the trees often, but scrambled and sank a couple of long putts to hang around par. At the ninth hole, a par 4, his game jelled as he nearly drove the green and then chipped in for an eagle. He was now two-under-par for the round and felt the adrenaline pumping.

He birdied the tenth hole and then made long par putts on the eleventh and twelfth holes. He added another birdie and as he strode up the sixteenth fairway, he was at four-under-par. He thought he might get into position to win $500 or $600. That would be plenty of money to pay Lowery back with some left over.

From the sixteenth fairway, he had a view of the leaders, Harney and Bob Inman, teeing off with irons to hit the tight fairway on the twelfth hole. Tony used a driver when he played the 12th.

"That's good," he thought. "Here are those two cautiously dillydallying around. They might just out-choke each other over there and I might slip in and win this thing."

He finished his round by sinking two very long putts for birdies on the seventeenth and eighteenth holes for a final round of 65. The putt on the eighteenth hole measured about 60 feet.

"I didn't think I had a chance in the world to hole it," Tony informed *The Oakland Tribune* via airmail after the tournament. Because it was a second-tier tournament, the paper did not send a reporter. "I was just trying to get it close, and the thing went in," Tony informed the paper.

Proud and energized after his round, he nevertheless did not give himself much of a chance to win. He started the day six strokes off the lead and felt that his 65 would not be good enough to catch the leaders. Harney had only to shoot a 70 to beat him by a shot. He returned to his favorite place at Barbara Worth—the bar.

He quickly drank down three Scotch and waters and was reaching for the fourth when a fan came bursting in. He informed Tony that Harney would have to get his ball up-and-down from the front of the eighteenth green just to tie him. Tony quickly pushed away the drink and stumbled out of the bar in time to see Harney chip to seven feet from the hole and then sink the putt.

Tony headed to the first tee for the sudden-death playoff. He arrived annoyed at himself for his activities at the bar when he should have been anticipating the possibility of a playoff. On the bright side, the alcohol did take the edge off the situation relieving some of the pressure he must have felt.

He and Harney were contesting for the first-place check of $1,000 while the loser would get $700. A tournament official suggested the two players split the $1,700 and play for the title only. During this era, splitting purses was a common occurrence on the tour. Purses were small and it was tough to make enough prize money to cover travel expenses so the players would ensure their financial payday, then playoff for the honor of a victory.

Tony quickly replied to the official's suggestion saying he was not interested in splitting the purse even before Harney could voice his wishes on the matter.

"Who the hell do you think you are, anyway?" the official asked.

"I'm the guy in this blasted play-off," Tony answered.

In the playoff, he teed off first with a good drive. Harney blasted his drive 40-yards past Tony winding up pin high to the right of the green on the short par 4. Using a wedge for his second shot, Tony ended up on the back edge of the green, about 20 feet above the hole leaving a tough downhill putt. Harney chipped his second shot to four feet with a much easier uphill putt. Tony continued his great putting for the day by draining the long putt for a birdie. Shaken by seeing this, Harney was barely able to coax in his four-footer.

The second hole was another short par 4 that doglegged to the right with a pond guarding the left side of the green. The smart shot was a drive down the left side leaving a safe angle to approach the green. That was too easy for Tony. He attempted to cut his drive around the trees and ended up putting too much cut on the ball which flew into the woods, hit a tree and kicked out into the fairway. Harney hit the perfect drive down the left side setting up an easy second shot.

When Tony walked to his ball, he surveyed his prospects for his second shot. Partially stymied by a tree, he would have to hit a career shot to reach the green. His only hope was to take a seven-iron and carve it around the tree with a huge slice. He had to aim at the pond guarding the green and if it did not slice, his bid for victory would find a watery grave. Despite the prospects of pulling off such a difficult shot, he could see the shot in his mind's eye. This gave him the confidence that he could pull the shot off.

After hitting the shot firmly, he watched as the ball headed toward the pond. After what seemed an eternity, the ball finally reacted to the spin he imparted on the shot. It started to slice towards the green finally coming to rest about 10-feet from the pin.

He recalled, "Harney must have figured by this time that he was contending with a freak that used black magic."

Whatever he was thinking, Harney left his nine-iron second shot short of the hole. Then he left his first putt short.

Tony used all his "black magic" to drain his birdie putt to win his first meaningful professional tournament. As the putt fell into the hole, he felt a tremendous release of nervous energy, replaced with excitement and joy. As the two players headed back to the clubhouse with their caddies and the thousand or so spectators, Tony realized he had just won a check for $1,000. This was a huge payday for the young pro, and once again, the thought of doing this for a living crossed his mind.

He realized he won the tournament despite the fact he started so poorly. He started getting good breaks, his game jelled, and he was able to take advantage of it. Instead of getting down on himself, or angry, when things were going poorly, he kept plugging away saving strokes where he could.

With a victory under his belt, he had one more tournament left to play on his vacation; the Phoenix Open. This was a star-studded event on the winter tour. The field contained big names such as Arnold Palmer and Billy Casper. Tony made the cut and cashed a small check.

At this point after the Phoenix Open, he would have taken his winnings from his trip and immediately gone out on tour. However, he was due to report for his new job as head pro in Elko, Nevada.

It was only a 9-hole municipal course in the middle of nowhere, but he was a head pro at the tender young age of 22, and took the job seriously. Tony would quickly find out that Elko had a few amenities that kept his life interesting.

8 THE PRO FROM ELKO
1957 - 1958

Reluctantly, Tony left the tour behind, drove up to Elko, and began his new job as head pro at Ruby View Golf Course. He heard about the job opening at the newly built course through the grapevine of professional golfers in the Bay Area. Due to the remote location, there were not a lot of other applicants so, despite his tender age, he landed the position.

Elko is located in northeastern Nevada near the Idaho and Utah borders. The ill-fated Donner Party traveled through the area, as did many of the '49ers on their way to the gold fields of California.

With gambling legalized in 1931, the town received an economic shot in the arm, becoming a tourist destination for residents of Idaho and Utah. It may not have been Las Vegas, or even Reno for that matter, but visitors and locals could find a little excitement in the few casinos in town. The Stockman's Hotel and the Commercial Hotel were the largest gambling houses.

Into this sleepy little town blew Tony Lema, 22-years-old and a winner on the PGA Tour. He settled into his new job at the municipal golf course located on the north side of town. Shortly after arriving in town, Tony became friends with Bing Crosby, and his sons, who all played golf at Ruby View. Bing purchased a cattle ranch in Elko in the 1940s to escape the rigors of Hollywood, located on a terrace just east of the course.

The workload at Ruby View was easy. The course, municipally owned, meant Tony was a city employee. He ran the modest pro shop, gave the occasional lesson, and organized the tournaments for the men's club and women's division. The light workload left a lot of time for him to work on his game. He would play two balls during 9-hole practice rounds imagining one ball as Ben Hogan's and one ball as his own. Hogan never had a chance in these matches. He would play similar fantasy games when he was practicing his putting.

As Tony conceded in *Golfer's Gold*, these fantasies sounded childish but "in a backwater of Nevada it's surprising the number of things you will do to put some juice in the daily routine."

With all the practice, he started to gain even more confidence in his game. Since his victory at Imperial Valley, the thought of going out on tour kept percolating in his mind. His confidence soaring, he believed he had the game to compete on tour, after all.

The fantasy practice games he played were not the only things he found to put some juice in the daily routine. Actual juice would work just fine. With not much to do in Elko when not playing or practicing golf, he turned to drinking, gambling, and women to pass the time. He enjoyed all three, sometimes to excess.

The Commercial Hotel and The Stockman's Hotel and Casino became familiar haunts to him. He fell into a familiar after-work routine of gambling at the casino tables with friends, oftentimes the Crosby boys. Martinis accompanied the gambling before dinner, and sometimes the martinis would substitute for dinner. After dinner, he would return to the gambling tables, fueled by more drinks. It was not long before the casinos ended up with all of his wages, as well as some IOUs. The owner of Stockman's, Don Bilboa, was an avid golfer, so credit was particularly easy for Tony to arrange.

Stockman's was located downtown, where it took up most of the 300 block of Commercial Street. The three-story building featured bright neon signs, including a large neon billboard on the roof with a figure of a steer and the slogan "World Famous Steaks"—Stockman's became a second home to Tony.

When he was not in Stockman's, Tony found time to test his game in regional competitions. He won the Montana Open in August 1957 at Hilands Golf Club in Billings, Montana. Purses in state opens were usually a few thousand dollars with the winner taking home $700. The fields were comprised of pros and talented amateurs from the region.

He opened with a 67, trailing the leader Gene May by two strokes on the par-71 layout. After the second round, he sat tied for third place, still two strokes behind the leader. Tony came out with guns blazing in Sunday's 36-hole final round shooting a 69 in the morning round and 66 in the afternoon round. Smiley Quick from Los Angeles, also playing well, fired a 66 in the morning round. Tony won the tournament by one stroke when he made par at the final hole, while Quick three-putted for a bogey. He pocketed $750 for the win and, even though it was just a state open, the victory filled him with pride and confidence.

A few weeks later during the first weekend of September, Ruby View hosted the Nevada Open. Despite the burden of playing the role of host pro, Tony managed a course record 61 in the third round. He bested Bill Johnston's course record 63, set two days earlier in the first round. His great round put him into the lead but Johnston came storming back with a final round 65. Tony could only manage a 70 and finished second, three strokes back of Johnston.

He played in the Idaho Open at Hillcrest Country Club in Boise, Idaho the next week, and again finished second. Cliff Whittle, the defending champion finished fourth with the aid of a third round 65.

Whittle was one of the head pros from the region that Tony befriended while playing in the tournaments that made up what was known as the Intermountain Circuit. Another good friend from the circuit was Jim Chenoweth, and the three men often traveled together sharing many adventures along the way. Because he made friends easily, Tony never had any problem finding other players who wanted to carouse with him. Fueled by liquor, the young men sowed their wild oats while away from their jobs.

Whittle was head pro at Blue Lakes Country Club in Twin Falls, Idaho. He piloted his own plane and flew Tony, as well as some other pros, to the tournaments on the circuit. One pro who traveled with the group was Don Knapp. On one trip, Whittle was making his final approach to a small airfield in Wells, Nevada to pick up Tony and Knapp. As he looked out the plane windshield, he saw the two players attempting to hit the airfield windsock with wedge shots.

Both Whittle and Chenoweth knew Jim Malarkey of Sun Valley, Idaho. Malarkey, adopted by a wealthy Pacific Northwest lumberman, was a trust fund baby and lived a life of leisure. He would split his time between Sun Valley and Portland, Oregon, where he played high stakes card games at the Astoria Country Club. Tony's new friends introduced him to the rich, young sportsman.

Malarkey often popped in from Sun Valley to Elko for some drinking, gambling, and golfing. The only one that he had any talent was the drinking.

Even so, Malarkey and Tony had a fine time pursuing all three activities. Malarkey soon took quite an interest in Tony's golf game. Tony viewed Malarkey as a friend as the two began to spend a great deal of time together. They also spent time with Cliff Whittle.

Whittle flew Tony and Malarkey into Sun Valley where the three scheduled to play in a pro-am event. The pros stayed at Malarkey's house in Sun Valley, a house he rented from the actor Ann Sheridan. The huge house was located across the street from the Sun Valley Lodge. When not on the golf course, the three spent their time drinking. After a few drinks one night, Whittle came up with an idea.

"Jim, why don't you put Tony out on the tour?" he asked.

Malarkey did not bat an eye as he replied, "Fine, I'll do it."

Tony thought it was the drinks talking, but Malarkey was serious about sponsoring him on tour. Later, they shook hands on an oral agreement whereby Malarkey would advance him $200 a week against Tony's winnings. Tony would split his winnings above that amount with Malarkey receiving a one-third share. The arrangement provided Tony with the cash needed to cover expenses while Malarkey stood to make a profit in the event Tony was successful.

They made plans for Tony to play some of the last tour events of the 1957 season, known as the fall tour. His pro career would begin in earnest in the first stage of the 1958 tour, known as the winter tour.

The PGA Tour was very different than what it would evolve into over the next decade. Television coverage of tour events was in its infancy, mostly local broadcasts, and broadcast rights revenues to pad tournament purses were still in the future. As a result, tournament purses were very small compared to what they would become in a few short years.

Most touring pros had to find a way to travel on the cheap. They would find a fellow pro to share the driving duties to get from one event to another. Rarely did they travel by air. Even Arnold Palmer pulled a camping trailer behind his car as he and his wife Winnie traveled the tour in his early days.

To help defray expenses, many pros utilized a sponsor to establish themselves on tour. Often this would be a member—or a group of members—from the pro's home course, who would pool their money to put "their guy" on tour. While making a profit was a possibility, the sponsor's motivation was as much to help a young pro, as it was to make money. Staking a horse in the race gave the sponsor bragging rights around his friends.

The arrangements usually called for the sponsor, or group of sponsors, to advance money to the pro to pay for expenses. The group split the winnings of the player, in some fashion, to pay the original investment off. The pro would continue to split his winnings for a predetermined time providing a potential profit on the investment.

Sponsorship deals eventually ended with the pro washing out on tour while the investors absorbed the loss. In other instances, the pro pays off the original investment, along with a profit, for the duration of the agreement. After the agreement ends, the pro continues with his career using his own resources to cover expenses. Some pros avoided sponsorship agreements, as they did not want the added pressure of being beholden to a group of investors, nor did they want to share their winnings.

After building up huge gambling debts during his time in Elko, Tony's sponsorship deal with Malarkey represented his only chance to get on tour. Malarkey, and his money, was his ticket out of town.

He returned from the Idaho Open to Elko to start preparing for his launch onto the PGA Tour. Malarkey also agreed to pay Whittle's way during the fall tour with the three of them travelling together. The two pros would play in the mini-tournament Monday qualifiers to gain entry into the main events. Malarkey would play in the pro-ams.

Originally, the three men planned to meet in Twin Falls, Idaho, the last week of October. They would stay with Whittle until he closed his shop at the course for the winter on November 1. Then it would be off to the tour. They all thought it would be one big party.

Shortly after arriving in Twin Falls, Tony and Malarkey quickly became bored. After a couple of days, they informed Whittle they were going to Las Vegas. They suggested he fly his plane down to meet them once he closed his shop for the winter.

Malarkey withdrew money from his trust account, with the aid of his mother, to cover travel expenses on tour. With the $25,000 in his pocket, he and Tony departed for Las Vegas with the bright idea of adding to the grubstake.

Of course, it did not work out that way. The day after arriving in Las Vegas, Tony called Whittle to inform him they lost all $25,000—in one day. This was an enormous sum of money in 1957, about $200,000 today. With Malarkey's wealth and the ease in which he could get his hands on it, they became reckless. Their gambling losses spiraled out of control.

Tony told Whittle that there was no problem, though. Malarkey placed a phone call to his mother and flew to Portland, Oregon, where he would get another check to replace the $25,000.

Tony finally met up with Whittle in Elko. When Whittle arrived at his apartment, he found a beautiful blonde helping him pack for his trip. Tony finished his packing and informed Whittle he needed to see some of his "sponsors" before leaving town. He invited Whittle to ride along to the meeting. He then drove to one of the legal brothels near town and the two went into the bar.

Behind the bar was a huge blown-up photograph of Tony in action on the golf course. Whittle learned that the girls in the brothel provided financial help with some of the IOUs at the casinos that Tony accumulated. The two golf pros drank and visited with the girls before returning to Tony's house.

Even with the girl's and Malarkey's help, Tony still had a large outstanding IOU at Stockman's Hotel. With this IOU, he did not need any help. The owner Don Bilboa, an avid golfer, told him not to worry about the IOU because he wanted to see him play on the tour. Tony promised Bilboa that he would pay off the IOU, as quickly as possible. With his gambling debts now taken care of— in one form or another—he and Whittle headed for the tour.

The two aspiring touring pros played the Hesperia Open, the San Diego Open, and the Long Beach Open while Malarkey played in the pro-am events. Tony did not make any money in these events although he did make the cut at San Diego and Long Beach.

While at the San Diego Open, Malarkey asked him if he was serious about playing the pro tour full-time. Tony insisted he was.

However, what he really wanted was to get out of Elko. He had put in his one year at Ruby View and felt like it had been too much. Too much booze, too much womanizing, and too much gambling. He would have left sooner if it were not for the fact that he was up to his ears in gambling debts. Now that he had Malarkey's financial support, he phoned the city and tendered his resignation while in San Diego.

To Tony the tour looked like a great life, an escape from the bad situation he had made for himself in Elko. He thought that Malarkey was a great guy, and that with his backing, he would see the country while playing golf for a living. He viewed it as an adventure, as if he were heading off for a two-year vacation.

He and Malarkey decided he should play in the last event of the 1957 tour, the Mayfair Inn Open in Florida. The San Francisco Giants, owners of the inn that served as their headquarters during spring training, sponsored the tournament.

He made the expensive, cross-country trip to play in the tournament. The plan was to make the cut and automatically qualify for the next event on tour, the season opening Los Angeles Open. A pro could avoid Monday qualifying for the next tournament on the schedule by making the cut in the preceding tournament.

The Mayfair did not present a problem when it came to qualifying. Because it was the final tournament of the year, many of the regular touring pros skipped the event electing to start their short holiday vacation. To fill the field, the tournament allowed any PGA pro, including head pros, to play without the need for a Monday qualifier. With the goal of making the cut, Tony entered the Mayfair. He managed not only making the cut but earned a good check in the process. He shot rounds of 73-66-69-67 to finish in a tie for sixth and a check of $725. He now set his sights on the 1958 tour and his rookie season as a tour pro.

9 ROOKIE ON TOUR
1958

With his made cut and healthy check at the Mayfair, Tony prepared to play the tour full time. He made a trip to Sun Valley to visit Malarky and one night, the two wandered into a bar in the town of Ketchum. A young woman, Shirley Donovan caught Tony's eye. He made his way over to the group she was with and asked her to dance to the live band playing. The two hit it off and spent a great deal of time together during his visit.

"He seemed like a pretty decent guy," she recalled in a 2000 interview with golf journalist Frederick Burger. "He looked like a very shy guy. He had no idea what Jim Malarkey was like. Quite frankly, I felt sorry for him. Like he was a little kid and needed some protection."

Donovan worked in the accounting department at the Challenger Inn and Lodge, owned by the Union Pacific Railroad and knew everybody in town. Tony peppered her with questions about the different powerful personalities in the ski resort. After his visit, they kept in contact by phone regularly.

As he made his plans for 1958, he did not have the benefit of an in-house travel agency to rely on, as do today's pros on the PGA Tour. He made all of his travel arrangements himself. He would have to learn, the hard way what hotels were closest to the golf courses each week. In the days before restaurant chains, with their uniform menus from city to city, a rookie had to learn the best places to dine within their budget.

The mode of travel on the nomadic tour in the late 50s was almost exclusively by automobile. Malarkey insisted his boy travel in high style, so Tony made the down payment for a new Plymouth and Malarkey would make the monthly payments. Tony made the long drives to unfamiliar courses that he needed to become familiar with quickly.

The rookie had to learn these things, for the most part, on his own. The veterans on the tour did not go out of their way to make life easier. Why would they? The rookies were trying to get their hands on the small amount of prize money that was available on tour at that time.

Some veterans, such as Jerry Barber and Sam Snead, could be very cold to a rookie. A few others, like Arnold Palmer and Dow Finsterwald, could be quite helpful.

To shorten the learning curve, a nascent player would hook-up with one or two players of similar status. Players found natural cliques with other players and would begin travelling together to spread the cost of travel. Tony eventually met Johnny Pott, Tommy Jacobs, and Jim Ferree. The four travelled together sharing expenses.

Malarkey sent Tony $200 a week; about what it took to cover expenses on the tour each week. During his first year on the tour, Malarkey traveled with him from time to time. Tony introduced him to the other pros, then Malarky would go back to Sun Valley and brag about being a bigwig out on the PGA tour.

The payments from Malarkey did not always arrive in a timely manner. A few times Tony sat in his hotel room, broke, waiting for a money wire.

The opening event of the 1958 season was the L.A. Open, played the first week of January at Rancho Park Golf Course. Tony drove down from Oakland, where he spent the holidays with his family, and checked into a hotel. He headed out to the course and made the unhappy discovery that his hotel was a full 90-minute drive to the golf course. Once he finally arrived at the golf course, he learned that no one particularly cared whether he was there or not. Registration desks could never get his name right. Locker room attendants were always too busy with other duties to assign him a locker, and when they finally did, he usually had to share it with another unknown pro.

The L.A. Open, a top-tier event, had a rich history with a long list of well-known former champions including Ben Hogan, Sam Snead, and Byron Nelson. The purse was $40,000 with the winner's share being $7,000, making it one of the better paying stops on the circuit. Tony opened with a 76 placing him well down the leader board.

Tony rallied to make both the 36-hole cut, and the 54-hole cut (needed because the field was so large) with a pair of two-under par 70s. His last round 75 for a 291 total placed him well back in the pack behind the eventual winner, Frank Stranahan. Although he won a $93 check, after subtracting his expenses of $200 for the week, it actually cost him $107 to play the event.

From L.A. the traveling caravan of the tour moved north to the Monterey Peninsula for the annual Crosby Clambake, a pro-am tournament. Pros teamed up with famous celebrities to play a two-man best-ball tournament in addition to their individual tournament.

The Crosby had a lively, party atmosphere with the addition of celebrities from the entertainment world, sports teams, and wealthy business executives. Bing Crosby started his tournament in 1937, and one year, after inclement weather washed out the first round, the host simply moved the party over to his house located on the back nine at Pebble Beach.

While the rain fell, Crosby threw some steaks on the grill and sang a few songs on the patio. He made sure the drinks continued to pour while young women materialized helping to keep the party going. Ever since, it was a highly desirable invitation for the amateur participants, while pros circled the date on their playing schedules each year.

The stars were there to party. There was a room at the Pebble Beach lodge, where most players stayed, called the "snake pit." In the "snake pit" high stakes card games took place with the professional golfers usually winning large sums of money from the celebrities.

Crosby nurtured the party atmosphere of the event. He distributed hand-made ceramic fifths of bourbon, whiskey, and brandy—packaged in little cloth sacks—to the participants each day of the tournament. Tony fit into the easy-going party scene at the Crosby. He always enjoyed a good time, especially one that included plenty of drinks, pretty starlets, and gambling.

The Crosby was one of the first tournaments broadcasted nationally on television, starting in 1956. Folks around the country tuned in from their cold winter regions to watch the professional golfers and their celebrity partners on the beautiful California coast.

While it was a fun, party-like event, the pros played for serious money. The purse for the Crosby increased from $35,000 in 1957 to $50,000 in 1958, with the winner taking home $4,000. The quality of the golf courses used for the Crosby added to the popularity, as well as the challenge, of the event. The tournament utilized three courses—Monterey Golf Club, Cypress Point, and Pebble Beach.

Tony played those courses many times as a teenager; Lake Chabot held an annual Dick Fry Day event at Pebble Beach. He Monday qualified for the Crosby in 1957, the year he fell off the cliff while hitting a shot. There was also the time when, as a youth, he snuck into the tournament with a friend.

Tony opened the tournament with a lackluster 75 in the first round, but was able to follow up with a superb round of 69 in the second round to make the cut. Disaster struck in the third round as he struggled to an 80 earning him a spot in the first group off the tee Sunday morning at 7:15 a.m.

The highest scores tee off first on the weekend so the television broadcast can feature the leaders later in the day. Tony managed to pull things together in the last round shooting a 70 to earn a check for $175.

While in California, Tony signed a deal to play out of Silverado Golf Club in Napa. Silverado was a new resort looking for publicity and figured that having a promising local rookie on the tour would be a good way to advertise. For the touring pros, this was a common avenue used to generate additional income. A pro would sign an endorsement deal with a resort or country club and make a few appearances during the year at the course. He would then register at tournaments in the club's name and be introduced on the tee as "playing out of" the club. Even though he called San Leandro home, Tony now stepped onto the first tee to the introduction, "Tony Lema, playing out of Silverado Golf Club in Napa, California."

While he was learning his way around the tournament venues on the tour, Tony realized he still had a great deal to learn to become a good player. To him, the most important thing to understand was the mental side of the game. During his first year, he collected what he called, "a checkbook full of fines" from the tour for temper tantrums.

After the Crosby, Tony loaded up the brand-new Plymouth and headed south to the next stop at the Tijuana Open. From Mexico, he followed the tour up to Arizona, first to Phoenix, won by Ken Venturi for his second victory in as many weeks, and then to Tucson. Tony had his first taste of the glory contending in a PGA tournament in Tucson.

The El Rio Country Club, labeled by many of the pros as a "pitch-and-putt" course at a short 6,434 yards, hosted The Tucson Open. The pros feasted on the layout scoring birdies with abandon.

Tony got his week off to a good start finishing second in the opening pro-am event by shooting a 63 before opening the tournament proper with a 66. He credited good putting, as well as a good caddy, for his four-under-par score.

His caddy for the week, Del Taylor was a pro golfer playing on the African-American tour conducted by the United Golf Association. Taylor stopped in Tucson to earn extra cash while on his way to Florida to play in a UGA event. Tony gave Taylor a great deal of credit for his good play in Tucson.

His 66 put him two strokes back of the leaders, Frank Stranahan, Billy Johnston, and Manuel de la Torre. The next day he shot a 65, giving him the lead at 131 with Johnston.

Tony's iron game was red hot with birdie putts of less than 10-feet on four holes, making them all.

In his feature column, "Open Notebook," Lou Povlovich in *The Tucson Daily Citizen*, described Tony as being visibly nervous after his second round 65.

"Sure, I'm nervous," Tony told reporters. "I have great respect for the name golfers I'm playing against, but I'm not in awe of them. Someday I hope to be up there with them."

Tony surrendered the lead after the third round to Don January, who shot a 64. Tony was three-strokes back in third place after his round of 70.

Tony still thought he had a good chance to win the tournament. He felt confident even though he faced the pressure of contending for a top-tier PGA title for the first time. He readily admitted that this was a brand-new situation and that he did not really know how to react to it.

He went to bed early, but hardly slept a wink as he tossed and turned plagued with fitful, strange dreams. He laid awake thinking of the strangest things, like what he would say at the trophy presentation ceremony. He finally fell asleep around 4 a.m. He felt good the next morning, despite the lack of sleep, until the pressure hit him like a sudden electric shock on the first tee.

Paired with the leader January, and veteran pro John Barnum, he was able to hit a decent drive that left him with an easy 9-iron into the green. His nerves began to get the best of him as he failed to catch his 9-iron cleanly and left his approach some 18 to 20-feet from the hole. He left his putt two-feet short and marked his ball with a coin. He stepped back as his fellow competitors putted.

As he stood there, he could feel himself going to pieces. He wrote in *Golfer's Gold* that his knees went shaky and his breath came in short bursts. His mind began to race with the worst sort of thoughts. By the time he got over his putt, he had no chance. He was shaking so badly that he did not even threaten the hole with his putt. The short course suddenly looked to his eye much more difficult than it was and he saw nothing but trouble.

The pressure of being in contention had completely undone him. His game spiraled out of control until he realized he was totally out of contention to win the tournament. He birdied the last hole for a 75 and a total for the tournament of 276, a full 11-strokes behind winner Lionel Hebert. He fell into a tie for 14th place.

He won $327.50 for the week, but what he gained from his initial experience of being in contention was far more valuable. A player must face the pressures that come with being in contention to learn how to handle the situation.

From Arizona, the tour moved across Texas into Louisiana, and then into Florida as the winter tour ended and spring arrived. The education of Tony continued, sometimes painfully and awkwardly. At one stop, he arrived at the course late on Monday and only had time for a nine-hole practice round. Jerry Barber, a veteran, was about to tee off and Tony thought that playing with him would provide insight on how an experienced player went about a practice round. He approached Barber, asking if he could join him.

What he did not know about Barber was that he could be one of the coldest players on tour, especially to rookies. Tony quickly detected from Barber's tone that he was not thrilled to have a rookie tag along with him. Nevertheless, Barber allowed Tony to join him and the two players set off on their practice round.

The first hole was a short par-5, reachable in two shots. Tony hit a poor second shot, then immediately dropped a second ball to try the shot again. He wanted validation that he had used the correct club for the yardage. Even though this was against tour rules, players routinely ignored the rule.

"Hey, kid," Barber said in a gruff tone of voice, "you can cut that out right now. Don't you know you are not allowed to hit practice shots here?"

Not all the veterans could be so cold to the rookies. Arnold Palmer handled a similar situation, with more tact, at the Buick Open later that same year. Tony, who was having trouble with the difficult sand on the course, Warwick Hills, snuck out on the course to practice in the bunkers. He waited until he thought that all the other players had completed their practice rounds before he and his caddy made their way out to the third green. Tony started to hit a few explosion shots from a bunker. Again, this was a violation of the tournament rules prohibiting practice on the course.

Suddenly, Palmer and Dow Finsterwald appeared over a hill, playing a few late practice holes. Palmer, seeing Tony in the bunker, his caddy on the green collecting balls, approached him.

"I know that you know you're not supposed to be practicing this way." Palmer said in a calm and friendly manner. "I guess you feel you need it very badly, but so do all of us. What you're doing will mark up the green and make it difficult for the greens keeper to keep it in shape. I'm not a policeman or anything, and I'm not going to order you to stop, but I can suggest a way of practicing that will be just as good for you and not nearly as hard on the golf course. Play a few holes and deliberately hit a shot now and then into one of these sand traps."

Finsterwald nodded in agreement before the two men played on. Palmer had just won the Masters two months before and was, by far, the biggest star on tour. He handled the whole situation with grace. Tony felt great that the tour's biggest star would give him, an unknown rookie, tips on how to practice. His admiration for Palmer grew because of this encounter.

The inexperienced pros on tour flocked to one another for companionship. The players Tony befriended during his rookie year, Johnny Pott, Jim Ferree, and Tommy Jacobs had personalities that meshed with his. Johnny Pott, a 23-year-old, exhibited a great sense of humor, as did Jim Ferree.

Jacobs, a quiet, deep-thinker from Denver, Colorado, is the older brother of John Jacobs, who also played the tour after occasionally caddying for Tony in the early 1960s. The elder Jacobs was very popular with the other players, but he was also one of the least known players by the public. He had a great record as an amateur winning the National Junior title in 1951. He was slender and was one of the finest balls strikers on tour, with the ability to shoot low scores.

Pott, along with the late Dave Marr, created corporate golf outings in the early 1960s, where PGA stars entertained and played golf with a corporation's executives and clients. Professional golfers played exhibitions to make extra money since the early barnstorming days of Walter Hagen and Gene Sarazen; however it was Pott and Marr who made the innovation to market, and customize, the concept to corporate America.

Pott went on to serve on the PGA Tour Tournament Committee in the early 1960s and was instrumental in developing the PGA Tour's standard for television programming and packaging. The huge television contracts the PGA Tour enjoys today resulted, in part, to the founding work done by Pott and the Tournament Committee.

Jim Ferree, grew up in Winston-Salem, North Carolina, learning the game of golf from his father, Purvis, a golf pro. He attended the University of North Carolina starring on the golf team. Known as one of the very best strikers of the ball tee to green, his weakness was his putting.

Ferree later played the Senior PGA Tour, now known as the Champions Tour. Former commissioner, Deane Beman, chose him as the model for the Tour's logo with his trademark plus fours, sometimes called knickers. The Senior Tour plastered the logo on everything from clothing to the leader boards around the course. Ferree told *Sports Illustrated* in 1999, that, "even though I've gotten older and my game is deteriorating, I'm still at the top of the leader board every week."

These four men traveled, roomed, ate, drank, and played practice rounds together. They cajoled each other, laughed and cried with each other, all the while helping each other over the rough spots that the Tour throws at the younger players.

10 MAKING THE CUT
1958

Tony made cuts as a rookie, which meant he was exempt from qualifying for the next tournament on the schedule. As a result, he kept playing week after week. Nobody wanted to Monday qualify, and the easiest way to avoid it was to make cuts. Playing every week was physically exhausting, but Tony persevered through the spring, picking up small checks that usually did not cover his expenses.

Tony, like most players, did not adhere to a physical fitness program. "The only running we did back then was to run to the bar after our rounds," said Mike Souchack, a former Duke football player who played the tour. Even so, Tony's young body held up to the rigors of playing every week.

Tony played the New Orleans Open, Pensacola Open, and the Azalea Open, making the cut in each winning small checks. The Azalea Open was the last stop prior to the Masters.

Tony watched the Masters, the first major tournament of the year, on television. He did not qualify for the invitation-only tournament. Players earned an invitation into the Masters by being a past champion, winning a PGA tournament, finishing high on the money list, or high finishes in the other major tournaments.

Tony watched as Arnold Palmer won the 1958 Masters emerging as a major sports superstar. The Augusta victory laid the foundation of what would become the Palmer legend.

The first stop after the Masters was the Greensboro Open at the Forest Country Club in North Carolina. Tony opened with a fine round of 69, just two strokes back of fellow Bay Area native Don Whitt.

Tony posted another 69 in the second round remaining in second place, two strokes behind the new leader, Al Balding.

In the 36-hole final round, Tony knew he was going to win the tournament as he stood on the final green. He fired a 70 in the morning and followed that up with a 69 in the afternoon. Art Wall, playing alongside him, needed to sink a 15-foot putt on the last hole to tie Tony. Sam Snead, playing in the group right behind Tony, also needed to birdie the last hole to tie Tony.

In *Golfer's Gold,* Tony wrote:

While Wall was lining up his putt, I strolled over to the scorer's table by the edge of the green wearing a mood of confidence as if it were a brand-new alpaca sweater. There I was informed not only that Don January had finished with a sizzling 64 that tied me, but that Bob Goalby had shot a 66 and would certainly win the tournament by at least two shots.

To make matters worse, Wall made his putt and Snead birdied the last hole resulting in a five-way tie for second place. Tony experienced mix feelings; he was thrilled to cash a check for $1,080, his largest check so far as a rookie, but he was also disappointed. What he really wanted was the victory. Goalby was also a rookie in 1958 and won his first PGA tour title. Tony impatiently wondered when his time would come.

The tour moved to Louisville, Kentucky, for the Kentucky Derby Open. Tony got off to another good start shooting a 69. Gary Player, the South African who had also joined the tour in 1958, was riding to the course with Tony each day. Player kept an optimistic patter about how happy he was to be playing against the American players and how much he enjoyed the tour.

Tony, playing good golf, spent an enjoyable first two rounds paired with his pal Johnny Pott. Pott witnessed Tony's hole-in-one on the 138-yard thirteenth hole. Tony used a nine-iron for his ace and finished the second round with a sizzling 67, tying for the lead. The weather was hot in Louisville that week, so when Tony, Pott, and Player arrived back at their motel, they decided to cool off at the pool.

Pott lounged at the side of the pool, giving the pretty girls the eye, while Tony decided to give the girls a show displaying his diving skills. He gave an extended performance exhibiting graceful dives and swam around the pool for far too long. Golfers learn quickly that swimming and golf do not mix well. The arms feel like sandbags the next day throwing off a player's timing.

Feeling the effects of his aquatic performance, he was lucky to shoot a 75 in the third round. In the final round, he birdied three of the last four holes to manage a 70 for a four round 279. Gary Player won the tournament for his first U.S. victory with a 274, $2,500 for his victory, while Tony won $950.

With the high finishes at Greensboro and the Kentucky Derby Open, his good first two rounds at the Azalea Open, and his performance at Tucson, Tony started to gain attention. His received an invitation to the prestigious Colonial National Invitational played in Fort Worth, Texas, known as Ben Hogan's tournament because he won it a record five times. Unfortunately, for Tony, he opened the Colonial with a 74 in the first round, followed with a 73 in the second round and finished out of the top

25.

Tony finished well down the money list the next week in Detroit at the Western Open winning $248.75. The tour returned to Texas for the Dallas Open the first week of June. Tony opened with a 66 but finished 10-strokes off the winning pace and won $180. It was a disappointing finish to what appeared, at the start, a promising week.

Tony failed to qualify for the next tournament on the schedule, the U.S. Open at Southern Hills. He watched on TV, again, as the big boys played for a major title. Tommy Bolt won the Open, his first major championship of his career, beating Gary Player by four strokes.

Tony returned after the U.S. Open for the Buick Open in Flint, Michigan, at the Warwick Hills Golf Club. Buick was a new corporate sponsor and had plans of adding a great deal of prestige to the event. They increased the purse making it one of the richer stops on tour.

"Everybody wanted to play," recalled Billy Casper, the eventual winner of the event. "A lot of guys said if they put up money like that, we'd tee it up in the streets."

Corporate sponsorship was still in its infancy and the newspapers did not know exactly how to handle it. In their reports, they alternated names, sometimes it was the Flint Open and other times it would be the Buick Open.

Tony's week got off to a rough start when he opened with a 75 in the first round and then followed it up with a 77 in the second round barely making the cut. Warwick Hills, a year-old course, quickly proved a stern test for the touring pros.

"It was a tough golf course," Casper said. "If you shot par that was a good score."

Tony finished much stronger with a 72 in the third round and a 70 in the final round to win $900. It was very different from Casper's huge payday of $9,000 for first place, but he salvaged a good check after a shaky start.

Tony enjoyed the next week on Long Island for the Pepsi Open at Pine Hollow Country Club. When he arrived in town, he flipped through his little black book of girlfriends and called a woman he knew from back in the Bay Area. She relocated to New York City to pursue a successful modeling career. He did not spend any more time at the course than it took to complete his rounds.

The model showed Tony all the hot spots in the Big Apple, with Tony picking up the tab each night. They wined and dined at the best restaurants and then danced the night away in the nightclubs and hip discothèques. When Tony had late tee times, he simply stayed over in the city.

As he would admit in *Golfer's Gold*, "The golf course was just a place I was forced to spend four or five hours away from this beautifully built female."

He played unremarkable golf but did make the cut and won $150. However, this did not come close to covering his nightclub expenses for the week.

Tony played in the Eastern Open finishing out of the money and then had another week off because he was not eligible to play in the last major of the season, the PGA Championship. Dow Finsterwald won the Wanamaker trophy at the Llanerch Country Club in Havertown, Pennsylvania. The PGA, for the first time, conducted the championship at medal play. Up until 1959, the PGA played a match play format.

Tony returned to the grind of the tour after the PGA Championship in August in Milwaukee for the Miller Open. This was another example of the influx of corporate sponsorship with the brewer taking over the Milwaukee Open.

Tony made headlines in *The Steven's Point Daily Journal*—but it was premature. UNKNOWN'S 66 TOPS WARMUP FOR MILWAUKEE OPEN screamed the headline. The headline underscored the ambiguity the press felt with corporate sponsors replacing the traditional civic names of tournaments. Tony shot a 66 in the practice round with a 34 on the front nine and a 32 on the back nine. Then, just for the heck of it, he went out, played the back nine again, and duplicated his score of 32.

Only trouble was, he could not keep it going. He shot a 69 in the first round and followed that up with rounds of 72, 69 and 68, good enough on the easy course for only a tie for 26th place and a check of $345.

Sitting Duck Keller Course and the St. Paul Open were next on the schedule and Tony shot a red-hot 64 in the third round. His round featured a 30 on the front nine that tied a tournament record. He opened the tournament with a nice 67, but as he did so often this rookie year, he threw a high score into the mix. This time, it came in the second round when he shot a 74. He finished with a solid 67 in the final round for 272, nine strokes behind the winner, Mike Souchak, and cashed a $656 check.

Tony continued to score well as the tour moved to Edmonton, Alberta for the Canadian Open at the Mayfair Country Club. He opened with a 66, one-stroke back of the leaders, Don Fetchick and Don January. He was still in the hunt with a second round 67 before falling back with a 73 in the third round. He finished with a 70 in the fourth round, nine-strokes back of Wes Ellis, the champion. Tony earned another $218 for his week's work.

The pros traveled across Canada, to the west coast, for the Vancouver Centennial Golf Tournament. Tony and his traveling mates, Ferree, Pott and Jacobs, arrived in town and set themselves up in a single apartment in the very posh Georgian Towers in downtown Vancouver.

The course, Point Grey Golf Course, was a pleasant layout that did not challenge the tour pros. Ferree opened the tournament with a 67 landing him in second place, one-stroke off the lead. He got hot in the second round firing a sizzling 11-under-par 61 for a two round score of 128 and held the lead. Tony was well back of Ferree's torrid pace with a two round 147, making yet another cut.

Ferree continued to lead after Saturday's third round. At the time, there was a blackout in Vancouver on professional sports on Sundays. To keep the players entertained, tournament organizers arranged a pleasure cruise up the Straight of Georgia. Ferree had to deal with the pressure of leading the tournament for two nights. However, the pressure never seemed to bother Ferree as he fought off Billy Casper to win by one.

Ferree captured his first victory on the PGA Tour, and won a check for $6,400. It was the first victory for Tony's group of friends. Ferree was a huge hit with the galleries in Vancouver with his easy-going style and his quips to the press. He sported a goofy, small straw hat during the week that he donated to the tournament after his victory. The club made a bronze replica of the hat to display in their trophy case.

In Vancouver, Tony's impatience and temper got the best of him in the first round. After missing a short putt, he jabbed with a backhanded stroke at the remaining tap-in and missed that one, too. He then compounded his mistake by backhanding the next putt with the same result. The lapse in self-discipline cost Tony two strokes as well as $450 in prize money. It was an expensive rookie mistake.

Tony and the tour moved on to St. Lake City for the Utah Open with a $17,000 purse. Tony opened with a 67 over the Salt Lake City Country Club and trailed Jimmy Turnesa of Elms Ford, New York, by three strokes. He finished with solid rounds of 68-71-70 and added another $550 to his official earnings for the year.

After the Utah Open in Salt Lake City, the tour moved on to Denver, Colorado. They were playing the Denver Centennial Open at the Wellshire Municipal Golf Course. Tony roomed with Jacobs, a native of Denver. Jacobs opened with a 65 and found himself on top of the leader board while Tony opened with a pedestrian 72.

Tony got the opportunity to observe, up close, the pressures that a leader has to deal with while rooming with Jacobs that week. Jacobs continued to lead after the third round shooting another 67. With a one-stroke lead going into the final round, Jacobs took Tony out to dinner with some of his local friends. As they were returning to the motel, their car broke down. They popped the hood and started working on the car by the side of the road. They both hunched over the engine, elbow deep in the greasy mess, for a couple of hours before they finally got it running. They

eventually arrived back at the motel around 1 a.m.

Tony was surprised how well Jacobs seemed to be handling the pressure, but that impression changed the next morning. He awoke and noticed that the ashtray on Jacobs' nightstand was overflowing, evidence that Jacobs spent a restless night smoking instead of sleeping.

In the final round, Jacobs managed the pressure even though he lost his putting touch during the middle holes of the front nine. He shot his third consecutive 67 for a 266 to capture the title. Tony finished strong with a 67 for a 274 total and won $930.

Tony was now not only making cuts, he was making good checks. He was climbing up the official money list. However, he was somewhat frustrated. While he was happy for his friend's recent victories, he was impatient for one of his own.

He kept plugging away the next week in the Mojave Desert at the Hesperia Open. He opened with a 71 while John McMullen shot a 69. Both players being rookies from the Bay Area, and Lucius Bateman students, comparisons between the two were inevitable. McMullen had won $6,325 in winnings for the year compared with Tony's $8,902.

McMullen kept his nerves through the four rounds, shooting 68 and 67 in the next two rounds before fighting off Gene Littler in the fourth round to shoot 67 for his first win. His first place check for $2,000 lifted his earnings to $8,325. Tony could do no better than a tie for 20th place and won $180.

While he led McMullen on the money list, Tony did not have a victory while McMullen did. Yet another rookie player had captured a tour victory before Tony.

As the year wound down, Tony reunited with Cliff Whittle, returning for the Idaho Open at Whittle's home course, Blue Lakes Country Club in Twin Falls, Idaho. In the final 36-hole round he shot a 128 to win by six shots over Whittle and Al Feldman of Tacoma, Washington. He won $500 and pushed his earnings, both official and unofficial money, to over $11,000 for the year.

Malarkey made the short trip from his Sun Valley home to watch Tony and Whittle play in the Idaho Open. The three spent the evenings in the town's bars and the drinks flowed freely. The morning of the final round, Tony knocked on Malarkey's motel room door, but the big man was in such bad shape from the night before that he could not answer the bell. Tony left him behind and departed for the course.

As Whittle and Tony, playing together in the final round, strode off the first tee, Malarkey finally arrived at the course.

"Good luck, Tone!" he yelled down the first fairway.

Tony made a caustic remark to Whittle and ignored Malarkey.

"Tony," Whittle started to explain, "Jim will get $3 million on his 31st birthday next month. You might want to be nice."

"Oh, *really?*" Tony asked, suddenly interested. He then turned around, gave a big wave over his head, and yelled back to the tee, "I'll see you after I've won this thing!"

The three men got together after his round to celebrate his victory.

In early November, Tony landed a spot in the select field playing in the Havana International Golf Tournament. Havana's casino resorts were sponsoring the tournament that featured a plump $45,000 purse. The casino operators invited the top-30 money leaders on tour as well as ten at-large invitations. Tony was inside the top 40 money winners for the year and received one of the at-large invites.

On the way to Cuba, he played in the Carling Open, the first week of November, in Atlanta, Georgia where he finished in a tie for 12th winning a check for $775.

In Cuba, the casino resort owners resembled the orchestra on the Titanic who played while the ship was sinking. At the time, Fidel Castro and his guerilla army where pushing the fighting in the Cuban Revolution from the mountains towards Havana. Yet, the golf tournament was an unrestrained party.

The players, treated lavishly off the course, played for a rich prize purse of $45,000 on the course. For added excitement, a Calcutta pool auctioned the players to gamblers. The Calcutta pool reached $39,000 with Sam Snead garnering the most action in the bidding selling for $5,500. Tommy Bolt, second in the bidding, sold off for $4,000. Players who made money for Calcutta participants could expect a cut from his owner. The winning bid on Tony went unreported, but he surely went for far less than the name players did.

Tony tied for fourth in the tournament and won a check for $1,600 in unofficial money. His Calcutta "owner" enjoyed a nice payday and, one would hope, cut Tony in on his winnings.

The players returned to the mainland for the West Palm Beach Open Invitational where Tony got off to a fast start shooting 69 in the first round. He cooled off in the second round shooting a 71 but came roaring back in the third round with a 66. His disappointing final round 73 was still good for a tie for 13th place and a check for $425.

The top-40 money winners on tour, including Tony in the 36th spot, made a return trip to Havana in December for the Havana Pro-Am Invitational, another lavish tournament sponsored by the casino resorts. Cuba was just weeks away from Castro's overthrow of the Batista government, but the party went on for the PGA players. They once again received lavish treatment from their hosts with free rooms at the best hotels, chauffeured limousines and cocktail parties at private haciendas.

"I was getting a taste of being an international playboy and it seemed pretty intoxicating," Tony wrote.

He enjoyed his time in Cuba with the Latin women, gambling and drinking, all played out to a Mambo beat.

Tony finished out 1958 by traveling to Puerto Rico for the unofficial Dorado Beach Open where he won $392. His year ended where his PGA Tour career started a year earlier; at the Mayfair Inn Open in Sanford, Florida. He opened with rounds of 70 and 72 but skied to a 77 in the third round. Exhausted, he withdrew and headed back to San Leandro for the holidays.

The rigors of living on the road continuously for the last 12 months took its toll. The life of a PGA pro was definitely not the carefree vacation he envisioned back in San Diego when he tendered his resignation from Ruby View. Living out of a suitcase, eating restaurant and take-out food, sleeping in unfamiliar beds had worn him down. His exhaustion resulted from competing in over 40 tournaments and pro-ams. His only breaks from competition were the forced layoffs during the weeks of the Masters, the U.S. Open and the PGA Championship—all tournaments he did not qualify to play in.

His hard work resulted in a successful year for him as he won a little more than $10,000 in official money. That figure climbed closer to $16,000 with his unofficial money added. He made the cut in nearly every tournament he entered avoiding the pressure of Monday qualifying.

Tony returned to the Bay Area for the holidays and felt pleased with his first year performance. His biggest disappointment was that he was unable to capture a victory in an official event. He had his chances; first at Tucson, later at Memphis, and his best chance, at Greensboro. Jacobs and Ferree managed to capture victories, and Tony felt confident that he was ready to do the same.

With the desire to become more competitive on tour, he decided that he would make a few minor changes to his game. He wanted to hit the ball on a higher trajectory with a left-to-right fade that would help land the ball softly on the greens. This would help him be able to get the ball close to tucked-in pins.

These adjustments, as Tony wrote, would, "make me a big winner, a top star, a rich man."

They almost put him out of business.

11 SOPHOMORE SLUMP
1959

It happens to every golfer. In an effort to improve, they adjust their swing and in the process ruin their game. As they fumble through various solutions, trying to get their swing back in a groove, they resemble a bungling safe cracker. They spin the dial from one number to another in a vain attempt to find the right combination and unlock the secrets. The player flits from one swing thought to another, becoming confused while losing his confidence.

Before long, they find themselves in a prolonged slump. During Tony's time on tour Ken Venturi, Mike Souchak and even Arnold Palmer, all suffered through slumps. In the modern era, Ian Baker-Finch and David Duval experienced the same thing. In Baker-Finch's case, it drove him from competitive golf.

Tony's goal was to make a few small adjustments that would change his ball flight from a natural draw, where the ball curves from the right to the left, to hitting a fade where the ball curves in the opposite direction. A ball hit with a fade will travel on a higher trajectory and will hit more softly with backspin and less roll. He felt that he could attack pins better with a fade. His thinking was sound, but he went about implementing the changes incorrectly.

He first changed his grip rotating his hands counterclockwise on the club. The result was a weaker grip that minimizes the power of the right hand making it easier to keep the clubface open through contact producing a fade. He also moved the ball back in his stance. This adjustment was the one that threw his game off.

Because of the changed ball position, he was coming down into the ball with his hips and hands too far ahead of the ball. Combined with the grip change, the result was a ball flight that started right and then faded *further* right.

While implementing these swing changes, he took a small holiday trip to Sun Valley, Idaho, to visit Malarkey. While there, he and Malarkey drew up a new sponsorship agreement for the 1959 season. The new contract, a written agreement, differed from to the oral agreement they operated under in 1958. The new agreement called for an increase of his advance to

$14,000 for the year. Of course, Tony's winnings would have to cover the increase.

Since he had his clubs with him in chilly Sun Valley, he decided to put on a little driving exhibition. He wanted to impress Sigi Engl, the head ski instructor at Sun Valley, and his staff. Tony was belting balls down the first fairway towards the green about 331-yards away. As he bombed out shots, he succeeded in impressing his audience. The ski instructors murmured their amazement at the length of Tony's drive. He loved to hit the driver, one of his favorite clubs, and he had owned this particular driver for a long time.

Rising to the enthusiasm of his gallery, Tony really belted one that stopped on the front edge of the distant green. He bent over to tee up another ball, caught a glimpse of his driver and almost got ill. The persimmon wood had shattered completely at the neck where it attached to the shaft. The wood could not handle the continued pounding he was giving it, combined with the cold temperature. He felt like a boy who had just seen his dog run over by a car.

A pro forms a special bond with the driver and the putter; the two clubs in the bag used the most. It was not a good omen for Tony to enter the new season searching for a new driver. He experimented with different persimmon, deep faced drivers before settling on a MacGregor model designed by Toney Penna.

He also spent time with Shirley Donovan while in Sun Valley. The two talked by phone often and enjoyed nights on the town during his visit. She knew everybody in the Sun Valley area and liked to show Tony around.

The first event of the year, the L.A. Open, started well for Tony. With his amateur partner, baseball great Bob Lemon, they finished in a tie for third in the opening pro-am event. Tony was a great pro-am partner who made the day enjoyable for his partners. Tony made beneficial long-term relationships with some of his pro-am partners including television star James Garner and television producer Danny Arnold.

Tony followed up his good play in the pro-am with some solid play in the tournament. With rounds of 73-69-73-72, he finished in a tie for seventeenth and won $680. His second season on tour was off and running with the sky as the limit, or so it seemed. The second time around the tour's schedule is much easier for the sophomore tourist. The pro now knows where to stay, eat, and he is familiar with the courses.

For Tony though, the year quickly deteriorated. It began when he wrenched a disc in his back forcing him to withdraw from the Crosby. The next week at the San Diego Open his back felt better but he found other ways to sabotage his tournament. He putted very well in the first two rounds shooting a 68 and 67. His putting stroke deserted him in the third round as he soared to a 74.

After the third round, Tony returned to his room at the Stardust Motel, which was located near the course. His phone rang, and on the other end was a very attractive model who he met at the tournament the year before. He invited the young woman over for dinner and the two spent a very enjoyable, albeit a very long night together.

He wrote he could play in a golf tournament any time, but how often do you have a chance to spend the night with a model that resembled a Greek goddess? Predictably, he stunk up the course in the fourth round shooting a 79. He finished out of the money.

It was never difficult for him to meet and entertain women; they were everywhere at the tournaments. They were at the course, in the hotels and in the bars. They were there to meet famous professional golfers.

To these groupies, it did not matter whether or not a pro was married. More than a few marriages broke up on tour because of a pro's infidelity. However, single players like Tony were particularly attractive to the women looking to hook-up with a pro.

In *Golfer's Gold*, Tony categorized the types of women who haunted the tour into four classifications. He felt that these categories probably applied to anyone who was in the public eye including entertainers, politicians, and other sporting figures. As was proven by Tiger Woods in late 2009, this easy access to women could prove calamitous.

The celebrity hounds made up the first category of women. This type of woman, one who craved attention, believed that the notice the celebrity attracts washed off on her. While this type of woman hung all over you in the public eye, she cooled off considerably in the bedroom. Tony wrote that the best plan with this type of a woman was to plead a sick headache and take her home early.

The next category was women who were golf nuts. They wanted to learn all about the game even though golf is the last thing a pro wants to talk about with a woman. Again, Tony advised the sick headache as the best way out of this type of date.

The final two categories were his favorites. One was the normal, fun loving woman who saw the players not as celebrities, but as men. They were moderately interested in golf, but they were more interested in having a good time with an eligible man. The final category was the impulsive, aggressive girls who make no bones about the fact that they were out to have a good time and that a pro golfer offered an excellent opportunity at doing just that.

These women, full of confidence and dressed in colorful dresses, stood where the golfers could not help but notice them. If that failed, they had no compunction about using the telephone to arrange trysts with the players.

Tony wrote a fictionalized, yet representative, version in *Golfer's Gold* of a phone dialog with this type of woman. The phone rings while he is watching television in his hotel room. On the other end is a woman who was on the course that day watching him play. One thing leads to another before he invites the young woman to the hotel for an exciting and fun night.

He believed that a player should try to live the kind of lifestyle out on the road that he would back home. If a player was single and dating, then he should date out on tour. If a player liked to enjoy a cocktail, or two, at home, then go ahead and do the same on the road.

Many of Tony's friends and family believed that his trouble with bad rounds during the weekend related directly back to his off-course habits. After grinding out good rounds on Thursday and Friday, he would then spend too much time partying that led to poor results on the weekend.

Like most bachelors, Tony kept a little black book with the phone numbers of women he met during his travels on tour. Along with the woman's phone number, he would add a small comment that would help him remember the encounter. As the black book filled with names, the comments became more important. Of course, he made sure the information on the Greek goddess-like model was up to date in the little black book.

The pattern that he set in California, playing well in the pro-am and mediocre in the tournament, continued as the winter tour moved through Arizona and into Texas. He made cuts and small checks, but he never really got things rolling, never built up any momentum.

The tour moved to Florida and he shared the lead after the first round in St. Petersburg. To him, the hole looked like it was the size of a garbage pail, instead of just $4\frac{1}{2}$ inches, as he sank putts from everywhere.

In the second and third rounds, his putting returned to normal and he shot a 76 each day knocking him out of contention. His enthusiasm for the tournament drained as his scores soared. By the fourth round, he lost all desire. He did not give a damn what he shot.

He played in the final round with Walter Burkemo and Chick Harbert, veteran players he considered friends. He was striking the ball well during the round. He came to a tough par-4 hole where he hit his three-wood second shot within 15-feet of the hole.

He ran his birdie attempt about a foot and a half past the hole. Carelessly he then missed the short tap-in. He became so enraged that he reached out with his putter and slapped at the ball. When that did not go in he began whacking the ball, back and forth, in a half-hearted attempt to get it in the hole. Finally, the ball somehow found the hole ending his nightmare.

"Give me a 12 on the hole," Tony snarled at Harbert who was keeping his card.

"No, goddamnit," Harbert replied with a chuckle as the two walked off the green. "You made an 11, but I lost a lot of cash on you—I bet Walter here you'd get down in 10."

Harbert was trying to add a little humor to the situation, but Tony did not think it was too funny. Therefore, Harbert turned serious with him on the way to the next tee.

"Look," he said, "if you're not going to try, then don't even bother to come out here and drive yourself crazy. Some days you are just going to have to work very hard to shoot a 74 or a 75. If you're not willing to put up with it, then you're in the wrong business."

There were other embarrassments for Tony during this dark time—missed backhanded tap-ins, thrown and broken clubs. At one tournament, he accidentally hit his ball, while taking a practice swing with his putter, off the green and into a sand trap. The result was a double bogey on a hole where he was originally putting for a birdie.

Many of his fellow players tried to help him. Professional golf is one of the few sports where a fellow competitor, a person who is trying to beat your brains out, offers a tip, loans you a piece of equipment or pulls you aside for a pep talk when needed. Tony felt fortunate that there were fellow players that cared enough about him that they tried to help. The Hebert brothers, Dow Finsterwald, Ken Venturi and others tried to advise him on improving his attitude on the course.

His behavior off the course was not helping matters either. Tony, trying to forget about the sad state of his golf game, tried to find solace in the bottle and the company of women. Yet his attitude on the course continued to spiral downward. Filled with self-loathing, he began to hate golf. At the Azalea Open, the week after St. Pete, Tony produced one of his worst scores as a professional going 79-75-80-79 for a 313 and finished out of the money. He now found himself fully mired in a slump.

In Chicago, at the Gleneagles Open, he missed his first 36-hole cut since coming out on the tour full-time. He then proceeded to miss his next three in a row. He was becoming impatient during his rounds, trying too hard to make something good happen and when it did not, he lost his temper.

Despite his bad attitude, he finally managed to get himself into contention at the Portland Open, during the first week of October. He followed an opening round 65 with a 68 in the second round that earned him a tie for the lead with Billy Casper. His third round 69 left him alone in second-place, two strokes behind Casper.

On the first hole of the final round, his tee shot took a bad bounce off the left side of the fairway and ended up under a tree. His only play was to chip back into the fairway resulting in an opening bogey. On the second tee, he impatiently told himself that he had to get that lost stroke back—

immediately. He hit his approach shot to within 15-feet but got too aggressive with his birdie putt, running it several feet past the hole. He missed his next putt and found himself two-over-par while the other leaders were firing birdies.

On the third hole, a short hole requiring only a drive and wedge, Tony aggressively went for a back pin and overshot the green winding up at the bottom of a slope. He continued his aggressive style trying to hole the chip shot and ran it by the hole. Two putts later and he had his third straight bogey.

Now realizing that he was out of contention to win the tournament, he gave himself a pep talk. Settle down and make a good check, he told himself. Stop charging for birdies in a lame attempt to get lost strokes back and start playing solid golf. Be patient and stop forcing the issue with blind aggressiveness.

He turned things around and played the last 15 holes in two-under-par, good enough to tie for fifth place and a check for $1,000. It was his highest finish and best check of the dismal year. His previous best finish was in Milwaukee at the Miller Open where he tied for twelfth winning $900. Still, his finish in Portland was not enough to salvage a horrible year.

A discouraged Tony headed back to Oakland. On the plane home, he mulled over his year in an attempt to analyze exactly where he went wrong. He realized he had developed a bad attitude while riding an emotional rollercoaster from one extreme to other on the golf course. When he blew-up on a hole, he allowed it to ruin his entire round resulting in a high score.

He understood that he had lost confidence in himself and his game. He had seen the same thing happen to other players, but he had seen most of them turn things around for a comeback. He chalked up 1959 as just a bad year. He hoped things would get better in 1960. He vowed he would start playing up to his potential.

12 THE YEAR OF THE KING
1960

Tony tried to put on an optimistic outlook for the new year of 1960, but his career continued to ride the escalator down. The year got off on the wrong foot when he was roughhousing with his brother Harry, resulting in Tony cracking a rib. He explained to the press that his injury was the result of a fall while skiing in Sun Valley. He had been in Sun Valley where he hooked up, again, with Shirley Donovan.

The injury kept him out of the opening event of the year, the L.A. Open. Tony started his year by playing in the Yorba Linda Open, the second event of the new season, and shot a blazing 66 in the first round.

His play fizzled out after his opening round, and he could do no better than a tie for 25th place winning only $112.50. It was a disappointing week after such a good start.

The next week, in San Diego, he won the pro-am event before the tournament with a 67 and then went out and missed the cut. He continued this pattern of playing the pro-am event loose and relaxed, and then the tournament tight and tense. It was a clear indication that his attitude had not improved any from 1959.

He was blaming things on bad luck. He blamed his cracked rib on bad luck and his high scores on lousy breaks. He often gave up after a bad shot, or bad hole.

Things did not get any better at the Bing Crosby National Pro-Am, where he opened with a dismal 78 in the wind at Cypress Point. With a 68 in the second round, he managed to make the cut, but mediocre third and fourth rounds left him with only a meager check of $100.

With his dark outlook, he entered the next tournament that featured one of the richest purses on tour at $100,000. It was the new Palm Springs Desert Classic with a format, an idea of Bob Rosburg, which was frenetic and confusing. The pro-am event resulted in a very large field, requiring the use of four different courses. The players, especially the amateurs, were never quite sure of their schedule or what course to play. The pros played with a different three-man amateur team each day. Amateur teams combined their scores with each different pro each round. To top it off, it was a 90-hole tournament played over five days.

Arnold Palmer negotiated his way through the confusing format to win the first-place prize money of $12,000 shooting a score of 338 over five rounds. It was the largest purse of Palmer's five-year career, his previous biggest payday at the Masters in 1958 where he won $11,250.

For his part, Tony started the tournament well with a 67 that placed him in a tie for the lead. However, he followed with lackluster rounds finishing in a tie for 53rd, collecting a small check of $139.58. In his first round, he drew as one of his amateur partners, the television producer Danny Arnold. The producer took an immediate liking to Tony.

After the round, Arnold invited Tony to stay at his house for the remainder of the tournament, an offer Tony quickly accepted. He checked out of the hotel where he was staying and moved in with the affable producer and his equally engaging wife, Donna. Tony felt staying with the Arnolds, eating home-cooked meals, beat the hell out of a hotel and restaurant food.

Tony fell in love with the Arnolds. They were warm, caring, and engaging. Tony needed somebody to talk to, somebody who would listen and help him turn his attitude around. Danny Arnold fit the bill perfectly.

Arnold noticed that Tony was overemotional on the golf course. He felt Tony did not have the properly serious attitude that the game required, and told him so. Arnold recognized that Tony had a fine swing, but his temper and negative attitude killed his talents.

Arnold advised him to control his temper.

"Don't throw away strokes because you are pissed off about something that happened on the last hole, or the last shot," he advised Tony.

Arnold's advice actually penetrated the thick layer of self-pity Tony had built around himself. But his well-ingrained bad habits, would take some time to fix.

Tony left Palm Springs with new life-long friends, and supporters, in the Arnolds. In the future, he would stay with Danny and Donna whenever he was in Palm Springs or Los Angeles, where they also had a home. He often called them from the road and felt comfortable talking to Danny about his deepest feelings and thoughts. Tony, a regular letter writer, also kept in contact by mail with the couple while he was traveling the circuit.

Even after Arnold's talk with him about his attitude, Tony continued to stumble through the winter tour. When he made cuts, he would finish far down the leader board, but worse, he was missing far too many cuts.

By August, he had fallen to 87th on the money list. He was miserable. Nothing was going right; he was not sleeping or eating well, and he continued to drink and womanize too much. Friends tried to make him realize that his poor scores, especially on the weekends, were a result of his hard partying. He was trying too hard to play good golf, but his off-course behavior was carrying him in the opposite direction. He lost all sense of values both on the course and off.

The other players became concerned, and tried to talk to him about the state of his game and his mind. Because Tony was so popular with the other pros, they wanted to help. At first, Tony did not listen to them. He was determined to work himself out of this slump.

Professional golf was all Tony knew. He wondered what else could he do for an income, especially an income as lucrative as the kind of money he knew he was capable of making on the tour. His only option was to find a head pro job at some country club, something Tony had already done and was incomparable to the life of a tour pro.

Finally, when the tour made its annual stop in St. Paul, Minnesota, things had hit rock bottom. Dow Finsterwald asked Tony to stop by his room for a talk. Finsterwald liked him enough that he thought a stern, man-to-man talk would do him some good.

"Look," Finsterwald began. "Don't you think you could give it a better try out here if you got hold of yourself, all the way down the line? Cut out the nonsensical drinking. You can't belt down a half a bottle of scotch at night and expect to play halfway decently the next day. Don't go out on the golf course all pissed off at the world, either. Develop a more cheerful and hopeful mental attitude or you will never be able to play well again."

Arnold Palmer, who had a soft spot in his heart for Tony, also took him aside to tell him he had a choice: he could be a player or a playboy. He could not have it both ways.

Finally, Tony began to listen to the advice and lectures from his friends. He realized he was lucky that there were people out on tour who were his friends and cared enough to try to help him.

While Tony went through a living hell in 1960, Arnold Palmer was setting the golf world on fire. His year would see the transformation of the popular golfer into "The King." It started at the Palm Springs Desert Classic, where he ran away with the tournament, then he rode a hot streak through the winter tour with victories in the Texas Open in late February, the Baton Rouge Open a week later, and the Pensacola Open the week after that. It was the first time since 1952 that back-to-back-to-back victories occurred on tour. Even Tony, deep in self-pity, recognized that Palmer was setting a new standard.

Palmer added the Masters title in April with a birdie-birdie finish to beat Ken Venturi by one-stroke. In June, at the U.S. Open at Cherry Hills in Denver, Palmer amazed the golf world with one of his now patented charges. Starting his afternoon round of the 36-hole final seven strokes behind the leader Mike Souchack, he drove to the edge of the par 4 first green.

He two-putted from the fringe for a birdie and started an assault on the leaders with a birdie barrage. As Souchack withered, the afternoon boiled down to a three-way race between Palmer, Nicklaus, and Hogan; a battle between professional golf's past, present and future.

Palmer arrived at the seventeenth tee at four-under, tied with Hogan. Nicklaus's inexperience contributed to him falling out of contention by this point. The seventeenth hole at Cherry Hills is a par 5, impossible to reach in two shots, because of water protecting the island green. Palmer watched from the fairway as Hogan, playing the same hole, tried to shave his short third shot close to the pin located on the front of the green. The shot spun back off the green into the water resulting in a bogey that ended Hogan's chances at an unprecedented fifth U.S. Open title.

Palmer safely coasted home with pars on the seventeenth and eighteenth holes to capture the title with one of the most thrilling rounds in U.S. Open history.

Palmer did not have time to savor the victory as he departed for St. Andrews, Scotland, to play in his first British Open.

On the flight to the British Isles, Palmer suggested to his business manager, Mark McCormack, as well as newspaperman Bob Drum, that if he could add the British Open and the PGA championship to his Masters and U.S. Open titles he would hold all four titles in one calendar year. He proposed that he would then hold the modern equivalent of Bobby Jones's Grand Slam. Jones won his Grand Slam in 1930, which consisted of the U.S. and British Opens and the U.S. and British Amateurs.

Golf had changed in the decades since Jones's achievement and it was unrealistic for a player to win those same four tournaments. An amateur had not won the U.S. Open since Johnny Goodman captured the title in 1933. Drum took Palmer's idea of a modern, professional Grand Slam and trumpeted it with his readers raising interest in Palmer's first attempt at a British Open.

Caddy Tip Anderson helped Palmer navigate the tricky links Old Course at St. Andrews. In the end though, they came up one shot shy of capturing the third leg of the new modern Grand Slam. Kel Nagle captured the Claret Jug, but the idea of the Slam lives on to this day. Palmer's performance jettisoned him into international superstar status, and Tony took notice. He saw what winning the U.S. Open meant for Palmer and wanted a national open title of his own. First, though, he needed to start playing better.

Palmer finished out his year by winning the Insurance City Open and the Mobile Open. After the Mobile Open, Palmer and Tony accepted an invitation to spend a few days on a mutual friend's yacht in New Orleans. The two flew down to New Orleans, enjoyed a night on the town with a cocktail party the following afternoon.

They spent the final night on the yacht rooming together in quarters that featured a bunk bed. Tony, in the top bunk, was having trouble sleeping. After tossing and turning for about a half an hour, he called down to Palmer's bunk, asking if he was asleep. Palmer was also awake, so the two lit up cigarettes and talked.

"Do you realize what you have really done this year?" Tony asked.

"What do you mean?" Palmer replied.

"Well, winning what you have the way you have," Tony, explained. "Finishing birdie-birdie to win the Masters. Shooting a 65 in the last round to win the Open. It seems so fantastic, so superhuman, to have done these things in that way."

Palmer thought for a moment, exhaled a stream of cigarette smoke and then said, "I never thought of it in those terms. I just kind of see what it is I have to do, and I just make up my mind that I'm going to do it. If I have a long putt to make, I just think about making that putt. I shut from my mind the thought of missing it or all the other stuff that would come from my missing it."

The talk with Palmer inspired Tony. He got a glimpse inside Palmer's head, seeing how he thought while he was charging towards a title. Palmer liked Tony, and he often helped him by giving him equipment and advice.

Tony took this newfound inspiration into the last event of the year at the West Palm Beach Open and won the opening pro-am event with a smooth 67. He then promptly missed the cut in the tournament.

His year over, Tony headed back to the Bay Area for the holidays. On the plane ride back to Oakland, Tony went through his customary year-end self-examination and review. He realized that in every tournament he had at least one good round, that there was something to build on.

He realized that the year had been a struggle, and the cause was his self-destructiveness. After a good round, he did not allow himself to think he was doing something correct. Instead, he would go out and party all night while his negative thought process convinced him that he would not be able to keep up his good play the next day. The whole year had been a trip through a mental hell.

It was inevitable that Tony and his traveling mates, Tommy Jacobs, Johnny Pott, and Jim Ferree would drift apart. They were still close friends, but Jacobs and Pott had gotten married in 1959. Married players on tour traveled in different circles than the bachelors. Pott had also finally won his first tournament, the Dallas Open in 1960, a tournament where Tony missed the cut. Players with victories on tour also traveled in different circles than players who had yet to win.

As his plane traveled westward, Tony thought that he would give the tour just one more year, and that would be it. He was getting sick of the travel, even sick of playing the playboy. The hotels and motels were becoming boring, as was the dining out every night. The nightlife, once exciting, was wearing thin. Tony realized he had lost his determination and his desire to play good golf. At this point, he hated to look at a golf club, or a golf course.

Malarkey, who Tony now owed about $10,000, wanted him to quit. He offered, more than once, to forgive Tony's debt if he would give up tournament golf. Nevertheless, Tony vowed to keep persevering, for at least one more year. If things did not get better, he would find a head pro job at a country club.

When he got home to Oakland, he finally began to relax. He spent time with his family and old friends like Bill Craig. He left the pressures of the tour behind.

"When Tony came home from the tour, he was just Tony," his brother Harry remembered. "He wasn't a pro golfer; he was just a part of the family."

Tony particularly enjoyed dating the hometown girls who did not know a thing about golf. Out on tour, the women who flocked to the bachelor pros were hanger-on types. At home in San Leandro, where the phone rang off the hook as old girl friends called, he could spend time with women who did not care that he was a professional golfer.

He loved Cleo's home cooking and he would start his holiday meals by loading up his plate with her dressing. He gobbled up the dressing, washing it down with a big glass of milk before returning to fill up his plate with the other food.

While in Oakland, he vowed to return to the tour with a new attitude. He swore he would control his temper and keep his emotions under control. He would try to be more optimistic. He was not sure it would work, but he was resolute that he was going to give this next year the best effort he could. Then, if he had to walk away from tournament golf, at least he could do so knowing that he had given it his best shot.

13 LATIN RENEWAL
1961

During the winter, the PGA helped sponsor an offshoot tour, known as the Caribbean Tour. This mini-tour was a five-week excursion through Latin America with about 50 U.S. professional golfers invited to compete. The U.S. contingent was made up of about 40 teaching pros, who were basically on vacation while their home courses were shut down for the winter, and ten, or so, touring pros.

For the touring pros, the Caribbean Tour offered a break away from the routine of the regular tour. Money won on the Caribbean Tour would not count as official money towards the money list. However, the pros relaxed knowing they had a guaranteed $200 each week against their winnings.

The pros received their $200 guarantee from local sponsors at each stop. The sponsors covered expenses for food, travel and lodging. In addition, Seagram's liquors, a co-sponsor of the tour, offered a "Pot of Gold" for the leading point winner of the tour. The pros accumulated points according to their finish in each of the five tournaments determining the champion who would collect the "Pot of Gold" $2,000 bonus.

Tony received an invitation to join the tour after Bob Toski dropped out because of business commitments. The year had started out indifferently for Tony, so he jumped at the invitation offered at the Palm Springs Desert Classic in early February.

When his name came up for consideration as a substitute for Toski, it did not garner a lot of excitement.

"Sure, why not? Nobody is going to miss him on the PGA Tour, anyway," one tour official said.

He only had $170 in winnings from the Bing Crosby National Pro-Am to show for his efforts in the New Year. At the event in Palm Springs, Tony finished with a horrible 80 to finish out of the money. A highlight of the week was a reunion with Danny Arnold.

Before joining the Caribbean Tour, he flew home to Oakland to pack before departing for Los Angeles. There, he joined the other touring pros for the flight to Panama and the Panama Open. Other touring pros making the trip included Billy Maxwell, fresh off his victory in the Palm Springs Desert Classic; Ernie Vossler, making his third Caribbean Tour trip; fellow Californian and Lucius Bateman student, Don Whitt, and Jim Ferree. Dow Finsterwald also made the trip; however, he would be playing in the first tournament only. Tony's roommate for the trip was Whitt.

For Tony, the Caribbean Tour represented a chance to be in contention every week and learn how to play under the pressure. As there was not a 36-hole cut in any of the events, he could work on putting four good rounds together—an area that he needed to improve.

The trip also provided him with an opportunity to work on his game. Back home, on the winter tour, the fields were so large that finding space on the practice tee was often difficult. It was all one could do just to get a patch of grass for a warm-up before a round. On the Caribbean Tour, Tony could put in some of the hardcore work required to get his game back on track. He finally abandoned the grip change he made two years earlier and went back to his natural draw.

His account of his time on the Caribbean Tour, written in *Golfer's Gold* reads like a hilarious travelogue. With their travel expenses and entertainment expenses covered, the pros enjoyed their pampering, but the schedule was brutal. They had to play in oppressive heat, were always on a plane, and dealt with language barriers.

The players settled into the Panama Hilton Hotel, a large modern hotel on the edge of the city with a view of the Pacific Ocean a few miles to the south. The course they played was a baked-out track with wide, dry cracks in the clay soil of the fairways. White stakes, driven into the hard ground on both edges of the fairways, right up to the green, marked the area where players could play preferred lies. Inside the rows of white stakes, rules allowed a player to move the ball onto a patch of grass within a few inches of their original lie. Drive your ball outside the white stakes and the result was a crapshoot; you could encounter any type of horrendous lie.

Tony had a tough time with the Panama City course and finished in 23rd place. Despite his poor play, he and Whitt were having a good time off the course. They relaxed between rounds while enjoying the shopping and nightlife of Panama City.

Tee times on the Caribbean Tour started in the late morning and the two would grab a quick breakfast before heading downtown for some shopping. Panama City was a free port with great deals on jewelry, cologne, and electronics in the shopping district. The boys then returned to the hotel for lunch by the pool before going to the course for their rounds.

After golf, they would return to their room, enjoy a few cocktails made from the free bottles of Seagram's left in their room, and relax. They grew fond of the frozen daiquiris at the hotel bar that helped take the edge off the broiling temperature. Later, it was off to dinner and a nightclub before returning to the hotel around midnight or 1 a.m. Tony found the routine relaxing.

Pete Cooper won the tournament and the $1,200 first prize with a 273. After the completion of the tournament, Tony tried going to bed early but the pre-Lent carnival was going on in full-force. There was a big celebration in the hotel and the loud music kept him awake.

Never one to pass up a good party, he got out of bed and got dressed. He went downstairs to the party with music blasting, the crowded dance floor moving to the beat. In the center of the dance floor, the crowd made a clearing for the beautiful Carnival Queen. She dazzled the crowd in her white gown and golden crown as she danced with her partner. Tony dragged his eyes away from the Latin beauty long enough to glance at her partner. What he saw floored him; keeping pace with the Queen was Whitt, who happened to be a graceful dancer.

Whitt was very absorbed by the music and Tony watched as he jumped up on stage. He grabbed a couple of maracas, started to shake them to the music, leading the orchestra. The crowd was ready to anoint him the King of the Carnival. Whitt looked the part with his long sideburns and dark complexion.

It was no wonder why the group of Americans showed up at the airport the next morning sleepy, dazed, and nursing a hangover. They boarded a plane for Venezuela. Once on the ground, they almost went into a state of shock. Maracaibo, the city they landed in, was a hot, flat and dusty oil town with a wind that blew off Lake Maracaibo.

The golf course however, was beautiful. Located about 15-miles outside downtown Maracaibo, the club utilized an $18,000 maintenance budget, a huge amount in 1961 dollars. Most of the budget went to pumping a million and a half gallons of water on the course each year. The result was green fairways and lush, elevated greens. Players had to keep the ball in the fairway, however, as trouble lurked beyond the well-maintained short grass. Iguanas ruled in large numbers in the desolate wind-swept rough. The course was long, measuring 7,000-yards.

In the tournament, Whitt played almost perfect golf beating Argentinean Roberto de Vicenzo to win the tournament.

Tony played well and even thought he had a chance to win the tournament himself. He got impatient, becoming greedy, while trying to win the tournament on the first few holes of the final round. He three-putted the first three holes on his way to a closing 79 that put him into a tie for tenth with his old pal, Jim Ferree.

His caddy, barely four feet tall was about fifty years old. He dressed in oversized coveralls and a straw hat and he was barely bigger than the golf bag. After Tony would hit his shot, the caddy humped the bag onto his shoulder and set off, at a very quick pace, for the ball. Tony tipped the man an extra $10 that made the caddy ecstatic. He went around showing the bill to anyone that would look at it.

After the squalor and oppressive heat of Maracaibo, all the players looked forward to the next stop, Caracas. They had heard that it was a beautiful city and, at an elevation of 3500 feet, it would be much cooler than Panama City or Maricaibo.

The climate may have been cool, but the political climate was not. The government of Venezuela recently changed from a dictatorship to democracy, resulting in unrest from various factions. When the players got word about a bomb threat at their hotel, it was enough for at least one club pro, Dick Chase of Pittsburgh, to call it quits and high tail it back to the states to play the PGA winter tour.

Despite the political chaos surrounding them, the pros enjoyed the beautiful metropolitan city. Whitt played well again in Caracas on the demanding, narrow course that measured only 6,200-yards. The course weaved along a hilly setting above the city. He won the tournament easily, by eight-strokes.

Tony had his moment in the spotlight negotiating the narrow course in the third round. He was six-under-par for the first 15 holes and he began to entertain thoughts about shooting a 60. In typical Tony fashion, he was going for all the gusto. All he needed to break the course record, a 65 shot by De Vicenzo in the first round, was to par out. Instead, he was greedy. He wanted to shoot a 60.

On the sixteenth hole, he nearly hooked his four-wood drive out-of-bounds. Luckily, a clump of tall grass stopped his ball. On the seventeenth hole, he again hooked a four-wood drive, this time into deep grass. On the eighteenth, he hit his four-wood tee shot through the fairway where he ended up barely two feet from being out-of-bounds. He did manage three pars to tie De Vicenzo's course record.

He parlayed the round into a third place finish, his best showing so far on the Caribbean Tour. The players received their checks at a festive dance held at the club after the tournament. A band called Billo's Caracas Boys played Latin and American dance tunes that kept the joint jumping.

During a band intermission, the pros received their checks. It was a lively affair and Tony spent the night on the dance floor in the arms of a young woman. Entranced by the girl's dark eyes, he invited her to spend a night on the town, along with her aunt who acted as a chaperone, following the festivities at the club. He did not get to bed until dawn and spent most of his winnings from the week entertaining the two women.

The tournament ended on a Saturday because Sunday was census day in Venezuela. The residents of the country served what amounted to house arrest while the golf pros remained sequestered at the hotel. Fortunately, for the pros, the hotel they were staying at, the Tamanaco Hotel, had all the amenities to keep them occupied. The pros enjoyed the sweeping view of Caracas from the hotel nightclubs, bought English-language newspapers and magazines at the newsstand, or lounged around the pool. There was even a pitch and putt golf course on the grounds.

The hotel manager decided to stage a tournament on the par 3 course so the pros could entertain the other guests. He dubbed the tournament the Tamanaco Open, and it got the pros' competitive juices flowing. Alcoholic juices flowed, as well. Whitt and Tony, for instance, fortified themselves with a couple of frozen daiquiris before they hit the pitch and putt course for the tournament.

The pros stumbled around the course in their bathing suits, half hung over with drinks in hand. Bob Watson, a teaching pro from the New York area won the tournament with an eight-under-par score, which did not exactly qualify him for the Masters.

After the tournament, the pros congregated at the pool. Tony grabbed a wedge that Jamaican player Caleb Haye had. He jumped in the pool to demonstrate the art of hitting a ball out of a foot of water. He splashed around accomplishing nothing more than soaking himself, and everybody around the pool.

Other players also attempted the impossible shot. Ernie Vossler tried the shot after jumping into the pool still wearing his shirt and wire-rimmed glasses. He started thrashing around in the water, keeping a running commentary dripping with his Texas twang, for a full five minutes, laughing the entire time.

"There's no way you can get this ball out of here," he kept shouting.

While frolicking at the pool, Whitt found a way to put an end to his two-week winning streak. Usually a good diver, the mambo king attempted a somersault off the high diving board and he threw out his back. He was in so much pain from the injury that he could hardly swing a club the next week in the Puerto Rico Open.

The trip to Puerto Rico did not go smoothly due to an airline strike. The strike forced the cancellation of the tour's Pan American flight and tour supervisor, George Hall, arranged a charter flight. Of course, Whitt and Tony made things difficult. The previous day's fun in the sun, along with evening cocktails, exhausted the pair. The next morning, they overslept causing them to miss the bus to the airport. The two caught a taxi, took the hour-long trip to the airport before finally rejoining the group. There they sat around in the heat for two hours while waiting for the preparation of the plane. They finally boarded the plane for the four-hour trip to Puerto Rico.

Once it landed, a grumpy group deplaned into the heat of San Jose. The pros felt burned out and exhausted. All they wanted to do was to finish the tour and return to the good old U.S.A. The heat, the difficulty of dealing with language barriers and the non-stop travel were all taking a toll.

San Juan was crowded with too much traffic and too many big hotels. The course, Berwind Country Club, was a "goat track." Ditches, inhabited with huge toads, crisscrossed the fairways. The heat made it difficult enough to play, but when a giant toad jumped out of a ditch in the middle of your backswing, it was downright unnerving.

Whitt was out of contention early because of his wrenched back while Tony was out of it due to a bad attitude. He kept trying to lay up short of the ditches with an iron or a three-wood from the tee only to watch his ball bound across the hard, dried out grass into the ditch he was trying to avoid.

To make matters worse, the room that Whitt and Tony shared had only one good bed. Whitt's bad back did not curry any favor from Tony when it came to choosing beds. The boys made a wager to decide who would get the good bed. The low score won the bed while the high score had to suffer on the foldout couch. Tony managed to beat the injured Whitt for the bed three out of four nights. However, he felt he was spending more time in Berwind's ditches than he was in that bed.

During one round, he attempted to layup short of a ditch but watched as his ball trundled across the hardpan fairway and into the trench. It happened again on the eighteenth hole and by now, Tony had enough. He unleashed his temper, going temporarily insane. He walked up to the ditch, hurled his three-wood down into the muck, and then he grabbed his bag from his caddy and threw it in on top of the three-wood. He turned around to face his caddy with a crazed look. The caddie's face turned white as a sheet with fright and he started to back away from the lunatic American.

"No, señor, no, no," the caddy pleaded, with his palms extended. "Por favor, por favor," he continued as he turned and fled down the fairway.

With the same lousy frame of mind he had back in the states, Tony was back to hating golf. His fellow competitors understood his frustrations; everyone was on edge from the arduous trip.

From Puerto Rico, the troupe boarded a flight for Jamaica and the final stop on the Caribbean Tour. After the flight landed, the golfers, and tour officials, posed for pictures on the tarmac and gangplank of the plane.

The picture ran in the local paper, *The Gleaner*, the next day portraying a ragged and worn-out group of men. Tony, at the top of the gangplank in the rear of the group, is leaning out over the handrail and looks exhausted.

Jim Ferree won the Jamaican Open by six shots. Tony and Whitt returned to form and they played good golf. Billy Maxwell won the Seagram's Cup, along with a bonus of $2,000.

Once the tournament ended, the golfers let off some steam. They gave an impromptu, alcohol-induced, clinic for the few fans that remained at the course.

The men cajoled each other and pulled off practical jokes whenever possible. They generally acted with the release of men who had just completed a tough, long job, which they had. When Tony was asked to hit a six-iron, he snuck a four-iron out to the tee which he hit 190-yards. Normally he hit a six-iron about 160 to 170-yards. The next player, hitting a five-iron, appeared to be a weakling when his shots were falling woefully short of Tony's "six-iron" shots. The other players got a big laugh out of this.

The exhausted players returned to their hotel, the Courtleigh Manor, and went to bed early. All of them except Tony, that is. He was feeling frisky, so he headed out for a night on the town. He returned to the hotel at 4:30 in the morning in just the right mood to play another practical joke. He bribed the night desk clerk to ring up each of the players' rooms with a wake-up call. The clerk then explained a change in their flight plans with a much earlier departure.

Of course, the plane was not to leave until late morning. When they finally boarded the plane for Miami, the players complained loudly about the hotel's screw-up. Tony had to join in the chorus or else reveal his role in the cruel prank.

After the plane landed in Miami, the group avoided close inspections of their golf bags at customs. Their bags were loaded with perfume, liquor, bolts of cloth, and other trinkets they bought on their trip. They were looking to avoid the high duty they would be required to pay if officials discovered their treasures. They pulled out golf balls and stuffed them in the pockets of the inspectors playing the role of PGA pros to the hilt. The ploy worked, the officials processed them quickly after only cursory inspections.

Whitt was returning to California for some rest with his family so Tony loaded him up with everything he had bought on the trip, shouted his goodbye, and hopped a plane for St. Pete to rejoin the Tour.

Tony felt that he had found his game again while on the Caribbean Tour. He did not win an event as he had hoped to, but he got in a lot of practice and felt like he made some improvements in his game. He was ready to get down to business for the remainder of 1961.

14 THE HARD CLIMB BACK
1961

Tony was exhausted physically from his five weeks on the Caribbean Tour, but he felt rejuvenated mentally. He finally started to feel good about his game. He won $1,938 on the Latin tour, even though it did not count towards his official money winnings. He gained valuable experience, put together some good rounds, and he felt that his swing was back to form.

He rejoined the tour at the St. Petersburg Open, the scene of his meltdown two years prior when he slapped the ball around the green before receiving a lecture from Chick Harbert. Because it was so dry, the fairways were running fast at The Pasadena Golf Club, and the course played very easy.

Tony got his week off to a good start when he finished second in the opening pro-am. He played well in the tournament with rounds of 71-66-68-66. His 13th place finish was worth $590.

Tony had his work cut out for him to climb the money list. Mired in 80th place on the money list when he left to play the Caribbean Tour, he fell 30 more spots by the time he returned. The check from St. Pete improved his position to 73rd and his goal was to make it into the top 40 by year's end. Being in the top-40 would get him in the invitation-only tournaments.

He found his finish in St. Pete encouraging, and he eagerly headed down to Miami Beach for the Sunshine Open. He stayed where most of the pros were staying in Miami, at the Miami Racquet Club. The amenities of the hotel proved to be a distraction to him.

He arrived at the Racquet Club very late at night and, after checking in, went immediately to bed. He woke the next morning to the distinctive sound of female laughter coming from the pool area just outside his room. He peeked through the curtains and saw a gaggle of young women swimming, laughing and sunning themselves. It was going to be a long yet fun week, away from the golf course, at least.

At The Racquet Club, the guests did not have a care in the world. In addition to the large swimming pool, the Racquet Club also featured several tennis courts. The hotel, located on one of the canals of the Florida Intracoastal Waterway, had docks with expensive yachts moored. Of all the pros staying at the Racquet Club, the single men had the most fun. The place was crawling with women and the week was one long party. Tony jumped in with both feet.

He started each day with breakfast by the pool before rushing over to the golf course to get that golf business out of the way. As soon as his round was complete, he would hurry back to the hotel. Once there, he sat by the pool enjoying drinks while mixing with the women. Later, he would wander down to one of the yachts moored at the hotel's docks for a relaxing cocktail party.

Predictably, he missed the cut leaving him a weekend full of free time. He decided to fill his time taking tennis lessons. He did not really want to improve his tennis game; he wanted to get closer to the woman giving the lessons. Tony amused himself during the lessons by teeing off on serves from the instructor. He sent the balls in a high arc over the restraining fence and out into the canal. He got a big charge out of this, but the result was a bill for both the instruction and the lost balls. At least the instructor was a good dancer.

At the Racquet Club one late afternoon, Tony and a few of the other players enjoyed cocktails down by the canal in the company of a few young women. One of the pros wondered how far it was to carry the canal with a golf shot. They haggled, back-and-forth, about which club would carry the water. They finally settled on a seven-iron. Of course, they made a few wagers, before they selected one of the pros, Gerry Priddy, as the player to attempt the shot.

Priddy had a big wild swing that could send the ball great distances making him the natural choice for the shot. With the small gallery watching, Priddy lashed wildly at the ball and dumped it in the water. He tried again with the same result.

Tony, fortified with bravery of a few cocktails, tried next. He gave himself a nice fluffy lie and whacked the seven-iron shot high over the water where it landed safely on the distant shore. The women were duly impressed and applauded the conquering hero.

Priddy, not to be outdone, attempted the shot one more time. This time, he caught the ball flush and it soared on a high trajectory over the water, over a house on the other side and over some trees in the backyard of the house. He hit a seven-iron, a club that usually produced a shot of 150 to 160 yards at least 210 yards.

Tony, unable to qualify for an invitation, had to settle on watching the Master's on TV, yet again. Gary Player won the year's first major, beating Arnold Palmer down the stretch and became the first non-American to capture a green jacket. For the remainder of April, Tony languished in the mid-eighties on the money list as the tour wound through Greensboro and then into Texas for the Texas Open Invitational and the Waco Turner

Open Invitational.

The Waco Turner was a relaxing tournament. Held opposite the Tournament of Champions, a tournament that featured a select field of tournament winners during the prior 12-months, the Waco offered the opportunity for non-winners to compete. Waco Turner was a huge golf fan who put on his tournament at his lodge and country club, in Burneyville, Oklahoma. He liked to add spice to the competition by awarding a $15 bonus for each birdie, $50 for each eagle and $25 for chip-ins from off the green.

Tony found this stop on the tour far more relaxing than Miami Beach and the Racquet Club. Players booked into Turner's lodge for next to nothing and the town did not feature any distractions. In fact, there was nothing to do in Burneyville. The town lacked so little nightlife that the players had to entertain themselves with card games and drinking in the clubhouse.

A relaxed and focused Tony played good golf at the Waco Turner. He opened with a 70 and followed up in the second round with a 73. Turner's course was flat, but extremely long, requiring two good shots into each of the par 4s, usually with a stiff wind blowing. Tony carded a third round 71 before closing with a 74 for 288. It was good for his first top ten finish since Portland in early October of 1959. The seventh-place check of $802 moved him from 84th place on the money list to 68th.

He followed his good showing at the Waco Turner by missing the cut at the next tournament. He bounced back two weeks later finishing tied for 16th at the Hot Springs Open Invitational.

Tony's comeback was rolling along smoothly until he ran into trouble with his putting after the Hot Springs Open. His confidence on the green was in shambles. Short putts became monstrously difficult for him.

With his confidence in his putter shaken, he traveled to the Western Open near Detroit in Grand Rapids. A friend in Detroit named Ed Addis loaned Tony his car to make the three and a half hour drive to Grand Rapids. Once there, his game went sour, and combined with his awful putting, he missed the cut.

Tony drove back to Detroit to return Addis's car. When he arrived, he discovered his friend was not home. He settled down to wait for Addis's return but, as he sat in the driveway, he realized that Detroit was the home of Horton Smith, one of the game's greatest putters. Smith won the inaugural Masters tournament in 1934. He stormed the tour in 1925 at the age of 20 and racked up 49 victories on tour before his 25th birthday. He made a lucrative living, for a professional golfer in those days, by enduring an exhaustive exhibition schedule once booking 100 exhibitions with Walter Hagen in a six-month period.

Smith grew up putting on sand greens and believed the experience helped him see the track of the ball and aided him in developing a great feel. Tony, introduced to Smith a few years earlier on tour, decided to call him to see if he could arrange a putting lesson.

Tony phoned Smith, who remembered meeting him. After explaining that he had a putting problem, Smith invited him to the club for a lesson.

"You come right on over," Smith said. "I'm sure all you've lost is your confidence, but you come over and we'll get you back to a good putting stroke."

Tony immediately felt relieved as he drove over to the Detroit Country Club. He spent about an hour with Smith on the putting green talking about what a putting stroke should be and how Tony could improve his putting. Even as Smith talked and gave examples of a good stroke, Tony could feel his confidence returning.

Smith's putting technique emphasized the importance of the stroke being a right-handed stroke while the left hand kept the blade square. The putting surfaces on courses during this era ran much slower than greens in the modern era. Players had to rap the ball much harder using the wrists and right hand for power. Smith demonstrated a drill for Tony where he stroked putts using only his right hand. Immediately, Tony's stroke returned, as did his confidence. He was very touched by Smith's gracious help, as well as extremely grateful.

Excited about the lesson, Tony was eager to put it into action. He jumped back into Addis's car, and instead of returning to Detroit, he headed straight for Flint, Michigan to play in the Buick Open. Once there, his putting touch returned, as did his confidence. His long game deserted him in the third and fourth rounds, but his putting remained solid.

After the Buick, he finally returned Addis's car to him, a week late in early July. He then departed for the St. Paul Open where he played very solid. He opened with a round of 71, followed by a 70 in the second round. His game really jelled in the third round resulting in a fine 66. A final round 71 put Tony in a tie for 15th place with a $670 check that jumped him up to 63rd on the money list.

After the final round, Tony returned to his hotel suite at the St. Paul Hotel. A group of players, including Tony, planned to catch a late train to Winnipeg for the Canadian Open. With time on his hands, and feeling good about his play in St. Paul, Tony was in the mood to celebrate. He hastily threw together a little party in his suite for the other players. He met some girls in the hotel's hospitality room and, using his substantial gift of persuasion, convinced them to attend the celebration.

The cocktails flowed with the expected, and desired, effect on all. Everybody had a delightful time and it was not long before the boys looked to pump some excitement into the festivities. One of them came up with the bright idea of hitting balls out a large window. The pros took turns driving balls out the window down onto Market Street. The inebriated group finally made their way to the train station where they poured themselves onboard for the trip to Winnipeg.

Tony started to really hit his form in Winnipeg; he shot a blistering 65 to take the first round lead over rookie Jacky Cupit, Jon Gustin, and Bob Pratt.

TONY LEMA ASSUMES OPEN LEAD read the banner headline in *The Winnipeg Free Press*. A story that documented the first round ran above a picture of Tony wearing a blazer, with a golf club in his hand, as he crouched down pointing at a group of balls arranged in the numerals "6" and "5" representing his first round score.

He shot a second round 70, which tied him for the lead with Cupit. The putting lesson from Smith was paying off as he holed a number of putts for birdies. In addition, he made key par putts on a number of holes on the back nine.

His game cooled off in the third round, what *The Winnipeg Free Press* described as "blowing up to a 72," because the course was playing so easy. He finished with a 70 in the fourth round, tied for seventh place, winning $1,200.

The Milwaukee Open was next, conducted over the North Hill Country Club course that measured only 6,410 yards. Tony opened the tournament with a 69, followed that up with a 68, and was one-stroke off the leaders.

Tony faltered in the third round with a 72, but came roaring back in the fourth round with a 66. The score was the low round of the day, an honor he shared with Tom Nieporte. Tony finished in a tie for sixth, along with Nieporte, and Jack Nicklaus playing as an amateur. The trio finished three strokes back of the winner, Bruce Crampton, from Australia, who scored his first PGA victory. Tony's finish was good for a check of $1,300 and he jumped to the 47th spot on the money list.

Tony had an epiphany after his final round. He started the fourth round tied for 18th place. After 10 holes, he was three-under-par and had closed the gap with Crampton, the leader, to four shots. However, he bogeyed the eleventh, twelfth and thirteen holes. He got angry with himself for blowing a good round. Things got worse on the fourteenth hole when he missed a short putt for birdie. He was just about to launch his putter in anger, but caught himself.

As he walked to the fifteenth tee, in an attempt to calm his emotions, he gave himself a pep talk. He told himself to bear down, play the last four holes and see what he could salvage of the round. After the round, if he still wanted to get mad, he could, but while he was out on the course, he was going to give it his best.

After gathering himself, Tony managed to finish with four straight birdies. On the eighteenth hole, a par 5, he hit a poor drive and his second shot from the rough ended up under a tree about 80-yards from the green. From there he choked up on a 5-iron and ran the ball up onto the green within eight-feet of the cup and made the putt for the birdie.

What he learned about managing his emotions on the back nine was worth as much as the $1,300 he won. He realized that a tour pro must keep his anger in check—that he cannot even *feel* like getting angry.

15 BACK IN THE WINNER'S CIRCLE
1961

Although his game and mental outlook were improving, Tony did not qualify for yet another major championship. He watched on television, as Jerry Barber won the PGA Championship at Olympia Fields in an 18-hole playoff over Don January.

Tony played next in the Eastern Open at the Pine Ridge Golf Club in Baltimore, Maryland, the first week of August. VENTURI, LEMA TIED FOR LEAD read the headline in *The Oakland Tribune* following the first round. The paper dubbed the two, who both shot 68, the "Mike and Ike of Golf."

Tony fashioned a 72 in the second round and now trailed Venturi, who still held the lead, by three strokes.

During the tournament, the PGA announced the field for the rich American Golf Classic, an invitation-only event at the end of August, at Firestone Country Club. Tony made the list, another sign that his stock was rising.

His 69 in the third round left him within striking distance of the leaders: Venturi, Gay Brewer, and Doug Sanders. Sanders played great golf all year. In the fourth round, Sanders won the tournament when Venturi missed a five-foot putt on the last hole that would have tied him. Tony shot another 72 and finished in a tie for 13th winning $827.50.

Tony fit in a pro-am, the Piping Rock Pro-Am, on the Monday following the Eastern Open, winning $283 before traveling to Nevada to handle some personal business. A few weeks earlier Tony received a phone call from Shirley Donovan, one of his many girlfriends that he knew from Sun Valley and Elko. She informed Tony that she was pregnant. Furthermore, she said he was the father.

With his strong faith, and a sense of responsibility, he agreed to marry Donovan. He first explained to her that it would be marriage in name only as he planned to get a divorce as soon as the child was born.

"No kid should be born into the world without a name," he explained when he broke the news to his family.

He traveled to Nevada where he and Donovan wed in Carson City. It was a quiet civil ceremony with Bill Craig standing in as Tony's best man. He and his family succeeded in keeping the whole affair secret from the other players on the tour, the press, and all but his closest friends. Tony was ashamed and embarrassed with the whole episode. After signing a letter that acknowledged that he was the father for Donovan's lawyer, he agreed to pay $75 per week in child support after the baby was born.

He rejoined the tour in time for the Insurance City Open, played on the Wetherfield Country Club course in Hartford, Connecticut, the next week. He played mediocre finishing in a tie for 30th place. He bounced back at the Carling Open in Silver Springs, Maryland where he tied for 11th and won $900. He was now in the 45th spot on the money list.

Next up was the strongest field Tony would face all year in the American Golf Classic at Firestone Golf and Country Club. His performance in this premier event was not particularly notable. His rounds of 72-73-75-76 for a 296, placed him well behind the winning score of 278 shot by Jay Hebert and Gary Player. Hebert garnered the first prize money of $9,000, beating Player on the first sudden-death playoff hole.

The next stop on the tour, in Dallas, got Tony excited. It was one of his favorite towns on the circuit, but not for golf reasons. Dallas, an airline hub, was full of attractive flight attendants. His scores for the week reflected his distraction; he shot 288 finishing well down the leader board.

He regained his focus in Denver the next week. At the Denver Open, he managed to put together rounds of 70-68-65-70 over the 6,843-yard Meadows Hills course. He finished ten strokes behind Dave Hill, who won his second victory of the year, this one in his hometown. Tony won $850 and moved up two spots, to 44th, on the money list.

The day after the completion of the Denver Open, on September 11, Shirley Donovan gave birth to David Anthony Lema. Tony made a detour on his way to the next tournament, the Greater Seattle Open. He stopped in the Bay Area where he picked up Bill Craig and flew to Carson City, Nevada to see his new son.

While in Carson City, Tony and Craig participated in David's baptismal and photos of the event show Tony holding the boy. From Carson City, he flew to Seattle.

He played well in Seattle, including a third round 64, and finished in a tie for 18th place worth $490. The next week, in Portland, Oregon for the Portland Open, he tied for 14th place. He earned a $653 check that finally landed him inside the top-40 on the money list.

The next stop, a new tournament on the schedule, the Bakersfield Open, featured offbeat prizes, in addition to cash, for the pros. In an attempt to highlight the agricultural and natural resources of the area, tournament officials came up with the inventive prizes. The winner would receive oil royalties for one year that could possibly add up to a tidy sum.

The runner-up would take home 16 steers ready for the table. Third place would receive a 500-pound bale of cotton, fourth place two sheep and fifth place would win a year's supply of grapes. How the organizers expected the pros to get the prizes home was anybody's guess.

Tony did not have to worry about that as he could only manage a tie for 25th place and a check for $167.50. Exhaustion now set in. He had been on the road since January, including the five-week whirlwind trip that was the Caribbean Tour. Most of his breaks came during the weeks of the Masters, the U.S. Open and the PGA Championship, all tournaments where he failed to qualify. In addition, his trip to Nevada to get married was not a relaxing break from the tour.

He needed a vacation, needed to go back to San Leandro and spend some time with his family and old friends. Nevertheless, before he could, he still had tournaments to play. First up was the Hesperia Open, a two-round unofficial tournament. It was a favorite stop among many of the touring pros because it was a low-key, fun event.

Playing well in both rounds of the 36-hole tournament, Tony won the event. Played on a Sunday, he shot a 71 in the morning placing him in a tie for the lead. In the afternoon round, with the aid of an eagle and three birdies, he shot a 67 and won the tournament by three strokes over Jerry Steelsmith of Glendale, California. Even though it was an unofficial tournament, it was a victory, his first since the 1959 Idaho Open. He won $1,200 with a victory giving his confidence a huge boost.

His remaining tournaments before his break included the Ontario Open, the Sahara Pro-Am, the Orange County Open, the Almaden Open and the Mexican Open. After that, he looked forward to visiting his family and enjoying some down time.

He finished out of the money in Ontario and finished in a tie for fourth in the Sahara Pro-Am, winning $750. While in Las Vegas for the Sahara, he found himself in an uncomfortable position. With his gift of gab, he proposed to two different women convincing both of them that it was true love. Neither woman obviously, was what he considered his one true love. He invited one of the women to spend the week in Las Vegas with him while he played in the tournament. Unbeknownst to him, the other woman, who lived in Los Angeles, decided to fly to Vegas to surprise him. The woman succeeded in surprising him, and he was no longer engaged to two women, or even engaged at all.

In Orange County, he picked up his ball and withdrew after only six holes in the first round because he was playing so poorly.

He finished in a tie for 17th in the Almaden Open and then traveled to Mexico City for the Mexican Open conducted on the Club de Golf. The course, euphemistically described as "rugged," was not up to the standards, or the condition, the pros usually played. Its yardage was a long 7,100 yards, but the altitude made it play shorter.

Tony opened with a four-under-par 68 to tie for the lead, with Mexican amateur Roberto Halpern. Only eight other players managed to break par. Tony rode a hot putter in the second round to shoot a two-under par 70 while Halpern skied to a 77. Tony was only one of four golfers able to break par in the second round.

He had a three-stroke lead over Antonio Cerda, the host pro at Club de Golf, and fellow Mexican Ramon Cruz. Phil Rodgers of La Jolla, California and Bob Stone were tied for fourth another two strokes back.

Tony continued to play solid, steady golf in the third round to record another 70. He then coasted to the winner's circle with a final round 72 to win by six strokes. Cerda finished second, while Phil Rodgers captured third.

Again, it was not an official PGA victory, but it was a victory in a national championship, played over four rounds on a tough golf course. Coupled with his win at the Hesperia, he began to learn what it took to win professional golf tournaments. Now he just needed to win an official tour title.

Finally able to take his long-awaited two-week vacation back in the Bay Area, he began to unwind. He visited with Dick Fry at Lake Chabot, offloading extra equipment he collected during the year. Fry would take the equipment and resell it in his pro shop. Tony still had two tournaments left on his schedule for the year, but for now, he could relax.

The two weeks passed quickly and, before he knew it, it was time to get back on the road. He packed his suitcase and golf clubs, and set off for the West Palm Beach Open that started on November 31. Stuck in the 42nd spot on the money list, he needed to play well at both West Palm Beach and the next week at Coral Gables to squeak into the top-40.

He did play well in West Palm Beach finishing in 11th place after shooting rounds of 73-68-70-72; however, it did not move him up the money list. The next week at Coral Gables, he opened with a 68 in the first round, but followed up with a 74. He eventually ended in a tie for 24th place and a check of $102.72. He fell short of his goal of making the top-40 of the money list, finishing in the 43rd spot.

Although he failed to crack the top-40 on the money list, Tony's confidence was sky high. He had made a good comeback from the hellish years of 1959 and 1960, once again establishing himself as a promising player on the tour. He turned his putting around, thanks to the lesson from Horton Smith, his long game was sound, and he was getting control of his temper and emotions on the golf course.

Officially, he won $11,505, but that figure climbed to well over $20,000 with the addition of the unofficial money from pro-ams, his Mexican Open title, and his winnings on the Caribbean Tour. He felt close to capturing his first official PGA tour event. He was no longer the depressed and sullen Tony Lema that received lectures from the other pros—he was the life of the party again. He felt that 1962 would be his year.

Tony with his brothers and sister. From left to right; Tony, Harry, Walter and Bernice
Photo courtesy of the Lema family

The Lema Family (front row) Tony and Harry (back row) Bernice, Cleo and Walter
Photo courtesy of the Lema family

Tony and his brothers, Walter (left) and Harry (Middle)
Photo courtesy of the Lema family

Tony's graduation photo. He had to attend summer school in order to receive his diploma
Photo courtesy of the Lema Family

Part Two
Breaking Through

16 KNOCKING ON THE DOOR
1962

Tony spent the holidays resting in San Leandro with his family. For him, the time bantering with his brothers and sister, as well as Cleo, was the closest he came to relaxing.

"Tony never relaxed," his brother Walter recalled. "He always had to be moving, had to be doing something."

In San Leandro, away from the rigors of travel, he recharged physically, mentally, and spiritually. As he had gotten older, he realized just what an amazing job his mother had done to raise four children alone. Cleo still worked hard, everyday reporting to her job at the Washington Pharmacy on West 150th.

Tony knew he had not made life easy for Cleo. He remembered how he conned his sister and mother to avoid the chore of washing dishes. How he told them the dishwater would ruin his hands for golf. While home on his break, he purchased a portable dishwasher for the house at 270 Sybil Street.

He also went through his annual evaluation of the past year while he formulated his goals for the coming year. It was a much more optimistic picture heading into 1962 than the despair he felt the year before. His game and attitude were better as the unofficial wins he notched boosted his morale and confidence. He felt like it was just a matter of time before he broke through to win an official event on tour. That was the overarching goal for 1962.

Tony also took a good look at his personal life. He determined he needed to be more serious and healthier. It was time to break out of the playboy mold. His episode in Las Vegas with his two fiancées made that clear.

To get his body in shape, he went to a friend, Jim Powers, a firefighter in Oakland. Powers ran a gym on 73rd where McArthur Boulevard met Foothill Boulevard. He put Tony on a conditioning and strength program to help him endure the rigors of travel and the pounding that playing golf every week put on his body.

Tony also started to eat better and resolved to get a handle on his drinking. He was determined to enter the 1962 schedule with a healthier body and a better mindset.

As he considered the 1962 tour, he thought it was time to cut his financial ties with Malarkey. He was under the impression that he could terminate the contract at any time. While this was true during the first year under their oral agreement, the written contract he signed the next year locked him into a long-term commitment. Still, he approached Malarkey at the start of the 1962 and asked for his release from the contract.

He proposed that he pay back the approximately $11,000 debt that had accrued during the slump years of 1959 and 1960. After that, he wanted the contract terminated.

Malarkey was not interested in settling on just getting his investment back. Also feeling confident and optimistic, because he saw the improvement in Tony's game, he felt there was an opportunity to profit on his investment. His sponsorship of Tony represented the only real tangible thing he had accomplished in his life to date. With Tony, Malarkey could play the big shot as the financial backer of a major league sports figure. It gave him an identity. He was not eager to have the arrangement end. It was not so much a money issue—he had his family wealth—it was a status issue.

Tony was green behind the ears when he signed his contract in 1959. He did not read it very carefully, or review it with a trusted friend or attorney. Malarkey assured him that the contract was just a way to get Tony accustomed to the ways of business. He assured Tony that all he had to do was say the word if he wanted out of the contract. However, he would soon learn that gaining his release from the agreement would be more difficult than Malarkey led him to believe.

Two items in the contract should have alerted him to potential problems. The first was a stipulation that required Tony to travel first-class. He sold the Plymouth and began to fly from one stop on the tour to the next and he stayed in the best hotels. Travel on the tour was in a transitional stage from the automobile to air travel. Tony was in the vanguard of that movement even though his status did not warrant it. Malarkey increased the advance to him from $12,000 a year to $14,000 and then again, later in the year, to $16,000 to cover the increase in traveling expenses. Tony had to pay these advances back from his winnings.

The other clause that would cause him problems was that it was a three-year contract with options in place that allowed Malarkey to extend the contract through 1966. Malarkey, meanwhile, continued to assure Tony he could opt out of it at any time.

The agreement required that any debts incurred at the end of one year would carry forward to the next year. Unless Tony quit the tour entirely, he would have to pay all the accumulated debts. In the hellish years of 1959 and 1960, he dug himself a deep financial hole. He earned a total of $15,000 in those two years while racking up $30,000 in expenses.

Even though he did well in 1961, he was unable to reduce the mountain of debt he had accrued the previous two years. A light bulb went on when Tony finally realized that this deal was not in his best interests. He understood that he could not have gotten his start on tour without Malarkey. He had paid off Tony's gambling debts back in Elko, and provided the financial means to travel the tour. He was grateful for the help Malarkey provided. But he also felt that he should be able to put more money in his pocket and less in Malarkey's pocket.

He put his contract concerns on hold as he started out the new season at the L.A. Open where he finished in a tie for fifth, worth $1,900. His check far outweighed that of the most talked about rookie on tour.

The L.A. Open marked the professional debut of Jack Nicklaus who shot a 289 winning his first check for a grand total of $33.33. After a stellar amateur career that included wins in the U.S. Amateur, a NCAA championship, Walker Cup appearances and contending in the 1960 U.S. Open, Nicklaus was destined for great things on the pro tour. His $33.33 was inauspicious for his pro career start.

Tony played well in the L.A. Open due, in no small part, to the fact that he was staying at the home of Danny and Donna Arnold. Since meeting him at the Palm Springs tournament early in 1961, Tony kept in contact with the Arnolds. The couple insisted that Tony stay with them at their house during the L.A. Open. Tony trusted and confided in Danny who returned the trust with solid advice and friendship.

"He was a very likable guy with a great talent as a golfer," Arnold later recalled to *Sports Illustrated* writer Gwilym S. Brown. "My wife and I invited him to stay at our houses in Palm Springs and Los Angeles. We found out he was emotional about his game but not very serious about it. He wasn't much different than any young kid. But, we got to know his problems. He needed someone to talk to and someone to talk to him."

"Danny would talk to me by the hour," Tony told Brown. "He built up my confidence in myself and my game. He was like a psychiatrist. He convinced me that bad putts and bad shots weren't necessarily caused by an unjust fate or a weakness in me. That if I stayed calm and kept the ball in play, the breaks would come my way, too. It began to work. Every golfer has rounds when he's not playing well, but I found I could now shoot 71 or 72 on those days instead of 76 or 78."

Arnold imposed a curfew on Tony when he stayed at his house during a tournament. He locked the door at 11:30 as Tony found out the one time he challenged the curfew. He returned late, from a date, and found himself locked out. The Arnold's made him sweat it out on the stoop before finally allowing him to enter the house. Arnold also suggested that he curtail dates with women after Wednesdays so that he could better concentrate on golf.

At the Bing Crosby Pro-Am the third week of January, Tony was just six strokes off the lead after three rounds. The famous Crosby bad weather plagued the tournament, including snow that postponed play in the final round. The next day, in the re-scheduled fourth round, played in high winds, Tony nullified an otherwise good week by blowing up with an 82.

After the Crosby, the pros moved north to San Francisco for the Lucky International Open at Harding Park. Tony looked forward to playing a familiar course he played many times as a kid. He enjoyed playing in front of hometown fans.

Both Tony and Venturi received a lot of press being local pros. Many newspaper accounts commented on the similarity of their looks. Both were similar in height and weight and both had the same "widow's peak" hairline. Both also knew Harding Park very well.

Tony opened up the tournament with a 68, even though he book-ended his round with bogies on the first and final holes. He was three strokes behind the leader, Gene Littler.

After the first round, *The Oakland Tribune* ran a story in the sports section, under the byline of Ed Schoenfeld, with the headline: MR. GOLF NOT FOR LEMA. The sub-head read "Too Many Demands." The story stated that Tony was not interested in trading places with Arnold Palmer as "Mr. Golf."

"Sure, there's a fabulous amount of money and a lot of fame attached to being the top man, but it's too demanding," he was quoted. "A man like Palmer is not left alone. People are always hounding him, disregarding his privacy and imposing on him.

"Palmer looks very, very tired, worn out and I think it is affecting his performance," he concluded. Palmer had gotten off to a slow start in 1962 having won only $1,650.

"Through all of this Arnold has stayed one of the greatest guys on the tour," Tony said of his friend. "And without a doubt he is the greatest thing to happen to golf in the last 15 years."

Even though he was not interested in becoming "Mr. Golf," Tony's confidence was soaring. A second round 70 put him right in the thick of the battle. Tied for second place with Billy Maxwell, and his good friend Tommy Jacobs, he was five strokes back of the leader Gene Littler who followed up his opening round 63 with a 68.

Grouped with Gene Littler in the final group for Saturday's third round, he watched as Littler scrambled his way to another great round, a 68. Tony, meanwhile, shot a 70 and dropped to fifth place, eight strokes back.

After attending Sunday mass with his mother in San Leandro, Tony headed across the Bay Bridge to Harding Park for the fourth round. He was once again paired with Gene Littler. After his warm-up on the range, he spoke with Ray Haywood of *The Oakland Tribune* at the edge of the putting green.

"The purses are getting so big now—$1,500,000 this year—that if you play even adequately you can make a good living. I know that every week I am getting closer to being a better than adequate player."

Tony went on to explain his propensity for throwing a bad round in with three good rounds.

"That's bad thinking, too. I get to trying too hard and forget to play one shot at a time. I forget that this is a game of patience. You win a tournament with four steady rounds. I don't have these bad rounds because I go out on the town or anything like that. Bachelors always get that kind of reputation if they are seen out after midnight. Actually, if being home early meant winning golf tournaments, I would be the greatest."

Those that knew Tony must have choked on their morning coffee when they read that quote. Even though he had gotten more serious about his game, he still had his little black book filled with women's phone numbers and still enjoyed a night on the town.

After talking with Haywood, Tony reported to the first tee where he hit the ball well past his two fellow competitors, Littler and Casper. There was little hope that he or Casper could catch Littler with his six-stroke lead. They were fighting it out for second place money, along with George Knudson and Bob Rosburg.

The crowd was enormous and completely ringed the first hole. They watched as Tony hit his approach over the first green. His chip shot stopped five-feet from the cup and then he missed the putt. He went up to his four-inch putt and attempted to backhand it into the hole. Of course, he missed that putt, as well. What should have been a par four ended up being a double bogey six.

He made another double bogey on the eighth hole and was out of contention for winning, or even finishing second. He made the turn shooting a 40 on the front nine. His 76 dropped him into a tie for 22nd. What could have been a profitable week, resulted instead in a check of only $625.

He and the tour now headed to the desert for the Palm Springs Desert Classic where he would again stay with the Arnolds. He put in a lackluster performance and finished out of the money, but he did enjoy his time with the Arnolds, as always.

Tony again accepted an invitation to return to the Caribbean Tour. He left for the Panama Open upon the completion of the Palm Springs Desert Classic and he would again be rooming with Don Whitt. Keeping in line with his new, more serious attitude about his golf game, his approach to the 1962 Caribbean Tour was less like a kid on spring break and more workman like.

Tour pros making the trip in 1962 were Jacky Cupit, winner of the Canadian Open in 1961, making his first Caribbean Tour trip and Al Geiberger, also a Caribbean Tour rookie. Jim Ferree, Billy Maxwell, a long time Caribbean Tour player and one of Tony's favorite players to be paired with, his roommate Don Whitt, and Caribbean Tour veteran, Pete Cooper rounded out the group. Doug Sanders made the trip to play in the first event, the Panama Open, before returning to the regular tour to defend his title at the New Orleans Open.

Tony and Whitt picked up the routine in Panama City they established during the Panama Open the year before; a relaxing breakfast, followed by shopping in the duty free zone and then on to the golf course for the day's round. Both played well as Whitt finished three strokes behind the winner, Jim Ferree, while Tony finished seven strokes back.

Ferree continued his hot streak the next week in Maracaibo, but the young Canadian club pro George Knudsen managed to catch him. Knudsen finished Ferree off in a sudden death playoff for the title. Tony again played steady golf and finished in a tie for fifth, while Whitt finished in fourth place.

The next week, in Caracas Al Geiberger captured the title. Tony and Whitt again played solid golf and shared fifth place. Tony was in fourth place in the point standings for the Seagram's Cup while Whitt was in third place.

The Caribbean Tour made its way to Puerto Rico, while back in California *The Hayward Daily Review* announced plans for a dinner honoring Tony. Ed Voorhees and Augie Benites of the Hayward Chamber of Commerce were the organizers of the event. As soon as they could co-ordinate with Tony's busy schedule, they would choose a date.

Back in Puerto Rico, Whitt came out firing with a first round 67 that included 12 one-putt greens. Tony shot a solid, if unspectacular, 71. Whitt cooled off in the second round with a 74. He came back with a solid third round and was only two strokes back, while Tony followed up a second round 71 with a third round 70 putting him just three strokes back of the lead set by Knudsen.

Knudsen managed to hang on for the win with a four round 280. With a steady final round of 70, Tony finished in a tie for second along with Geiberger and Whitt. Whitt was firmly in the lead in the Seagram's Cup with a total of 68 points. The next three players in the standings were neck and neck; Knudsen, in second place, at 60 points, Tony in third place with 59½ points, followed by Geiberger with 57 points.

The troupe headed for the final event on the Caymanas Golf and Country Club in Kingston, Jamaica. The local company that was sponsoring Tony, paying his expenses for the week, was the Kingston Industrial

Garage. An unknown pro, Henry Williams, hung on to win the Jamaica Open while Tony played a very steady tournament and with the aid of a final round 67 managed a seventh place finish. Don Whitt won the Seagram's Cup while Tony finished third in the final point standings.

Although he did not capture the win on the Caribbean Tour that he desired, he played very steady golf and finished in the top ten in every event. His unofficial earnings for the tour totaled $3,388 and his confidence continued to soar. He was itching to get back to the regular tour where he was in 22nd place on the money list at the start of the Caribbean Tour but had fallen to 41st place during his five-week absence.

Meanwhile, in Hayward, the announcement of the date and location of the dinner to honor Tony was set. The tribute would be on May 17 at the Sequoyah Country Club.

Tony made his return to the regular tour at one of the tougher stops, the Doral Open. The players found Doral Country Club's length a stern test. In the first round, Tony shot himself in the foot when he came out and stumbled to an 82. The old Tony would have allowed that score to sabotage his entire week.

However, the new Tony kept his composure, worked hard and salvaged a check. He had a 71 in the second round to make the cut and then followed with a 72 and a 73 and made a $47.14 check. Not a huge sum, but much better than a missed cut and no check at all. He actually derived a great deal of pride out of the check because he realized how far he had come in his efforts to control his temper on the course. His new serious approach was starting to pay dividends, albeit in this case, small ones.

Despite his drop in position on the money list, Tony was confident enough in his game that he scheduled a break from the tour for a visit back to San Leandro. He did not want to exhaust himself the way he had the year before after returning from the Caribbean Tour. He also planned to play in the Northern California Open at the El Macero Country Club just outside Davis, and the Northern California PGA Medal Championship in Sacramento at the Mather Air Force Base Course.

In the Northern California Open, a 54-hole tournament, Tony shot an opening round 70 and then followed that up with a 68 in the second round. Young George Archer, an amateur due to report to the Army, was fighting Tony for the lead. John McMullen, who had given up life on the pro tour to become the teaching pro at a San Jose driving range, also challenged for the lead.

In the last round, Tony fell one stroke behind Archer who eagled the 15th while Tony could only manage a birdie. Tony then birdied two of the final three holes for a come from behind victory. The title was worth an unofficial $750.

He then traveled the short distance to Sacramento to play in the Northern California PGA Medal Championship, a one-day 36-hole event. Tony felt that being a touring pro from Northern California, he needed to support the chapter by playing in its championship. Coming down the final hole, Tony found himself two strokes down to Gary Loustalot as they battled for the title. Tony birdied the hole while Loustalot bogeyed requiring a sudden death playoff. On the first sudden death hole, Tony managed a birdie to take the title and the check of $304. He also won an exemption into the PGA Championship with his victory.

After the enjoyable trip to California, complete with the two wins adding to his already high confidence level, it was time to rejoin the tour in Houston.

17 LOVE AT FIRST FLIGHT
1962

While Tony was dominating the competition in Northern California, an exciting Masters took place in Augusta. Arnold Palmer, Gary Player and Dow Finsterwald were involved in a three-way 18-hole playoff that Palmer won, keeping his streak of winning the Masters in even numbered years alive. He previously won the green jacket in 1958 and 1960. Palmer's stardom reached insurmountable heights as he was attracting new fans, new interest in the tour and numerous commercial endorsements.

Tony rejoined the tour for the Houston Classic. He shot a first round 70, followed up with rounds of 70, 73 and 72 and finished in a tie for 15th place worth $1,075. He finished out the Texas swing by playing in the Texas Open where he finished in a tie for 28th. At the Waco Turner Open, in Oklahoma, he finished in a tie for 18th, while his friend, Johnny Pott, won by six shots. Of his original travel group from his rookie year, Tony was still the only one without an official victory.

He was now doing most of his travel by air, primarily because of Malarkey's obsession with first-class travel. He was not a huge fan of flying but it was part of his job. With his restlessness, he always had to be moving and found planes too confining. He tried to pass the time on flights by reading or playing cards.

After the Waco Turner, he caught a flight in Dallas to return to the Bay Area. As he boarded an American Airlines flight, an attractive flight attendant greeted him. During the glamorous heyday of jet travel, stewardesses, as they were then known, were almost in the same class as movie actresses and models. Tony's black book was filled with the names and numbers of many of these alluring and exciting women of the skies. Tony and the flight attendant exchanged pleasantries before he settled into his first-class seat.

The flight was a quiet one and shortly after takeoff, the flight attendant, Betty Cline, sat down with him. The two became involved in a gin rummy game. Both were enthusiastic card players, and Betty's favorite game was gin. He would play any card game—especially if you could bet on it.

Betty, like most women, was immediately attracted to Tony. He found her attractive with red hair, a pert nose and a vivacious personality. He later described the first meeting as "love at first sight." They saw each other on a few more flights before taking the next step in the relationship and started dating. He did not give up the women around the tour, the ones that filled his little black book, but he started to have feelings for the flight attendant from Dallas. They tried to get together whenever their hectic traveling schedules found them in the same cities.

His schedule for 1962 was different from his past few years because he was picking and choosing which tournaments to play in. He was conserving himself for a strong late season push instead of exhausting himself playing in every single tournament. With his experience of the past few years, he now knew which courses fit his game and which did not.

He made a trip to California in May to play in the Duden Invitational, a relaxing pro-am event that helped raise $2,000 for five East Bay boys clubs. He made it a habit to play in fundraisers, or donate his appearance fees from exhibitions to children's causes. He found it quite easy to be generous when it came to helping kids.

Another reason for the trip home was the festivities surrounding "Tony Lema Day" in San Leandro on May 17. He kicked-off the day with the groundbreaking for a new municipal golf course in San Leandro. In the evening, the Chamber of Commerce dinner honored Tony as the "Athlete of the Year" in San Leandro. After dinner, a film showing Tony in action entertained the attendees.

Mayor Jack Maltester presented Tony with a key to the city while the Chamber awarded him the "Athlete of the Year" award. John Fry, his old golfing friend and competitor attended, as did his family. After dinner and the awards, Tony addressed the crowd. He approached the lectern and looked sheepishly down at the police chief. He remembered the chief once told him to get out of San Leandro and go back to Oakland, "where you belong."

Smiling at the chief he said, "It's so nice to be home—where you're wanted."

After speaking, Tony posed for pictures including one that ran in *The Oakland Tribune* showing him poised to hit a chip shot off the mayor's balding head.

While in California, the daydreams Tony had while playing Lake Chabot with Fry came true. He signed a deal with Fernquist and Johnson, a small golf club manufacturer, to produce a line of clubs with his name on them. Both Tony and Ken Venturi signed contracts with the company who forged the irons to their specifications. Venturi did the design work incorporating Tony's request for irons with a squared off toe while his own featured a rounded toe.

He had one other piece of business to attend to while he was home in the Bay Area—getting through local qualifying for the U.S. Open.

The day before the local qualifier, Tony won a pro-am event held at Sequoyah Country Club in Oakland with a five-under 65 to beat the venerable Dutch Harrison by a stroke.

"I guess I'd have to say I'm playing pretty well," he understated.

In the local qualifier for the Open, a 36-hole event, he shot a 66 in the morning round and followed that up with a 71 in the afternoon. He played in front of a gallery of about 250, a large gallery for a local qualifier. His 137 total was good for medalist honors and advanced him to the sectional qualifying round. He would play in the sectional at Memphis when the tour made its annual stop there.

In late May, Tony returned to the tour to play in the 500 Festival Open, part of the festivities surrounding the Indianapolis 500 auto race. This was one of his favorite stops on tour. Both he and Venturi were big fans of racecar driver Johnny Boyd who was from San Francisco. That year they went to extraordinary lengths to see Boyd race in the Indy 500.

After the tournament, where Tony finished in a respectable tie for 15th place, the two flew down to Memphis for the sectional qualifier for the U.S. Open. The two played a practice round on Monday at the Memphis Country Club, the course used for the qualifier. On Tuesday, they headed over to Colonial Country Club to play a practice round for the Memphis Open. Tuesday night, they flew back to Indianapolis to watch Boyd race in the 500 the next day, before flying back to Memphis to tee off Thursday morning.

The crammed travel schedule took its toll on Venturi who failed to make the cut in the Memphis Open, and then failed to qualify for the Open.

The travel, however, had no effect on Tony who opened up in the Memphis Open with a fine round of 68. After an even better round of 67 in the second round, he found himself just four strokes back of the leader, Gary Player. His third round 69 kept him in contention just six strokes back of the third round leader, Jay Hebert. A lackluster 72 in the final round put him in a tie for 13th place.

The U.S. Open sectional qualifier was a one-day, 36-hole affair held the day after the Memphis Open. He managed to qualify and would return to the U.S. Open for the first time since his 1956 appearance at Oak Hill.

He had one event to play before the Open, the Thunderbird Classic at the Upper Montclair Country Club in Clifton, New Jersey. He did not drive the ball very well at the Thunderbird finishing well down the leader board. It was not a good sign to arrive at a U.S. Open with a balky driver. Open courses are always set up to put a premium on accurate driving. The Oakmont Country Club, host of the Open, not only required accurate drives, but long ones, as well.

In the first round, Tony continued to have trouble controlling his driver and the tough Oakmont course ate him up as he missed the cut by one stroke. Forced to watch from the sidelines, he watched as one of the most exciting and historic U.S. Opens unfolded.

A cast of pros, including Palmer and Nicklaus, battled for the title during Saturday's 36-hole final round. During the morning round three players, Palmer, Gary Player and Bob Rosburg, all held the lead at one point or another. Nobody seemed to be paying any attention to Nicklaus as he negotiated the course for a 72 to position himself two shots back of the leaders. Palmer, Phil Rodgers, Bobby Nichols and Rosburg sat atop the crowded leader board at the conclusion of the morning round.

The majority of the record-setting crowd at Oakmont, estimated at 23,500, followed the hometown hero Palmer.

In the afternoon round, Nicklaus bogeyed the first hole but he came roaring back with birdies on the seventh, ninth and eleventh holes. He was now even with Palmer. Rosburg was in the process of shooting himself out of the tournament with a 79. Rogers and Nichols also faded from contention.

Nicklaus focused intently, while tuning out the raucous partisan crowd, and handled the pressure extremely well, especially for a rookie. After he got his par on the final hole, recording a 69, he watched as Palmer played to the final hole. Palmer missed a 20-foot birdie attempt to win and the stage was set for an 18-hole playoff the next day between the hometown hero Palmer and the pudgy young challenger, Nicklaus.

In the playoff, Nicklaus built up a four-stroke lead after eight holes and fought off a Palmer charge to capture the title. With the victory, he became the first man to hold both the latest U.S. Amateur and the U.S. Open titles since Bobby Jones.

With a weekend off after missing the cut at the Open, Tony used the time to work out his problems with the driver. He also visited Manhattan where, in a nightclub, he ran into Gwilym S. Brown, who wrote for *Sports Illustrated*.

"Tour life is crazy," he told Brown over drinks. "I'm going to write a book about it."

"No, you're not," Brown replied, "because I'm going to and I write faster than you."

Before the night was over the two decided to collaborate on the book and the idea of *Golfer's Gold* was born. They decided that they would have some fun while writing the book; they would arm themselves with a tape recorder and put the whole thing on tape "while we lie on a beach at Acapulco for a week."

They never made it to the beach, and the project took much longer than a week. Tony carried the tape recorder with him as he traveled the tour. Brown would come out on tour and the two met in various hotel rooms while Tony recounted his exploits on the tour into the recorder. Brown implored him to bring his deepest introspection into the story, which made the taping sessions wearing on Tony. Finally, the two set a two-hour time limit on the taping sessions.

Tony later said, "An hour with Gwil is harder than 18 holes of golf. It's close to a psychoanalytic experience."

The extra work he put in with his driver started to pay off the next week, at the Eastern Open. Even though he started poorly in the first round, stumbling to a 75 on the Mt. Pleasant municipal course, he jumped back into the tournament with a 67 in the second round. The round shot him up the leader board into a tie for sixth. He felt confident as his accuracy with the driver returned and he was putting well.

He moved up two spots on the leader board to a tie for fourth after a steady 70 in the third round. A very solid 69 in the final round, his best final round in a month, gave him a third place finish and a healthy check of $2,200—his largest official check on tour.

He was riding a wave of confidence as the tour headed to Chicago for the $50,000 Western Open at Medinah Country Club. Upon arrival at Medinah, Tony met his caddy for the week. Max "Jerry" Winters had joined the caddy corps at Medinah for the summer with the sole intention of working the Western Open. During the summer, the PGA required that pros use local caddies, who were on summer vacation from school, as opposed to the regular caddies who traveled the tour.

Tony liked Winters's work ethic and his knowledge of the course. It could be a haphazard proposition when employing a local youngster as a caddy but, in the case of Winters, it was a hit. The two formed a close friendship and kept in touch over the next several years.

A great final round of 69, the second best score of the day, helped Tony climb the leader board into a tie for 13th place and another healthy check of $1,125. This put him inside the top-40 on the money list for the first time since his return from the Caribbean Tour.

The Buick Open in Grand Blanc, Michigan, at the Warwick Hills Country Club, was next on the schedule. In the first round, veteran Art Wall shared the lead with Ken Still, both shooting 69. Tony, tied with Venturi and nine other players, was two shots back. In the second round, he staked a claim to the lead with a round of 69 that tied him with Pete Cooper. The first round leaders, Wall and Still, fell from contention with a 78 and 77 respectively.

Tony retained a share of the lead after a steady one-under-par 71 in the third round. He now experienced, for the first time since his rookie year, the uncomfortable experience of sleeping with the lead going into a final round. Would this be his time? Could he finally notch his first PGA tour victory? He tossed and turned while these thoughts, and others, raced through his mind.

The next day he stood in the second fairway, a par 5, and visualized his second shot. The hole bent around a stand of trees, but with a good drive, it was possible to fly the second shot over the trees to the front of the green for a good opportunity at birdie. Tony selected a five-iron, and at impact, thought he had hit just the shot he visualized in his pre-shot routine. From the feel, he was sure he would carry the trees. As he looked up and caught the flight of the ball he could see it heading for the top of the last tree he needed to carry. He figured that even if he caught the tree, it was so wispy up near the top that it would not affect his ball. However, he watched in horror as the ball hit the top of the tree, ricocheted straight left, and high across the fairway, out-of-bounds.

"Son, that's the worse piece of luck I have ever seen a man have on the golf course," his fellow competitor in the group, Pete Cooper said.

The old Tony would have become angry at this unfortunate turn of events. He would have started throwing clubs and strokes away, as well as any hope of a sizable check. The new Tony, however, kept his temper under control. He decided to work as hard as he could for the next 16 holes and let the chips fall where they may.

Bearing down, he played the remainder of the round surrendering two more strokes to par. His 76 did not look good on the leader board or in the papers the next day under the headline: LEMA BLEW UP. Nevertheless, Tony felt a large sense of satisfaction that he was able to keep his round under control. He dropped into a tie for sixth place, and on the bright side, it was his third straight top-15 finish in as many weeks. He won a decent size check for $1,825 and moved up to 34th place on the money list. In the last three weeks on tour, he had made $5,150 and his confidence continued to soar.

He found it difficult to split these large checks with Malarkey. He had put the contract issue on a back burner since the start of the year, but now he was making some good money bringing the issue to a head. He had no problem with paying Malarkey back for his initial investment, plus some profit, but he was ready to go his own way without a sponsor. He spoke with Malarkey who assured Tony he would have his lawyers draw up the necessary papers to terminate the agreement.

With a separation from Malarkey on his mind, Tony started to pay more attention to his expenses. Malarkey's insistence on traveling first-class and staying in the best hotels was racking up the expenses. To retain more of his winnings, he realized that he needed to cut back.

Instead of flying to every tournament stop, as Malarkey insisted, Tony started to drive. Players often had a car at one tournament, but planned to fly to the next tournament. They hired caddies, or enlisted players who could not afford to fly, to drive their car to the next stop. On more than one occasion, Bob Rosburg had Tony drive his car. Mike Souchak once lent Tony his car providing him his gas company credit card, as well.

"In those days, Tony was almost like a gofer for us," Bob Rosburg recalled decades later.

Still trying to ride his hot streak after the Buick Open, Tony played in the Motor City Open, but shot a lackluster 286 and finished out of the money. He pushed himself hard during this stretch. While his new physical fitness regime, begun earlier in the year at Jim Power's gym, kept his body strong, mentally he was exhausted.

Despite this, he played in his third career major championship at the PGA Championship the next week at the Aronomink Country Club. After a poor opening round of 77, and a second round 72 he withdrew. Burned out, he needed a break. He flew back to the West Coast to get some rest and tend to some business.

His business was sitting in a lawyer's office while Malarkey instructed his attorneys to draw up the necessary papers to dissolve their contract. Malarkey and his lawyers assured Tony the termination of his contract would occur soon and he left the office satisfied.

He had some personal business to take care of, as well. He flew to Montana where he and Shirley Donovan got a quick divorce. With David Anthony Lema born, and given a name, there was no longer any need for the two to be married. Despite Donovan's claim to Frederick Burger in a 2000 interview to the contrary, it was never a marriage made of love. "I think that there was a lot of love involved," Donovan (now Shirley Kozy) declared to Burger.

Rather, it was a marriage to provide the child with a name and baptismal. He and his family had been successful in keeping the news of the marriage secret and continued to do so with the divorce.

With his personal business attended to, he headed back out on tour for the American Golf Classic in Akron, Ohio, where he finished in a tie for 23rd. The next stop on tour was St. Paul, where he had held his hotel party the year before, complete with players hitting shots out the window over downtown St. Paul. An opening 69 placed Tony just three strokes back of the leaders. He followed with rounds of 70, 71 and 70 and a tie for 15th place.

The tour moved on to Oklahoma City, which was the hometown of his new girlfriend, Betty. He got off to a terrible start shooting a 77. He then made a great rally with rounds of 68, 70 and 70 to finish in a tie for fourth.

Once again, Tony gave part of the credit for his high finish to Danny

Arnold. Arnold had taught him the need to keep plugging away, even after the disastrous opening round 77. He felt good about his ability to comeback from that bad first round to finish high on the leader board. His hard work earned him another $1,800.

The next week, at the Dallas Open, he finished out of the money and his mediocre play continued the next week, in Denver.

The tour headed up to the Pacific Northwest for the Seattle World's Fair Open. Rain and clouds greeted the pros. The rain softened up Broadmoor Country Club and the pros took advantage of the situation to go low with their scores.

The Seattle event featured a strong field, including what the press started calling "The Big Three" of golf, Arnold Palmer, Jack Nicklaus and Gary Player. Mark McCormick managed all three and nurtured the nickname resulting in fantastic endorsement opportunities.

Young Dave Hill captured the first round lead with a 64, a round in which he hit every green in regulation. Nicklaus was three shots back along with Casper, while Player was another stroke back. Palmer shot a 70 and Tony was eight strokes back with a 72.

Billy Casper came out hot in the second round and, despite the rain, shot a course record 63 taking over the lead by two strokes. Nicklaus remained in the hunt with a 65 tying for second with Billy Maxwell. Player maintained his position with a 67. Tony fashioned a round of 66 that moved him up a few spots on the leader board, but he was still six back and not threatening the leaders, at this point.

The third round saw the rain and clouds replaced with brilliant sunshine, but the course still played soft, especially the greens. The players could not have asked for better playing conditions. Nicklaus, with his length, played a driver-wedge-putter combo on nearly every par 4 hole resulting in another 65. He now led the tournament, by two strokes over Player who fired a 64. Casper had fallen into a tie for third. Tony sat tied for 14th, seven strokes off the lead, after a second consecutive 66.

Teeing off several groups in front of the leaders in the fourth round, Tony started red-hot going five-under in the first four holes. He sank an 18-foot putt on the first hole, a par 5, for eagle, and followed up with two birdies, both made from 18-feet. A kick-in two-footer for birdie on the fourth hole kept his momentum going. He continued to play well on the front side and made the turn in just 28 strokes, the lowest nine-hole score on the tour up to that point in the year.

Murmurs traveled through the galleries watching other players.

"Tony Lema's hot," they said. "Let's go follow him, he's going low."

With his gallery growing on each successive hole, he pulled even with Nicklaus for a share of the lead after he birdied the twelfth hole. On the sixteenth hole he hit his approach shot to within six-feet, but then missed the putt derailing his momentum.

"If I would have sunk that birdie putt on the sixteenth, I think I would have had a good chance," he later told reporters, after his round.

Trying to finish strongly, he hit his approach shot long and left on the seventeenth hole, ending up in the gallery. He chipped short and missed the par putt. At just about the same time, Nicklaus eagled the fifteenth hole.

He later explained what happened on seventeen to reporters. "Yeah, I was keyed up," he admitted. "I tried to cut a 6-iron right to the pin, but I had way too much club."

Despite faltering towards the end of the round, Tony finished up with a 63. Feeling good about his round, Tony chatted with the press while Nicklaus played the final holes. As he bantered with the press, one of the reporters jokingly asked him if he was hoping that Nicklaus would break a leg.

"Oh, no," he answered. "A sprain would be enough."

He was getting very good at sparring with the press and he was always quick with the quip making him very quotable.

Nicklaus finished steadily for the victory avoiding broken bones or massive sprains. Tony finished in solo second place winning a check for $3,000 and jumped up into the 31st spot on the official money list. He felt pleased he was able to overcome his slow start in the first round. However, there was also a feeling of disappointment as he came so close to victory only to come up short. Despite his disappointment, his confidence continued to be sky high as he wrote in *Golfer's Gold*.

"After that burst of golf I figured there was nothing I couldn't do and that my first tournament win must be just a lucky break away."

He headed for Portland, the next stop on tour, in a good mood. He was playing good golf, continuing to climb the official money list, and he was in love.

He had fallen head-over-heels for Betty Cline and they were spending as much time together as their busy schedules would allow. They tried to synchronize their travel schedules so that they could be in the same city at the same time. He found the well-grounded Betty had a stabilizing effect on him and he felt more focused on the golf course since falling in love.

The only thing that was not going well was progress concerning his contract with Malarkey. As September turned into October, the papers Malarkey had assured Tony would be ready, still had not arrived.

The two met in Portland, Malarkey's hometown, while Tony played in the Portland Open. Malarkey assured Tony he would have the papers by Christmas.

During the fall stretch, Tony focused on earning more money while racking up Ryder Cup points. He wanted to represent his country in the Ryder Cup, a biannual match between pros from the U.S. and Great Britain.

There was also a bonus pool available, put together by the Western States Golf Sponsors. The group consisted of the organizers of the tour stops in Denver, Seattle, Portland, Las Vegas and Bakersfield. The organization devised a point system that allocated points for high finishes in each tournament. The winner received a check for $5,000, with $3,000 and $2,000 going to the second and third place, respectively. With his tie for 22nd in Denver and his solo second in Seattle, Tony had put himself in good position for a healthy bonus.

An invitation to the Masters was also up for grabs to the player with the best record during the fall. All of this motivated Tony to push through his mental exhaustion and ride his wave of confidence through the fall events.

18 CHAMPAGNE KID
1962

Both Jack Nicklaus and Tony arrived at the Portland Open riding a wave of momentum from their first and second place finishes, respectively, in Seattle. Scores were low at the Columbia-Edgewater Country Club as 80 players broke par in the opening round. Nicklaus, with a first round 64, led Tony by one stroke.

With his confidence at a high point, Tony was playing beautiful golf. He had a good frame of mind allowing him to be relaxed and composed on the golf course. He truly felt that his first victory could come at any time.

Despite a two-stroke penalty for slow play, Nicklaus still held a one-stroke lead after the second round. Tony, meanwhile, had slipped back into the pack after his 71 put him three strokes off the lead. He dropped further off the pace with a 70 on Saturday.

Long hitting George Bayer, a former offensive lineman for the University of Washington, came out strong in the final round. He made a charge shooting a 65, but in the end, it was not enough. Nicklaus held on to win by one stroke.

Tony finished with a 71 that placed him in a tie for 14th place earning him a check for $551, which kept him in the 31st spot on the money list. His earnings for the year were just over $22,232 in official money.

After his victory in Portland, Nicklaus returned to Columbus to finish classes in order to graduate from Ohio State University. He added the $3,500 winner's check to his nearly $60,000 in official money. He also won $50,000 in unofficial money when he captured the World Series of Golf making for a very profitable rookie season.

Tony hooked up with Wally Heron, a regular tour caddy, at the Portland Open. Heron proved adept at reading Tony's state of mind and was an expert at keeping him relaxed on the course. Tony found great comfort in having him on the bag and the two hooked up the next week in Las Vegas, at the Sahara Invitational.

The Sahara was a pro-am event and therefore an unofficial event. Even so, it featured a rich $30,000 purse attracting a strong field. There were also points in the Western Golf Sponsors Association bonus pool available at the event. The tournament played over two courses, Paradise Valley and the Las Vegas municipal course, to accommodate the 360 amateurs and 120 pros in the field.

On the first day, Tony was the recipient of a good break concerning the weather. He completed his round at Paradise Valley, shooting an uncomfortable 75. His discomfort came from a feeling that his alignment had been off. He looked at the leader board and saw quite a few low scores posted from the morning group of players. He shrugged his shoulders in resignation and returned to his hotel for a nap before an evening of gambling and dancing with Betty. His relationship with Betty was growing more serious as he began to entertain the thought of spending the rest of his life with her. She arranged her schedule to spend the week in Las Vegas with Tony.

Once back at his room, he no sooner laid down on the bed than the phone rang with a friend on the other end.

"Man, are you lucky," the friend stated. "It rained so hard over at Paradise Valley that the first round has been postponed."

The rule on tour at that time was if rain washed out any participant's round, none of that day's scores counted.

Tony was incredulous when he heard the news, so he wandered down to the hotel lobby to investigate further. In the lobby, he gazed out the window and saw typical Las Vegas weather—warm and sunny. He thought his friend was pulling a cruel prank.

He was just about to spin on his heel, return to his room and get down to the business of his nap when a group of golfers came trudging into the hotel. His jaw dropped when he saw the soaking wet players. One of them stopped to tell him that it had indeed rained—hard—at Paradise Valley in the afternoon. It was official; the rain had washed out the round, granting Tony a reprieve.

Because of the rain cancellation, players teed it up for a replay of the first round on Friday, with the second round set for Saturday and the final 36 holes on Sunday.

Tony felt the rainout was an omen, so he cut his nighttime activities short and requested an early wake-up call. The next morning he got out to the course early, put in extra time on the practice range and he adjusted his alignment making sure he was square to the ball and his intended line. Soon he was back in the groove feeling comfortable once again over the ball. He stepped to the first tee brimming with confidence.

He took advantage of his good fortune concerning the weather with a smooth 69 in the replay of his first round putting him five strokes off the lead. He continued to hit the ball well Saturday carding a 67, for a two round 136, one stroke back of the leaders, Billy Casper and Jon Gustin.

In Sunday's 36-hole final round, Tony grabbed the lead, shooting the best round of the day, a 66, in the morning. In the afternoon, he kept it going strong and he never relinquished the lead shooting a 68 to win by three shots.

It was his first important victory on the tour, even though it was an unofficial victory. He headed off to Bakersfield with the winner's check from the Sahara of $2,800 in his pocket and his confidence sky high.

Unlike the previous year, the Bakersfield event was not offering up the added prizes of stakes in oil wells, or dressed sides of beef. Instead, they increased the purse to $40,000 making it the richest stop on the fall tour.

Tony played very well in the first round on his way to a 68 placing him in a tie for second place with Butch Baird, one stroke behind the leader, Dave Hill. The next day, he continued his fine play resulting in a 69 that kept him in second place, now tied with Jimmy Powell and Mason Rudolph.

In the third round, he culminated his round by sinking a 15-foot putt for birdie on the last hole and his 68 tied him for the lead at 205 with Casper whose putter was red-hot.

Casper's putter remained hot in the final round as he blazed to a 67, which was good enough to top Tony. Tony finished with a 71 that secured a solo second place finish, four strokes back of Casper. The Bakersfield Open was the final stop of the Western Golf Sponsors Association bonus pool. Don January entered the event with a slight lead over George Bayer. By the conclusion of the event, Bayer was able to overtake January and collect the $5,000 first-place bonus. Casper got $3,000 for finishing second while Tony captured the $2,000 third-place money. Don January barely made the 54-hole cut and fell to sixth place collecting $1,250 from the bonus pool. In addition, Tony added $3,600 in official money and moved up ten spots to 21st on the official money list.

In January, at the Los Angeles Open, Tony won the largest check of his career, $1,900. In June, at the Eastern Open, he set a new high water mark when he cashed a check for $2,200. Then in the middle of September, he bettered that at the Seattle Open with $3,000. At Bakersfield, he improved his personal best with his $3,600 check.

He continued his arduous fall schedule at the Ontario Open, played in the third week of October at Whispering Lakes Golf Club east of Los Angeles in California's "Citrus Belt." Even though he was on the verge of exhaustion, he played on. He was playing so well, and coming so close to an official victory, there was no way he was going to break the hot streak with a week's vacation.

As players prepared for the Ontario Open they discussed in the locker room the news that U.S. reconnaissance photos revealed the construction of missile bases in Cuba. With these bases just off the coast of Florida, Cuba, and its ally Russia, could launch missiles into America with little or no warning. Americans watched the developments with a concern that soon bordered on panic.

Tony opened the tournament with a 69 putting him in a good position on the leader board. He was three back of the leader, Bob Pratt. In the second round, he found a groove. The headline in the October 20 sports section of *The Oakland Tribune* read TONY LEMA LEADS AFTER TORRID 66. The lead paragraph began; "Handsome Tony Lema, the hottest player on the PGA Fall Tour, continued his torrid play by shooting a five-under-par 34-32—66 yesterday for a one shot lead at the halfway mark of the $25,000 Ontario Golf Open."

His only errors of the round were a three-putt green at the ninth hole and a bunkered approach at the sixteenth, both resulting in bogeys. He offset these errors with seven birdies. He was ecstatic with both his round and how well he was playing.

In the third round, Tony had putting difficulties en route to a three-over-par 74. His 54-hole total was 209, three strokes off the lead, now held by Al Geiberger.

Geiberger, fighting a cold all week, shot another 70 in the final round to capture his first win in three years. Tony's friend, Tommy Jacobs made a charge with the best round of the day, a 65, to finish in a tie for second place. Tony finished with a solid 69, but his third round 74 dropped him into a tie for seventh place, worth $987.

Despite feeling good about his game, Tony was frustrated. He was playing great golf, his confidence was high, but he just could not break through. He desperately wanted to get the monkey off his back. Even though he was tired and needed a break, he decided to ride his hot streak and play one more tournament. He headed off to Costa Mesa, California for the Orange County Open, played at the Mesa Verde Country Club.

At the conclusion of the Ontario Open, United Press International ran a syndicated article on Tony. The article, picked up by newspapers around the country, focused on the factors that were contributing to his hot streak. *The Hayward Daily Review*, one of Tony's local papers, ran the story under the headline; NEW APPROACH PAYING OFF, LEMA SHOOTS FOR MASTERS.

Tony, quoted at length in the article, spoke about his new, more serious approach to his game. The influence of Danny Arnold was very apparent in his words.

"I'm enjoying the best year I've ever had and I attribute it to my better mental attitude towards the game," Tony said. "I have forced myself into accepting the bad with the good and not becoming either too enthusiastic when I play well or too depressed when things go wrong."

Tony went on, "Not too long ago I decided that blowing my top hurt my game, so I set out to change my mental attitude. I used to act like a kid by cursing and beating my clubs when I hit a bad shot. But then I got to thinking. I figured it would be better for me to try and salvage whatever I could from such a situation. If I lost a chance for birdie, why not try for par?"

Then he got philosophical, saying, "I think how fortunate I am to be doing something that I enjoy that is paying me well. I believe the more pleasure I get out of golf, the better my game will become. I don't want to give the impression that I take the game lightly. I study every situation on the course and try to do my best on every shot. But, I think here's the secret of good playing; once I make a shot, I've learned to feel that's the end of it. I don't worry where it goes. I've done my best, and I'll worry about the next shot when I get to it."

The article pointed out that in the Fall Tour point race, Tony held the lead in the competition for a Masters invitation. The top two players, based on points awarded for play during the fall, would receive the coveted invitations. He had accumulated 75.67 points during his fall hot streak and led Al Geiberger, who had 67.5 points. It was very important to Tony to qualify for the Masters.

"I'd give my right arm to compete at Augusta. I've got the chance and I'll do anything I can to keep from losing it," he said.

He made the short drive to Orange County feeling confident. His one sore spot remained his contract with Malarkey. Malarkey and his team of lawyers were dragging their feet producing the paperwork that would bring to an end the sponsorship contract. Tony had high hopes that the papers would arrive before Christmas.

On October 22, President Kennedy addressed the nation; "It shall be the policy of this nation to regard any nuclear missile launched from Cuba against any nation in the Western Hemisphere as an attack on the United States, requiring a full retaliatory response upon the Soviet Union."

The Cold War was heating up. President Kennedy authorized a naval blockade of Cuba, and on the night of October 23, the Joint Chiefs of Staff instructed the Strategic Air Command to go to DEFCON 2 for the only time in history. The world was at the brink of nuclear war and Americans began to build backyard bomb shelters.

The players had to put the disturbing national news aside as they went to work in Southern California. Tony got off to a good start at the Orange County Open, winning the pre-tournament pro-am with 33-32—65, six-under par. He had never played Mesa Verde Country Club as well in the past. The year prior, he withdrew in disgust after only six holes in the first round. In three years of playing the event, he won a grand total of $70. He felt he turned a corner with his 65 alleviating the prior frustrations he felt about the course.

At the end of his pro-am round, Bob Rosburg swapped putters with one of his amateur partners, actor Bob Wilke.

Rosburg, utilizing the new putter very effectively in the first round, took only 23 putts and grabbed the lead with a course record 63. He enjoyed a three-stroke lead over his closest pursuer, Jerry Steelman. Tony was five strokes back.

Rossie cooled off in the second round with a 70. George Bayer caught him after carding a 66 and both sat tied at 133. One shot back of the two leaders was Tony. He toured the front nine in just 31 strokes, including an eagle two on the par 4 ninth when he holed out his eight-iron from 135-yards.

During the second round, Tony looked at his fellow competitor, Rosburg, and said, "I'll tell you what Rossie, if I don't win this thing, that's it. I'm done. I've been out here five years and I don't have a victory to show for it, I'm frustrated. I just might not be cut out for this. I think I might be better off just getting a club job."

In fact, he had been discussing a head pro job at the new San Leandro municipal course that was under construction.

Fog delayed the start of the third round by 45 minutes. Once it finally got under way, Tony took control of the tournament with a brilliant 64. The round catapulted him into the lead with a 54-hole total of 198—one shot shy of the lowest 54-hole total of the year. Both Rosburg and Bayer continued to play well with Rosburg at 200 and Bayer at 202.

Tony's round featured eight birdies and one bogey. He showed great resiliency on the sixth hole after he hooked his tee shot into a weedy ditch littered with bushes.

"The turning point came on the sixth hole," he later recalled for reporters. "I almost hooked my ball out-of-bounds but a couple of bushes kept it from going out. I was just going to hack it out with a wedge and the ball really took off flying about 80-yards down the fairway. I was able to make par on the hole, and that gave me a big lift."

Tony addressed the group of reporters in a makeshift press area in a small room in the clubhouse. The room usually served as a card room for the members. There was not a large group of reporters covering the event as football season was in full swing. In addition to the ever-present Associated Press and United Press International beat reporters, the only other reporters there were from the local papers, The L.A. Times, The San Diego Union-Tribune, and The Long Beach Independent Press-Telegraph.

While Tony answered the reporter's questions, he helped himself to a bottle of beer from a cooler in the room. When he finished answering the reporter's questions, he ended his session with an aside.

"Okay fellas," Tony stated as he looked down at his beer bottle. "If we're in here tomorrow, I guarantee you we won't be drinking beer. We'll celebrate with champagne."

Playing with Rosburg and Bayer in the final group, Tony started shaky in the final round, bogeying two holes on the front nine. Rosburg applied pressure with a steady round, making up the two-stroke deficit to catch Tony. Tony managed to make a shaky par, barely toppling in a three-foot putt, on the final hole that he needed to tie Rosburg, who shot a 67. The two players prepared for a sudden-death playoff.

Rosburg, winless on the tour since capturing the 1961 Bing Crosby National Pro-Am, was eager for a victory. Of course, Tony was desperate for an official PGA title. As they headed for the tee to begin their playoff, Tony's nerves were on edge. Luckily, Danny Arnold and his wife, Donna, were in the gallery. They had a reassuring and calming effect on him.

Utilizing a draw, it was determined that Rosburg would tee off first on the dogleg right par-5 first hole. He stepped up and hit a perfect drive down the middle of the fairway. Tony, his nerve ends raw, sent a big sweeping hook that was heading out-of-bounds. Both players thought the shot was out-of-bounds, so Tony hit a provisional ball. The two players, and their caddies, then walked to where they thought Tony's drive was. Much to their surprise, they found the ball, in-bounds by only a yard. Tony continued to be a jangle of nerves despite what seemed to be an act of providence.

Tony tried to take advantage of the good luck, but instead sliced his second shot across the fairway into the rough a good 40-yards from the green. Rosburg, meanwhile, playing from the middle of the fairway, hit his second shot to the front edge of the green setting up a putt for eagle. Tony then hit his 40-yard pitch onto the green.

In *Golfer's Gold,* Tony wrote that he pitched his third shot to three-feet of the hole, while Rosburg, in an interview 40 years later, recalled that Tony's ball was 15-feet from the hole. Either way, Tony did not have a tap-in putt for birdie.

Rosburg routinely two-putted for his birdie and Tony lined up his must-make putt to extend the playoff. Nervously he drew the putter back and stroked the putt straight into the hole. The two players headed for the second tee.

The second hole at Costa Mesa is a short par 4 with an elevated green. Rosburg played his approach shot first, sending a nice smooth wedge up to the green and out of view of the two players. Tony, hearing the resulting cheers from the gallery, figured the shot must have been within three feet of the hole. This slightly unnerved him, and he hit a very shaky wedge to the back of the green. When the two players climbed up and saw the green, Rosburg's ball was actually six-feet from the hole.

Tony stroked his dangerous and long downhill putt to 18-inches from the cup, a truly great lag putt. It was now Rosburg's turn to be unnerved.

He missed his simple, straight uphill putt. The two players made their way to a third playoff hole.

The third hole was a par 3 with another elevated green. The pin, cut on the left side of the green, required a shot that would draw from the center of the green and curve in towards the hole. Rosburg hit exactly that shot leaving him a 10-footer for birdie.

Tony was having trouble hitting a draw. Instead, he decided to go with a shot that was working for him, a fade that would start left of the green and bend in towards the hole. He hit the shot just as he had planned and ended up about a half-foot outside of Rosburg.

Tony, putting first and suddenly filled with confidence, could visualize clearly the line of his putt as he got over the ball. He had no doubt he was going to make the putt, and furthermore, he was certain that once he did make it, he would win the playoff.

This time he drew his putter back and stroked through the ball with conviction sending it right down his intended line. The ball tracked exactly on that line and dove straight into the cup. He threw his head back, kicked out a leg and trotted to the hole to retrieve his ball from the cup. He then walked to the edge of the green to watch Rosburg putt.

As he watched, he could not stand still, fidgeting with excitement and nervous energy. Rosburg stroked his putt, it tracked towards the hole, but he had hit it too hard. Both players watched the ball hit the back of the cup, pop up in the air and remain above ground.

When Tony saw the ball land on solid ground he felt as if a big pressure relief valve had opened. He was exhilarated at finally winning his first official title. He leaped into the air and flung his golf ball well back up the fairway. In *Golfer's Gold*, Tony admitted that he was sure he kissed Danny Arnold and shook hands with his wife.

Tony accepted congratulations from a downtrodden Rosburg, the caddies and the fans that followed the playoff. The whole crowd headed back from the third green to the clubhouse. Once there, Tony returned to the card room to meet with the press. As promised, the champagne arrived, corks popped, and the sportswriters enjoyed the bubbly along with Tony.

"But all the sportswriters there couldn't have drunk as much as I did that night," Tony recalled years later.

The winner's check was good for $2,800 and moved Tony up to 18th on the money list.

Donald Webster "Doc" Giffin, the press secretary for the PGA, was present as the sportswriters toasted Tony while interviewing him. The reporters called Tony the "Champagne Kid," or "Champagne Tony." The reporters wrote about the champagne celebration in their columns the next day and used Tony's new nickname thus guaranteeing that it would endure.

In front page news, Soviet Premier Khrushchev issued an order to dismantle the weapons in Cuba after the United States agreed to remove Jupiter and Thor missiles from Turkey averting nuclear war. It was the closest the two superpowers had ever come to Armageddon and it put fear into the American public. In addition to backyard bomb shelters, schools started conducting air raid drills teaching children to "duck and cover."

After his victory in Orange County, Tony decided to forgo his vacation electing instead to continue playing to take full advantage of his hot streak. He very much wanted to play at Augusta and he needed to lock up one of the two invitations available to the top finishers on the fall tour. After playing in a pro-am he committed to, he headed for Lafayette, Louisiana and The Cajun Classic. There, he would try to rack up more points towards a Masters Invitation and a Ryder Cup spot.

The other pros at the Cajun Classic offered him congratulations on his first tour win. He had always been very popular with the other players. Many knew of the struggles he had gone through in '59 and '60, and they were genuinely happy for him. As tired as he was, he could only manage a tie for 19th, worth a check for $256. The small check was still enough to move him up one place, to 17th, on the money list.

He kept pushing on to Mobile, Alabama for the Mobile Sertoma Open played at the Mobile Municipal Golf Course. In the first round, an unknown teaching pro from Hinsdale, Illinois, by the colorful name of John Paul Jones, took the lead with a blazing seven-under-par 65. Tony got on a hot streak scoring four straight birdies on the front nine and posted a 67, which could have been a 66. On the ninth hole, Tony reverted to one of his bad habits when he carelessly stabbed at a two-foot putt and missed it.

The next day, he fashioned a very nice 68 in a strong wind. Jones did not handle the wind well and carded a 71 for a 136 two-round total. Tony had possession of the lead at 135 with Pott, the hometown favorite, two strokes back, tied with George Knudsen.

"I was hitting the ball real well," Tony said after his round. "My drives were getting me into position to knock the ball stiff to the pin."

His 68 in the third round gave him a seven-stroke lead. The UPI report of his round described him as "even tempered." It was testimony that his new approach to the game was working.

"I played almost flawless golf. I didn't make any mistakes," he said recapping his round.

He slept soundly on his lead, and woke feeling relaxed. He remained relax and focused as he shot a very steady 70. He won in a cakewalk. He was able to stroll up the eighteenth fairway with the tournament well in-hand and bantered with the gallery.

"Hey, Tone," somebody in the gallery yelled. "You think your eight-shot lead is safe?"

"Yes," Tony yelled back. "I think it is, if I play it careful here."

Tony did play the hole carefully, scoring only his fourth bogey in the tournament, to win by a comfortable seven-stroke cushion. After his round, Tony met with reporters. With another champagne celebration, he lived up to his new nickname and firmly solidified his new post-victory tradition.

Both Tony and Doc Giffin, the PGA press secretary, recognized the value of a colorful persona and "Champagne Tony" fit the bill perfectly. They both latched onto the image and trumpeted it to great effect.

"Oh, he played that to the hilt," recalled Butch Baird, a close friend.

The relationship between Tony and Betty continued to grow as the two began to discuss plans for their future. Tony never had feelings about a woman like the ones he had for Betty. He was ready to settle down with her and felt that his recent success was due, in large part, to his falling in love with her. Tony proposed to Betty, although they would wait to make a formal announcement.

The Carling Open in Orlando, the final tour event of the year, featured a large purse, by fall tour standards, of $35,000. The rich purse attracted a large field. Tony shot himself out of the tournament with a second round 75, and finished in a tie for 23rd. Although he did not earn a decent check, he still sat comfortably in the 15th spot on the money list.

The final tournament of the year for Tony would be a return to Mexico City to defend his Mexican Open title. His brother, Harry, made the trip to Mexico City to watch him play. Harry and Tony did not spend a lot of time together growing up because Harry had been away at seminary school. Tony invited Harry to accompany him to Mexico City so the two could spend time together.

He began his defense of his Mexican national title by setting a course record 64 to win the opening pro-am event. Then, in the first round, he stumbled to a lackluster 73 but came back with a nice 69 in the second round. He started the third round in third place, six strokes back of the leader, Don Massengale. With a third round 68, he was able to make up the difference, and then some, entering the final round with a one-stroke lead.

Harry was having a great time following Tony on the course marveling at his great play. The two spent evenings dining and drinking in Mexico City accompanied by Massengale. Tony loved his family and was grateful for this time with his oldest brother.

In the final round, Tony missed only three greens in regulation on his way to a 71 and a four-stroke victory. The victory, his fourth of the year, was worth $3,000 in unofficial earnings. Harry stayed in the background while Tony addressed the press, with champagne, of course. When he was done with the press, Harry approached Tony, offering his hand in a congratulatory handshake.

"Even though it was a small tournament in Mexico, Tony was very excited," Harry recalled. "When I shook his hand, it was like sticking your finger in an electrical outlet. I could feel how excited he was. It was pretty exciting for me, as well."

It was now finally time for Tony to take a break from the tour. A very happy Tony and Harry headed back to San Leandro to spend the holidays with the rest of the family.

This year, Tony enjoyed his customary review of the year. He had finally proven that he could win and that he belonged on tour. His goals for the upcoming year were to continue winning and to play well in the majors. He would be getting his first chance to play in the Masters having earned an invitation by winning the points total on the fall tour.

Betty wanted to get to know her future in-laws and made the trip to San Leandro as well. She loved the closeness of the family and the way they bantered back-and-forth. The two formally announced their engagement, although a date for the wedding was not set. Tony wanted to work out his contract with Malarkey before embarking on married life. His earnings for the year, both official and unofficial, came to $48,000 getting him back even with Malarkey. Malarkey continued dragging his feet on producing the papers that would dissolve their business relationship.

Aside from that, all was well with Tony Lema. He had won his first official tour victory, quickly added another and he was in love with Betty. He had enough money left over, after paying Malarkey his share of his winnings, to purchase a mink coat for his mother, Cleo. Giving his mother that mink coat was as good as the day he brought home the silver service he won in the Oakland City Amateur. He loved presenting her with the Christmas present. He enjoyed showing his love for her, recognizing all she had done in raising the family, and supporting him. It was a happy Christmas for the Lema family and Tony looked forward to 1963. He wanted to prove that the fall of 1962 was not a fluke.

19 A STAR IS BORN
1963

Tony spent a relaxing visit in San Leandro, visiting with family and friends, all the while unwinding from the pressures of the tour. He felt great pride in the way he had finished out the 1962 season, but he also felt pressure to prove it was not a fluke.

Tony was eager for the 1963 season to begin, eager to prove that he was for real. His confidence level was high and his new attitude was serving him well. He knew that if he just played his game, his success would continue to skyrocket.

While at home, Tony continued his work with the youth of the Bay Area. *The Oakland Tribune* ran a picture of Tony with Berkeley Pontiac car dealership owner, Don Doten, an old friend from Lake Chabot. The picture ran on the automotive page and showed Tony behind the wheel of a brand new 1963 Pontiac station wagon. Doten smiled at the camera as he hands the keys to the new car to Tony through the open window.

Both men are smiling at the camera and the car has "Oakland Boys Club" emblazoned on the door. Doten donated a car to the Boys Club each year, and Tony, a former member of the club, helped promote the event. Working with Doten, Tony became interested in finding other ways to help the Boys Club where he participated in the basketball program as a teen.

The work for children's causes made Tony eager to start his own family. He and Betty discussed their engagement, as well as possible dates for the wedding. The only thing holding them back was the uncertain state of his finances. He was still having problems resolving his contract with Malarkey. He felt he needed to be on his own before he took on the added responsibility of providing for a wife. The two decided they would marry as soon as he could terminate the contract with Malarkey.

The two also discussed his previous marriage, his son, and his divorce. He explained, and Betty understood, that the episode had nothing to do with love, that it was nothing more than a terrible mistake. They also discussed his reputation, as a lady's man out on the tour, something that she would have to deal with. Even though she battled insecurity issues, she felt that she would be able to handle Tony's reputation. She and Tony planned to travel the tour together, so she would have the chance to keep a close eye on him.

Soon it was time to get back to the grind of the tour. He returned to the familiar routine again, starting the year at the L.A. Open. By this time, the tour had become Tony's real home. The nomadic lifestyle fit his restless nature.

His fall finish had elevated his status, making him a featured player in any tournament he entered. Sportswriters mentioned Tony Lema as a favorite in pre-tournament coverage at every event. He was assigned preferred tee times. No longer did he tee off early in the morning with the "Dew Sweepers" or late in the afternoon with the "Garbage Brigade." No longer did he have trouble with inattentive locker room attendants or reception committees who had difficulty spelling his name.

His disappointing 74 in the final round of the L.A. Open put him in a tie for 35th while Arnold Palmer rode a final round 66 to capture the title. The tour then moved south for the San Diego Open played on the short and flat Stardust Country Club.

Although he did not strike the ball well in the first round, Tony managed a 65 that tied Gary Player and Stan Leonard for second. Billy Casper enjoyed a one-stroke lead over the trio. Tony was all over the course, but took advantage of a few good breaks and made some long putts. On the very first hole, he holed out an 80-foot chip for eagle.

The next day, Player shot another 65 to grab the halfway lead at 130. Tony was three strokes back after a 68. Player, with another 70, held onto the lead through the third round. The course played much more difficult in that round because the wind had kicked up. Tony managed a 71 nicely positioning him on the leader board at 204, four strokes off Player's pace.

Playing in front of the leaders during Sunday's final round, Tony came out and made a charge up the leader board. He finished with a very nice 67, which gave him the clubhouse lead at 271. When he finished his round, Tony sat in the pressroom and listened to a radio broadcast of the action as the final groups came down the stretch.

Player, who believed he was engaged in a head-to-head battle with Casper, was surprised when he saw a leader board.

"I didn't realize anyone was so close until I got to the 18th green. Then I found out I had to sink that putt to win," Player told the press after the round. "I knew I had better win now because I haven't been so good in playoffs. In fact, I've been in eight playoffs and lost every one."

The putt that Player referred to was an 18-foot putt from the fringe to save par and finish one stroke ahead of Tony. Tony listened to the radio broadcast while Player stroked in the long putt for the title. Deeply disappointed hearing the news, he threw his hands up in the air in disgust, got up from his chair and quickly exited the pressroom. There would be no pithy remarks to the press after this tough loss.

It was a bitter pill for Tony to swallow, finishing second. He did not think that Player had a chance of making his putt. Because he had played so well in the fourth round, he was eager for a playoff. Instead, he was back in his car for the drive to the Bay Area and the Bing Crosby National Pro-Am.

While in the Bay Area, Tony took time to visit Bill Bishop, the physical education director at the East Oakland Boys Club. Bishop remembered seeing Tony and a friend walk into the boys club 15 years prior. At that time, he had watched Tony go through a basketball workout and figured that he was a natural for the club's team. Bishop put Tony on the team, and he quickly became a star leading them to two championships.

"I don't think I would be where I am today if it were not for the boys club," Tony told Bishop. "Golf is a solo game, but I don't think I would have been successful at it if it were not for the discipline of working with a team."

He played solid but unspectacular golf in the Crosby National Pro-Am with rounds of 74-72-74-71 to finish in a tie for 15th. Palmer, disqualified after an inadvertent rules violation, ended a 47-tournament streak in which he had finished in the money.

The pros then made the short trip to San Francisco for the Lucky International. Tony played well, shooting a second round 67, the lowest score of the day, on his way to a tie for eighth earning $1,600. He got his year off to a solid start and sat in seventh-place on the official money list.

Tony headed next to the Palm Springs Desert Classic and a reunion with Danny and Donna Arnold, spending the week at their home. The Arnolds hosted a dinner party, with some of their Hollywood friends as guests.

In *Golfer's Gold* Tony wrote, "The more people from his world that I met in Danny Arnold's house the more I began to realize why there is such an affinity between show people and golfers on the tour. We are all performers, of course, and a mutual admiration society seems to have developed."

He had another solid week in the desert finishing in a tie for 8th place earning a healthy $1,450. Nicklaus won the Desert Classic defeating Player in an 18-hole playoff. "The Big Three," of Palmer, Nicklaus and Player dominated press coverage as each had a victory in the new season.

As the tour moved on to the Tucson Open, played in 1963 at a new course, the 49er Country Club, *Golf Magazine* hit the newsstands. It featured a story about Tony's new positive approach to the game. In the article, Tony explained how he was more relaxed on the course, in total control of his emotions. His temper was no longer sabotaging his game.

Butch Baird, paired with Tony in the first round at Tucson, had read the article, as did many of the other pros. On one green, Baird finished the hole and stepped to the edge of the green to watch Tony finish putting. Tony had a short putt and missed it. Baird turned his back as he headed for the next tee. All of a sudden, he heard a whizzing noise go past his ear. After holing out his putt, Tony had angrily whacked his putter against the heel of his shoe. The head snapped off, went flying through the air, right past Baird.

"Tony," said Baird, "I can see that new relaxed mental approach is really helping."

"Shut up," Tony replied. "I'm not taking any shit from you."

The two men then chuckled at the incident and their exchange. Tony had to use another club, probably a one- or two-iron, as a putter for the remainder of his round.

Tony planned to play in one more event—the Greater New Orleans Open-before taking a couple of weeks off. He scheduled a meeting, back in San Leandro, with his lawyers concerning the situation with Malarkey. He also planned to spend some time with Betty. He played well in New Orleans, finishing in a tie for second, winning a check for $3,050. This moved him up to fifth place on the money list for the year. It was now time to go home to San Leandro, rest up, and prepare for his first Masters.

He spent the first week of his break relaxing around his mother's house with Betty. Again, they discussed their wedding plans and they decided to announce their engagement to the papers. *The Oakland Tribune* published the engagement news as well as the plans for a wedding "somewhere in the Bay Area sometime in September." Tony felt that he would have his contract situation with Malarkey resolved by the end of summer.

He found time for a little vacation fun defending his Northern California PGA Medal Play Championship in Salinas at the Corral de Tierra golf course. He pulled out to a two-stroke lead in the first round of the two-day tournament and then socked it away with a 71 in the second round to win by six strokes. The win again qualified him for the PGA Championship.

Tony rejoined the tour for the Doral Open. Also at Doral was Fred Corcoran, a sports impresario with a distinguished career. His resume included being the tournament supervisor for the PGA Tour; one of the founders of the LPGA; business manager for Ted Williams, Sam Snead and Babe Didrikson Zaharias, among others; and manager of the 1937 and 1953 Ryder Cup Teams. While at the Doral, he searched for new talent to represent as a manager.

He was nosing around the tournament with a list, compiled by a former Masters champion, of possible clients. On that list were ten names of the most promising young golfers on the tour. Corcoran showed his list to Chick Harbert before asking for a candid appraisal. Harbert scanned the list quickly before he handed it back to Corcoran.

"It's a good list," Harbert stated, "but there's one name missing. I'll take him and you can have the other ten."

"Who's that?" asked Corcoran.

"Tony Lema," replied Harbert. "He's got 'winner' written all over him. He's got every shot in the bag and I think he's got the temperament to win, and that's important. Why don't you go out and take a look at him?"

Corcoran did just that, and he liked what he saw. He watched Tony play the last four holes and could clearly see that Harbert was correct; this guy was good. Corcoran also saw that Tony had "something there that struck sparks."

Tony reminded Corcoran of Ted Williams. He described it as "the way he handled himself, the way he stood off and surveyed the crowd with quiet amusement. It was there in his loose-gaited walk. Prospectors must get the same charge when they see yellow glint in the face of a canyon wall."

Corcoran's timing was impeccable, as was usually the case in his business affairs. Tony felt he was missing endorsements, a valuable supplement to what a pro golfer earns on the course. He felt he needed someone of Corcoran's ability to promote him in order to land those product endorsements. For his part, Corcoran felt that Tony would be a very attractive spokesperson for a number of companies. With Corcoran's legal contacts, he could also be helpful to Tony in his battle with Malarkey, which seemed headed towards litigation.

Corcoran was impressed with Tony's finish in the Doral. Tony fired a 69 that jumped him up the leader board into a solo third place finish, three-strokes behind the winner, Dan Sikes. The third place finish earned him a check of $3,000 and moved him into the fourth-place spot on the official money list. He would be heading into his first masters, on top of his game, one of the top five money earners on the tour.

20 AUGUSTA
1963

Tony, for the first time in his career, joined the privileged pilgrimage of 82 players, pros and amateurs, to Augusta, Georgia for the Masters. The first real inkling that the Masters was an extraordinary event occurred to Tony in 1956, when Ken Venturi nearly won the event as an amateur causing quite a stir around the Bay Area. Tony realized how important, and special, a Masters victory could be.

Tony next heard about the elite nature of the Masters when he qualified for the U.S. Open the same year. There, he played the last day with Walker Inman, Jr. a young pro from Georgia. Inman's goal during that day was not to win the U.S. Open—he was too far back to have any hope of accomplishing that. His goal was to finish in the top sixteen and earn an automatic invitation to play in the Masters. This was the first time that Tony became aware of the fact that the Masters was an invitation-only tournament.

Once out on tour, Tony continued to hear what a great privilege it was to play in the Masters. Failing to earn an invite, he watched the tournament on television, year after year. He finally earned his invitation to the 1963 Masters with his strong play during the fall of 1962.

His play earlier in the year, with his many top-ten finishes, made him a favorite in his first Masters, according to sportswriters and fellow players. Despite not winning a tournament during the winter swing, he was in the fourth spot on the money list with $11,831 in official winnings. He enjoyed his new prominence, but still he thirsted for victories, not just prize money.

He began to receive some national press in the weeks leading up to the Masters. *Golf Digest* ran a feature that painted Tony as a playboy out on tour, constantly surrounded by beautiful women. *Sports Illustrated* ran a profile of Tony by Gwilym S. Brown, who was also collaborating with Tony on the book that would become *Golfer's Gold*.

It was the first real national press that Tony received and the profiles did not quite fit the image he had of himself. He felt the hard-partying playboy profile went too far. At least in the case of the *Sports Illustrated* article, Brown portrayed the playboy image as outdated, pointing out Tony's engagement to Betty.

Although considered one of the favorites, a role he was not entirely comfortable with, he was not at the top of the list of favorites. Most experts felt Palmer, Player or Nicklaus were locks to win the green jacket. There was such conviction by the press that one of these three players would win that many of the other players were slightly peeved.

"It's ridiculous," proclaimed Jimmy Demeret, a veteran of the tour and a television commentator. "You would think only three men were playing. In a tournament of this caliber, there are 30 men who could win it."

Demeret made his own prediction naming Don January, Tony and Johnny Pott as his picks to finish in that order.

In the April 1 issue of *Sports Illustrated*, the esteemed writer, Alfred Wright, handicapped the field in a preview of the Masters. He noted that "The Big Three" won more than 15 percent of all prize money distributed on the winter tour and that they won five of the nine tournaments conducted. One of the three placed second seven times—Player accounting for five of those runner-up finishes. However, he also pointed out there were chinks in "The Big Three's" armor.

Palmer was struggling with his attempt to give up cigarettes, and it was affecting his game. He felt he needed tobacco to relax during his round. He gained ten pounds during his cold turkey attempt to quit the cigarette habit. Still, he had won in Los Angeles, Phoenix, and Pensacola.

Bursitis that first occurred in San Francisco at the Lucky International bothered Nicklaus causing him to miss his first cut as a pro. Fortunately, the pain disappeared as suddenly as it appeared on the Friday before the Masters. Player, playing fantastic golf, secured a victory in San Diego in addition to his five runner-up finishes. The only cause for concern was that his playoff record was still woeful. In nine playoffs, he was able to win only one.

"I'm playing so well now it scares me," Player told Nicklaus during a practice round at Augusta.

Wright went on to handicap the other players who might be able to challenge "The Big Three." He noted that Billy Casper had the best winter tour of his ten-year career. Wright also wrote about Tony's chances, pointing out that he was playing great golf.

Tony was determined to play well in his first Masters telling Wright, "I've waited too long for this opportunity to mess it up. I think my game is good enough to win and I think I can hold up under pressure—my nerves are in pretty good shape."

Once he got to Augusta, though, suddenly his nerves were not in great, or even good, shape.

Approached by a reporter while on the practice tee at Augusta he said, "I'm sorry if I seem to be preoccupied, but this is my first time here and

I'm still trying to get my bearings. A man who is invited here for the first time and doesn't feel the magnitude of this event would have to be numb."

In the secret and unsanctioned betting in Augusta, Palmer drew 4-1 odds as the favorite on the tote board. Nicklaus and Player came next at 6-1.

A poll of 14 past champions gave Palmer ten first-place votes, while Nicklaus received only one vote. The others receiving first-place votes were Tony, January, and Jerry Barber.

Interestingly, Palmer, who participated in the former champion's poll, did not cast his vote for himself. His was the one vote for Nicklaus. Herman Keiser was the past champion who picked Tony to win.

Even though Palmer had voted for Nicklaus, he was optimistic about Tony's chances. "I realize no first timer ever has won here before, but that doesn't mean it can't happen. And if it can happen, Lema could be the boy to do it. Man, have you seen some of his drives? He hits 'em clear out of sight. I like the rest of his game, too."

Jay Hebert also liked Tony's chances in his first Masters.

"Ordinarily, you have to stick with Palmer and some of the boys who have done it in the past, but don't sell a fellow like Lema short. I like the way he's been playing lately and he has the equipment to win here," Hebert said.

"He's one of those long knockers who can carry most of these hills with his drives," Hebert went on. "The first time out here is always rough. You gotta get used to hitting in the water and you gotta know when to go for it and when not to. But, if one of these new boys is going to do it, I'd put my money on Lema. He looks like he knows what to do with those 14 sticks."

As soon as Tony turned off Washington Street onto Magnolia Lane towards the antebellum clubhouse, he fell in love with Augusta National. Greeted like a visiting dignitary upon his arrival, his clubs were whisked off to the caddy house by a doorman while he registered.

Led upstairs to the locker room, his locker assignment was located directly under a picture of Bobby Jones sinking the winning putt for the Grand Slam. He also viewed pictures of such legends as Gene Sarazen, Craig Wood, Byron Nelson, and Sam Snead. As he strolled around the clubhouse, he ran into these same legends in the flesh. He saw Freddie McLeod, winner of the 1908 British Open and Jock Hutchinson who won the same tournament in 1921. The two men acted as the honorary starters hitting the first tee shots in the Masters each year. The atmosphere around the clubhouse sent a shiver down Tony's spine. He felt he was present in a real life picture book on the history of golf.

His enjoyment continued once he got out on the golf course. The weeks leading up to the Masters had been dry and warm and the course was alive with color. The verdant fairways and greens, framed by blooming dogwood trees, pink and white azaleas, and rhododendrons make Augusta one of the most beautiful venues in golf. Tony felt it was the finest course he had ever seen or played on.

"I wanted to lie down and roll around on it, it looked so beautiful," he wrote in *Golfer's Gold*.

Tony and Bo Wininger accepted an invitation from Ken and Connie Venturi to share a rented house near the course. Accommodations were difficult in Augusta with hotel and motel rooms reserved months in advance of the tournament. Many Augusta residents rented their houses and then "got out of Dodge" during the hectic week.

Tony found the house comfortable, compared to the cramped quarters of a hotel. Its close proximity to Augusta National made the commute to the course easy and relaxing. He also enjoyed the camaraderie of sharing the house with friends. Tony, Wininger, and Venturi played their practice rounds together, joined by Venturi's former teacher and good friend Byron Nelson.

Venturi and Nelson chatted about shots they hit in past Masters. They speculated about where they thought the location of flagsticks for each round would be and what they would do on certain holes when the wind blew. Tony paid very close attention and felt the information would pay big dividends once the tournament started.

He also learned that although the fairways at Augusta were wide and spacious, it was imperative to place your tee shot precisely. The key on the challenging course was to get in a position for the best angle to the pin on approach shots. Length was an asset at Augusta National, but not at the expense of accuracy.

Being a gutsy player at Augusta was also important, Tony discovered. He realized that you had to cut corners on the doglegs and know when to attempt to carry a water hazard. Nicklaus, for one, decided that he would go for broke more in the 1963 Masters. He recognized that Palmer played Augusta National with abandon, as if he owned the place. To compete with Palmer in the Masters, he too, would have to gamble.

With their final practice round complete, Tony asked Nelson how he thought he was playing. Nelson gave him a good long look with the eyes of a teacher.

"I've watched your swing for three days now," Nelson began in his soft Texas drawl. "I've observed you pretty carefully and I cannot see a thing wrong. I think you're swinging and hitting the ball beautifully."

This comment sent Tony's confidence soaring and made him feel like doing a little dance right there on the veranda of the clubhouse. He could not wait for the tournament to start.

The next morning, however, standing on the first tee, his confidence gave way to his nerves. Like most first time players in the Masters, he wondered if he was going to be able to make contact with the ball. He pegged his ball, stood back and took a deep breath. He addressed his ball and then hit it as hard as he could. He looked up and saw the ball soaring down the middle of the fairway about 300-yards. He was off and running in his first Masters.

What a Masters it turned out to be, both for Tony and for the fans. The dry weather turned the greens hard and unreceptive to approach shots while the wind was gusty and hard to gauge. The conditions contributed to a great many high first round scores.

"Where's your "Big Three," now?" asked Demeret of the press after the first round.

Mike Souchak and Tony's housemate, Bo Wininger shared the first round lead at 69, while Palmer and Nicklaus shot 74 each. Of "The Big Three," only Gary Player seemed to be in the hunt having shot an opening round 71.

Wininger utilized his short game to produce his 69, chipping to within two-feet, or less, on five different occasions. He also sank three putts over 20-feet. Souchak birdied three straight holes starting at the par 5 thirteenth.

Tony recorded a 74 in the opening round, a round where he admitted that he was tense. He did not drive the ball as well as he knew he could, and he was out of position for his approach shots. With the tough conditions, he felt satisfied with a 74 except for a costly double-bogey on the eighth hole that was particularly vexing.

In the second round, he played with Sam Snead who shot a first round 70. Tony played well and even hit some shots that earned a "nice shot," from Snead, known to be stingy with complements. He fashioned a fantastic 69, one of the better rounds of the day, to Snead's 73. His round included an eagle on the 475-yard, par 5 thirteenth hole where he hit a four-iron second shot to ten-feet and sank the putt.

The best round of the day, a 66, belonged to Nicklaus. He identified the round as one of the best of his career, while Alfred Wright, writing for *Sports Illustrated* called it one of the "finest single rounds ever shot at Augusta." He went bogey free for the round while scoring six birdies. His 66 was just two shots off the Masters record of 64, carded by Lloyd Mangrum in 1940. His hot round resulted in a move up the leader board to second place, one shot off the lead.

"I just can't play much better," Nicklaus, told the press after his round.

Mike Souchak had the mid-point lead at 139 after following up his 69 with a fine 70 in the second round. The co-leader in the first round, Wininger, recorded a second round 72 and was three off the lead.

Tony returned to the rented house in high spirits, as did Wininger. Ken Venturi was happy for his friends but disappointed with his own play. He was far down the leader board. Even though he seemed out of the tournament, Venturi continued to talk to Tony about how to play Augusta National, where to go for broke and where to play cautious. As the players prepared for bed, it began to rain. The rain continued to pour all night long.

The next day, Saturday, the course was soggy from the overnight rain and the weather remained ominous. It continued to rain off-and-on, making for a miserable day out on the course.

In the sodden conditions, Nicklaus was attempting to become the youngest Masters champion at 23-years-old. Byron Nelson, the current holder of the youngest champion honor, won his green jacket when he was just 25 years old in 1937.

Out on the wet course, Souchak completely lost his composure on the thirteenth hole. He hit a fine drive into the center of the fairway that left him only a mid-iron into the par 5. His drive came to rest in standing water. Entitled to a free drop from the casual water, he had trouble locating an area to take his drop—there simply was not a dry spot on the fairway.

"Why don't we call it off?" Souchak snapped at a rules official. "The fairways and greens are under water; the course is unplayable."

"Mr. Roberts says, 'play on'," explained the official as he shrugged his shoulders.

Finally finding a semi-dry place for his ball, he was never able to regain his composure. He skied to a 40 on the back nine and shot a 79 for the round. Nicklaus, who witnessed Souchak's unraveling, immediately dismissed him as a challenger. Nicklaus had the ability to focus during bad conditions, able to plod along stringing pars together while other players became unnerved.

Even though he remained focused, Nicklaus did not play the third round flawlessly. He started the round with a wildly hooked tee shot ending up between the first and ninth fairways, but managed to salvage par. He birdied the fifth hole, but missed short putts on the sixth, seventh, eighth and tenth holes.

However, he continued to grind out one par after another while other players faltered. As he approached the eighteenth green, he looked over at the scoreboard to gauge his position in relation to the rest of the field. Nicklaus, partially colorblind, had trouble reading the scoreboard with the system employed at Augusta for the Masters. The scoreboards list the player's scores in relation to par with under-par scores in red numbers and over-par scores represented in green. Nicklaus could not tell the red numbers from the green ones on the scoreboard. He finally had to ask his caddy to help him.

"By gosh, Willie," Nicklaus asked, "are we leading this thing by three strokes?"

"Yes, Boss," came the answer.

Nicklaus felt a surge of adrenalin at this news and said, "Well, let's see if we can make it four."

He was unable to increase his lead, which actually shrank as Ed Furgol, playing in a group behind him, narrowed the margin to one.

"I played a lot better than I scored," Nicklaus told the press after carding a 2-over 74.

One of the better rounds of the day belonged to Chen Ching-Po, a golfer from Formosa who now lived in Tokyo. Ching-Po fashioned a 71 in the wet conditions and moved up the leader board into a tie for sixth. Julius Boros fired a very steady 71 and was just two strokes off Nicklaus's lead.

Tony shot an uneventful 74, although he maintained his position on the leader board because of the wet conditions and high scores. His 217 put him in third place, tied with Snead at one over par for the tournament.

Playing in just his third major championship, and contending, did not faze Tony at all—in fact, it fired him up. Arriving at the golf course for the final round, Tony went upstairs to the second floor of the clubhouse at Augusta. He was studying the pairings and standings when Dan Sikes, the former attorney who now played the tour, came up behind him.

"Tony," he drawled in his Florida accent, "you just might be able to win this thing."

"Attorney," Tony responded, "I feel so charged up I could just walk out the door to the porch over there, walk right through the railing and float straight to the first tee."

That feeling stayed with him the whole day. The weather matched his mood as sunshine replaced the cold rain of the previous day. He felt that if he could shoot a good score on the front nine he would be in very good position to win. He accomplished that goal when he made the turn at one-under-par, now even par for the tournament. As he walked to the tenth tee, he paused to study the leader board and learned he had gained one shot on Nicklaus.

Nicklaus admitted to nervousness and butterflies in his stomach before and during the fourth round. He made a rare mental mistake when he left the first green. He neglected to check the hole placement on the eighth green, visible from the first green. The eighth green is elevated, so players cannot gauge exactly where the flagstick is located from the fairway. When he got to the fairway on the hole, he guessed that the cup location was on the right side of the green.

He played his one-iron to the left giving him plenty of green to work with in the event that he missed the green, which he did. As he climbed the hill to the green, he was shocked to see the hole was actually located on the left side of the green. He now faced a tough, little chip shot with no green to work with. He had to chip a six-iron into a bank and try to trickle the ball down to the cup. The chip shot hit the bank, which killed the shot short of the green, resulting in a bogey.

Tony, playing with Chen Ching-Po, split the tenth fairway with his drive, but then selected the wrong club for his approach. Hitting a five-iron, when a four-iron would have been a better choice, he hit the green, but was approximately 100-feet from the hole. The result of his mental mistake was a three-putt bogey.

Meanwhile, Snead and Player started making birdies in front of Tony. Now he was behind not only Nicklaus, but Player and Snead, as well. On the twelfth hole, a tricky par 3, Tony hit a good shot to eight-feet. He needed to drain the birdie putt desperately. When he missed the putt, Tony's temper got the better of him.

The gallery on the twelfth hole is contained behind the tee so only the players and their caddies are on the green. Tony tapped in for his par and then unleashed an angry stream of "the filthiest language I had used since mustering out of the Marines."

After retrieving his ball from the hole, he straightened up and looked at Ching-Po who wore a quizzical expression on his face. Tony walked over to his fellow competitor, who was having difficulties in the fourth round, and apologized for using such vile language in front of a guest in his country.

"Is all right," Ching-Po replied in broken English. "If I knew those words I would use them myself." Tony laughed, no longer feeling angry and headed for the par 5 thirteenth hole.

He followed up a great drive with another good shot resulting in a birdie that got him back to even par for the tournament.

The tournament was down to five competitors and the action was getting hot and heavy. Alfred Wright described the action in *Sports Illustrated* writing, "For the next hour and more, the respective positions of these five players were scrambled and descrambled so rapidly that one might have thought the scoreboards around the course were being operated by the dealer in a five-card Monte game."

The five players were Nicklaus at one-under par playing the twelfth hole; Sam Snead, one-under playing the fifteenth; Gary Player, even par also playing on fifteenth; Tony, even par teeing off on the fourteenth; and Julius Boros at one-over playing the twelfth with Nicklaus.

Nicklaus found trouble on the twelfth hole when his tee shot on the par 3 found the front bunker. The sand was wet from the prior day's rain. His shot came out hard, running across, and off the green. He elected to use a putter for his next shot rather than risk chipping to the downhill sloping green towards Rae's Creek. Still, his putt ran eight-feet past the hole.

He marked his ball and watched as Boros ran his 12-foot putt for birdie straight into the hole to put him at even par for the tournament. Nicklaus had to make his eight-footer to remain even with Boros, as well as Tony, and avoid losing ground to Snead and Player who had birdied both the fifteen and sixteen. Nicklaus studied the putt, stood over it for an eternity and then finally stroked it into the hole for his bogey.

The leader board now read:
Snead (through sixteen) - 2-under
Player (through sixteen) - 2-under
Nicklaus (on thirteen) - even
Boros (on thirteen) - even
Lema (on fourteen) - even

Things got wild as Player took bogey fives on both the seventeenth and eighteenth holes flushing away his chance at a second green jacket. Snead hit his tee shot on the par 3 sixteenth hole badly, winding up at the front of the green and three-putted for a bogey. He also bogeyed the eighteenth falling out of contention.

Tony managed to secure pars on the fourteenth through seventeenth holes to remain at even par. Nicklaus added a birdie on the par 3 sixteenth to his birdie on the thirteenth to go two shots in front of Tony. Boros was unable to secure the birdie down the stretch he needed to catch Nicklaus. Tony knew his only chance to pull off the upset victory was to birdie the last hole and hope that Nicklaus would bogey either seventeen or eighteen.

The eighteenth hole is a difficult hole to birdie. The tee shot, from out of a chute of pine trees, demands a precisely placed shot on the dogleg right hole that plays uphill the entire way. Bunkers on the right protect the narrow green while a drop off on the left results in a very difficult chip shot. Two ridges divide the green into three distinct plateaus and makes putting very difficult.

Although Tony was tense, it was a good kind of tension. It focused his mind. He hit a good tee shot that left an approach shot to a pin located on the middle plateau of the green, slightly favoring the right side of the green. Tony knew if he landed the ball just off the green on the right side it would bounce towards the pin, but this also meant flirting with the bunker. He settled into the shot with positive thoughts. He hit a firm four-iron that hit his target and bounced up, and onto, the green, 22-feet above the hole.

Alfred Wright, in *Sports Illustrated*, wrote that Tony "looked over this scary putt with a poise that denied the torment inside him. For all one could tell, he might have been playing a $2 Nassau on Wednesday afternoon back home in San Leandro."

He took off his glove as he and his caddy, Pokey (most Augusta caddies had colorful nicknames), looked over the putt. He tossed away his cigarette and got over the putt they read to break two ways. First, the putt would break to the right before curling back to the left closer to the cup. In addition, it was a slick putt, downhill all the way.

When he hit the putt, he knew it was good. He watched as it started on line and, as he thought it would, the ball started to break right. It held that line for an instant before it gradually swung back to the left and headed straight towards the hole. As the ball turned towards the hole, Tony began to chase it, moving to his left. When it disappeared into the hole, it was as if an explosion went off inside him. He roared in approval as he jumped into a little jig. The crowd around the final green erupted with one of the famous Augusta roars heard around the course.

A picture of Tony, by James Drake, shows Tony giving a fist pump with his right hand while he raised his left leg in the first step of his celebratory dance. Drake's camera caught Tony with his mouth wide open releasing an ecstatic yell.

Nicklaus heard the huge roar that erupted from the eighteenth green. He delayed his second shot on the seventeenth hole until he could learn the reason. Before playing the seventeenth, he glanced at a leader board and discovered that only one player left on the course had a chance to beat him—Tony.

The leader board near the seventeenth green soon registered Tony's birdie, so Nicklaus now knew he needed pars on both seventeen and eighteen to win. He managed a par on the seventeenth hole and headed for the tee at eighteen.

After his round, Tony felt wrung out and excited at the same time. He signed his card before officials escorted him to Cliff Roberts's private office in the clubhouse. This was the same room where Venturi had watched on television as Palmer had birdied the last two holes in 1960 to defeat him. The same room where Gary Player had watched Palmer double bogey the eighteenth hole to hand him the green jacket in 1961.

In the room were Roberts and Bobby Jones, who Tony was meeting for the first time. Also in the room were Arnold Palmer, who as defending champion would participate in the green jacket ceremony, and Labron Harris who was low amateur for the event. There was a television set in the room providing tournament coverage as well as a television camera to record reactions in the room.

Palmer was glum and downhearted about his play in the tournament. Still, he heartily congratulated Tony on his fine play, as did the other men in the room. Servers poured drinks while everybody sat down to watch

Nicklaus play the eighteenth hole.

"I didn't try to play conservative golf at any time," Nicklaus later explained, "but neither was I about to get reckless on the eighteenth."

He hit his drive down the left, the safer side, of the fairway, where it ended up in a muddy patch. After a free drop to a drier spot on the fairway, he looked towards the green that appeared very small to him. From that side of the fairway he could only see the top half of the pin, the huge gallery and the gaping bunkers.

Nicklaus mapped out courses with precise yardages from landmarks, one of the few pros who did so at the time. He paced off the distance to his yardage marker, the last tree on the right, and calculated that he had 160-yards to the pin. The distance called for a normal six-iron for him. His approach left him a 35-foot putt from above the hole.

Watching the television, Tony knew how difficult Nicklaus's downhill putt would be. He thought it was quite possible that Nicklaus could three-putt.

Nicklaus took his customary lengthy time studying the putt before he stood over the ball. After a long pause, he at last struck the putt. He thought he hit a very good putt, thinking it was going in the hole. Instead, the putt ran three-feet past the hole.

Nicklaus again deliberated for a lengthy time studying the short, difficult putt. He stood, as if frozen, over the putt forever before he finally stroked the ball. When Tony saw his second putt, he did not think it had a chance to go in. Somehow, the ball held its line, climbed the hill and finally dove into the hole.

After his putt went in, Nicklaus took off his white ball cap and flung it towards the front of the green. He turned back towards the television camera with a huge smile on his face as his father, Charlie, ran onto the green and gave his son a big bear hug.

"I was kind of surprised when my first putt didn't go in," Nicklaus admitted after the round, "and I was even more surprised when my second one did."

When the putt dropped, Tony felt as if every bit of emotion drained from him. He felt as if he would never be able to muster up the effort to get out of the chair he was sitting in. He felt deflated, almost numb.

Nicklaus signed his scorecard and then, on cloud nine, arrived at Robert's office. All present in the room congratulated him before preparing to move to the presentation ceremonies held on the practice putting green.

Venturi was waiting for Tony just outside the office, grabbed him and ushered him into an unused room in the clubhouse. There the two talked as tears welled up in both their eyes and they "stumbled around the room like two blind people, trying to regain our composure," as Tony described it. They both now knew, and felt the heartbreak, of coming so close to a

Masters green jacket.

Finally, the two made their way to the presentation ceremony where they watched Palmer help Nicklaus into a size-44 regular green jacket. During the ceremony, Tony could not help but think back to that damn double-bogey on the eighth hole during Thursday's first round. He could not help but ponder what might have been, if not for that costly mishap.

Nicklaus won a check for $20,000 while Tony had to make do with the second-place prize of $12,000. This was more money than he won in his first full year on tour, more than he won in the bleak years of 1959 and 1960 combined. The check also moved him up to third place on the official money list bumping Palmer from third to fourth.

Still, the check was not big enough for Tony's tastes. He met with the press after the awards ceremony and said, "You'd have had champagne—the best—in the press tent, and all you could drink, if I'd have won. I would have been glad to have blown the whole $20,000 first-place money."

Instead, there was only beer in the tent.

The numbness of his narrow defeat wore off and he was starting to feel philosophical, even proud of his performance. He admitted that he was "too stupid" to realize that no first-timer had ever won the Masters.

"I think I have it made," he told reporters. "Even though I finished second, they've already asked me to appear on at least two television matches next year."

"When I started out in golf as a caddy in my teens I decided I was going to adopt Walter Hagen's philosophy of life—'smell the roses along the way.' Well, I've smelled them and I'm going to keep on smelling them."

He pointed out to the press how valuable Ken Venturi's help was during the tournament.

"Had I won, I would have given him half the trophy," Tony said. "Here was a guy, who was in the field against me, yet I played four practice rounds with him, and he told me everything he knew about the course. I never would have done as well as I did had it not been for Ken. I want to pay him tribute. I have a fine family, the best. I never made college, I barely got through high school, but it wasn't my family's fault; they are gods to me. So is Venturi. He's quite a guy."

Across the country from Augusta, back in Oakland on that Sunday, John Fry was working in the pro shop, at Lake Chabot, when the phone rang. On the other end was a local reporter who asked Fry if he knew that Tony was married. Seeing the tournament on television, Shirley Donovan called a local paper to inform them that she was Mrs. Tony Lema, mother of Tony's son. The reporter called Fry in an attempt to verify the story. Fry told the reporter that he knew nothing about Tony having a wife, or a child.

Later, a well-placed member of San Francisco Golf Club made a phone call to the paper, which subsequently spiked the story.

Back in Augusta, after Tony met with the press, he attended a dinner hosted by Cliff Roberts. Also present was the new champion, Nicklaus and his wife Barbara, Palmer and his wife Winnie, Gary and Vivienne Player, Billy and Shirley Casper and Charlie Coe, one of the finest amateurs in the country and a member of Augusta. Everybody toasted the winner, as well as Tony, and they enjoyed a convivial meal. The sting of defeat had worn off and Tony felt proud to finish second in such a prestigious event.

After dinner, Arnold Palmer took him aside for a man-to-man talk. He told Tony how well he played. Referring to Nicklaus, Palmer felt that Tony could "beat that kid." He also told Tony he considered him a close friend and this particularly touched Tony. Their friendship, always warm, grew tighter after this conversation.

21 WEDDING BELLS AND CHAMPAGNE TOASTS
1963

Tony's performance in the Masters transformed him into a burgeoning celebrity. He quickly signed Fred Corcoran as his business manager to help handle the requests for his time that poured in. Endorsement opportunities started to "spring up like gushing oil wells," as Tony described it. His putt on the eighteenth hole at Augusta, witnessed by hundreds of thousands of golf fans in the gallery and on television, gained him new fans. Many more saw Drake's photograph of Tony celebrating after the putt went in. Reporters called the putt the most exciting shot of the 1963 Masters. Many reports described him as "bursting onto the scene" after his performance.

Offers came in for televised golf matches including Shell's Wonderful World of Golf. The Shell show, a travelogue-style visit to exotic locals and famous golf courses, featured matches between players from all over the world.

Corcoran sifted through a myriad of offers for everything from equipment to clothing to power tools. Complicating matters was the ongoing clash with Malarkey concerning his sponsorship contract. A provision in the contract required Tony to split endorsement income with Malarkey.

Popular professional golfers could make substantial sums from endorsements and exhibitions. Golf entered into its "golden age" in the early 1960s as it experienced a huge popularity explosion. Mark McCormick made huge stars of Arnold Palmer, Jack Nicklaus and Gary Player. Tournament purses on tour were skyrocketing as the country went golf mad.

While not in the same class as "The Big Three," Tony still benefited from the increased popularity and interest in professional golf. Advertisers sought his style, grace and easy-going personality to help sell products or entertain during exhibitions and television matches. Palm Beach Sportswear wanted to tap into that style and flair with a clothing contract, while Buick wanted to add him as spokesperson. Tony and Corcoran jumped on this sweetheart deal, one that Buick extended to a few other players, which provided a brand-new car at each tour event. Buick also provided a new car each year for his personal use when he was home.

Al Laney, of the *New York Herald Tribune*, in his report on the Masters, focused on Tony. He wrote that "The Big Three" might become a quartet with the addition of Tony.

"He had very much the look of a man who can win the big ones and he is one of the most personable golfers now playing the circuit," Laney wrote. "He has all the attributes of a winner; long, accurate tee shots and irons, a smooth putting touch, boldness now tempered by judgment and, above all else, golfing style. Lema seems to have that elusive thing called class."

With his new fame, Tony was flooded with fan mail. He felt it important to respond to all his mail, especially from the kids. No matter how busy his schedule was, he found time to dash off a handwritten response to his fans. While playing in tournaments, or exhibitions, he made it a point to interact with the people in his gallery adding to his popularity. The press soon dubbed these fans "Lema's Legions."

In The Greater Greensboro Open the week after the Masters, Tony tied for 28th earning a paltry check for $365. It was a difficult week, a letdown after the excitement of Augusta.

He tried to push on and play the Houston Open, but withdrew late on Tuesday before the start of the tournament. He traveled to San Leandro instead for some well-deserved rest. While there, he evaluated his endorsement offers as he and Betty began making plans for their wedding.

With the large check from the Masters, and the prospect of additional endorsement income, his felt secure enough, financially, to move up the wedding date. With characteristic impatience, he wanted to marry Betty as soon as possible. The couple chose April 28 to tie the knot in San Leandro. The change in date caught Betty's family off-guard and only her sister, Mary, would be able to attend.

It was imperative for Tony to get his situation with Malarkey settled. He did not need the financial support any longer and particularly felt the sting of handing over Malarkey's share of his Masters check—$6,000. Malarkey, for his part, felt that he was starting to enjoy some of the profits for his investment that started back in late 1957. He financed Tony through the dark days of 1959 and 1960 and now wanted a piece of the action in the good times.

Tony consulted with lawyers seeking council on how to buy his way out of the agreement. Tony understood that buying Malarkey out was his only option to disentangle himself from the burden of the flawed contract he signed.

His bride-to-be, Betty, was the eldest child of Lowell Harold Cline and Louise Cline. The family included her two sisters, Mary and Virginia, as well as a brother Jim. Even though she was quite shy in high school, she made many friends and earned good grades as a bright student. When she was 19-years-old, her father died of a heart attack, at 48-years-old, and she entered the work force after graduation, helping with the family's expenses.

The family was a working, lower-middle-class family in Oklahoma City and a college education for their eldest daughter was beyond their means. Betty went to work for a legal firm doing administrative duties before landing the job with American Airlines as a flight attendant. She regularly sent money home to her mother, who remarried.

Betty was a petit, pretty woman with deep green eyes and natural light brown, almost red, hair. Her green eyes and petite nose highlighted a smooth beautiful olive complexion. She wore the latest fashions exhibiting the same classy style as Tony. Her friends and family described her as "down to earth" and "level headed." She loved to read, shop, play cards and dominoes.

They were both very much in love. For Tony, Betty provided a stabilizing force in his hectic life. He left the partying playboy life behind once he fell in love with her. He later credited his love for her as the source for his focus in his career.

"When we got serious, I got serious," Tony later said.

The two worked feverishly arranging plans for the wedding. She resigned from her flight attendant job in preparation of her new life as the wife of a PGA professional. Tony planned to play in the Tournament of Champions in Las Vegas, scheduled for the first week of May, immediately following the wedding. He phoned the tournament officials to ask them to reserve the honeymoon suite at the Desert Inn. This would be his first chance to play in the Tournament of Champions, which featured a field made up of tournament winners from the previous 12 months.

Tony made a curious selection for his best man choosing Malarkey. His brother Harry later explained the choice came at Malarkey's request. He made the request as a ransom, of sorts, towards Tony's release from the contract. Of course, he still wanted a substantial amount of money in addition for the buy-out of what he felt was a valuable arrangement. Tony would have much rather had Bill Craig, or Chet Smith, stand as his best man.

Malarkey arrived in San Leandro for the wedding and wanted to see the town. Tony's brothers, Harry and Walter took him to a few of the local bars.

"The thing I remember," Walter recalled many years later, "was that he never went into his pocket to pay for a round, once."

A day before the wedding, Walter suggested that Tony give him his annotated, little black book full of women's names and phone numbers.

"You're not going to need it after tomorrow," Walter said.

Tony chuckled before joking, "No, I don't think you could handle it."

On Sunday, April 28, in a small wedding ceremony at St. Leanders Church in San Leandro, Tony and Betty exchanged their wedding vows. Tony and Malarkey were both dressed in conservative dark suits and ties with boutonnières attached at the lapels. Malarkey sported a full beard. Betty was stylish and beautiful in a tailored soft blue dress, that hit just below the knees, and matching small circular veil.

Tony's family and a few friends, including Bill Craig and Chet Smith, attended the ceremony. From Betty's family, only her sister attended the service. The local papers ran a picture of the happy couple descending the church stairs as friends and family showered them with rice. There was a short reception afterwards before the newlyweds departed for the airport and their honeymoon in Vegas.

In Vegas, bookmakers were offering 8-1 odds on Tony in the casinos, while Nicklaus was listed at 4-1, Palmer at 5-1 and Casper was at 6-1. The odds on Tony moved all the way down to 6-1 before gamblers got wind of his newlywed status. Once word spread that he was on his honeymoon, the odds shot up to 15-1, before stabilizing back at 10-1.

For his part, Tony felt relaxed, ready to play. He looked forward to having Betty travel with him. He also expected to maintain his high style of travel.

"I won more than $40,000 in 1962," he informed Don Johnson of *The Pasadena Star-News*, "but I don't have much to show for it now. I went through about $25,000 in expenses last year, and I figure I'll spend at least that much this year, regardless of how much I make. I like to travel first-class. It's the only way."

He went on to explain his regard for money when he said, "I never had any before. And now that I have a few bucks, I want to enjoy myself while I'm young."

The press had gotten wind of his situation with Malarkey. In his "Once Over Lightly" column in *The Long Beach Independent Press-Telegram*, Dave Lewis described Tony's sponsor noting, "Malarkey was a Portland millionaire who owns half of Sun Valley and a huge plywood company." Malarkey informed Lewis that his investment in Tony since late 1957 was near the $90,000 mark.

"I thought all along I had potentially the greatest golfer of the bunch," Malarkey disclosed to the reporter.

In his article, Lewis continued, "Tony wants 'out' when the current contract runs out on June 1." However, Lewis failed to mention the options that Malarkey held that could extend the length of the contract through 1966.

The newlyweds arrived in Las Vegas amid a great deal of publicity. An

Associated Press photo of Tony ran in papers around the country the day after he got his first look at the golf course. He is hard at work on the driving range, while his new bride sits on the ground nearby with her dress fanned out around her while she watches her husband work. In another photo, by Unifax, he is carrying her across the threshold of the bridal suite at the Desert Inn. He is dressed in a suit and tie while Betty, with a bouquet of his golf clubs in her arms, is stylish in a light colored dress adorned with a corsage and high heel shoes.

Every pre-tournament article mentioned him as one of the favorites in the Tournament of Champions. Of course, Nicklaus, Palmer and Player came first in the lists of favorites.

"He's playing beautifully," said Billy Maxwell before the tournament. "Lema should be the co-favorite with Nicklaus."

The small field of tournament winners enjoyed themselves off the course in Vegas. Palmer spent most of Tuesday night teaching Nicklaus the intricacies of shooting craps, and then on Wednesday night, he stood in as a celebrity dealer at the blackjack tables. Tony and Betty spent their honeymoon evenings dining, dancing and playing cards.

Once the tournament started, Nicklaus took control with a nearly unbelievable eight-under-par 64 setting a new course record. He simply overpowered the course with seven birdies, one eagle and one bogey. Tony finished his round of 72 and then rushed back to the hotel to resume his honeymoon. He followed up with rounds of 69 and 71 that shot him up the leader board.

Nicklaus cruised to a wire-to-wire victory with a four shot cushion. He won a cloth sack filled with 13,000 silver dollars. The real excitement of the final round, however, was the fight for second-place. Palmer teed off in the final round playing with Casper. After eight holes, Casper developed pain in his left hand, due to a mysterious nerve injury, and withdrew. Palmer continued his round alone until he caught the twosome in front of him, Tony and Ted Kroll, and joined them.

Tony was in the process of scoring the low round of the day. At this point in the tournament, it was obvious that the battle for second-place was down to him and Palmer. Tony felt that Palmer joining him and Kroll was an advantage.

"It was a tremendous help being able to play him face-to-face instead of wondering how he was doing," Tony told reporters. "He had me by two shots at that time but I thought I could catch him."

By the time they walked onto the eighteenth tee, he had caught him. The difference in prize money between second and third place was $2,500. Tony drove his ball past Palmer, and Palmer shooting first, sent his second shot near the back of the green, leaving a 50-foot putt for his birdie. Tony hit his second shot below the hole, and faced a 15-foot birdie putt. Palmer putted first, and his deviously long, difficult putt started down the green, rolled over a slight rise, and oozed across the left edge of the cup.

Tony recalled the action in *Golfer's Gold* when he wrote, "I stood there with my mouth open and my eyes hanging out. Then I looked up and Arnold was coming across the green, hitching up his pants the way he does when things are going his way, and looking at me. He had a grin as big as a slice of watermelon on his face and it said as clearly as words could have, 'Aha, you s.o.b., I almost got you there, didn't I?' Then he started to laugh at the look of shock still on my face and I laughed too."

Tony, unnerved by Palmer's putt, missed his own birdie attempt. Even so, he had blazed over the final nine holes in 32 and tied Palmer for second-place. He won a good-sized check of $5,300 and moved up into the second position on the money list behind Nicklaus.

He attracted even more press attention with his high finish during his honeymoon. Art Rosenbaum, a San Francisco scribe, wrote, "Tony Lema got married one day in San Leandro, headed immediately for the bridal suite in Las Vegas, and was on the Desert Inn Golf Course the next morning practicing for the Tournament of Champions. Would you call Mrs. Lema an instant golf widow?"

Every male golf fan watching on television, or in the gallery, must have envied Tony. What other guy could play golf four days straight on their honeymoon?

His honeymoon golfing activities were not the only thing attracting press attention. Oscar Fraley wrote a syndicated United Press International article that ran under the headline: "SAME SWING AS SAMMY—LEMA JOINS 'BIG FOUR.' " He wrote that Tony, despite not having won a tournament all year, deserved mention right along with Nicklaus, Palmer and Player.

"Getting serious, and deciding to get married, put my mind in a much better state," Fraley quoted Tony.

Tony's new business manager, Fred Corcoran, speaking with Fraley, compared his new client's smooth swing to that of Sam Snead in his younger days. He also said that Tony's demeanor was similar to that of Ted Williams.

The pro tour moved to Texas and the Colonial Invitational where Palmer was the defending champion. Tony played solidly in the Colonial finishing in a tie for fourth with Sanders. His week's work earned him a check of $2,800.

The USGA released the list of players exempted from qualifying for the upcoming U.S. Open. Tony's name was on the list because he was one of the top-10 money leaders. He would not have to go through the rigors of local and sectional qualifying rounds to play in the next major championship on the schedule.

Tony took a week off, planning to play next at the Memphis Open. He spent the week entertaining Betty with a second honeymoon in New York City, where they enjoyed the sights and nightlife. While there, Tony fit in a practice round at the Westchester Country Club, site of the upcoming Thunderbird Classic, scheduled for the middle of June before the U.S. Open. Oscar Fraley, of the United Press International, and Don McLeod of the Associated Press caught up with Tony at Westchester for interviews. Corcoran most likely set the interviews up.

The *Oakland Tribune* ran McLeod's interview that quoted Tony saying, "Arnold Palmer is the greatest golfer in the world—don't bury him yet."

He did not agree that Nicklaus had overtaken Palmer as the number one man in golf.

"Not at all," Tony insisted. "I'm getting a little fed up with this talk that Arnie is a has-been, and you've been hearing it more and more lately. It just so happens that Palmer is tired and in a temporary slump and Nicklaus is riding a hot streak. But, Arnie will snap back—mark my words. He's still the best."

Tony went on to say, "Everybody is entitled to a letdown. Arnie is having his now. With a little rest, he'll be back strong as ever."

Tony then spoke about his own game and said, "I've finished second in four tournaments this year; the Masters, Las Vegas, San Diego and New Orleans. I'm not satisfied with that. I don't want to be a runner-up; I want to be a champion."

McLeod concluded the article writing, "The handsome 6'1" Californian, a matinee idol type who hails from San Leandro, announced plans to concentrate on the 'big ones'."

Fraley's article highlighted Tony's history as a professional golfer from the time that Jerry Kroeckel pulled him over for speeding to the present. It also pointed out that Tony competed against players who forged their games with competition in college and in major national amateur events, both beyond his means. Fraley wrote of his prior playboy reputation and the dark years of 1959 and 1960.

"I still didn't think I was very good," Tony admitted. "For five years my theory was that I'd probably never be back to any of those places on tour again, so I'd better have a good time."

Tony concluded by saying, "It's a whole lot better than working in a cannery. I'll never be able to thank that policeman (Kroeckel) enough."

A few days later, *Golf Digest* hit the newsstands and included a preview of the upcoming U.S. Open at Brookline Country Club. The publication handicapped the field and placed odds on the top players. "The Big Three" and Gene Littler were listed as the co-favorites at 6 - 1 odds. Tony, Casper and Sanders came in next at 8 - 1 odds.

Bobby Jones, quoted in an Associated Press article, declared that the days of Palmer's domination of the tour were over.

"It could be that neither one (Palmer or Nicklaus) will dominate the game," Jones said. "There are too many good players. Tony Lema isn't very far behind them."

After their brief respite in New York, the newlyweds returned to the tour for the Memphis Open held the last week of May. A refreshed Tony got right back in the thick of things with a 67 in the first round to share the lead with seven other players including Johnny Pott. Over 20 pros broke par despite a chilly wind that blew throughout the morning.

In the second round, Tony experienced a substandard performance on the greens, including a trio of three-putt greens. However, he was able to calm his putting stroke and birdied four straight holes on the back nine on his way to another 67 putting him at 134 with a two-stroke lead. Harold Kneece carded the best round of the day—a 65—placing him in a tie for second with Tommy Aaron, George Knudsen, and Jerry Edwards.

Rain washed out Saturday's round before half the field was able to tee off and Tony never made it out of the locker room.

After the announcement of the postponement, Tony joked to reporters in the locker room, "At least I'll hold the lead for one more day."

Rain again washed out the 36-hole final round on Sunday forcing Tony to sleep on his lead for another night. As he wrote in *Golfer's Gold*, "By the time we teed off on Monday I had been leading the tournament for four days. If ever a player figured to blow a lead it was me."

He almost blew it. He lost the lead to Kneece after Monday's morning round, while Tommy Aaron played well, too. Kneece was at 201, Tony and Aaron at 202. In the afternoon, during the fourth round, the tournament boiled down to a battle between Tony, Aaron, and Jerry Edwards after Kneece shot himself out of contention. Aaron, playing with Tony, held a two-stroke advantage as the two reached the seventeenth tee.

The seventeenth played as a 186-yard par 3 with an elevated green. Aaron had the honor and hit a four-iron that covered the flag. Both players thought the shot was stiff to the pin, but the crowd reaction told them otherwise. Initially the crowd began to cheer, but the cheers died away quickly. Tony figured that the ball must have ended up short and well below the hole.

He then decided to switch clubs from the four-iron he had intended to use, to a three-iron to make sure he got his ball up to the hole. He hit his shot and watched as it flew deep into the green. The crowd's reaction was explosive; he knew he was close to the hole.

When the players crested the hill to the green, they saw the results of their shots. Aaron's ball was 20-feet below the hole while Tony's ball sat just six-feet from the hole. After Aaron two-putted, Tony got over his putt and stroked it straight into the cup for a birdie two. Aaron's lead was down to one.

The eighteenth hole, a par 5, was reachable in two shots—at least in theory. Tony, unable to reach the green in two during the first three rounds, now felt the adrenaline pumping through him. He smashed his drive into perfect position giving him a chance to reach the green with his three-wood. His shot landed on the green, and held, giving him a putt for an eagle. The shorter hitting Aaron hit his second shot well short of the green, in the rough near a tree. Aaron hit a wonderful recovery winding up 15-feet from the hole.

Tony faced a long putt that broke down the green. He hit the putt and thought it had a chance to go in for an eagle, but the ball trickled over the edge of the cup and he had to settle for a tap-in birdie. Aaron then lined up his 15-footer for the win. He missed the putt and the two players prepared for a sudden-death playoff.

On the first playoff hole, Aaron made a mess of things on his way to a bogey, while Tony made a routine par, winning his third official PGA tournament. The victory was an immense relief for Tony. Despite winning a bunch of money, he had yet to notch a victory for the year. Finally securing the victory was extremely satisfying. He was proud that he did so with birdies on the final two holes and a solid par in the playoff. In addition, he topped a quality field made up from most of the top earners on tour.

The headlines the next day read, "LATE FOR WEDDING—LEMA STACKS UP $9,000, TOSSES CHAMPAGNE PARTY."

After his playoff victory, Tony ordered champagne for the pressroom, "The best you've got," he said.

With three tournaments remaining on the schedule before the U.S. Open, Tony's confidence was sky high at a particularly good time. With the victory in Memphis, he regained the second spot on the money list. He was certainly one of the golfers to be favored in the Open. He had cemented his spot among the top players. His style, humor and champagne parties made him one of the most popular players, as well.

In the weeks leading up to the U.S. Open, you could not pick up a newspaper without seeing Tony's name mentioned as one of the favorites. First among the favorites, of course, were "The Big Three" of Nicklaus, Palmer, and Player. Some writers, including Red Smith and Oscar Fraley, felt, and wrote, that "The Big Three" be renamed "The Big Four" to include Tony, even though he had yet to win a major.

With the U.S. Open in his sights, Tony and Betty traveled from Memphis to Indianapolis for the Festival 500 Open. The course used for the tournament, the Speedway Golf Course, featured nine holes inside the racing oval. The Indianapolis 500, run the weekend before, had left the course trampled down from the huge crowd that watched Parnelli Jones win the race.

Fred Hawkins grabbed the lead with a seven-under 64 as the course played easy. 51 players broke par including Tony at one under par 70.

Tony had a fine second round shooting a 64 that included two eagles, five birdies and one bogey. His first eagle came when he holed out a wedge shot from 60-yards on the tenth hole and his second resulted from a fine second shot into the final green, a par 5 and he sank the 20-foot putt.

In the third round, Dow Finsterwald and Julius Boros took over the lead. Boros, nearly as hot recently as Tony, had a 65 while Finsterwald came in with a 64. Tony's 69 put him at 203, three strokes back.

In the fourth round Finsterwald shot a 68 for a 268 total and captured his first win since the New Orleans Open three years earlier. His round was steady as a rock, and he avoided a five-way playoff with a birdie-par finish. Tony birdied the final two holes for a 67 to finish in a tie for second-place winning $3,400. He remained firmly ensconced in the second spot on the official money list that now read:

Nicklaus - $57,615
Lema - $47,697
Player - $39,065
Boros - $34,325
Palmer - $31,545

A story appeared in *The Oakland Tribune* on the Sunday of the fourth round of the 500 Festival. Above the byline of Norm Hannon, ran the headline GOLFER TONY LEMA ARRIVES AS A STAR.

The story's lead paragraph stated, "They call him 'Champagne Tony' and he's the glamour guy of the world of golf these days as he hops from course to course around the country, a beautiful bride on his arm, a man with game, color—and great promise."

He wore his new celebrity comfortably. He carried a presence that attracted attention, and fans found him easy to approach. He always found time to sign autographs and converse with his fans.

"He was one of those guys, like Arnie, who would light up a room when he entered," Butch Baird recalled. "He was a real star."

Betty was going through a crash course learning the minutiae of professional golf tournament play. One has to wonder what she thought of these first weeks out on tour with Tony's continued success. She might have thought that this professional golf thing was a walk in the park, a license to print money. If she did think that, Tony surely dispelled the notion right away. More likely, she must have wondered how Tony could do it. How could he birdie the last two holes to get into a playoff, and then win the playoff? How could he do it with television cameras and thousands of people watching? How did he handle the pressure?

He tried to explain the importance of playing one shot at a time, staying in the moment and trusting his golf swing to her.

They were enjoying the fruits of his hot streak, living the high life on tour. The only blip on their radar was the continuing delay on his contract negotiations with Malarkey.

22 BATTLE AT BROOKLINE
1963

With the recent win at Memphis, the newlyweds arrived in Flint, Michigan for the Buick Open the first week of June on top of the world. With his game red-hot, Tony's confidence was soaring.

He started the Buick with a torrid round of 67. The weather during his round at Warwick Hills was perfect, sunshine and 90 degree temperatures. He shot a front nine 34 and followed that up with a 33 on the back nine.

Unfortunately, a thunderstorm hit the course before a third of the field could complete their rounds. The result was a postponement of the first round with all completed rounds washed out. A year earlier, at the Buick, lightning struck and killed a spectator, so officials were extra cautious at the first signs of trouble in 1963. Tournament officials rescheduled the first round for Friday.

In the re-start, his game cooled off as he recorded a 71 leaving him five-strokes behind the leader, Julius Boros. He finished with rounds of 74, 73 and 71, finishing nine strokes behind the winner, Boros, in a tie for tenth. He earned a decent sized check of $1,300.

The next week, at the Thunderbird Classic in Rye, New York, Tony tried to focus on the job at hand, but his mind was preoccupied. The U.S. Open, just a week away, consumed his thoughts. Every newspaper he picked up mentioned him as a favorite in the Open, including an article written by Arthur Daley for the *New York Times*.

"Not until after he had become deadly serious about his golf did Tony Lema get a nickname that has all sorts of frivolous implications, 'Champagne Tony.' The timing was wrong. If he had earned it, it was during the carefree, dilettante days of his earlier years," Daley wrote.

In the article, Daley identified Tony as a favorite for the Open, but Tony wondered why he was the focus of so much attention since he had yet to win a major championship.

"What's all the fuss about?" Tony asked Daley with a quizzical grin. "I haven't won anything yet—except money."

Privately, Tony was frustrated that a lot of that money was going to Malarkey. He also was accumulating legal bills trying to extradite himself from his contract with his sponsor.

In his negotiations, the sticking point continued to be the options written into the contract. The options, that Malarkey desired to exercise, would tie Tony up through 1966. Malarkey felt that these options were of value, and he was not about to surrender them unless he was justly compensated. The lawyers for each side were attempting to determine a value of the options and ultimately, the cost to buy-out the contract.

At the Thunderbird, his preoccupation with the U.S. Open cost him. He barely made the cut and finished in a tie for 55th earning a measly check for $240. The small check dropped him to number three on the official money list.

While Tony struggled at the Thunderbird Classic, Palmer returned from a month-long break rejuvenated. He won the Thunderbird in a sudden-death playoff over Paul Harney and set off for the U.S. Open with renewed confidence.

Despite his poor performance in the Thunderbird, Tony was also riding a wave of confidence. His performance in the second half of 1962, and his fine play in 1963, placed him in the third spot on the Ryder Cup points list. The Ryder Cup, a biennial event, at that time pit American pros against pros from the United Kingdom. The 1963 matches, scheduled for early October, would take place at the East Lake Country Club, in Atlanta, where Bobby Jones learned the game as a young boy. The chance to represent his country in the match inspired and motivated Tony.

After the Thunderbird Classic, Tony decided to drive from New York to Boston and The Country Club at Brookline for the U.S. Open. He wanted to show Betty the scenery of New England. The sights were beautiful, but they ran into bad traffic that delayed them. They finally arrived at their hotel, the Ritz-Carlton, much too late for him to get in a practice round at Brookline. He eventually got his first look at the course on Tuesday and what he saw put him into a state of shock.

He could not believe how difficult the course was. After his practice round, he did not know what his score was, but he was sure it was in the mid-80s. The next day, his practice round went better—he shot pretty close to par—and he began to feel a little more confident and comfortable with the course.

The Country Club at Brookline was the scene of Francis Ouimet's startling playoff victory over Ted Ray and Harry Vardon in the 1913 U.S. Open. The U.S. Open returned to Brookline to commemorate the fiftieth anniversary of Ouimet's historic win.

Many of the other pros in the Open field agreed with Tony on the difficulty of the course. Brookline was an old-fashion golf course with small, elevated greens that required accurate approach shots. The players had to play these shots into the green blind, with only the top of the flag visible, making it very difficult to gauge which club to use. Although Brookline was not a long course, it put a premium on shot making.

Arthur Daley, of *The New York Times* wrote, "This is a gigantic game of blind man's bluff because the target is hidden on fifteen of the longer holes."

To make matters worse, the United States Golf Association set the course up in the typically challenging U.S. Open style. High, heavy rough pinched in the fairways putting a premium on accuracy off the tee.

Daley, describing the rough in *The New York Times*, wrote, "The greens committee apparently seeded it with barbed wire."

Mother Nature added her challenges to the proceedings. A severe winter resulted in winterkill, a disease caused by the sun burning through accumulated ice adversely affecting grass growth. Fairways were ragged and as a result, the maintenance crew grew the grass to a longer length than normal. This resulted in more grass coming between the ball and the club at contact, commonly called a "flyer." A "flyer" has little backspin making it difficult to hold the small circular greens at Brookline.

The condition of the greens also presented problems. Many underwent re-seeding after the severe winter, resulting in inconsistencies from green to green. To make matters worse, the application of dye to three of the greens were required to make them look presentable.

The U.S.G.A. prepared these inconsistent greens as fast as they could. They cut them as short as possible, then, they rolled them with heavy rollers until they were as slick as glass.

Julius Boros described the challenge saying, "Trying to hold the ball on these greens is like putting on a flight of marble stairs and trying to stop it on the next-to-last step."

The U.S. Open had changed dramatically, as had all professional golf, since Tony first qualified for the event as an assistant pro from the San Francisco Golf Club in 1956. In the seven years since he first played in it, the purse had jumped from $24,000 to $86,000. The endorsement opportunities available to a winner of the U.S. Open also increased significantly. A victory could mean hundreds of thousands of dollars in off-course income to the winner.

Along with the pressures presented by the prestigious tournament, the players encountered added challenges from the weather. In the first round, the wind kicked up, and along with the typically high temperatures and humidity of a New England summer, only two players managed to better par. One was Jacky Cupit who recorded a 70. The other, Bob Gajda, was an unknown pro from Bloomfield Hills, Michigan who fashioned an almost unbelievable 69.

Often an unknown player surprises everybody, including himself, by jumping into the lead in the first round of a U.S. Open. Eventually, the magnitude of the situation, along with all the other pressures a national open exerts, conspire to see the unknown drop from contention quickly.

Managing the conditions fairly well during his first round with an even par 71, Tony was in a tie for third with Boros, one stroke back of Cupit. Palmer bested his "Big Three" brethren with a 73, one better than Gary Player and three in front of defending champion, Jack Nicklaus.

The wind had been vexing, as it was constantly changing directions, seemingly at whim.

"When you looked over your shot, you'd think the wind was with you," Tony explained to the press. "When you'd take your stance, it would be a crosswind. When you were in the process of swinging, the wind would seem to be against you. It was confusing."

The complicated winds continued in the second round, actually increasing in velocity. Par again put up a formidable defense as only three players could break it. One was Palmer with a 69 for a two-round 142 that placed him in a tie for the lead with Jacky Cupit who shot a 72. Tony remained in the thick of the battle after a 74 gave him a 145. He sat in a tie with Boros and Davis Love, Jr.

Gajda, as expected, soared to an 80 in the second round. Things would not get any better for him, either. He finished the tournament with an 84 and an 80 to become the first player in history to finish a U.S. Open without a score in the 70s.

U.S. Open Saturday was, by tradition, a grueling 36-hole death march. The windy conditions at The Country Club magnified the usual hurdles present during this endurance test. Since the cut eliminates players who are playing poorly, the average scores in the last two rounds of an Open are usually lower than those before the cut. However, in 1963 the average scores in the last two rounds were actually higher. The third round scoring average was 78.2, the highest average score of the week, while the fourth round average score was 77.4, only slightly below the first round scoring average of 77.5.

"These scores look like a caddy tournament," remarked Mason Rudolph.

In an effort to relax, Tony spent the night before the final round attending a baseball game with his business manager Fred Corcoran. The pair witnessed the Boston Red Sox murder the New York Yankees in a night game at Fenway Park. Betty remained back at the hotel with a good book.

He arrived at the course for Open Saturday under sunny skies and the wind still howling. It gusted to 40 miles an hour at times, again exhibiting caprice when it came to direction. He felt good and well rested, having left the baseball game early to be in bed by midnight. He played adequately in the morning round with a 74 that moved him to within one-stroke of the leader Jacky Cupit. Still, it could have been a better score. He bogeyed the fifteenth, sixteenth and seventeenth holes—all considered easier holes. He was upset about his finish but heartened that he actually had gained ground on the leaders.

"It's not too bad out there," Tony told reporters after the morning round. "I only got blown down twice."

He had lunch with Betty in the clubhouse where he wolfed down meatloaf with a couple glasses of milk. He changed his shoes before returning to the course for the afternoon round. He felt good as he prepared for his final eighteen holes.

"I felt a serenity that is rarely with me. Everything seemed to be falling into place. I seemed fated to win," Tony wrote in *Golfers Gold*.

He played the front nine with eight pars and one bogey and remained one shot behind the leader, Cupit, who was playing two groups behind him. Palmer, in the group directly behind him, trailed Cupit by three-strokes, while Boros, playing in the group right in front of him, was two off the lead.

On the tenth hole, Tony hit a fine drive, but his six-iron approach skipped over the green and into the thick rough. He chipped from the rough leaving a ten-foot putt to save his par. The putt refused to drop, resulting in a bogey.

Right in front of him, on the eleventh hole, Boros dunked his shot into the water and took a double-bogey six. Tony figured Boros was out of the tournament. Tony managed pars on the eleventh and twelfth holes and stopped to study the leader board on the thirteenth tee. He was eight over par, Palmer was nine over and Cupit was six over. (While Tony was playing the thirteenth, Cupit was mangling both the eleventh and twelfth holes scoring a bogey on each.)

On the thirteenth, a long downhill hole that was playing right into the teeth of the wind, Tony hit a good drive and then found the green with his 4-iron. He was playing with Walter Burkemo and Tony was the first to putt and left his putt about 18-inches from the hole.

"Do you mind waiting while I putt out?" Tony asked Burkemo.

Burkemo said he did not, so Tony went about cleaning up his short little tap-in. He stroked the ball and the ball hit the hole, took a rollercoaster ride around the lip and stayed out.

The missed putt shocked Tony and it changed the whole complexion of the tournament for him. He believed that he had to force things in order to get back that lost stroke. Tony's lack of experience in major tournaments cost him greatly in this instance.

On the fourteenth hole, a par 5, he was just shy of the green in two shots. His chip shot left him an eight-foot putt for birdie. With his confidence damaged by the missed short putt on the thirteenth hole, he made a timid attempt at the easy birdie. Because he did not hit his putt firm enough, the ball trailed off-line.

After his disappointing par on the fourteenth, he made a routine par on the fifteenth. He paused for another look at the leader board just off the green. The tournament was changing rapidly around him. He was now nine over par, tied with Palmer, while Boros was 11-over and Cupit led at eight over. The field had bunched up with no one player taking control of the tournament. All of the leaders made mistakes in the tough, windy conditions.

He still believed he had to do something on the last three holes if he was to win. Instead of playing within himself, posting a score that the players behind would have to beat, he pressed the issue trying to score birdies.

The last four holes at The Country Club make a loop so that the finishing hole winds up just south of the fifteenth green. Each fairway was lined, four deep, with a raucous gallery.

"We were the Roman legions marching through the crowded boulevards and the crowds were cheering themselves hoarse," Tony described the scene in *Golfer's Gold*.

Boros birdied the sixteenth hole, right in front of Tony. However, Tony was not too concerned, with Boros still one shot behind him. On the sixteenth tee, a par 3, Tony plucked a few blades of grass from the tee and threw them up into the air in an attempt to gauge the wind direction. The blades of grass rose slowly before the wind caught them and then they blew straight up. The national television cameras caught the strange flight of the grass and the viewers at home, along with the gallery that surrounded the tee, enjoyed a good laugh, as did Tony, relaxing him.

He selected a five-iron and hit his shot to about 12-feet giving him an excellent birdie opportunity. Again, he hit his putt timidly, and it died off to the right of the hole. Even though he secured a par, he knew that he let a good chance for a birdie slip away.

On the seventeenth hole, he hit a great drive right down the middle of the fairway leaving nothing more than a smooth seven-iron shot into the green. Before he could hit his shot, the whole tournament changed around him, again. As Tony was walking down the fairway, he heard a huge eruption from the sixteenth green behind him and knew immediately that Palmer had birdied the hole.

He walked another dozen or so paces and heard another huge roar go up from the gallery around the fifteenth green. Cupit, who backed off his shot when the crowd's reaction to Palmer's birdie distracted him, calmly re-addressed his chip shot and sank it for a birdie. The miraculous shot put him two in front of Tony, and one ahead of Palmer.

As Tony reached his ball in the fairway, he watched Boros, on the green in front of him, ram in a 20-foot birdie putt. He and Boros were now tied, two behind Cupit. Tony began to have a feeling of desperation, a sign of his lack of major tournament experience. He now felt he had to birdie the final two holes to have any chance of winning.

On the seventeenth, he studied his shot. He decided that instead of hitting the seven-iron, he would try to cut a six-iron in an effort to get the ball close to the hole. In order to get close to the pin he would have to bend his shot around a tree. He was going for broke, eschewing the shot that would get him to the middle of the green, opting instead to go pin hunting. He hit the shot, from a slightly sloping lie, and the ball refused to fade flying dead straight. The ball landed on the green, took a big hop and bounced into the backside of a bunker behind the green.

He now faced an extremely difficult downhill bunker shot that he could easily leave in the bunker. He negotiated the slope in the bunker, so severe he kept slipping as he tried to take his stance. He was worried that the slipping and sliding would move his ball and he would incur a two-stroke penalty. He finally was settled over the ball, and successfully exploded out of the bunker. The downhill slope made it difficult to spin the ball and he watched as it rolled across, and off the green.

He chipped his next shot stiff to the pin, but still wound up with a damaging bogey. He now felt his chances to become the U.S. Open Champion in 1963 were dead.

Deflated, he drove into the deep rough on the final hole resulting in another bogey. After signing his card, he trudged into the locker room and watched the conclusion of the tournament on television. Boros was also in the locker room where he was drinking a beer.

Tony watched on the television in the locker room as Palmer missed a 20-inch putt for par on the seventeenth hole. Cupit then made a series of bad shots to double-bogey the same hole. On the eighteenth hole, Palmer faced a 35-foot putt for birdie that he left six-feet short. As he lined up his par putt, the gallery shouted at him to check the leader board, recently updated with Cupit's double-bogey.

"I thought I had a good one on that first putt," Palmer told reporters later. "Much to my surprise, it came up six-feet short. I really was certain when I hit it, the ball would be up to the hole. It looked like a tough putt as it was, but after Jacky put up that six it became a helluva difficult putt," Palmer admitted.

Palmer crouched over his six-footer and stroked it into the hole to tie Boros. "It was one of the biggest putts I ever made anywhere," he said.

Cupit played the eighteenth needing a birdie to win, a par to wind up in a three-way playoff with Palmer and Boros. Cupit hit a fine shot into the green leaving him a 15-foot putt to win. He thought he made the putt after he stroked it, but the ball slipped just past the hole. The Open would be decided in an 18 hole playoff the next day, Monday.

Tony was despondent. He kept going over the handful of "what ifs" that kept him out of the playoff. If he had not been so desperate, if he would have hit a normal seven-iron on the seventeenth hole instead of greedily going for the pin, if he would have played for pars on the last two holes, he would have been in the playoff, as well. As in the Masters in April, Tony could only ponder what might have been.

There was a great deal of excitement for the playoff the next day. Palmer, as always, was the favorite. However, Boros played a rock solid round, and he rendered the playoff anti-climatic shooting a 70 while looking relaxed the whole time. Cupit came in with a 73 and Palmer a 76.

In a special to *The Oakland Tribune* that ran after the final round fireworks, Tony talked at length about what happened.

"I tried to get cute on the seventeenth and I blew it. That one shot did it," Tony said. "Instead of putting it on the green with my second shot, I tried to fade around a tree to get closer to the hole and it went straight. One bounce and it landed on the back lip of the bunker."

"I knew then, my chances were through. I had been keyed up all day, but that one shot did it," Tony said.

Tony also admitted that the whole back nine had been something of a test. "I three-putted on the thirteenth, I missed a five-foot birdie putt on fourteen. I missed a ten-foot birdie putt on sixteen. And, I bogeyed seventeen and eighteen. That's the way the ball bounces. I had a chance and I blew it."

The story concluded with Tony stating that he had plans on returning to the Bay Area after the Cleveland Open, played the next week.

Although he was disappointed with his finish in the Open, Tony moved on to Cleveland for the Cleveland Open. The purse for the tournament increased in 1963 to an astonishing $110,000, with a first prize of $22,000. The tournament, played on the 6,618-yard Beechmont Country Club, featured Jack Nicklaus as the sentimental favorite son of the Ohio galleries.

Bill Eggers, an unknown, 30-year-old from Henderson, Nevada had a first round 66 to put him in a tie for the lead with Gary Player and Bo Wininger. Clyde "Moon" Mullins, a 29-year-old from Indio, California was in second-place with a 67. Nicklaus fashioned a respectable 68, as did Tony, Mike Souchak, Jim Ferrier (an Australian not to be confused with Jim Ferree), and Sam Snead.

U.S. Open Champion Julius Boros shot a 69 while Arnold Palmer could only muster a 71—and he needed a birdie on the last hole for that.

Beechmont did not put up much of a defense as 42 players broke par while an additional 27 matched it. The players continued to assault par in the second round as 51 players finished the midway point with scores below par. Wininger, Aaron, and Player stood atop the leader board with 36-hole scores of 135. Tied at 136 were Tony, Nicklaus, Goalby and Jim Ferree. Down the leader board, at 139, was Palmer.

In the third round, Tony grabbed the lead for himself in the mid-point of the round, but then threw it away with bogeys on two of the final three holes. He wound up with a 69 and was in a three-way tie with Nicklaus and Palmer for the lead. Palmer had shot lights out carding a 66 while Nicklaus, playing steady golf, made a 69.

Ferrier told the press that Palmer could have carded a 62 if his putting had been better. A reporter asked Tony how he felt after his faltering finish.

"I feel fine—has anybody got a knife?" Tony joked.

Although he was apprehensive at the daunting task of beating both Palmer and Nicklaus, he looked forward to the challenge. When reporters asked him about being tied with the duo he quipped, "They're in good company."

The fourth round was a wild and wooly ride as no fewer than 12 players were in contention to win at one point or another. It boiled down to Aaron, who birdied the final four holes for a 66, Tony, and Palmer. After Palmer and Tony both missed birdie putts on the fourteenth hole, they paused to study the scoreboard on their way to the fifteenth tee. Both realized they would need a birdie on one of the last four holes to beat Aaron.

Palmer then turned to his friend Tony and said, "It would almost be fun to tie with you, Tony. We could have such a good match tomorrow. But, now let's play just as hard as we can."

Aaron retired to the clubhouse to watch as Tony and Palmer played the last three holes. On the seventeenth hole, Tony bunkered his approach shot, and things looked dire. He blasted out to ten-feet and then made what he called, "a real money putt," to save his par.

On the eighteenth hole, Palmer put his second shot close, ten-feet from the cup, while Tony could only manage to get his second shot onto the fringe of the green. Tony putted from the fringe and lagged his first putt close, tapping in for par. The crowd grew still as Palmer addressed his putt to win the $22,000 first prize. He stroked the putt, which looked good all the way, but at the last moment, it slid past the hole on the high side. The three players, Tony, Palmer, and Aaron, departed the course to get a good night's rest before their 18-hole playoff the next day.

Jim Weeks, of *The Lima News* of Lima, Ohio, wrote, "Tony Lema, the 29-year-old California pro who is considered the most improved player on the tour this season has a huge following. The combination of 'Arnie's

Army' and 'Lema's Legions' kept getting larger as the tournament progressed until nearly one third of the 15,000 spectators were following the threesome."

Palmer took control of the playoff early and never looked back. He had a one-stroke lead after three holes. On the fourth, Palmer missed the green and chipped poorly to about 35-feet short of the hole. Both Tony and Aaron faced birdie putts and waited for Palmer to putt. Palmer calmly stroked his putt into the hole for a miraculous par. Both Tony and Aaron failed to make their putts, unable to make a dent in Palmer's lead.

Palmer continued to dominate the playoff until the players got in view of the nationally televised audience at the fifteenth hole. Then, inexplicably, Palmer began to make bogeys while Aaron and Tony began to card some birdies. Palmer usually saved his best performances for the television cameras, but here he was allowing a glimmer of hope for his two competitors.

Nevertheless, the lead that he built early in the round was too much for either Tony or Aaron to overcome. Despite a bogey on the last hole, Palmer won his fifth title of the year. The first place prize money, when added to what he won at the Thunderbird and the U.S. Open, gave Palmer earnings of $54,000 over the last three weeks. He was on a pace to break the record for money earnings in a year.

Tony delayed meeting with the press as he searched for Betty so that he could get money to pay his caddy. After paying his caddy, Tony and Palmer displayed their friendship during the post-round press conference.

"It was a great playoff—until we teed off," Tony joked. "I was stiff, tightened and nervous from too much playing and Arnie didn't help things with all those birdies."

Tony then grew serious and said, "I would like to say this; the professional golfers, all of them, are indebted to Arnie Palmer for the color he has added to the game, for getting the people to come out and see us, and for the high esteem in which professional golf is held. He is not only a great player, but also he is a great guy and I'm glad to have him as my friend."

"Arnie and I have one similar distinction—we're both Mobile champions, but after I won it they decided not to have it any more. I whipped you good that time," Tony said glancing at Palmer.

"Well, it won't happen again," Palmer quickly shot back as he clapped Tony on the back. "I've watched Tony come along since we roomed together at the Mobile tournament in 1960. We spent some time on the practice tee together and his driving and putting have really improved. I'll be disappointed if he doesn't keep coming."

After the Cleveland Open, Palmer, along with Nicklaus, traveled to England for the British Open. Aaron departed for the Canadian Open, while Tony headed back to the Bay Area for some much needed rest and relaxation. The day after arriving at his mother's house in San Leandro, Norm Hannon, a reporter for *The Oakland Tribune*, contacted Tony by telephone for an interview. He learned that Tony and Betty were opening their wedding presents.

"This is the first chance Betty and I have had to pull the wrappings off…I'm burning them in the incinerator now," Tony told Hannon.

Tony also visited the Wolff Buick Company in San Leandro where national representatives of Buick presented him with a brand-new car. He received the car as a benefit of his new endorsement deal with the company.

The newlyweds also spent time looking for an apartment in Oakland. In addition, there were lawyers to talk to about settling the Malarkey matter. Tony could see the end of the ordeal was near but was impatient to wrap up the negotiations.

Although packed with activities, Tony's brief rest recharged him. Now it was time to get back to work. He would dive right back into major championship action at the PGA Championship played at the Dallas Athletic Club. In the press, he was an 8-1 favorite to win the tournament while Palmer was at 4-1 and Nicklaus, Player and Boros were 6-1 favorites.

23 WORLD STAGE
1963

Tony's schedule for the remainder of 1963 filled up quickly. He was certain to make the Ryder Cup team in September, and he agreed to play on *Shell's Wonderful World of Golf* at the end of August. Off the course, his many projects included endorsement deals and his negotiations with Malarkey.

On the course, it was right back into the grind of another major championship—the PGA Championship at the Dallas Athletic Club.

In the first round, Tony turned in a nice 70, despite a double-bogey on the par 3 sixteenth hole. The weather was extremely hot and his four-iron slipped in his sweaty hands causing the ball to fly far to the left where it ended up in a ditch. He was one of the few players to play well in the afternoon. Most of the other good scores in the first round came from players with morning tee times before the huge field had a chance to leave their marks on the putting greens.

"I shocked myself with my putting," Tony admitted. "It's impossible to putt on those greens in the afternoon after 100 or more guys have trampled over them. I don't know how I got the ball into the hole."

Tony's 70 put him four shy of the leader, unknown Dick Hart who had a 66, one stroke off the course record.

Nicklaus handled the quick turnaround from the British Open just fine with a 69.

Hart, an assistant pro from Hinsdale, Illinois, did not wilt from the pressure or the heat in the second round. He managed the rough greens for a 72, retaining his lead, now three-strokes. Tony ended up with a 71, but like the first round, he showed brilliance on the front nine and careless play on the back. He putted very well on the front nine sinking putts for birdies on the third and fourth holes and then saved par with good putts on the sixth, seventh and ninth holes.

Tony was in a good position, three strokes back of Hart, tied with Julius Boros and club pro Shelley Mayfield. Nicklaus, too, was very much in contention, just four strokes off the pace. It took 151 to make the halfway cut, and the reduced field would provide some relief for the greens.

Oscar Fraley, of UPI, in an article after the second round wrote that despite his "Champagne Tony" nickname, Tony actually drank very little.

"Give me those guys who use that hard stuff," Tony said, "and I'll beat 'em just walking beside them."

Even in the age before media consultants, Tony had an inherent ability to control his image. It did not hurt to have the press on his side. With a plethora of endorsement deals on the horizon, it was important to present a marketable image and Tony was quite adept at managing his. Even though he had reigned in his drinking during the last two years, those who knew him recognized he was not a teetotaler, or that he avoided the "hard stuff."

Fraley's article ran nationally in newspapers around the country. The PGA attracted a large contingent of reporters and quite a few were not familiar with golf, or the stars on tour.

One obtuse reporter asked Tony, "How much do you really drink?"

"Not as much as you," he quickly replied.

"I don't drink," the reporter responded.

"That's funny," Tony, said, "I thought only a drunk would ask a question like that."

Tony was hitting his stride when it came to supplying the press with quick one-liners.

Another reporter asked, "How did you find the heat?"

"Why, I just walked through that door over there and it met me," Tony blithely answered.

In the third round, the wheels came off Tony's game as he blew to a 76. His carelessness during the back nine of his first two rounds carried over into his entire third round and resulted in a precipitous drop down the leader board. Bruce Crampton with a 65 took over the lead at 208. Dow Finsterwald was in second place two back while Nicklaus sat three off the lead.

Tony returned to form in the fourth round as he toured the course in 69 strokes and moved up the leader board. He finished at 287, eight back of the winner, Jack Nicklaus.

The Wannamaker Trophy, the prize for winning the PGA Championship, was on display in the hot sun during the final round. Nicklaus required a towel, used as a type of potholder, to hoist the trophy for photographers at the awards ceremony.

Upon completing his round, a police officer tracked Tony down to serve a warrant for his arrest. Before gathering up Betty for the ride downtown in the squad car, he paused to explain his situation to the press.

Back in 1961, Tony was speeding as he drove through Buda, Texas. A cop flagged him down and wrote him a ticket. He made an immediate appearance in traffic court, receiving a fine of one dollar for speeding and fifteen dollars for court costs.

"I paid the dollar, but refused to pay the costs because they were so exorbitant," Tony explained. "Now, I have to go with the officer and pay an extra $100 penalty."

Tony finished in a tie for 13ᵗʰ place, winning a check for $1,550 that took some of the sting off his legal fine. He remained in fourth place on the official money list.

After clearing his good name with the state of Texas, Betty finally got a chance to introduce her new husband to her family. Her brother, Jim, had predetermined that Tony would be a prima donna sports star. When he arrived at his mother's house to meet Tony, his impression immediately changed. He saw Tony down on the floor playing with Betty's nieces and nephews and discovered a down-to-earth nice guy, as opposed to a big-shot athlete. After playing with the children, Tony wanted to go get watermelon, one of the local crops.

After visiting with Betty's family, the couple returned to San Leandro where he worked on his game. He planned to play next at the Insurance City Open in Hartford, Connecticut.

The Insurance City Open, played on the Wethersfield Country Club, offered a $40,000 purse with $6,400 going to the winner. In addition to Tony, the field featured Nicklaus, Casper, and Boros. In the opening round, Wes Ellis fired a 67 to take the lead. Casper was one stroke back while Tony, tied with twelve other players, sat at 69.

Casper, off the tour because of his wrist ailment, served notice that he was going to make up for lost time as he won the tournament with a last round 65.

Tony's game went downhill after his fine first round and he finished in a tie for 21ˢᵗ earning a check for $532. He remained in the number four spot on the official money list.

The next week, at the American Golf Classic at Firestone Golf and Country Club, Tony tied for ninth place winning a check for $1,400 solidifying his hold on the fourth spot on the money list. He extended, to 30 tournaments, a streak of finishing in the money, the tour's longest current streak. Palmer, for his part, went over the $100,000 official earnings mark for the year, the first player to do so in tour history.

Johnny Pott went toe-to-toe with Palmer in the fourth round fighting off every effort that Palmer could muster. He produced a 70 to win by four and took home the $9,000 first place money, plus $2,333 in bonus money for holding the lead in the first, third and fourth rounds.

"When you beat Palmer, you beat the greatest," Pott gleefully said afterwards.

From Akron, Tony and Betty returned to California to pack their bags for an Asian adventure. They flew to Japan for his scheduled match against Chen Ching-Po, of Formosa (Taiwan), on the *Shell's Wonderful World of Golf* series. The recorded match would be part of the television series in 1964.

The Shell series, part travelogue, part corporate promotional film, and part golf match, visited all reaches of the globe usually pitting an American pro against a pro from the host region. This would be Tony's first appearance on the widely viewed series, and it would be Ching-Po's second appearance.

After the Masters, when producers of the show contacted Fred Corcoran about Tony appearing on the show, Tony specifically requested Japan. He wanted to return to Japan, where he had spent a large portion of his time while in the Marines, and show Betty the sights.

While flying to Japan, Tony spoke with a reporter from *Sports Illustrated* for a piece that ran in the magazine's "Scorecard" section—a section of the magazine devoted to short bits of news that did not warrant a full-blown article. Tony revealed to the reporter that he finally reached terms with Malarkey on the buy-out of his contract.

Tony informed the reporter that the disputed contract stipulated that Malarkey be entitled to nearly one third of all of his winnings and off-course income.

The reporter also spoke to Malarkey, describing him as a "wealthy Oregon and Idaho sportsman." Malarkey told the reporter that since the contract started in 1958, he had backed Tony to the tune of at least $16,000 per year and as much as $21,000 in some years.

"It was a great thing for me," Tony admitted to the magazine, "knowing that I had his backing."

Nevertheless, he implied that it was time to stop playing for someone else, that he had to start playing for himself and his new wife. In *Golfer's Gold*, he detailed his side of the accounting. He revealed that the cost of purchasing the options in the contract came to everything he was going to make in 1963, less expenses, and an additional $22,000 paid over the next two years.

He was flat broke and in hock up to his ears after a very successful year on tour—a year where the prize purses exploded. He was going to end up paying Malarkey well over $50,000 when all the dust settled. In the five and half years of being on tour, Tony had nothing in the way of assets to show for it, while Malarkey turned a profit of over $60,000.

It was time for Tony to start generating income in order to get out of the hole. The trip to Japan was a good place to start. Tony played in a couple of warm-up exhibitions with the legendary Gene Sarazen, who also provided on-camera commentary for the Shell matches. One exhibition, played at the South Camp Drake Golf Course, included Brigadier General Thomas R. Ford, the Kanto Base Commander. The gallery included many service personnel from the base, and Tony enjoyed entertaining them. As Sarazen was well past his prime, the matches were not competitive, but they were entertaining. Tony donated a portion of his fee to charity.

After his exhibitions with Sarazen, it was time to shoot the Shell match. Before the advent of lightweight, portable television and film cameras, the shooting of the first few seasons of the Shell matches could take up to four or five days. However, this was the 27th match staged for the series, and the production crew honed their skills to the point where the filming now required a mere 12 hours. This still left a lot of idle time between shots for the two competitors.

During the down time, a native female assistant set up folding camp chairs for Tony and Ching-Po. They sat and tried to relax while the production crew set up the cameras to capture the next shot. The cameras made a terrific amount of noise that players found distracting.

The Fuji Course of the Kawana Hotel and Golf Club in Shizuoka, about two hours south of Tokyo, hosted the match. The course, known as the "Japanese Pebble Beach," features stunning cliff views of the Pacific Ocean, situated in a pine forest. Many of the Charles H. Alison designed holes feature elevated tees and uphill approach shots.

The Korai grass on the Kawana course is a stiff wire-like grass similar to Kikuyu. The ball sits up on this type of grass in the fairways, but shots from the rough can be deadly. Putting on this grass can also be tricky with grain affecting the break. Tony described putting on these greens like "playing golf across the bristles of a hairbrush."

When aired, the show opened with background shots of famous points of interest in Japan, Tokyo and the area surrounding Shizuoka. The weather is cloudy, obscuring the view of Mt. Fuji, but the stunning views of the bay below the cliffs are on full display.

As the two players teed off, young women forecaddies, dressed entirely in white, including hooded helmets, marked the locations of the players shots for the cameras. The player's caddies were young women dressed similarly to the forecaddies pushing carts holding the players bags.

Tony dressed in black shoes, black pants and a white shirt, and as always, looked very stylish. Betty is briefly shown on-camera wearing a tangerine scarf and matching skirt with a patterned white blouse. Although the day is cloudy, she is wearing sunglasses.

During the entire broadcast, there are huge dragonflies visible around the players, caddies, and the golf balls. Ching-Po surged to a two-stroke lead after sinking a putt from the fringe on the third hole. Tony had to make a five-footer to avoid losing two strokes on the hole that would have resulted in a three-stroke deficit.

Tony started to turn the tables on Ching-Po on the next hole, a par 5 that he reached in two. Ching-Po, chipping his third shot with a three-iron from the fringe of the green, ran his ball well past the hole. Tony two-putted for his birdie while Ching-Po could only manage a par.

After Ching-Po again makes a poor chip resulting in a bogey a few holes later, the match was even. Both players finish the front side shooting 33, two-under-par.

The two players then joined the hosts, George Rodgers and Sarazen, at the edge of the green. They asked Tony what he thought about Ching-Po's first nine, especially his putting.

"I thought we left Billy Casper back in the states," he quips.

Ching-Po caught a bad lie in a bunker on the fourteenth hole resulting in a bogey while Tony secured a routine par to go one-stroke up in the match. On the fifteenth and sixteenth holes, both players secured pars.

Tony later called the seventeenth hole, "one of the toughest golf holes I have ever seen." It is a par-4, measuring 457-yards and plays uphill to a green guarded by two large bunkers in the front. Both players drove into the rough and while Ching-Po caught a good lie with his ball sitting on top of the Korai grass, Tony's ball had nestled down into the wire-like grass, under some weeds.

The two players waited about ten to fifteen minutes while cameras were set up before Ching-Po hit his approach shot into the grass face above one of the bunkers. Tony dug his ball out of the bad lie ending up in the first of the two bunkers guarding the green. As he slashed the shot out of the Korai grass, he felt a stab of pain in his left hand. Deeply involved in the match by now, he tried to ignore the pain.

Tony described what faced him in the bunker in *Golfer's Gold:*

"For fifteen minutes thereafter, while the cameras were shifted again and one of them moved in for a close-up of my lie in the sand, I smoked a number of cigarettes, but was damned if I was going to sit in my camp chair. I was faced with an explosion of about thirty yards that must clear the second deep bunker. Fifteen minutes is a long time to contemplate a shot like that."

Tony handled the shot expertly, exploding out to about 12-feet from the hole. Ching-Po now fidgeted and waited as the cameras moved into position for his shot. Once he got the go ahead from the crew, he set up for his shot, and fluffed it, leaving it 20-feet from the hole. Both players made bogey and Tony retained his one-stroke lead.

The winner's share of the match was $3,000 while the loser received $2,000 and the two split the $5,000 purse in the event of a tie. On the final hole, Tony needed two-putts from ten-feet to secure the victory. After holing his second putt, he flung his ball side arm into the small crowd following the match. The two players joined Rodgers and Sarazen, at the edge of the green, to discuss the match. Tony is very respectful to both Ching-Po and Sarazen.

"I really appreciated playing with you, Chen. Thank you very much," he said to Ching-Po.

The show concluded with pre-recorded tips from both players. Ching-

Po demonstrated the four-wood shot and Tony showed how to play a plugged shot from the bunker. The filming of the match took two days; four holes the first day and fourteen the second.

While they were in Japan, the White House confirmed press reports that President Kennedy would visit Dallas to kick-off his re-election campaign on November 22. Although politics did not interest Tony, he was impressed with Kennedy's youthfulness and he felt supportive to a fellow Catholic in the White House.

As they were flying back from Asia, Tony's thoughts turned to the upcoming Ryder Cup. He hoped the matches would provide the impetus to re-ignite the competitive fire within that had dimmed since his letdown following the narrow miss at the U.S. Open. He was eager to represent his country and to play in his first Ryder Cup with his fellow American pros as teammates. His schedule was to play in the Whitemarsh Open the first week of October and then in the Ryder Cup matches the following week.

Tony was exhausted from his trip to Japan and did not play well in the Whitemarsh. He managed to make the cut and despite a last round 83, won $230 extending his in the money streak to 33 straight tournaments. He remained in the fourth spot on the money list. It was now time to focus on the Ryder Cup.

On the Ryder Cup team with Tony were playing captain Arnold Palmer, Johnny Pott, Billy Casper, Julius Boros, Dave Ragan, Bob Goalby, Gene Littler, Dow Finsterwald, and Billy Maxwell. Jack Nicklaus was not on the team having not yet completed his five-year apprenticeship in the PGA to become eligible. The players unanimously elected Palmer the playing captain of the team.

The team from the United Kingdom consisted of Brian Huggett, Peter Alliss, Neil Coles, Dave Thomas, George Will, Christy O'Conner, Bernard Hunt, Harry Weetman, Tom Haliburton, and Geoffrey Hunt.

The American team was the overwhelming favorite to retain the Ryder Cup at East Lake Country Club in Atlanta, Georgia, the British having never won the cup on American soil. The Cup matches would not truly become competitive until, at the urging of Jack Nicklaus and Arnold Palmer, the British team expanded to include players from the rest of Europe in 1979.

At the start of the week, Palmer announced, "This team of ours is unbeatable."

Peter Alliss, the strongest player for the British side, agreed with Palmer, to a point.

"I'd say it was about a 60-40 thing and you'd have to put the 60 on the Yanks," he speculated.

Palmer scoffed at the suggestion the American team would feel pressure.

"When you're accustomed to stroking home thirty-footers for the kind of loot we play for, playing for a big silver cup makes it a pleasant holiday," Palmer told the press.

The talented U.S. team had earned a combined $459,386 on the tour to this point in 1963.

In his first team meeting, Palmer told his team, "Fellows, wouldn't it be great if we could win this thing 32 to 0?"

Oscar Fraley of the United Press International cornered Tony after a practice round and asked him his feelings about representing his country.

"We will be playing harder and with more inspiration because we're not playing for money, but for the glory of the United States," Tony explained to Fraley. "It's an honor we can't treat lightly."

"Money's nice," grinned Tony to Fraley, "but while maybe some folks might think I'm waving the flag, this is a tremendous honor to all of us and we intend to play harder than ever in our lives."

Tony concluded by saying, "You can't quite put your finger on it, but it's a wonderful feeling to have fellows like Palmer and Boros on your side backing you up, instead of running at you like they do the rest of the year."

The British and Irish players were incensed at the betting odds, 7-1, laid against them. Nevertheless, they were also cognizant of the challenge ahead of them.

"I'd be happy to break even on the foursomes," non-playing captain John Fallon told the press. "Because we always have done well over the years in the singles."

The British team decided to use the ball commonly used in the United Kingdom that was smaller than the ball used in the United States. The smaller ball was easier to control in windy conditions, but was much more difficult to apply spin making in more difficult to hold firm greens.

On Friday, the two teams assembled at 7:50 A.M. on the putting green for the opening ceremonies. A marching band played the "Star-Spangled Banner" and "God Save the Queen" for the large crowd assembled for the ceremony. As the music played, officials raised the Stars and Stripes and the Union Jack, and the full impact of the moment registered on all the players, including Tony. Tony admitted to a large case of nerves, and he could tell that the other members of the team felt the same.

Led by Palmer, the American team won the 1963 Ryder Cup by a score of 23 to 9. With his four victories for the U.S. squad, Billy Casper was the star of the team. Tony had reason to be quite proud of his record of 3-0-2, a fine showing for a rookie.

Tony, accompanied by Betty, returned to Las Vegas to defend his title at the Sahara Invitational. The format of the tournament changed, eliminating the pro-am aspect, making it an official PGA event attracting a strong field, with Palmer, Nicklaus, Casper, Littler and Tony all in the field. Tony never threatened to defend his title after rounds of 72-70-71-69 tied him for twelfth place and a check for $1,562.

At the Almaden Open, the next stop on tour, Tony admitted to a hand injury, later diagnosed as torn tendons between the thumb and forefinger of his left hand. He injured the hand while playing a practice round at Orinda while he was preparing for his appearance on Shell's Wonderful World of Golf. The tough Korai grass at the Kawana Club exacerbated the injury.

Tony tried to play through the pain, but it proved to be an uphill battle. He played poorly and missed the cut by one-stroke. His in the money streak ended at 34.

After the Almaden, in an attempt to rest his hand, he withdrew from the Fig Garden Village Open, a brand-new tournament in Fresno. He attempted one more start, at the new Frank Sinatra Open at the singer's home course, Canyon Country Club in Palm Desert. His hand injury led to mediocre play that resulted in rounds of 76-71-70-69 and a tie for seventeenth worth $875.

With his hand still bothering him, he and Betty returned to the Bay Area and consulted doctors. The doctors informed him the hand would not heal until he rested it, meaning no golf. The remainder of 1963 he spent resting and setting up house with Betty in their new apartment in Alameda. He reviewed various business opportunities with Fred Corcoran and he wrapped up final details on *Golfer's Gold*.

Considering the distractions that occurred, it was amazing that 1963 was a breakout season for Tony. Getting married, dealing with the Malarkey contract issue and working with Brown on *Golfer's Gold*, it was a wonder that he could compete with any effectiveness at all. He not only competed, but he became a star on tour.

Tony with Danny Arnold
Photo courtesy of the Lema family

Tony and Betty on the town
Photo Courtesy of the Lema Family

*Tony's new stardom required a publicity shot. The Golden Gate Bridge
Can be seen in the background
Photo courtesy of the Lema Family*

*With his victory in the Orange County Open, Tony began his tradition of sharing
champagne with the press
Photo courtesy of the Lema Family*

PART THREE
Super Star

24 CHAMPAGNE CLAMBAKE
1964

Due to his injury, Tony closed out 1963 at home resting in San Leandro. He hung around the new apartment with Betty, spent time with his family and visited friends. Golf was strictly off-limits. Tony hated sitting around; he liked to keep moving, doing something. While the rest was beneficial for his hand, he was soon suffering from cabin fever.

He read, talked on the phone, played cards, and watched television to relieve the boredom he felt. He watched with Betty the horrifying news coverage on November 22, 1963.

Lee Harvey Oswald shot President Kennedy that fateful day in Dallas and Tony and Betty watched the all-day coverage. The fact the tragedy occurred in her hometown was especially troubling to Betty.

In the wake of the assassination, the sporting world went dark, with most of the sporting events that weekend cancelled, including The Cajun Classic on the PGA Tour. The Cajun was the final tournament of the season.

Tony won $67,113 for the year, which placed him in the fourth spot on the official money list. He played in 25 events, won one, finished second six times, (which tied Gary Player for the most runner-up finishes in 1963) and finished in the top ten an amazing 16 times. *Golf Digest* named him the "Most Improved Professional Golfer" for 1963.

Melvin Durslag, a writer for the syndicated King Features, summed up Tony's year in an article that ran in many of the nation's newspapers on December 30. The lead paragraph began, "It has been a very good year to Tony Lema. He sent champagne to his friends, bought extravagant gifts for his family and otherwise reflected his good fortune in being engaged in a business showing distinct growth possibilities."

Durslag pointed out how professional golf was exploding. Increased attendance at events, television revenue and corporate sponsorship all contributed to the money pouring into tour events. Purses continued to increase with the total purses for 1964 reaching $2.5 million. The best professional golfers, with added off-course endorsement incomes, were making much more money than the best baseball, football or basketball players.

"Tony now attaches his name to pants, jackets, shirts and underwear,"

Durslag wrote, "not to mention assorted pieces of golf equipment."

While he was proud of the year he had, he envisioned much more for 1964. His goal was a simple one—win a major championship.

Feeling rusty from his forced layoff, Tony made the cut at the season opening L.A. Open, but finished out of the money. He was not the only pro who was feeling rusty from a layoff, however.

"I haven't hit a ball since November 12th," Arnold Palmer, told the press upon arrival in L.A. "There seems to be something wrong with all parts of my game."

Even though Tony did not play well in L.A., he continued to attract press attention. Hal Wood of United Press International wrote a piece on Tony at the conclusion of the L.A. Open that ran under the headline: WIN OR LOSE, LEMA STILL BUYS. He described Tony as "one of the most lovable young characters ever to stride down a fairway."

"I want to win one of the big four tournaments," Wood quoted Tony. "Sure, it's nice to win the others, and that $67,000 in prize money was mighty welcome. But, you have continuing contracts and prestige that lasts as long as you are in the golfing business after you win one of the big ones."

Tony sent champagne to the pressroom after he completed his fourth round in the L.A. Open despite never being in contention.

"I just think the California press did a great thing for me when they started calling me 'Champagne Tony,' " he said. "I'm not seeking publicity now, giving them champagne, I just want to express my thanks. I don't even have a tie-in with a wine company, but maybe I'll get one."

Either Wood misquoted him, or Tony was being coy. He signed an endorsement contract with Moet-Chandon whereby they would supply the champagne for post-victory parties. Company officials read about Tony's post-victory champagne parties in an article written by Doc Giffin. They contacted Fred Corcoran, who quickly struck an endorsement deal.

Other endorsement contracts came from Palm Beach Clothing, Floreshiem Shoes, and Buick. He continued to endorse golf clubs made by the Fernquist and Johnson equipment company.

The added income came in handy. He told Wood that it cost $32,000 to travel the tour in 1963. Still it was important to him to have Betty travel with him, despite the added expense they incurred.

"It's not much of a life going home to an empty motel room every night," he admitted to Wood. "So, as long as I travel, she'll be with me."

For Betty, travelling the tour meant she could keep an eye on Tony. It was not so much that she did not trust Tony as she did not trust the circumstances surrounding him. She had been to enough tournaments and saw the women, some quite bold, who flocked to her husband's gallery.

Besides, the two were madly in love. She could not picture herself back in the Bay Area puttering around the apartment alone while Tony was on tour. She also became hooked on the excitement when Tony played well and contended.

The two settled into a routine while they were on the road. Tony devoted a whole chapter in *Golfer's Gold* titled "Day With a Touring Pro" and chronicled his early rising to take care of business matters and answer mail. He took time to read all of the fan mail he was receiving and would answer them all. He wrote letters, or talked with Corcoran on the phone, while Betty slept. When she awoke, they would get ready and go to the course.

Once at the course, she would find some of the other wives to visit with while he conducted interviews and collected more mail. The PGA sorted and distributed the player's mail, forwarded from their mailing address to the various tournament stops. Betty walked the course during his round following every shot. He often scanned the gallery to locate her because, "I like to look at her."

After the round, she would wait around the clubhouse while he conducted more interviews, especially if he happened to be in contention. The two then returned to their hotel before going out for dinner, or more times than not, they ordered from room service.

A new course on the tour, the hilly Rancho Bernardo Country Club, hosted the San Diego Open, the second stop on the 1964 schedule. The course featured monstrous greens.

The tournament got off to a rocky start when a frost delayed the start of the first round. Thirty players could not complete their rounds due to darkness. Tony teed off in the morning and was one of the players able to complete his round shooting a 67 that included four birdies and a single bogey. He putted well as he made birdie putts of 35-feet and 15-feet. His 67 put him into a tie for second place with Julius Boros and Gay Brewer, one-stroke behind the leader, Bob Rosburg.

Frost again caused a delay the second day. The 10 players who were unable to complete their first rounds teed off first after the delay causing a backup for the rest of the field. Darkness fell before all players could complete their second round, including Tony. He, along with the other players who were unable to finish, returned the next day to finish their second round before playing their third.

When the second round was finally in the books on Saturday morning, Gene Littler, Tommy Bolt, and Bob Rosburg sat atop the leader board tied at 135, while Tony, tied with Bruce Crampton and George Archer, sat at 137.

At the end of Saturday's long day, Art Wall held the third round lead shooting a 68 for a three round 204. Rosburg was in second place two-strokes back, and Tony, still in the hunt after a third round 72, was five off the lead.

In the fourth round, Tony started with a disappointing 37 on the front nine. However, he caught fire on the back nine making five birdies with putts ranging from five-feet to twenty-feet, and was mounting a charge. He recorded birdies on six holes in a ten hole stretch on his way to a 30 on the back nine, but he was never able to narrow the gap between him and Wall to less than three strokes. Wall coasted to his first victory since the 1960 season. Tony finished in a tie for second and won $2,300.

Following the routine that Tony and the other players were so accustomed to, the tour traveled up the California coast to Monterey for the Bing Crosby National Pro-Am. Tony looked forward to playing with Father John Durkin as his pro-am partner. Father Durkin was a chaplain in the Air Force stationed in Japan who befriended him while he was in the marines.

This was Father Durkin's second appearance in the Crosby. The weather was impeccable in 1963 and Bing Crosby felt it was due to Father Durkin's divine intervention. Believing he was a good luck charm, Crosby invited him back, hoping to ensure good weather in 1964.

Because it was a pro-am, the Crosby was not an official tournament, but it did offer a healthy purse that attracted a stellar field. Jack Nicklaus and Arnold Palmer represented "The Big Three" while Gary Player was home with his wife Vivienne for the birth of the couple's fourth child.

In his first practice round, Tony played two balls on each of the first two holes. On the first, he scored two birdies and on the second, he scored a birdie and an eagle. He was ready.

Genial Canadian Al Balding claimed the first round lead with a 66 on the tough Spyglass course. Tony, also playing Spyglass, was in good position after carding a 70. He and Father Durkin were in second place in the pro-am with a 63, but they were five-strokes behind Mike Fetchick and his amateur partner Charlie Seaver.

Tony and Father Durkin, playing well, were having a great time. Tony's brother, Harry, with his fiancée, Judi, and their mother Cleo, made the short trip to Monterey to watch him play. Tony wore a bucket hat during the Crosby as a tribute to the tournament's host.

His game was starting to jell. In the second round, he was almost flawless, hitting 17 greens in regulation and did not suffer a single bogey. Tony won $1,000 for having the best pro-am score of the day. Even though his round of 68 was nearly perfect, like most golfers, he felt it could have been better.

"If I could have just made some of those putts," Tony lamented to the press. "I missed four putts that were makable, maybe more."

Al Balding retained his lead after the second round, shooting a 67 for a 133, while Tony sat five strokes back. He and Father Durkin caught

Fetchick and Seaver atop the leader board in the pro-am portion of the tournament at 123.

Nine of the top ten leaders had yet to play the more difficult Pebble Beach course that promised to separate the wheat from the chaff.

"I feel like a man going to the firing squad," was how Tony described the prospect of playing Pebble. "I've never been under 70 there."

The weather forecast for the third round called for high winds and rain, and the day turned nasty as predicted. Winds whipped the course driving a cold rain. After the third round, the headline in *The Oakland Tribune* blared in huge letters: LEMA RALLIES TO TIE BALDING.

He managed the weather and made up five-strokes on Balding. His only blemish on his way to shooting a 70 was a double-bogey on the seventeenth hole. After hitting into a bunker on the long par 3, he three-putted.

Despite the three-putt on seventeen, Tony was putting great. He made birdie putts ranging from three-feet to twenty-feet while shooting a 32 on the front nine.

He and Father Durkin were now just one-stroke back of Rex Baxter and his amateur partner, Dr. Bud Taylor, in the pro-am. Some sportswriters cynically wondered if Father Durkin's 13 handicap would be a major topic at the next ecumenical council in Rome. They suspected that he was violating an unwritten commandment—thou shall not sandbag.

On Sunday, before teeing off in the final round, Tony attended Mass, a special Mass for both him and his pro-am partner. Father Durkin conducted the ceremony while Tony served as his altar boy. Later, they would play the fourth round with divine inspiration.

The weather for the fourth round at Pebble Beach was atrocious. Winds whipped up to 30 miles an hour and drove a heavy mist that fell the entire day. Al Balding, tied with Tony going into the final round, succumbed to the weather and skied to an 88.

As Tony strode off the first tee, he confidently shouted back over his shoulder an order to put the champagne on ice. He hit his approach on the first hole over the green and then hit a mediocre chip shot that ended up 25-feet past the hole. He calmly surveyed the putt from all angles and then made the putt as the gallery erupted.

He birdied the third hole sinking a three-foot putt and then added another birdie on the fifth hole when he stuck his four-iron to ten-feet. The galleries started to murmur with excitement in the anticipation that a local boy was hot and could win the Crosby. He was threatening to run away with the tournament as his challengers were having difficulty handling the weather, which deteriorated as the round went on.

His round stalled though, when he went five over par during the tough stretch of holes seven through ten. He was coming back to the pack. On the seventh hole, he hit a beautiful five-iron that bore through the wind to the green but then three-putted. On the eighth, he failed to run a shot through a bunker resulting in a double-bogey. A bad chip cost him another stroke to par on the ninth hole. A short missed putt on the tenth cost him yet another stroke. He was leaking oil.

Tony finally turned things around with a good shot from a bunker on the fourteenth hole. He later identified the shot as being the most important shot of his round.

"I hit a real good drive and a three-wood into the front trap, right where I wanted to," Tony recalled after the round. "Then I blasted out to within eight-inches. I didn't even tremble over the putt. That was the shot in the arm I needed after blowing that putt on the tenth."

Tony came to the final tee with a three-shot cushion. The rain and wind had picked up to the point where newsreel footage of the final hole is shot through a rain soaked lens producing a blurry image of Tony, his tan rain pants soaked through, as he plays the challenging hole.

Tony hit driver off the tee, a beautiful shot that traveled 250-yards and found the fairway.

"Don't give me another wood until next week," he instructed his caddy as he handed him back his driver.

Tony made a routine par and then threw his ball into the crowd that surrounded the eighteenth green. He captured the title, as he predicted years before when, without a ticket, marshals escorted him off the premises as a sixteen-year-old.

Not one player was able to match par in the day's horrific weather. Bob Harrison, a pro from Palm Desert, California, carded a 12 on two different holes during his round and wound up shooting a 100. Bob Rosburg six-putted a green in the windy conditions.

Tony, jubilant after his biggest victory to date, entered the pressroom where reporters greeted him with champagne glasses. Smiling widely he popped the cork on a bottle of Moet, and celebrated with the press. He spoke with reporters for most of an hour.

He and Father Durkin finished in second-place in the pro-am, one back of the winners. He credited the priest with helping him maintain an even keel throughout the tournament.

"Father Durkin's influence throughout the tournament was a big help," he said. "I only swore once and apologized. He took it like the great guy he is. This was my biggest win and most gratifying one. This golf course is the greatest test of shot making and nerves. I won't kid you. I was scared for eighteen holes."

He acknowledged his appreciation to the gallery.

"I just can't say enough about the galleries. It was wonderful. The way they pulled for me and built me up day after day. I really felt bad when I started to choke."

After the celebration with the press, Tony and Father Durkin, dressed in full military uniform, attended the stag awards ceremony hosted by Bing Crosby. Dubbed the "Clambake and Victory Dinner" the evening featured entertainment from the stage by Bob Newhart while Crosby, Dean Martin, Phil Harris and Frank Sinatra sat in the audience. Tony mingled with the Hollywood stars comfortably becoming friends with many of them.

The tour made the short trip to San Francisco and Harding Park for the Lucky International. Hot off his win in the Crosby, Tony was a consensus favorite at the Lucky. Fans came out in droves, estimated at 2,000, to watch him in the first round and he gave them a show. He shot a 66 tying for the lead with Don January. Palmer and Jerry Steelsmith were one-stroke back. The press was already getting excited about another champagne party.

"I'd say it's a little early to worry about the bubbly yet," Tony warned.

He turned the front nine in four-under-par 32 and suffered his only bogey on the fourteenth when he three-putted. On the twelfth hole, a dogleg left, he hooked his tee shot. His second shot, a difficult blind shot, required him to hook a four-wood around the trees. He knocked the ball to 20-feet from the hole.

"I hit a high, quick hook around the trees and that shot really saved the day for me," he admitted.

In the second round, his putter went cold and he could not beg, borrow, or steal a birdie putt on his way to a 74. Palmer blazed to a 66 moving him into a one-stroke lead over January. As the two player's fortunes headed in opposite directions, many of the fans in "Lema's Legions" left to become recruits in "Arnie's Army" as Palmer's gallery grew to an estimated 3,000 strong.

On the seventh hole, Tony's sixteenth, he chipped to two feet, but he had a bad spot in the green between him and the hole. He attempted to chip the ball over the rough area and into the hole, but failed to pull the trick shot off. He had another disappointing day in the third round with a 73, and finished with a final round 70 placing him in a tie for 25th worth $587.50

In an exciting finish, Juan "Chi-Chi" Rodriguez, a diminutive Puerto Rican, birdied the eighteenth while January bogeyed. The two ended up tied and would face each other the next day in an eighteen-hole playoff, the first playoff of the new season. The next day, Rodriguez beat January in the playoff for his first PGA tour victory.

The following week, at the Palm Springs Golf Classic, Tony entered the final round just four-strokes off the lead. As he stood on the final tee, he was at one-over par. He drove his ball up onto a steep bank along the shore of a lake. He inspected his lie with the ball partly submerged in the water. His options included taking a drop with a one-stroke penalty. This would have been the safer option allowing him to collect a nice check. Alternatively, he could gamble on a heroic shot out of the water and possibly salvage par. If he gambled and was successful, he would make a much larger check.

After mulling his options, he elected to gamble and what transpired over the next twenty minutes was pure *opera buffa*. A good title for the production would have been "Shredding C-Notes." He removed his left shoe and assumed his stance putting his left foot in the water. The ball was lying well above his feet requiring him to choke up on the club almost down to the steel shaft. He swung at the awkward shot, producing a large spray of water, but topped the shot and the ball barely cleared the lake. It came to rest on the opposite shore.

Tony, again wearing a bucket hat with the back brim turned up, turned toward the gallery, photographers and television camera on the opposite side of the lake and burst out laughing. Again, he would have to stand in the water for his next shot, this time with his right foot. However, he neglected to remove his shoe and planted his right foot in the water while his left foot, still bare, was on land. The gallery roared with laughter at the show unfolding before them.

Adding to the ridiculous situation, the television camera crew now asked him to wait so that they could position their cameras for his shot. After a lengthy delay, he hit the shot, which came to rest under the clubhouse. He now took off his soaked right sock and shoe and finished the hole barefoot. He kept the gallery entertained with a steady stream of comments—all in a humorous vein—before finishing up the hole with a score of 13.

His antics on the final hole ballooned his score up to an 81 and he finished out of the money. After completing the hole, Arnold Palmer, who was commentating for television after finishing his round, interviewed Tony.

"I had $1,300 worth of fun in the water," Tony said explaining his final hole escapades. "Oh well, what's $1,300?" He laughed along with Palmer as he made his exit.

The press, and fans, found his happy-go-lucky reaction to the foolishness that unfolded on the final hole endearing. He could add fans to the "Lema's Legions" by shooting himself out of the money on the final hole of a tournament.

At the next stop on tour, the Phoenix Open, Mother Nature intervened forcing a delay in the start due to frost. Tony started in the afternoon on the back nine and barely completed his round before darkness forced a halt to the first round. His 68 was two shots back of the leader,

Don Fairfield.

He actually had a good opportunity to tie Fairfield but blew his chance when he trapped his approach at his seventeenth hole resulting in a bogey. He dropped another shot on his eighteenth hole after driving into the trees.

In the second round, he fought his putter and clicking cameras to successfully card a solid 68 and take sole possession of the lead. On the third hole, he noticed a fan with a movie camera and politely asked him not to film while he was putting. The fan abided by his wishes, but another spectator took a still photo while he was putting. The distraction caused Tony to three-putt. Then, on the next tee, it happened again when another spectator snapped a photo. He briefly lost his temper, but made a point of assuring reporters after his round that the galleries, for the most part, were good.

"The galleries were just fine," he said. "Everyone was quiet while we were shooting. That is everyone except the amateur cameramen."

There was a traffic jam at the top of the leader board after the second round as no fewer than 18 players were within three of the lead. Nicklaus ran off a string of seven straight threes on the way to a 66 and was just one off the lead. Player fired five straight birdies, shot a 65, tying Nicklaus. Player and Nicklaus, paired together, played in front of a huge gallery.

After his round, Tony sat down with reporters and while drinking a large glass of milk, went over his round.

"I was driving just terrific," Tony said. "I was cutting it and drawing it at will."

Big hitting George Bayer got into the mix in the third round with a 65 for a three round 202. Nicklaus remained hot carding a 68 for a 205 total. Tony suffered a miserable putting round resulting in a one-over 71 and sat at 207.

On the Sunday of the final round in Phoenix, golf fans around the country had a plethora of choices for viewing golf. In addition to the broadcast of the Phoenix Open, they could watch *Challenge Golf* or the *CBS Golf Classic*. Tony featured in both programs that Sunday, teamed with Phil Rodgers against Palmer and Player on *Challenge Golf* and paired with Sam Snead against the team of Gene Littler and Bo Wininger on the *CBS Golf Classic*. In 1964, CBS began using cameras on cranes to record the action during the *Golf Classic*. This was the first use of cranes that are still widely employed for televised golf today.

In the fourth round, Nicklaus used a driver on nearly every hole to overpower the course on his way to a 66 finishing at 271. He drove the 305-yard par 4 fifth hole and then drained the putt for an eagle two. His power game blew away the field giving him his first victory of the 1964 tour. Tony shot an even-par 70 for a four round 277 finishing in a tie for sixth place. His winnings of $2,067 moved him up to the tenth spot on the money list.

Ray Haywood, writing in the *Oakland Tribune* announced a testimonial dinner in Tony's honor on February 20 at the Athens Athletic Club in downtown Oakland. His friends and supporters were honoring him with a "Tony Lema Appreciation Night."

Haywood went on to write that, "Lema, through exercise, became stronger and through diligence learned to apply the power. He now rates as one of the finest drivers on tour, particularly when the course is narrow."

Ron Giblin divulged in *The Oakland Tribune* some of the plans for the "Tony Lema Appreciation Night" at the Athens Athletic Club. Music by Wally White's Five-Piece Band and a film of the 1963 Masters were just two of the items on the agenda. Tickets sold for $5.00 each and a crowd of 400 was expected.

On the night of his dinner, his fans flocked to the Athens Athletic Club to fete Tony. He arrived at the event on Clay Street in a classy convertible with Betty, looking young and vibrant, at his side. Lou Moschetti was the chairman of the event and local sportscaster Bud Foster was the master of ceremonies. Celebrities in attendance included football great Ernie Nevers, Willie Mays, Willie McCovey, Archie Matsos, Ken Venturi and Harvie Ward.

The Oakland mayor presented Tony with the key to the city while Mayor Maltester of San Leandro presented him with a plaque and an honorary deputy's badge. The Athens Athletic Club also awarded him an honorary membership.

After accepting these gifts, Tony, invited to say a few words, noted that he found the honorary deputy badge very ironic.

"Oakland and San Leandro have fought over me before—but it was the chiefs of police, then," Tony half joked.

He also spoke about the future of the tour. He warned that the PGA could end up without any tournaments if they greedily insisted on sponsors turning over all television revenues.

"We're beginning to think that we're better than you common people," Tony informed the gathered guests. "We want TV rights and all—we put ourselves above everyone else, and we'll put ourselves out of business."

Tony closed with a heartwarming tribute to his family.

"If any attention has been drawn to me, I feel that without a doubt it belongs to what is a regal family in my books; the Lema family; my mother, my wife and all the Lemas."

Bill Fiset, in his "Man Alive" column in *The Oakland Tribune* expressed surprise that a country club in the Bay Area had never extended Tony an honorary membership. Harlan Gelderman and John Sparrowk, developers of the Round Hill Country Club, immediately extended an invitation to Tony and Betty to join as "guest members."

25 SPRING FREEZE
1964

After receiving accolades in the Bay Area during "Tony Lema Appreciation Night," it was back to the tour for the Greater New Orleans Open at the Lakewood Country Club. Rain postponed the first round and once the tournament got underway, Tony showed signs of rust. After opening with a 75, he followed up with a 73 and a 78 and missed the 54-hole cut.

His season, one with a start-and-stop aspect to it, paused yet again as he and Betty traveled to New York City. Tony was one of the main attractions at the International Golf Show. The show was both a trade show and a consumer show.

He took the show by storm, outdrawing the other PGA pros appearing, including Sam Snead. After each of his three daily personal appearances, he stayed, for more than an hour, talking with fans and signing autographs.

While at the show, Bill McCormick, a writer for the syndicated Newspaper Enterprises Association, obtained an interview with him.

McCormick described him as "just like any other young man self-marked for success in a highly competitive business. His manner is as sincere as the silk necktie under his button-down collar. He has the poise and assurance of a junior executive married to the boss's daughter."

McCormick asked Tony about the state of his game.

He admitted his game was not in top form, saying, "I'm practically in one of my resting periods now. But, I'll work up to a peak by playing in the Doral Open and the Azalea Open."

Another factor that contributed to his herky-jerky schedule during this stretch was the demands of his newfound stardom. While providing additional income the personal appearances, exhibitions, televised golf matches and endorsement commitments all took time away from golf.

He returned to tournament golf at the Doral Open, but again missed the 54-hole cut despite shooting a 70 in the second round.

Days before the start of the Azalea Open, excerpts of *Golfer's Gold* began to run in *Sports Illustrated*. These excerpts were interesting in that they were not an exact reproduction of the book released a few months later.

Malarkey, given the alias of "Crocker" in the book, is "the Sponsor" in the excerpts. There were many other minor differences between the articles and the finished book.

His game started to show improvements in the pro-am before the Azalea Open when he shot a 69.

"I don't think you could say this round means I'm going to play well the remainder of the tournament," Tony told reporters. "Still, all in all, I hit some good shots and it's encouraging to know my swing is smoothing out again."

The main reason for the minor slump was inconsistent putting. He was experimenting with different putters alternating between a flanged blade putter and a Bullseye putter trying to find one that worked. His putting woes caused a loss of confidence, always an important aspect of his game.

Despite his putting problems, he managed a 70 in the first round of the Azalea Open putting him three strokes off Joe Campbell's lead. His putting did not improve during the second and third rounds as he recorded two rounds of 73 and finished with a 76 to finish in a tie for nineteenth and a check worth $325. His position on the money list fell to 28th place.

The next week, at the Greater Greensboro Open, he opened with a 71, but then was forced to withdraw midway in the second round, complaining of a muscle strain in his right arm.

"I played a little basketball before the second round, and going for a tip-in, I pulled a muscle. It was a real effort to play on Friday," Tony admitted a few weeks later.

In early previews for the Masters, Nicklaus was the odds-on favorite to repeat as champion. Julius Boros, after winning the Greater Greensboro Open, made his own predictions for the Masters.

"The field there will be tops," the big man told reporters. " 'The Big Three' will be there, and Lema will make it the big four. Perhaps you fellows can slip me in there as number five."

Excitement was building for the Masters as it did every year. Golf fans eagerly anticipated the year's first major after suffering through the cold winter months.

Heavy rains softened up Augusta National as players began arriving for practice rounds. A softer course made Nicklaus, with his prodigious length, a stronger favorite.

"Let it rain," Jack confidently stated.

Arnold Palmer snatched a share of the first round lead, along with Gary Player, at 69. Also at 69 were Davis Love, Bob Goalby and Kel Nagle. Tony had a dismal 75.

Palmer came into Augusta without a major championship victory since he won the 1962 British Open. Many speculated that his game was off due to his decision, back in January, to quit smoking and he came to Augusta packing a few extra pounds, the result of his incessant snacking.

The *Oakland Tribune*, taking advantage of the time difference on the west coast, reported on early action in the second round. The headline across the sports page read: LEMA NABS EARLY MASTERS LEAD. Tony putted brilliantly and posted a 68 for a 36-hole total of 143 and the clubhouse lead. His round featured an eagle on the thirteenth hole, a par 5, when he found the green with his three-iron second shot and then sank the 15-foot putt.

Many players, especially Palmer, played later in the day than Tony after *The Tribune* went to press, and his lead did not last long. Palmer played in his usual charging style and fired a blistering 68 to take sole possession of the lead at 137.

While a private plane trailed a streamer over Augusta National during the second round that said, "Go Arnie Go," Palmer extended his lead to four-strokes over Gary Player.

Palmer, with his army of fans growing with each passing hole, marched to a 69 in the third round for a 206 total and built his lead to five-strokes. Palmer was on track to win an unprecedented fourth green jacket while keeping his string of winning the Masters in even-numbered years intact. Palmer's nearest challenger was Australian Bruce Devlin who shot a 67 in the third round for a 211 total.

Tony had a disappointing 74 in the third round as the putting stroke that worked so magnificently in the second round deserted him.

Palmer coasted to the title in the final round, recording a 70. He comfortably held off a challenge by Nicklaus who came charging out of the pack with a 67 to tie for second with Dave Marr. Palmer won by a seven-stroke margin, but despite his huge lead, Palmer kept charging, even hitting a three-wood on the par 5 fifteenth hole for his second shot.

His playing partner, Dave Marr, thought he was nuts to gamble trying to carry the pond guarding the front of the green. Palmer lost the flight of the ball in the sun as it soared towards the green. Almost in a panic, he asked Marr if his ball got over the water.

Marr looked at him with a wry smile and said in his Texas drawl, "Hell, Arnold, your divot made it across."

The press speculated that the victory was worth an estimated half-million dollars to the newly formed Arnold Palmer Company. With his Masters victory, Palmer solidified his position as the most financially successful professional golfer.

Tony shot a final round 70 that placed him in a tie, with 51-year-old Ben Hogan, for ninth place winning $1,700. His four round 287 was the same score he shot in 1963 when he finished in second place, although he was nowhere near as excited in '64 as he was in '63. In fact, he was very disappointed in his play and his confidence was at a low point.

Tony, along with Betty, left Augusta Monday morning travelling to Gastonia, North Caroline for an exhibition. Once there, he taped an interview for television. During the interview, his sense of humor was on full display.

"You fellows must really be hurting for news," he stated. "The way I've been playing I doubt seriously if I could break par on a putt-putt course."

At the course, he conducted a clinic filled with quips that kept his audience entertained. One attendee asked Tony how to overcome the shanks.

"Lay off for a couple of weeks, then quit altogether," Tony advised. "Seriously, when you find a sure cure for shanking, let me know—we'll make a lot of money."

The mood of the exhibition round was light and entertaining for the approximately 600 fans that followed the players. As usual, Tony donated his fee, after expenses, to charity.

From North Carolina, the two traveled back to the Bay Area for some rest giving him a chance to work on his game. He was not happy with his play since the Crosby, bothered by inconsistent putting and his lack of confidence.

To correct his putting problems he kept returning to the advice he received from Horton Smith in Detroit back in 1961. Smith had emphasized the importance that confidence played in putting and he needed to get that confidence back. How to get that confidence back was the tricky part.

Golfer's Gold hit the bookstores and reviews began appearing in various publications. While not generating rave reviews, the book was an enjoyable read and a rare glimpse into the everyday life of a touring golf professional. Although tame by today's standards, his exploits during his bachelor playboy days raised eyebrows at the time.

Tony drove to Salinas to defend his title in the 36-hole Northern California PGA Medal Tournament. His three-under-par 69, on the Corral de Tierra course in the first round gave him a commanding four-stroke lead. He came back with a 73 in the second round that was good enough to win by one-stroke over Al Mengert. He then surprised the organizers of the event, and Mengert, when he refused the $200 first prize money, which Mengert received.

"I just wanted to play for the fun of it," he replied when asked about refusing the check.

Murray Olderman wrote a syndicated article that foretold of dissention in the ranks of the PGA pros. The touring pros were starting to talk about breaking away from the PGA, an organization whose main job was to administer to the hundreds of teaching pros at courses around the country. The touring pros thought that the tour was becoming too large for the PGA, and they had questions about the money they generated by their tournaments. The PGA had over $400,000 in its coffers, collected from entry fees and television revenues, not currently earning interest.

Mark McCormick, and his stable of superstars, was a major player in the discussions about a possible split from the PGA. Since signing Arnold Palmer, McCormick had added Jack Nicklaus and Gary Player to his client list earning each of these men, especially Palmer, vast sums of money through endorsements and television matches. He was adding more players to his client list, as well.

"McCormick's waiting until he gets 20 top players and then he'll break away (from the PGA). He already has 10 players," an unnamed tour regular explained to Olderman.

The PGA had a special committee in place to procure an exclusive television-broadcasting package. All parties knew that television would soon pony up huge fees for the rights to broadcast tour events. The thinking was that if McCormick could put together his own package of 20 top pros, he could launch a competing tour, completely televised.

"If he could pull it off," admitted Jack Dolph, CBS director of sports, "some network would put him on. It might be very attractive to us. Especially if he did it right—with starting times tailored for television and other angles to help the medium."

Not being a McCormick client, Tony was not too keen on the idea of a tour built around the agent's stable of players. He was intuitive enough to realize that such a tour would benefit McCormick's clients primarily.

While it was clear that the tour was quickly outgrowing its status within the PGA organization, it would be five more years before it would branch off on its own.

Tony and Betty celebrated their first wedding anniversary in Las Vegas while he again played in the Tournament of Champions. The elite field of 29 PGA tournament winners from the prior 12 months played on the Desert Inn Golf Course located behind the Desert Inn Casino and Hotel on the Strip.

With a 77 in the first round, Tony could finish no better than a tie for 24th place and a check good for $1,045. Despite the nice check, Tony fell from the 21st place on the money list all the way down to the 27th position.

The players headed for Texas and the Colonial National Invitational. Tony opened the tournament with a 78, but fought back with three straight rounds of 71 to finish in a tie for 17th and $1,150 check.

The next week, Palmer took over the number one spot on the money list, enjoying a slim lead over Nicklaus, when he won the Oklahoma City Open. Tony showed some signs of working his way out of his slump when he shot a 66 in the pro-am. He played with Palmer in the first two rounds, and both shot 75 in the opening round. Fortunately, for both, a thunderstorm washed out the round and rain on Friday pushed the round to Saturday. Tony managed a 70 in the re-start, while Palmer could do no better than a 72.

The second round, on Sunday, Tony fell back with a 72. Palmer, with a 69, sat three off the leaders, Lionel Hebert and George Bayer. The tournament wound up on Monday with both the third and fourth rounds played because of the rainouts. Palmer shot rounds of 69 and 67 to capture the victory by two-strokes over Hebert.

Tony blew up in the morning round with a 77 but came back strong in the afternoon with a 66, which earned him $1,400 for an eighth place tie. He made an upward move on the money list moving up to 23rd place.

In Monday's morning round, he finally succumbed to his frustration with his putting, and lost his temper. He decided to punish the offending putter and later admitted that he "crystallized" it beyond use by whacking it against a tree. Putting with a long iron, he finished the round and then replaced it with a back-up putter for the afternoon round.

After completing the Oklahoma City tournament, he played an exhibition with Palmer, British Open champion Bob Charles and Byron Nelson at Brook Hollow Golf Course in Dallas. The proceeds of the exhibition went to the Dallas Society for Crippled Children and the Cerebral Palsy Treatment Center. He teamed with Charles against Palmer and Nelson with the match resulting in a tie. With two holes to play, Tony had to leave early to catch a flight to Memphis where, as defending champion, he had commitments to fulfill and the host pro at Brook Hollow, Shelley Mayfield, filled-in securing pars for the team.

During the match, Tony received a gift from Arnold Palmer. Palmer knew all too well the trouble Tony was having on the greens. He had also heard about the destroyed putter. He thought he had just the thing to help.

"Here, try this," Palmer suggested as he handed him a putter. The putter was a flanged blade putter with a black finish, a Tommy Armour model manufactured by MacGregor. Tony putted with it, liked it and put it into his bag, thanking Palmer.

The next week, in Memphis he shot a 68 in the first round, three strokes back of Bob Duden of Portland, Oregon. He followed up with a stellar 66 in the second round and trailed the new leader, Casper, by a single stroke. He capped off his round with a superb scrambling birdie on the final hole after hitting his tee shot into the woods. He was able to hit his next shot out of the trees to the front edge of the green and then two-putted for his birdie.

He finished with a 69 in the third round and a disappointing 71 in the final round putting him in 12th place. The $1,110 winnings kept Tony in the

23rd spot on the money list.

The next week, at the 500 Festival Open, Tony missed the cut. He did gain attention when newspapers around the country ran news that he would travel across the Atlantic to play in his first British Open later in the summer.

As spring gave way to summer, he needed to get his game in gear. He was stuck far down the money list and he had been missing too many cuts. He still enjoyed the benefits of clothing and equipment endorsements, received invitations to play in televised matches, and for personal appearances and exhibitions. All of that could go by the wayside if he did not break out of his slump. He needed to boost his confidence. The best way to do that, and ensure the fruits of his stardom, was to start making cuts and win a tournament or two. The tour was heading into the purse-rich summer tournaments, including the three remaining major championships and it was time to make some hay.

26 SUMMER SIZZLE
1964

Fred Corcoran invited Tony and Betty to stay with him and his family, for a week, in Scarsdale, New York. Tony was playing in the rich Thunderbird Classic at the Westchester Country Club in Rye, a short five-mile commute from Corcoran's house. Tony loved kids and enjoyed playing silly little games with Corcoran's two young daughters. Overall, it would be a comfortable week.

Corcoran was very involved in the Thunderbird, once serving as the tournament director, and was currently a consultant for the event. With its large purse and the quality of the golf course, the Thunderbird was an important stop on tour. Corcoran was excited about Tony's chances in "his" event.

Palmer and Nicklaus, as usual, enjoyed the role as the pre-tournament favorites. With the U.S. Open at Congressional Country Club in Washington, D.C. a mere two weeks away, both players planned to use the Thunderbird as a warm-up, as did many players.

Ken Venturi was suffering through a slump that was much more severe than what Tony was going through. It had gotten so bad that he was having trouble getting into tournaments. He failed to Monday qualify for the Thunderbird, so he called Bill Jennings, the tournament director, to beg for a sponsor's exemption. Jennings informed him that there was only one exemption remaining.

Jennings asked him for some time to think about it and asked Venturi to call back the next day. Jennings then immediately called Corcoran.

The two men discussed it and agreed to give Venturi the exemption—almost as a gesture of sympathy. Venturi was determined to take this opportunity and make the most of it. He felt his game coming back into form and experienced a boost in his confidence when he qualified for the U.S. Open, a tournament he had not played in since 1960.

In the first round of the Thunderbird, unknown Canadian Jerry Magee blistered Westchester shooting a 66 for a one-stroke lead over Venturi and Phil Rodgers, who was also trying to battle his way out of a prolonged slump.

With a 68 in the first round, Tony joined a gaggle of nine other players two off the lead. In all, 43 players broke par on the Westchester course. In the second round, Tony caught fire aided by a birdie-eagle finish on his way to a 67 capturing the lead at 135.

Both Venturi and Mike Souchak, playing in the morning, posted half-way 137 totals. They enjoyed the clubhouse lead for three hours before Tony's finish eclipsed them by two.

Tony's round featured a chipped in eagle on the finishing hole. A photo, distributed by the Unifax syndicate, depicted him as he watched his chip shot approach the cup. In his raised left hand, he holds his club aloft, while his right hand is steering the ball towards the hole. A middle-aged female spectator, wearing a hat and sunglasses, seated in a folding wooden chair behind him, has both her arms raised above her head. The photographer captured the woman with her mouth wide open as she cheers in anticipation of the ball going in the hole. He carded a 32 on the back nine finishing 3-4-3-3-3.

The new putter from Palmer remained hot in the third round. He used it to sink a dramatic 20-foot eagle putt on the ninth hole. The eagle came just as his pursuers were applying pressure and he could feel them breathing down his neck. He shot a 70 and increased his lead, now over Bobby Nichols and Souchak, to three.

Venturi posted a 54-hole 209, four-strokes off Tony's pace and tied with George Bayer and Bob Duden. Drizzles and 20 mile an hour winds made the course play much more difficult than it had in the first two rounds.

"I sure hope I'm here Sunday night," Tony told the assembled press after his round. "Bring your sleeping bags. We're going to have a ball. It will be a long evening."

The reporters looked forward with anticipation to the possibility of a champagne party the next evening.

Tony provided a gem of a quote as he left the press saying, "It's funny how your swing gets a little tighter with $20,000 at stake. And I've got a little redhead (Betty) to help me spend it."

He attended Mass early Sunday morning and arrived at the course for the fourth round under dark clouds and showers. He was paired with Duden and Souchak, who got off to a very rough start when he double-bogeyed the first hole. Duden never really got into the mix during the round struggling to a 73.

Tony birdied the third hole while Souchak took a bogey and the lead was now seven. Souchak had cut the lead to six before hitting his approach, on the sixth hole, deep into the woods. The tournament looked over. Souchak, however, hit a miraculous recovery shot from the woods. He actually holed it for a birdie to cut the lead to five.

The fun really started at this point as Tony and Souchak entered into a head-to-head battle that Will Grimsley, writing for the Associated Press called "one of the most dramatic finishes in years on the pro tour."

Tony hit his approach on the eighth hole into a bunker, wound up with a bogey, and the lead shrunk to four. On the ninth, he put his second shot under a fir tree forcing him to crawl through the low-hanging branches to play his shot. To make a swing at the ball he had to assume a stance from his knees. The result was another bogey and the lead was now down to three. He managed a birdie on the twelfth hole, but Souchak went him one better with an eagle. The seven-stroke lead had now shriveled to just two.

On the fourteenth hole, a par 3, Souchak stuck his tee shot four-feet from the pin while Tony hit his tee shot into the crowd.

"It was just a terrible shot. And the chip was bad, and then I three-putted," Tony explained to the press after the round.

Souchak made his four-footer for a birdie, and coupled with Tony's double bogey, now found himself in possession of a one-stroke lead with four holes to play. Tony did not panic. He channeled the teachings of Lucius Bateman, Horton Smith, Danny Arnold and Fred Corcoran to marshal a positive mental attitude. He had let his big lead melt away, but he was determined to fight back and win the tournament.

Back in the clubhouse, headwaiter Frank Devito sat alongside the cases of Moet Champagne stacked in preparation for Tony's victory celebration. As he heard the reports from the course, he wondered if he should not get some lemonade on ice, just in case.

On the sixteenth hole, another par 3, Souchak placed his tee shot on the green, though it was a long way from the hole. Tony missed the green with his tee shot, but made a fantastic chip to 18-inches and tapped in for par. Souchak left his first putt six-feet short. He faced a tough putt for par, but managed to coax it in to retain his one-stroke advantage.

The showers turned to a driving rainstorm. Souchak utilized a towel, embroidered with "Westchester Country Club," over his massive shoulders in an attempt to keep dry.

On the seventeenth hole, Tony exhibited a great deal of heart as he wedged his second shot to a foot for a tap-in birdie. Souchak made a routine par and the two players were all even as they headed for the eighteenth tee. A spectator in the crowd unfurled a banner that read, "Lema's Legions."

It was Tony's wedge, again, on the par 5 eighteenth hole that provided him an advantage. He wedged his third shot to eight-feet setting up an excellent chance at birdie. Souchak tried to reach the green in two shots and came up short. After a weak pitch shot, he faced a long putt for birdie.

Tony scanned the gallery and found Betty, soaked by the rain, standing near the retaining ropes by the green. While Souchak played his pitch shot, Tony walked over to his wife.

"Honey, I sure made this thing interesting didn't I?" he asked her.

Souchak two-putted for his par and then stood off to the side of the green watching Tony. Tony took his time studying the eight-foot putt that "looked like 80-feet." He assumed his stance, but quickly backed off for another look. He setup, again, over his putt and rolled the ball right into the heart of the cup for the victory.

As the ball disappeared into the hole, he dropped his putter. He then did a little three-step jig while pumping both fists and letting out a yell. He retrieved his ball from the cup, and in what was becoming another victory trademark of his, he threw it up into the gallery. He was back in the winner's circle.

"I don't remember making the putt," Tony told Oscar Fraley of the United Press International. "I told myself, 'keep your stupid head still' and I almost did. I looked up just in time to see the ball fall in."

Frank Devito had no need for lemonade. He delivered the cases of Moet to the pressroom where corks popped and the bubbly flowed. An Associated Press photo of Tony depicts him with his hair wet and disheveled from the downpour, a towel around his neck and a wide smile on his face. He has a very large champagne goblet raised in his right hand toasting his victory.

An offshoot of the champagne victory parties with the press was that he spent a long time in the pressroom. With the wine flowing, loosening up inhibitions, Tony was a veritable quote machine. He related a story from the Sunday night after the recent Masters. He was dejected with his poor showing, did not feel right for some reason—did not feel charged up and his confidence was lacking.

That evening he went with Fred Corcoran and some other friends to a private club. Corcoran had noticed that Tony was not playing with confidence and decided to have a talk with his star client. He waved Tony into a backroom where they could be alone. The room was empty, except for some quarter and dollar slot machines.

"Look, Tony. You got the wrong slant on things. I want to tell you, right now, that the only thing you lack to become a great golfer is the power of positive thinking. Look at these machines," he went on as he pointed to the slot machines. "You can't beat them, right?"

Tony nodded slowly.

"Watch this," Corcoran said as he pulled a quarter from his pocket. He dropped the quarter into the machine, cranked the handle and watched the wheels spin before landing on a triple jackpot.

Tony's eyes bulged out in disbelief.

"Positive thinking," Corcoran, said unexcitedly. "Now, Tony, let me tell you, that's all you need."

Before the night was over, Tony and Corcoran had a whole stack of coins on their table.

"I told myself on the sixteenth tee," Tony told Corcoran in the pressroom while tapping his temple, "positive thinking."

For his part, Corcoran almost collapsed when Tony lost the lead and he sweated bullets all through the final nine holes. In the pressroom, he exhibited the signs of a man who had ridden an emotional rollercoaster over the past two hours.

Tony told the press, "Souchak's birdie putt at the fourteenth might have helped me. I was leading this thing so long; I was choking to death out there."

As promised, Tony partied with the reporters for a lengthy period before finally leaving Westchester en route to Corcoran's house. The press returned the love when writing their stories of the final round.

"Lema proved his class and his courage when he whipped a wedge to within a foot of the flag on the 346-yard, par 4, seventeenth for a birdie," wrote Fraley for the UPI.

"The perfectly poised Lema refused to become unhinged," Grimsley wrote about Tony's near collapse in his dispatch for the AP.

Tony told Grimsley, "I always felt I could hit a golf ball but I never had much confidence. Winning the Thunderbird—especially the way I did, when it looked as if I was going to blow it—gave me the kind of lift I needed. Now, I can go into the Open feeling that I can win it."

His victory, just at a time when he truly needed one, was worth $20,000 and shot him up the money list to the fifth position. More importantly, it gave his confidence a tremendous boost making him feel that he could compete against the toughest fields on tour. Only a week or so earlier, he was worried about his value in regards to exhibitions, endorsements and personal appearances. That was no longer a concern and his value was about to enter the stratosphere.

Tony joked after officials presented the $20,000 winner's check to him—three times. First, at a presentation ceremony for the television cameras, another for the still photographers and then finally, Tony received the check at the authentic presentation.

"Betty won't understand this," Tony explained. "She'll figure: 'you got three checks. That's $60,000 to spend.' As it is, this will just pay off Neiman-Marcus."

He also received the keys to a new Ford automobile from the New York area Ford dealers who sponsored the Thunderbird.

Venturi took advantage of his sponsor's exemption and finished in a tie for third and a check worth $6,250. Just as important, he automatically qualified for the Buick Open the next week—there would be no calls to beg for an exemption spot.

Four days after the completion of the Thunderbird, Milt Gross wrote in a syndicated story:

> *What you've got to understand about Tony Lema is that this is the guy who's boozed it up, spent nights around gambling tables and tomcatted around in the dark often enough to know the difference between good and bad, right and wrong and tough and easy.*
>
> *He finally decided that no man could drink it all and only an idiot keeps bucking the percentages at the card and dice games and writing IOU's. He found a girl with whom he fell in love and married and he found his golf game. Now, they call him Champagne Tony and he'll come up one of the favorites in the U.S. Open at Washington in a couple of weeks.*

Another syndicated story, under the byline "by Tony Lema as told to Murray Olderman" ran under the headline: PRESSURE LEMA PREFERS WOULD POP BUBBLY. Tony detailed the immense pressure players felt in the Open.

> *"I could feel it as we started the last nine at Brookline last year. The pressure. It grabbed my arms and squeezed like a guy tying a tourniquet. This was the U.S. Open, the tournament you dream about winning when you're a kid. For a golfer, it's the World Series or a heavyweight championship fight, one of the most important titles of all. It puts your name firmly into golf forever."*

He spoke of the stamina needed during the traditional 36-hole final day in the Open, as well as the challenges presented by the U.S.G.A. course setup.

He went on to identify the players he felt were favorites in the tournaments. It was a list of the usual suspects; Nicklaus, Palmer, Player and defending champion Julius Boros.

He concludes the article with, "Just in case Mrs. Lema's little boy Tony gets lucky, there'll be a man from Moet hanging around Congressional. That's the champagne I'm signed with, and they always have a man near me at every tournament. I'll be glad to pop every cork myself."

The press estimated that Tony poured $500 worth of the bubbly after each win. Tony joked to reporters that when he told the press the champagne would flow if he won the 1962 Orange County Open, "I meant for me—not them."

Nevertheless, his champagne victory parties were one of golf's most endearing trademarks; the press long ago dropped the quotation marks from his nickname. Champagne was an integral part of his image.

On the strength of their success in New York at The Thunderbird, he and Betty floated into Grand Blanc, Michigan, for the Buick Open. Both

Nicklaus and Palmer passed up the Buick, opting instead for practice rounds at Congressional in preparation of the Open, now just a week away.

Warwick Hills Country Club, a beast of a course measuring out at 7,238 yards, hosted the Buick Open. It was viewed by most players, as well as the press, as a good warm-up for Congressional, also a lengthy course.

Phil Rodgers took the first round lead with a 67 and he credited some advice he received from Nicklaus two months earlier for his fine round.

Tony continued to putt well tying with Mason Rudolph one-stroke back of Rodgers. Ever since Palmer gave him his putter, Tony had been magical on the greens.

"We had a fist fight and I won his putter," he joked to reporters when asked why Palmer made the gift. "Sometimes I think the putter still feels that Arnie is handling it."

The opening round got off to a bad start when Tony double-bogeyed the second hole after driving into the trees. Then, he bogeyed the next hole, but he bounced back with four straight birdies on the back nine. He was again in contention, attempting to win back-to-back victories, a feat not accomplished since Nicklaus won both the Seattle and Portland Opens, back-to-back in 1962.

In the second round, with all guns blazing, he rode a roller coaster of a round. He started with a birdie on the first hole, but then bogeyed two of the next three holes before he got back on-track. He reeled off six straight birdies, the last five holes of the front nine and the tenth hole. His gallery, which was the largest to follow any group at the start of his round, grew as news spread around the course about his round.

He finished with a remarkable 66 and enjoyed a three-stroke lead over Mason Rudolph. Dow Finsterwald was still within shouting distance of the lead, five-strokes, after shooting a 70 in both the first and second rounds.

"I had a very uninteresting round," Tony joked. "It was so consistent."

In the third round, Tony complained of the heat, humidity and wind. The tough playing conditions resulted in rounds that took over five hours to complete. The conditions caused Phil Rodgers, who started the day in fourth place, six back of Tony, to sky to an abominable 84 and he missed the 54-hole cutoff.

Tony played a solid round in the tough conditions in front of a huge gallery. He was two-under-par through sixteen holes, and then carelessly bogeyed the seventeenth and eighteenth holes to finish with a 70. His lead dwindled to two over Dow Finsterwald, who shot a third round 69, while Rudolph, with a 73, sat four back.

"The wind made the course a lot more difficult today," Tony, related to reporters. "I was real happy to reach number seventeen tee at two-under-par. Then I shot a three-iron 20-feet from the hole and went to sleep for the first time. I three-putted, and before I knew what was happening I had bogeyed the eighteenth after hitting the second shot into the trap. Nobody is happy to finish bogey-bogey."

The weather during the fourth round was still warm, however the winds abated somewhat. Tony played solid golf and was able to handle a challenge from Finsterwald, who fought to within one of the lead. Finsterwald's challenge fizzled as he bogeyed the penultimate hole after missing the green.

Tony's final round 70 included four birdies and two bogeys. His four round 277 was just three-strokes shy of the tournament record. With his 114 putts for the week, including just one three-putt, he was growing extremely fond of Arnold Palmer's putter. His winner's check of $8,000 gave him a total of $28,000 won in just eight days. He also won the keys to another car (to use for one-year), a brand-new Buick Riviera, and he would receive a new one each year, for the next five years. This in addition to the new Buick he received every year as a spokesperson for the company.

The Riviera was a luxurious and stylish car with two doors, a powerful 401 cubic inch engine that delivered 325 horsepower. The interior featured leather seats, a center console and floor shift. A tilt steering wheel, cruise control, power steering, windows and seats, as well as air conditioning rounded out the luxury appointments. Tony's car featured gold golf balls on the trim near the rear on both sides. When he was out on tour, Judi, his sister-in-law had custody of the car.

Tony met with the press after his victory and the man from Moet delivered the champagne to the pressroom. Tony sat with reporters unleashing a torrent of quotes, as usual.

"I was pretty worried when my second shot on fifteen landed in a trap," Tony admitted, "but I felt a little bit better when they told me that Dow also had trouble and had bogeyed the hole. I'm real happy with my game. I've got all my confidence back and, don't forget, I did lead from the 27th hole on."

Tony waxed philosophical about the vagaries of the game of golf when he said, "Some days it's the chicken, and some days it's just the feathers."

The reporters inquired about his chances in the next week's U.S. Open.

"You still have to go with fellows like Arnold Palmer, Jack Nicklaus, Billy Casper and Gary Player." Tony explained. "I'm going to the Open tired and worn out. I don't figure my chances are any better than they were last year when I finished in a tie for fifth. If I won it, I'd be very, very lucky, and lightning would have to strike about 999 times. I'm putting better than I have at any time since I finished second in the 1963 Masters."

After the trophy presentation, Tony, holding the large silver cup mounted on a wooden base, posed for photographers with Betty who was stylish in a sleeveless white top. He held the trophy while she was holding the $8,000 check. They hugged and kissed for the cameras.

With his victory, Tony moved up another spot on the money list to the fourth position. After the champagne celebration, he and Betty packed up their new Buick for the trip to Washington D.C. and the U.S. Open at Congressional.

27 DEATH MARCH
1964

The players arrived in Washington D.C. as the temperature sizzled and humidity hung in the air. Tony, hot off his two straight wins, was tired, both mentally and physically. Despite his exhaustion, he was oozing with confidence. He skipped the first day of practice at Congressional Country Club, but did participate in a *Sports Illustrated* reception. He joined Snead, Boros, Wall, and Casper in putting on a clinic at Hines Point. In the rain, they hit balls toward the Jefferson Memorial in the distance while Byron Nelson served as master-of-ceremony.

Congressional, the longest course played in U.S. Open history, suffered a drenching by heavy downpours in the days leading up to the championship. The rain softened the greens making them receptive to approach shots, but also made the lengthy course play even longer.

Tony assessed his chances in the Open with a trace of realism.

"Winning three in a row is out of line with the odds," he told reporters. "I'm tired, while the big two—Jack Nicklaus and Arnold Palmer—are fresh, with plenty of practice behind them."

In early first round action, Bill Collins shot a 70 to take the morning clubhouse lead. At 71, Tony and Pott were hot on his heels. Both players scorched the front nine shooting 33 but cooled off on the back nine with 38s. Both had a chance to tie Collins for the lead, but bogeyed the finishing hole.

Temperatures reached 90 degrees during the round.

Venturi continued to show improvement shooting a 72 in the first round, tying with Nicklaus, while young Ray Floyd posted a 73. With an afternoon starting time, Palmer had to battle the brunt of the heat, but handled it well with a 68 and took possession, by two-strokes, of the lead. He admitted to reporters that the round was one of his finest single 18-hole performances of his career. Only 46 players, less than one-third of the field, managed to break 75, while 31 players posted scores of 80 or worse.

The heat did not abate for Friday's second round despite a heavy rainfall just after dawn. The rains softened the greens making them more receptive to the long approach shots required on the lengthy course. Tony's friend, Tommy Jacobs, took advantage of the conditions and blazed to a 64—equaling the lowest round in U.S. Open history. The record dated back to 1950 when Lee Mackey, Jr. shot a 64 at Merion.

Veteran E. J. "Dutch" Harrison, playing with Jacobs described the round to reporters.

"It would have been a 58 on any other golf course," he asserted. "I still don't believe it. This course cannot be played in 64."

Palmer also played well in the second round finishing with a 69 but could not match the fireworks of Jacobs and was one off the lead.

"You must have been cheatin'," Palmer quipped to Jacobs about his unbelievable record round. "Either that, or we were playing different courses."

With a solid round of even-par 70, Venturi sat just six-strokes back of the lead.

Tony struggled through the afternoon heat and humidity for an unremarkable 72 and sat seven-strokes behind Jacobs, the leader. The next day, traditionally known as "Open Saturday," would be a 36-hole final round requiring stamina, both mental and physical, to win.

On Saturday morning, Tony saw a relaxed, but focused, Venturi on the putting green and approached him.

"You look great today, Ken," he said to his long-time friend. "You know something? I have a feeling it's going to be your day."

"I sure hope so, Tony," Venturi replied.

Venturi played with Ray Floyd in the final round and he played the first fourteen holes in the morning round like a well-oiled machine. He later called his five-under front nine "the greatest nine holes of golf that I ever played."

He cooled off a bit on the back nine, especially when he got to the seventeenth hole, as the effects of the heat began to take a toll. Feeling dizzy from the heat, he missed an 18-inch putt for par on the seventeenth green and then on eighteen, he missed another short putt for par. Despite these lapses on the putting green, he posted a 66 for the morning round.

Jacobs clung to his lead, now by two, with a fantastic back nine 34 to post a 70 fighting off Venturi's charge.

Palmer blew his chances at a second U.S. Open title with a disastrous 75 in the morning round. He hit just two fairways and two greens in regulation on the front nine.

After his round, Venturi admitted to reporters, "I almost blacked out on the fifteenth hole."

The heat severely affected him and dehydration set in. Under doctor's orders, he ate nothing during the break consuming only ice tea and salt tablets. As he lay prone in the locker room, Tony came up to him and put his hand on his shoulder.

He said, "You can do it, Ken."

With permission from the U.S.G.A., a doctor accompanied Venturi during the afternoon round. Dr. John Everett, a Congressional member and the doctor who administered to Venturi during the break (actually advising Venturi to withdraw), would monitor his condition while he played the final 18 holes.

A 75 in the morning round dashed Tony's hopes for a National Open title. He had difficulty in the hot conditions.

"They should have oxygen masks and ambulances at every hole," he half joked to reporters after the round. "I don't know how I can go out there again, let alone the older guys."

A rumor spread through the galleries that Venturi would withdraw because of dehydration. Venturi put the rumors to rest arriving at the first tee, albeit on shaky legs, to begin his afternoon round.

Things got tight on the leader board early in the afternoon round. Palmer resurrected his chances with a birdie on the first hole. Jacobs double-bogeyed the par 3, third hole and the margin between him and Palmer was down to three-strokes. Palmer's challenge withered however, with bogeys on two of his next four holes.

Venturi continued to play steady golf. He gobbled up salt tablets in an attempt to ward off dehydration as he trudged slowly down the fairways with his head bowed and his face ashen. Today we understand that salt tablets actually hinder recovery from dehydration, as did the caffeinated ice tea that he consumed during the break. In retrospect, it is amazing that he remained on his feet.

The tournament boiled down to a fight between Jacobs and Venturi. Venturi arrived at the ninth hole after eight straight pars, now tied with Jacobs. He hit a one-iron second shot winding up just five-yards short of a ravine that guards the par 5 green. He wedged his next shot to nine feet and drained the putt for a birdie that put him into the lead. He played steady golf over the next nine holes, even though he felt anything but steady. He resembled a marathon runner at the end of the race struggling to reach the finish line. His step grew slower and slower, his head drooped lower and lower.

His steady par golf was good enough to widen his lead, eventually to four-strokes, and he arrived at the eighteenth tee needing only a seven to win. He played the hole artfully saving par from the front bunker and capped off one of the most inspiring and gutsy U.S. Open victories in the history of the event. His 276 total was the second lowest 72-hole total in Open history.

When Venturi holed his putt on the eighteenth hole, his playing partner, Ray Floyd picked the ball out of the hole for the exhausted champion. When Venturi looked at Floyd, he saw tears streaming down the young player's face and he was sobbing. Venturi's eyes welled up with tears before he too, began to sob uncontrollably. He thought, "My God, I've won the Open."

Dangling at the end of a rope, Venturi came back from the abyss with his victory. He had won less than $7,000 in 27 starts in 1962 and won less than $4,000 in 1963. His comeback inspired golf fans around the world.

With another 75 in the afternoon, Tony wound up in 20th place earning a check for $700. At the completion of the tournament, Tony phoned Venturi's hotel and told the operator he wanted to be the first caller put through to his room. The operator accommodated his request and he was the first person to talk with his friend after he left Congressional.

"Congratulations," Tony said, "I knew you could do it."

Although he was exhausted, Tony moved on to the Cleveland Open. He felt confident about the tournament, one he nearly won the year before, losing an 18-hole playoff to Arnold Palmer.

Highland Park Golf Club in Cleveland provided a course in stark contrast to Congressional. The 6,821-yard par-71 layout was no match for the skills of the touring pros and 63 players broke par in the first round. Al Geiberger shot a course record 64 with birdies on six of the last 10 holes, but he held only a one-stroke lead over Tony, and a two-stroke lead over George Bayer. Palmer sat another stroke back, three off the lead.

Tony started the tournament by holing out a bunker shot on the first hole for a birdie. His playing partner, Gary Player, told reporters he was inside Tony on almost every green, but that Tony was, "putting them in from everywhere."

Player used 35 putts en route to a 69. Billy Casper shot a 66, as did Ray Floyd, while Nicklaus negotiated the course in 68 strokes. A tired Venturi suffered a post-Open letdown shooting a 75 on a course the other pros were eating up.

Low rounds were again the norm during the second round. Palmer's 131, the lowest 36-hole total for the year, gave him the lead. Richard H. Sikes, Jr, playing his first PGA tournament as a pro, was one-stroke off Palmer's pace. Both Palmer and Sikes equaled Geiberger's course record, barely 24-hours old. Jack Nicklaus, with a 65, sat another stroke back in third. Tony's 70 dropped him down the leader board at 135.

Palmer and Nicklaus, paired together in the third round, waged a head-to-head battle resembling a heavyweight title bout. Palmer cruised along until disaster struck at the thirteenth hole where he three-putted for a bogey from 40-feet. He exacerbated his troubles when he again three-putted the next hole for a double-bogey.

Nicklaus shot a 69 while Palmer limped home in 71 strokes and the pair sat atop the leader board at 202. Tony, with another 70, sat tied with Casper, Player, Don Fairfield and Sikes at 205.

In the final round, Nicklaus bogeyed the first hole and was never a factor thereafter. The putter that Tony received from Palmer turned red-hot and he started making birdies from everywhere, making five straight birdies, on the fifth through the ninth holes.

Palmer also was putting together a fine round and the tournament quickly boiled down to a mano-a-mano contest between him and Tony. Palmer birdied the fifteenth hole after hitting his seven-iron approach shot to five-feet.

Tony, at 15-under, played the eighteenth hole with the goal of making a birdie that would force Palmer to birdie the seventeenth and eighteenth holes in order to tie him. A birdie would also give him a 63 for the new course record. He hit a fine approach shot leaving him with a 12-foot putt for his birdie. He lined up his putt and stroked what he thought was a good putt. He was sure he made it, but as the ball neared the hole, it curled off, leaving an easy 12-inch tap-in. He took his time over the short putt, very carefully stroked the putt, and missed it. He signed his card for a 65 and settled in to watch Palmer finish.

Palmer hit his approach to the eighteenth green 20-feet from the hole and as he approached the green, the marshals lost control of the huge crowd. Arnie's Army was in full assault fighting to stake out positions for a view of the exciting finish.

The marshals struggled to regain control of the crowd before finally establishing a semblance of order. The gallery grew quiet as Palmer lined up his 20-foot putt to win the tournament. He assumed his trademarked pigeon-toed, knock-kneed and elbows akimbo putting stance and stroked the ball that tracked towards the hole. He had hit the ball with too much speed and as the ball hit the hole, it popped up in the air and refused to drop into the hole. Palmer tapped-in for a 68 and a sudden-death playoff with Tony.

Palmer won the coin toss and teed off first. He pulled a driver from his bag and lashed a drive that carried a creek that bisected the fairway.

"I was very happy to lose the toss of the coin for the playoff and have Arnie shoot first," Tony later told reporters.

He used a fairway wood on the first hole in the third and fourth rounds, laying up short of the creek.

"I hadn't used a driver in two days and didn't intend to there, but when he drove over the creek, I decided I might as well go out in style," he said.

Tony got lucky as his drive actually bounced over a crossing bridge spanning the creek. He then put his approach safely on the green with a good chance at birdie. Palmer hit his approach a little long and was on the fringe just off the back of the green. Electing to putt from the fringe, he rammed it ten-feet past the hole.

Tony surveyed his putt from every angle before settling over the putt. He drew his magical putter back and stroked the ball straight into the hole.

"Yes!" he yelled and flung his putter into the air as the ball disappeared into the hole.

The players, reporters and the huge gallery returned to the clubhouse where champagne waited in the pressroom. An AP photographer snapped a picture of Tony pouring a glass of champagne for Betty, and always cognizant of endorsement opportunities, has the bottle perfectly positioned so that the camera captures the Moet logo on the neck label. They both smile widely for the shot

Tony sat down with his glass and sipped champagne while he discussed the final round with reporters. The writers asked about the short missed putt on the final hole of regulation. Tony's answer began with the first putt on the eighteenth.

"It was no more than 12-feet and I thought I'd get it. I thought I'd get the course record with a 63 and go two ahead of Arnie," he explained. "I thought the first putt was going in. But even when it didn't I was kind of relieved it was so close. So I walked up there and took my time, but I guess it was anticlimactic. When I missed, I thought I had blown the tournament."

With his $20,000 winner's check, he brought his total won in the last four weeks to over $55,000 and vaulted into second place, behind Palmer, on the official money list. The fact that he won in Cleveland against a strong field that included "The Big Three" boosted his confidence further.

"It's been a wonderful month," Tony admitted in a vast understatement. "I'm glad it's happening to me."

Palmer, citing exhaustion and the time commitment involved, announced he changed his mind and would not travel to Scotland for the British Open.

At the beginning of the year, Tony had not been sure about playing in the British Open. At that time, it would have been necessary to qualify for the tournament requiring him to skip the Whitemarsh in order to arrive in Scotland in time for the qualifying round. He waffled throughout the year unable to make up his mind whether he would make the trip, or not.

"First he is going and then he isn't," complained Betty to John Lovesey of *Sports Illustrated*. "I don't know and, believe me, neither does he. Tell me; are other golfers like normal people?"

Once Palmer decided he was not making the trip, he offered to arrange for Tip Anderson, his caddy who was on the bag for both of his British Open victories, to carry Tony's bag.

The *Oakland Tribune* ran a story that said Tony would be making a trip home to the Bay Area in late July, but he would not be in town long.

"I'm just going to change clothes, practice a little and be off again for some exhibitions," Tony told the newspaper. "I'm going to the British Open in Scotland after the Whitemarsh, then back to the PGA in Columbus July 16-19 before going home."

The Whitemarsh Valley Country Club was ripe for scoring and the touring pros ripped it apart. Tony continued his hot streak making an eagle and five birdies on the way to a 66. He and three other players, young Tom Shaw, Chi-Chi Rodriguez and Al Balding sat at the top of the leader board.

Tony was running out of gas, though and told reporters, "I find myself starting to lose my temper quickly."

Still, he was able to muster a 67 in the third round before falling out of contention with a 75 in the final round and a sixth place tie good for a $3,917 check.

Two players who were not having any difficulties in the fourth round were Jack Nicklaus and Gary Player. Player charged up the leader board shooting a final round 69. In the end, his charge fell short as Nicklaus scorched the course for a 67. Nicklaus came from six off the lead to capture the title.

Tony, Player and Nicklaus, along with Doug Sanders, immediately departed from Whitemarsh for the airport and their flight to Scotland, for the British Open.

28 CHAMPION GOLFER OF THE YEAR
1964

"I just want to see how they operate things over there," Tony told reporters before his departure to play in the British Open.

The madcap trip to The Open in Scotland took 16 hours to complete. High over the Atlantic, he sat in a jet airliner next to Fred Corcoran who attempted to explain the subtleties of the St. Andrews Old Course, often referred to as "the home of golf." He spoke about the strategies required to negotiate a true Scottish links course with the diabolical winds that buffet the course and could change directions on a whim. He tried to prepare Tony for the strange bounces and unfamiliar shots he would face.

Tony listened patiently. At last, he turned his tall frame in his seat and fixed his keen green eyes on his business manager.

"Fred, I don't want to hear any more about it. Just let me tee up the ball out there, that's all I ask. I let them build the courses; I play 'em."

While Tony and Corcoran flew to Scotland, Betty returned to the Bay Area and the apartment in Alameda. Upon arrival in St. Andrews, Tony immediately went to the Old Course for a look around. With three titles in the last month, the locals greeted him as the celebrity he had become. He wore the mantle of his stardom comfortably, which added to his popularity.

Before making the trip, Venturi had given him some advice about playing a links-style course in front of the knowledgeable Scottish galleries.

"If you're in a position to win, remember this one thing," he counseled. "Don't you ever hit a wedge at eighteen. You run it up the valley. Trust me. That's the way to win in style and the crowd will really appreciate it."

Jack Nicklaus, Doug Sanders, Doug Ford, Dean Beamen, Phil Rodgers, Johnny Bulla and Bill Johnston, in addition to Tony, made up the American contingent. All, but Bulla and Johnston, arrived late and would attempt to familiarize themselves with the ancient course quickly. The Scottish fans thought the Yanks were daft and did not give them much chance to win on a course that they believed required a lifetime to learn.

Waiting for Tony at the clubhouse was a tall, pink-cheek Scot.

"I'm caddying for Tony Lema," Tip Anderson, a 28-year-old caddy at St. Andrews told reporters. "Arnold Palmer told him to take me on. I'm sorry Mr. Palmer isn't coming this time, but I'll do my best for Mr. Lema."

Anderson, a son of a former caddy at St. Andrews, knew the golf course as intimately as anyone did and that would serve Tony well. Tony could only complete ten holes of his first practice round but completed all eighteen holes in his second.

Nicklaus told reporters that he intended to use the smaller British ball during the tournament. He felt the smaller ball would be easier to control in the wind and he figured he could gain 25-yards on his drives. The British ball was identical in weight, 1.62 ounces, to the larger American ball; however, it was smaller in diameter at 1.62 versus the 1.68 inches of the American ball. Being denser, it bore through the wind better.

When the reporters informed Nicklaus that Tony intended to use the American ball, Nicklaus retorted, "Well, if the wind blows, good luck to him."

Before he teed off for his practice round, Tony told the press, "I've heard so much about St. Andrews and golf in Britain that I just had to get over here. I'm not worried about getting here late. I'll just have to meet the problems as they come up."

After just 28 holes of practice, Tony pronounced himself ready for the tournament. Members of the press misinterpreted his confidence, and laid-back approach, as a prediction of victory.

"I never said I would win," Tony complained to Corcoran after reading the newspapers.

"Well, you have now," replied his business manager.

The morning of the first round, as Tony walked onto the first tee, he spotted a coin in the grass. He picked it up, and looked around at the gallery.

"Look at this," he said holding the coin aloft. "I'm already the leading money winner in the British Open."

The Scottish fans around the first tee took to him immediately and became full-fledged members of "Lema's Legions."

The famous winds at St. Andrews were evident on Wednesday during the first round. It picked up in ferocity as the day wore on so that players teeing off early had a distinct advantage over the late finishers. Tony drew an early tee time, finishing his round just as Nicklaus was teeing off in the late afternoon.

On the par 4 eighteenth hole, Tony launched his drive to thirty yards shy of the green. He hit an indifferent pitch shot that ended up 50-feet beyond the hole, but made the long putt for a birdie and a 73. The crowd at the "Aberdeen Bench," the free spectator section at the corner of the green, gave him a rousing ovation.

The wind played havoc with the scoring in the first round—especially in the afternoon. Irishman Christy O'Conner and French-Canadian Jean Garaialde captured the first round lead at 71. Tony's 73 represented the lowest score of the eight Americans entered. Rodgers shot a 74, and Nicklaus, fighting the worst of the conditions, recorded a 76.

Between Tony and the leaders were Harry Weetman of England and Bruce Devlin of Australia both with 72s.

"I guess I was lucky to end up with a 76," admitted Nicklaus. "I hit the ball as well, if not better, than on other previous visits to Britain, but I putted awful. My eyes kept watering, and sand kept blowing in my face. I thought the wind got stronger later in the day and it was particularly tough around the loop."

The first six holes on the Old Course play away from the town of St. Andrews and the Royal and Ancient clubhouse. The seventh through the eleventh holes forms a loop before the course returns adjacent to the opening holes, back to the clubhouse. The wind off the North Sea can be particularly treacherous on the loop holes.

After his round Tony admitted to having difficulty with his chipping and pitching from inside 100-yards. He was attempting to make the transition from hitting high pitch shots to the bump-and-run shot played along the ground. The huge double greens on the Old Course were also difficult for him to figure out.

Fourteen of the holes at St. Andrews play to large greens used for two separate holes. These large greens are equipped with two flagsticks. On the first nine, the hole locations are located on the east side of the green, while on the back nine, hole locations are on the west side. One of the many quirks that make the Old Course special is that the holes sharing a green add up to 18. The fifth and the thirteenth share a green, the seventh and eleventh also share a green, and so on.

"I finally put the wedge back in the bag and said goodbye," Tony said. "Instead, I took a seven-iron and ran the ball to the hole."

"It's a tough son of a gun, this course," he said. "You can't afford to go to sleep on a single shot. I thought I played pretty well, but it's a fight at every hole not to lose a stroke. The biggest difficulty from the wind was in putting."

Asked which hole was the most difficult Tony quickly responded, "The first 18."

With his quick wit, he quickly won over the British press.

The morning of the second round, the wind continued to blow. As the day wore on, the breezes abated, giving the afternoon tee times an advantage. Tony, teeing off in the afternoon, again avoided the worst of the gales.

"I think the biggest thing that happened to Tony there was he had the weather on his side," Nicklaus recalled decades later.

Tony three-putt the fifth hole for a bogey, but from then on, he played fantastic golf. He birdied the sixth and ninth holes and, with the wind at his back, drove the 312-yard par 4 twelfth hole. He calmly stroked in the 25-foot putt for an eagle two.

He added another birdie at the fourteenth hole and nearly added another at the eighteenth where his birdie putt lipped out. He shot a remarkable four-under 68, described by one scribe as "one of history's great rounds over the St. Andrews Old Course."

He enjoyed a two-stroke lead over long-hitting Harry Weetman while Devlin and O'Conner sat one more stroke off his lead. Nicklaus shot a 74 that placed him nine-strokes off Tony's lead.

"I took 40 putts in that round," Nicklaus observed after his round. "That's a record for me. But, I took 39 putts in the PGA last year in Dallas in one round—and still won," he went on optimistically.

In addition to Tony and Nicklaus, three of the other eight Americans in the field survived the cut to play in Friday's 36-hole final round. The cut came at 153, Doug Ford sat on 149, Doug Sanders at 151, and Phil Rodgers made it on the number at 153. Johnny Bulla, well past his prime, missed with a 159, as did Billy Johnston at 158, and amateur, Deane Beaman, at 157.

When he saw the winds at St. Andrews, Tony wisely chose to abandon all thoughts about playing the larger American ball. In fact, he said he would have liked to play a marble.

"If we had played with the big ball, I doubt we would have finished," Nicklaus commented after his round.

The gallery and press reporting on the event could plainly see that the Old Course inspired Tony. The Scottish galleries were warming to him and his swashbuckling style of play. He began to sense that he was playing for something quite more than the $4,200 first place prize money.

Returning to his hotel, Tony stretched out on a sofa in his room, a whisky in hand, and talked with Lovesey of *Sports Illustrated*.

"That 68 I shot today was one of the finest rounds of golf I've ever shot, but I still don't feel confident. This is the most challenging golf course I've ever been on," he said. "You don't dare go to sleep one moment. And to finish second won't mean a thing. In the year 2064, when people pick up that record book, this is the kind of championship they will look up. You'll be remembered only if you win."

Later he tried to eat something for dinner but lacked an appetite because of his nervousness. He retired for the night early in an effort to get plenty of rest before the Friday finish—the most important 36 holes of his life.

The weather did an about-face, to sunny and mild, for the final rounds. The Open Championship featured the unique format of ending the tournament before the weekend for two reasons; Saturday was held in reserve for a possible 18-hole playoff if needed, and the Sunday Sabbath was strictly observed at St. Andrews with the course closed, allowing it "to rest."

Satellite television coverage that brings The Open to viewers worldwide was still years in the future, so a Friday finish did not result in lost television revenue. Fans back in the states would have to wait a week to see any of the action when ABC aired a delayed broadcast as part of its "Wide World of Sports" show.

Tony's lack of an appetite continued on Friday, he choked down a cup of coffee for his breakfast and prepared for his morning round.

On the fifth tee, Tony learned that Nicklaus, playing many groups in front of him, was five-under.

"I heard that Jack was five-under-par and there I was, three-over after four holes," Tony later said.

After a shaky start, he turned things around. He made par on the fifth and sixth holes and as he left the sixth tee, he passed Nicklaus going the opposite direction playing the thirteenth hole. The two players paused, looked at each other's scores, on the walking scorer's signs, and took stock of the situation.

Nicklaus looked confident, fiercely so, and Tony admitted, "I didn't feel so good."

On the sixth, Tony managed a par and then caught a Scottish fire by running off five straight threes, including three birdies, on the seventh through the eleventh holes. Nicklaus finished his round with a course record tying 66 and then was astonished to learn that Tony was also on track to shoot a sub-70 round. At one point during the third round, Nicklaus was able to narrow the lead to a single stroke until Tony went on his amazing run of threes.

Tony finished his round by making a 20-foot birdie putt on the eighteenth hole to post a 68. He had successfully held off the Nicklaus challenge surrendering just two strokes from his nine-stroke lead. Nicklaus knew his chances were as good as gone once Tony posted his 68.

During the lunch break, Tony tried to eat, but found it difficult because of his anxious stomach. He was only able to get down a few bites of a cold salmon sandwich.

In the afternoon round, he played cautious and carefully. He two-putted the first three greens before three-putting the fourth for a bogey. Despite his slim chances, Nicklaus continued to apply pressure playing another great round in the afternoon.

Tony pulled his drive on the fifth hole, but made a remarkable recovery shot with a three-wood to the front edge of the par 5 green. He two-putted for his birdie giving him the spark needed to ignite his round. He sank an 18-foot putt on the seventh and followed with a gutsy eight-footer for another par on the ninth. He played the tenth through the seventeenth holes conservatively. Nicklaus posted a 68 in the afternoon, but he knew it was too little, too late. Tony came to the eighteenth tee knowing that he could shoot a seven or less for the title.

Tony completed his magical week in Scotland in style. He drove the ball down the middle of the fairway, just short of the famed Valley of Sin that fronts the green. The mob of fans followed Tony filling the fairway behind him, a custom of the British Open. He then executed one of the prettiest pitch-and-run shots up through the Valley of Sin that finished 18-inches from the hole.

The mob swarmed around, engulfing him, as they jostled up the fairway in search of prime viewing spots at the front of the green. Lost in the sea of humanity, he fought his way through the crowd finally emerging. He ran his hands through his hair, mussed in the struggle through the crowd, and acknowledged the applause from the huge gallery raising his club high above him.

He tapped-in his short birdie putt and flung his ball back into the boisterous crowd. His score of 279 matched the third lowest score in British Open history, just three strokes shy of Palmer's record 276 at Royal Troon in 1962.

Coming off the course, Tony asked for a "cold drink" and a police officer obliged handing him a bottle of English ale. The crowd around Tony started to laugh at the irony of Champagne Tony with beer. Before he took a big slug off the bottle, Tony laughed, too.

Tony changed into a sports coat, a black and pale blue thinly striped jacket similar to seersucker that he wore over his black sweater and pale blue turtleneck. With his dark grey slacks, he presented his usual style as he accepted the Claret Jug during the awards presentation.

In the days before the live television broadcasts, the champion had time to prepare for the trophy presentation and the result was far more eloquent than today. After taking possession of the historic Claret Jug trophy, Tony addressed the crowd on the porch of the Royal and Ancient Clubhouse. Throngs packed the grounds in front of the clubhouse, while members watched from behind the huge paned windows of the historic stone building.

"I want to thank the gallery for giving me the gas I needed out there today," Tony acknowledged. "You helped me win it, when Jack started to pour it on. I felt that I owed it to myself as a golf professional, and one who loves the game, to visit where my great friend—the game of golf—was born."

Tony spoke of the historical ramifications of his victory saying, "I have read Walter Hagen's name and Gene Sarazen's name and other great names on this cup. Now mine will be added. I feel inadequate. I certainly will be back next year to defend my title. I never thought I would find myself speechless, but I am as close to that as I've ever been."

Servers popped the corks on magnums of champagne and all toasted his historic victory. A picture depicts him with a full champagne glass raised in a toast in his right hand with his left arm wrapped around the Claret Jug. In another photo, Tony cradles the trophy to his chest, as if it were a baby. His steely green eyes reveal the pride, and exhaustion, that he feels.

Tony paid Anderson, his caddy, $1,000, well above the going rate, which thoroughly won over the frugal Scots. The Scots fell in love with Tony, and his style, dubbing him the "Jolly Yank."

With cases of champagne in tow, Tony met with the press.

"The turning point was this morning when I was told Jack was five-under. Then I went and threw those five threes back at him and that's when I won it. The British Open is one of the world's four major tournaments and I'll be back for it again, and again," Tony promised reporters.

He described the mob scene on the final hole saying, "I got some bruises getting through there. But, I'm happy about those bruises."

The conversation then focused on his caddy, Tip Anderson.

"Tip Anderson was at least 50 percent of this team and I reckon to say 51 percent would not be too far wrong," Tony acknowledged. "Tip did it. He taught me the first lesson, to run seven-irons onto those tough greens. I put my wedge away at his advice and that's the best thing I ever did."

For his part, Anderson told reporters, "He's a great player. His swing is about as sweet as Sam Snead's. There's very little difference in his game when you compare it to Mr. Palmer's. He is more relaxed. When something goes wrong, like a six he took at the fifth hole Friday, he forgets immediately."

Asked if Tony ignored any of his advice he answered, "No, sir. Once at the fourteenth, I told him to shoot for the spire of a church, and he drew the ball a bit and we didn't come out of that as well as we might. But, he hit it where I told him every time."

Tony and Corcoran spent a great deal of time with the press, drinking champagne and answering their many questions.

Tony paid tribute to Nicklaus and his final round score that posed such a threat to Tony.

"Jack was never far from my mind all day," he said. "I knew he was the danger."

Tony's faith surfaced when he told reporters, "I got down on my knees last night and asked the good lord to give me this one."

He spoke with pride about securing his place in golf history.

"The money doesn't mean anything. It's the cup you want to win," he declared.

A phone call from the states interrupted his revelry with the press. On the line was Venturi.

"It's from the lad who won that *other* Open Championship," Tony informed the writers before departing to accept congratulations from his friend.

Tony and Corcoran finally made their exit from the pressroom and the hallowed grounds of St. Andrews. The next morning they departed for Paris with a few friends for a celebration in the famous city. They located a nice restaurant on the Left Bank, behind Notre Dame, and settled in for a night of merriment. Tony ordered champagne, but Moet was not on the wine list.

"Tony, we'll have to pay for that," Corcoran warned.

Tony never had to pay for Moet when dining out.

"Who cares?" Tony gleefully asked.

The group enjoyed a raucous meal before moving on to a nightclub— they called ahead to make certain that Moet was on the beverage list—and celebrated late into the night. The next morning, Tony and Corcoran awoke, a bit groggy from the night's festivities and prepared for an important visit.

Corcoran was an old friend of the Duke of Windsor, the former King Edward VIII. Upon learning Corcoran and Tony were in Paris, the Duke invited them to his home at 4 rue du Champ d'Entrainement on the Nevilly-sur-Seine side of the Bois de Boulogne.

"I understand you like champagne," the Duke stated after greeting the two Americans. "Well, that's what we'll have."

The small group split a bottle of champagne and talked golf for nearly an hour. As Tony and Corcoran bade the Duke farewell to prepare for their flight back to New York, the Duke presented Tony with a long white cigarette holder as a memento of the visit. Tony called the Duke "one of the most gracious and charming men I've ever met."

Reporters met the new champion when he deplaned at Kennedy International Airport in New York.

Tony called his victory the "highest achievement of my career. It was my first major championship and I doubt if anything will ever surpass it. I wanted it badly and I was fortunate to get it. The prize money was worth only $4,200, but it is worth a million dollars in prestige."

Tony described the playing conditions at The Open.

"This is really golf in its greatest and most invigorating form," he stated. "I thought that I had seen winds before, but they have the patent on them over there."

One of the first things he did once back in the states was to place a phone call to Arnold Palmer.

"Arnie, first I borrowed your putter and won three tournaments," Tony began, "and last week I borrowed your caddy at St. Andrews and won the Open. What else have you got that I can borrow? ...Like your bank book?"

While he was in New York, Tony received a phone call from a young woman in charge of lining up guests for the popular television show "What's My Line." She extended an invitation to Tony to be the mystery guest on the game show. Tony agreed even though the appearance fee hardly offset the cost in inconvenience that he would incur returning to New York for the taping.

He was now a major winner, a big star, and he was enjoying it.

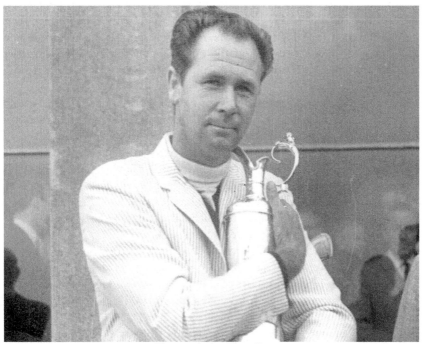

Tony with the Claret Jug
Photo courtesy of the Lema family

29 WORLD SERIES PAYDAY
1964

Tony arrived in New York the conquering hero enjoying the accolades of the press and fans. From there, Tony and Corcoran headed to Columbus, Ohio for the PGA Championship. In Columbus, he stepped off the plane, dressed nattily in a dark blue suit, with the wooden box containing the Claret Jug in his arms. Betty flew from Oakland to join him in Columbus. The scheduling of the PGA Championship, the week after the British Open, made it very difficult for the pros that played in both events.

"I'm emotionally drained dry after the British Open," Tony told reporters upon his arrival in Columbus. "I don't see how I can possibly get myself up for another tournament so quickly. If this weren't the PGA, if this were just another weekly tournament, I think I'd skip it."

"My big trouble will lie in my emotions," Tony predicted about his performance in the PGA. "I threw everything I had into winning at St. Andrews and when I finally won, I went up on cloud nine. I'm afraid I can't get my feet planted firmly enough in such a short time to be a factor."

Tony credited his putting for his hot streak.

"There was a time I felt lucky if I made a 25-foot putt a week," he stated. "Lately, I've been making one or two of them in almost every round, and I have been hitting on most of the important five and six-footers. I'm happy I'm having a good year. I owe it all to my putter, the one I got from Arnie Palmer."

After a practice round at the Columbus Country Club, Tony lounged in the locker room with reporters. He was smoking a cigarette using the new holder he received from the Duke of Windsor. He held it at a rakish angle and affected a thick British accent.

"A little gift from the Duke of Windsor in Paris," he said slightly condescendingly as he flicked ashes from his dark blazer.

Venturi walked into the locker room and tossed his shoes into his cubicle. He looked on with amusement as Tony held court with the reporters.

"Oh, you must be the fellow who won that American tournament," Tony said in his fake accent.

"That's me. And you're the guy with the champagne factory," Venturi replied. "What have you been up to lately?"

The two friends continued to rib each other and laughed giddily. They thoroughly enjoyed themselves and why not? The two were in the midst of a magical summer, Venturi having staged one of the greatest career comebacks in professional golf history, while Tony was breaking through to become one of the true superstars of the sport.

Fred Corcoran had exhibited impeccable timing when he signed the two as clients. Both were changed men, Tony in particular, whose experience in Scotland forever transformed him as a golfer and as a star. His trip to Scotland provided him a deeper respect for the game and its history, and he was now a member of the elite and exclusive club known as major champions. Gone forever was the young player who was never quite sure he was good enough to make it on the PGA Tour. In his place was a composed, confident, and steely competitor unafraid to match his game against the greatest players on tour.

Tony found himself in the rough all day in his first round of the PGA.

"The rough is impossible," Tony complained to reporters. "I'd like to get out there with a lawn mower for a day and even then I couldn't begin to cut all the high grass."

Bobby Nichols shot a course record 64 in the first round and led by three strokes over Nicklaus, the local hero, and Mike Souchak. Palmer, well placed after shooting a 68, sat three in front of Tony.

The day of the second round, the *Oakland Tribune* ran an article under the headline; LEMA HITS MILLION DOLLAR VEIN. In the article, Fred Corcoran disclosed that Tony could make $200,000 in endorsements in 1964. Corcoran went on to describe Tony as "the new Walter Hagen."

"Hagen was the first to make a million dollars out of golf and Lema's the first to come along with Hagen's great color," Corcoran explained.

The article mentioned that Tony was paid $2,500 for a two-minute television commercial and that he would be starting a nationally syndicated instructional newspaper feature. Arnold Palmer, Jack Nicklaus, and Sam Snead all did a one panel drawing instructional piece, and Tony would start a similar feature in August.

He signed a contract to appear, once again, on Shell's Wonderful World of Golf, this time competing against Carl Poulsen at the Rungsted Golf Klub near Copenhagen in September. Tony's exhibition fees were now $1,500 for a weekday event and $2,500 for weekends.

"It's fantastic how Tony is taking the world by storm," Corcoran gushed. "When we were leaving England they wanted to know when Tony would be back. They want him for a month of exhibitions."

Corcoran went on, "They are fascinated by his swing and enraptured by his personality. You should have heard Tony and the Duke of Windsor talk golf for a solid hour. Obviously, Tony is going to have to keep on winning. And he is having a great year. So far he has won about $80,000 in prize money."

Nichols remained in the lead at the end of the second round after a 71 that gave him a 36-hole total of 135. Venturi was just two-strokes back after shooting a solid 67. Tony shot a 68 and was four off the lead and Nicklaus and Palmer were lurking within striking distance.

Utilizing some timely miraculous recovery shots, Nichols retained his lead after the third round. His 69 gave him a total of 204. Palmer, with a 69, vaulted up into second place, one behind Nichols. However, the big news of the day was the 68 posted by Ben Hogan for a 210. He led Tony, who had a 72, by one-stroke.

Nichols completed a wire-to-wire win with a 67 in the final round, finishing at nine under par. He held off a charge by Jack Nicklaus who blazed to a 64 ending up in a tie with Arnold Palmer at 274, three off Nichol's pace. Tony managed to tie the legendary Hogan at 282 after a 71. He won $2,300 and retained his position in the third spot on the official money list.

Exhausted, Tony went back to the Bay Area after the PGA Championship to rest. The *Oakland Tribune* caught up with him and the story appeared under the headline: WEARY LEMA HOME, SAVORS BRITISH WIN. The reporter, Ron Giblin, visited with Tony and Betty in their apartment.

"I had a much better time over there than I expected," Tony recalled about his British Open experience. "The people were very considerate."

He recalled his experience fighting through the mob on the eighteenth fairway.

"I was laughing like hell," he recalled. "I told the crowd that I had to get up there to the green, but it was just like a big wave. First, we'd go up and then back. Finally one time, on a surge toward the green, a policeman reached out and hauled me on the green."

He went on, "That wind was something else, too. The last day it died down to 18 or 20 miles an hour. They consider that a calm day over there."

Betty told Giblin, "I wish I had gone with him. I almost died waiting for the scores to come each day."

Tony took the Claret Jug down to the Airway Heights driving range to show it to Lucius Bateman. He also took it up the hill to Lake Chabot and handed it over to Dick Fry.

"I want you to keep the trophy at Lake Chabot," Tony told Fry.

Fry kept the trophy at Lake Chabot, displaying it proudly, for three months.

"It was so valuable," Fry, recalled years later, "I was afraid to leave it at the course. I took it home with me every night."

Following his victory, Lake Chabot had made Tony an honorary lifetime member.

His stardom and popularity escalated now that he was a major champion. The first week of August, the first installment of his instructional feature ran in the *Oakland Tribune* and focused on the subject of putting. His first advice was to sleep in a draft, get a stiff neck that would keep your head still, avoiding the tendency to look up.

After his brief rest, Tony was off to New York for a dinner honoring the major champions of 1964. Along with Tony, the dinner paid tribute to the Masters champion Arnold Palmer, U.S. Open champion Ken Venturi and PGA champion Bobby Nichols. The dinner was the first stage of a promotional campaign for the upcoming World Series of Golf, a two-round event contested between the major championship winners at Firestone Country Club.

While at the dinner, reporters asked about comparisons between him and Walter Hagen.

"It's not fair to Hagen when people mention me in the same breath with the great Sir Walter," Tony said about his hero. "But I love it."

He got a great thrill in meeting Hagen at the recently completed PGA Championship.

Tony tried to get back into the swing of competitive golf at the Western Open. He finished in a tie for sixth place, worth $1,960 that kept him in the third spot on the official money list.

Tony next teed it up in the American Golf Classic at Firestone Country Club in Akron, Ohio—the same course he would play in the World Series of Golf. The long course played even longer due to heavy rains that lasted through the mid-afternoon of the first round. Arnold Palmer shot a 68 to capture the lead, but Tony was hot on his heels shooting a 69. The two were the only players in the field who managed to break par, 72.

"I was disappointed because the course played so short today," Tony joked to reporters after his round.

With a 66 in the second round, Venturi grabbed the lead at 137. Palmer, after a disappointing 73, was four-strokes off the lead, a stroke behind Tony who added a 71, for a 140.

With a 69 in the third round, Venturi continued to lead, now two in front of Mason Rudolph who fashioned a 70. Tony also carded a 70 to place him third on the leader board, four off the lead. Nicklaus and Palmer were deadlocked at 212, six behind Venturi.

In the fourth round, winds that blew up to 25 miles an hour greeted players and the scores reflected the tougher playing conditions. Venturi continued his amazing comeback story by shooting a final round 69 to capture the title by five-strokes. The wind blew Tony off his game as he soared to a 76 finishing in a tie for fifth and a check for $2,200.

Murray Olderman of the Newspaper Enterprises Association wrote in his column "Between You'n'Me" that Tony's beverage of choice was a light blend of scotch, not champagne.

Olderman spent time with Tony when he was in New York for the World of Series of Golf dinner. The interview took place at Corcoran's house while a New York Yankees baseball game played on a television in the background. After seeing Roger Maris strike out, Tony commented that the Yankee player, "choked." He then went on to provide a rare glimpse into the psychic of an athlete when he faces a pressure situation.

"I backed off from that putt because I couldn't take the club back," Tony explained about the final putt of the Thunderbird Classic. "I was tightened up, if I ever get any tighter, I'll never swing a club again. I don't recall ever being so tense. I choked. Guys give you a lot of baloney and blame what went wrong in a tight spot on everybody but themselves. Especially in golf.

"I'd like to be like Arnold Palmer was at Augusta the first time I saw him win the Masters. He hit a six-iron and the camera focused on his hands. They didn't move at all, like he was fixing a watch."

He finished his dissertation on choking by saying, "It's all right for me to say I choked, but if somebody says it for me, he better be ready for a fight."

He planned to do his promised appearance on "What's My Line?" during this same trip to New York. However, after Bobby Nichols won the PGA, Tony got a call from the same young woman production assistant who arranged his appearance in July.

"You know Mr. Lema," the young woman began, "we try to keep very current on our show..."

She stammered some more attempting to get to the point.

"What you're coming to is that you don't want me on the show after all," Tony interrupted. "Isn't that it?"

"Well," the woman said somewhat gratefully, "we do try to be current, you know, and after all, you didn't win the PGA..."

"Gee, I'm sorry," Tony, said mischievously. "I won four of the last six tournaments, then I won the British Open, but I slipped up last week. So now I suppose you've got Nichols?"

The young woman admitted that she did. "Maybe we could have you on some other time," she suggested, "after you win another tournament."

Tony agreed that sounded like a good deal.

"Tell you what," he said. "Why don't you set up a time that will be convenient for your people to have me on the show. Then let me know and I'll arrange to win the tournament that week for you. Or, better still...I'll win three in a row. How would that be?"

A moment of silence came from the other end of the line before the woman gushed, "Oh, Mr. Lema! Would you *really?*"

Tony went from New York to Cleveland to be the guest of honor at a champagne lunch co-sponsored by the Chamber of Commerce and the Cleveland Open, where he was the reigning champion.

From Cleveland an exhausted Tony set off for the Carling World Open. He arrived in Detroit for the tournament nursing a very bad cold and felt golfed out, mentally. He coughed and sneezed his way to rounds of 72, 71 and 70.

Earlier in the summer he had signed a contract with ABC Television to give commentary from the eighteenth hole tower whenever he finished before the leaders. After the third round, he told Max Winters, his caddy, that he did not feel up to doing his TV work. He ducked his job in the tower, while announcers kept informing their audience that he was "expected shortly." He and Winters snuck off to a quiet place where they talked and relaxed.

"How old are you, Jerry?" he asked, using the name Winters went by in his caddy days.

The teenager responded by saying he was nineteen.

"Boy, I wish I was 19 again," Tony said.

Not only did Tony realize he would have done things differently if given another chance to be 19, but the responsibilities of being a star on the PGA Tour and his hectic schedule were wearing him out. He longed for the carefree days of youth.

In the final round, he blew to a 75 finishing ten-strokes off Bobby Nichols winning score. After the Carling, the demands on his time did not abate. He teamed up with Arnold Palmer for a pair of exhibitions, first in Baltimore and then in Quincy, Massachusetts.

Before the match in Quincy, Tony made a personal appearance in a Boston department store. He signed autographs, many for children who stood in line for nearly an hour.

"What do you want to be when you grow up?" Tony asked one young boy.

"I want to be you," the boy answered.

"That's good," Tony replied. "I want to be Arnold Palmer."

The day after the exhibition, *The Fitchburg Sentinel* sports page carried the headline: QUITE A SHOW BY TONY LEMA. Tony fired a nine-under 63 at the Wollaston Golf Course and defeated Palmer by eight strokes. Tony was nursing a bruised left foot—he dropped a suitcase on it—and noticeably limped through the round before he finally accepted an offer to ride in an official's golf cart. His round featured six birdies and an eagle and equaled the competitive course record at Wollaston while 2,500 fans enjoyed the show.

The newspapers the next Sunday, in the Parade magazine insert, contained a feature on Tony. Jack Ryan authored the piece that recounted Tony's career and the fantastic year he was having. He also spoke to his mother, Cleo, who disclosed that Tony was "a little hot-tempered when young."

Ryan spoke with Tony about his playboy image during his bachelor days.

"That playboy stuff was exaggerated. Golf is my life and always came first. Sure, I liked the girls, dancing, and good times, but nobody ever saw me out late if I had to play the next day," Tony related.

The press began to gear up for the World Series of Golf played at Firestone Golf and Country Club in Akron, Ohio. Nearly all of the experts were picking Palmer, the Masters champion, to win.

"I can understand why Arnie would be the favorite," Tony reasoned. "He has the best record of all of us on this course and he's been playing very well lately. But don't rule out Venturi or Nichols. They've both been on hot streaks."

The World Series of Golf was not an official PGA tournament; it was more of a televised exhibition. The players treated the tournament as an exhibition as well, even though they were playing for a $50,000 first prize.

Tony was the first of the four players to arrive in Akron. He laughingly told Milton Richmond of UPI that with only four players, he rated his chances at 4 to 1.

The other players arrived on Friday and all four players enjoyed a casual practice round in preparation for Saturday's first round.

Venturi came out of the blocks fast, with a 33 on the front nine, on his way to a 69 and took the lead. Tony was one back at 70, while Palmer had a disappointing 74 and Nichols struggled with his control and limped in with a 77.

Tony scrambled his way through the front nine. On the third hole, he drove up against a tree forcing him to chip out to the fairway. He managed to get his next shot on the par 4 green, however he was still a long way from the hole. He calmly stroked the putt in saving his par.

Tony began to apply pressure on the back nine shooting his own 33 and narrowed Venturi's lead to a single stroke. Venturi three-putted the final green for his only bogey of the day.

Tony continued his scrambling Sunday in the final round repeatedly making saving pars from unlikely spots. He caught Venturi on the second hole when Venturi bogeyed and he took the lead outright on the fourth after another Venturi bogey. Venturi tied it back up with a birdie on the sixth hole, but Tony got the lead right back with a birdie on the par 3 seventh against yet another bogey by Venturi.

On the ninth hole, Tony's second shot hit a mound and took a huge bounce before ending up on a patch of scratchy grass in front of the pro shop.

"I couldn't loft the ball because there were branches in the way," Tony later explained to reporters. "So, I decided to bounce it along the walk and have it bounce up to the pin. It worked. You need breaks like that on this course or you simply can't win. It's too big."

The crowd following the four players was immense, estimated at 8,000. In the crowd, several teenage girls sported signs that read, "Go Tony, Go!" and "Tony Is The Most."

As Tony and Venturi battled for the title, Palmer looked at Nichols, who also had no chance to win, and said, "What are we doing out here?"

Nichols chuckled and said, "I don't know, but those two guys are playing for $50,000."

The par Tony saved on the ninth hole helped him maintain his lead. He still held it as the players arrived at the fourteenth tee. Tony walked up to the front of the tee, bent over, plucked a few blades of grass from the ground, and tossed them in the air to judge the wind.

A loud spectator asked, "That champagne looks pretty good, eh Tony?"

Tony slowly turned and said quietly, "It don't look too bad."

He socked away the victory on the sixteenth hole when he made birdie and Venturi suffered another bogey. He enjoyed a leisurely stroll down the eighteenth fairway on his way to a $50,000 payday. He shot a 68 beating Venturi by five-strokes. Nichols rebounded from his nightmare 77 in the first round with a steady 70 on Sunday edging Palmer for third place— academic since third and fourth place paid the same amount.

Tony, accompanied by Betty, celebrated with the press, pouring champagne for all.

He informed reporters, "I'm dead tired and I'll play very few tournaments the rest of the year. I've had only four days off since April and I didn't like myself the past two days. I couldn't get up for the Carling Open (two weeks ago) and I really had no desire to play here."

Arnold Palmer then entered the pressroom, glanced at the champagne before asking, "Where's mine?"

After Tony quickly offered a glass, Palmer declined saying, "I don't want any of that stuff. I hate champagne."

He gave Tony a roguish smile and a wink.

"Wait until Uncle Sam gets done with you, you may want to borrow a little from old Arnie," he said nodding towards Tony's check.

Tony received letters, telegrams and phone calls congratulating him on his victory. One call came from Jerry Wright, an official with the Buick Open.

"That was a nice year you had last week," he joked.

Adding his $50,000 in unofficial money to his official earnings brought the total to $122,555. Throw in his other unofficial money won during the year took it to $133,714—and this didn't count what he won in exhibitions. In just the British Open, Bing Crosby National Pro-Am and the World Series of Golf, all unofficial events, Tony won $60,000, more than he had in any year on tour, except for 1963. In fact, his weekend exhibition fee was approaching what he won in official money in 1960.

With his income soaring, Tony began to explore investment opportunities. He began an annuity account for when his playing days were over. He also began looking for vacation property in the mountains northeast of Oakland near Twain Harte Lake.

After his huge payday at the World Series, Tony and Betty headed home for some badly needed rest. They had been in the fast lane all summer long, especially Tony with his trans-Atlantic trip. Plus, he was scheduled to make another in a couple of weeks, to London, to participate in the inaugural Piccadilly World Match Play Championship. On this same trip he would play his scheduled match against Carl Poulson in Copenhagen for *Shell's Wonderful World of Golf*.

While resting in the Bay Area, a testimonial dinner at the San Francisco Golf Club honored Tony. The members bestowed an honorary membership to their former assistant pro, a measure of how far the once unruly teen from the wrong side of the bay had come. He now rubbed shoulders with the titans at the ultra-exclusive club.

After his much too brief break at home, he was off to London for The World Match Play Championship. The new tournament, a brainchild of Mark McCormick, matched eight golfers battling one-on-one in 36-hole matches. The winners of each match advanced while the losers went home. The field was comprised of McCormick's three prized clients, Palmer, Nicklaus and Player, as well as Tony and Venturi. Neil Coles and Peter Butler of England and Bruce Devlin of Australia rounded out the international field.

The west course of the Wentworth Club outside London, known as the "Burma Road" due to its difficult walk through a parkland setting, played host to the new event.

On October 4, Venturi, fresh from being awarded the "Player of the Year" award (Tony finished third in the balloting, behind Nichols, while Palmer finished fourth), and Tony went to New York City. They were in town to appear on the *Ed Sullivan Show*. On the show, Sullivan talked golf with the two national title winners in between acts of Sid Caesar doing comedy, Louis Armstrong performing "Hello Dolly" and Pat Boone singing "Beach Girl." Tony and Venturi boarded a plane for England the next day.

Once he got a look at Wentworth, Tony struggled through his practice round.

"It's all these trees," he complained to the press. "They stick out everywhere."

The bookmakers in the U.K. listed Tony as the favorite.

Tony scoffed at the odds and told reporters, "I hear someone says I am the favorite, but in fact I do not care too much for match play. You hit a few bad ones and you are out the first day. In medal play I figure I always can catch up."

The matches for the first day pitted Tony against Neil Coles, Palmer versus Peter Butler, Venturi would play Player and Nicklaus would take on Bruce Devlin.

Before his first match, Tony spent a fitful night without any sleep. He picked up something that bothered his stomach and the next morning he felt weak. He tried to play, even though he felt lousy, but before he knew what hit him, he was five holes down after just six holes. He battled back, thanks to some good putting, to cut into the lead Coles built up, but could not fight all the way back. The result was a two-down deficit after the first 18 holes.

In addition to feeling poorly, he was up against an opponent who was playing magnificently. In his weakened condition, Tony did not stand a chance and succumbed to Coles 3 and 2.

Palmer won his first match and at the end of the first day, was the only surviving American in the field. Venturi lost his match to Player 4 and 2 and while he returned to the States, Palmer captured the first Piccadilly World Match Play Championship. Tony moved on to Denmark where he met Carl Poulson in the Shell match.

He beat Poulson in the match at Rungstad Golf Club in Denmark. Poulson was one of the few people who Tony met that he did not like.

"He thought he was a jerk; he didn't like that guy," Tony's brother Harry recalled years later.

Tony stayed in Copenhagen for a couple of days, seeing the sights with Betty, before heading back to the Bay Area for some rest.

Meanwhile out on the tour, at the season ending Cajun Classic, both Palmer and Nicklaus staged a battle for the honor of being the top money winner for year. The two normally passed on a tournament this late in the schedule, especially one that offered a meager prize purse the size of the Cajun Classic. In the days before the advent of the FedEx Cup, the money list was the barometer of who was the best player on tour for the year.

Palmer held a slim $319 lead over Nicklaus.

On the final hole, Gay Brewer missed a putt of just over 15-feet that would have given him sole possession of second-place. Instead, he ended up tied with Nicklaus who eked out the money title by a mere $81.13 over his rival, Palmer. If Brewer had made the putt, Nicklaus would have only received third-place money allowing Palmer to capture the top spot on the money list.

Tony finished the year with $74,130 in official earnings, placing him fourth on the money list. At the end of November, Tony pulled out of the Mexican Open citing a shoulder injury. Papers also carried the news he would be making his acting debut in an episode of the *Hazel* show on television. Tony portrayed himself in the typically simple sitcom plot of the times. Hazel loses his golf clubs while he is unaware the clubs are missing. Hilarity ensues while a search is conducted for the clubs before they are eventually found, with Tony none the wiser.

In early December, he told Ed Schoenfeld of *The Oakland Tribune*, that he was spending time at home resting, restricting his sports interests to being an Oakland Raider fan. Tony had attended the most recent game where Art Powell of the Raiders intercepted a pass by Buffalo Bills quarterback Tom Flores as time expired to preserve an upset win.

"Aren't those Raiders something?" Tony asked rhetorically.

He told Schoenfeld he would soon begin work to get ready for the 1965 tour with practice at Lake Chabot, Round Hills, Orinda Country Club and San Francisco Country Club, where he recently received his honorary membership.

Venturi informed reporters that he would like to team with Tony in a challenge match against Palmer and Nicklaus. He proposed a best three out of five series conducted on five different outstanding courses.

"Let us put up $10,000 each and they put up the same," Venturi proposed. "Let television sweeten the pot for perhaps a $100,000 purse and see what happens. I'm sure Lema would be all for it."

Venturi approached Corcoran with the idea of the challenge match. Dutifully, Corcoran sent out feelers to Mark McCormick about the idea. McCormick showed no interest in exposing his prized players to the risks inherent in such a match.

"You think I'm crazy?" Venturi reported McCormick as saying. "I've been building The Big Three. If those two guys beat my guys, I have no case."

McCormick sold his Big Three matches to television where Palmer, Nicklaus and Player played a medal play match between the three of them. He was not about to dilute this television deal, worth a lot of money to the players, as well as McCormick, with a match against Venturi and Tony.

Still, the idea intrigued Roone Arledge, vice president of sports for

ABC Television. He announced to the Associated Press that ABC was willing to offer $25,000 to the winner of a Venturi and Lema challenge match against a team of Palmer and Nicklaus.

In early December, Tony headed out on the rubber chicken circuit. With his ascent into the realms of a superstar, the demands on his time for personal appearances skyrocketed.

"It's getting so I am having breakfast in Los Angeles, lunch in New York and dinner in San Francisco," Tony, only half-jokingly, told an audience at a bank convention in Passaic, New Jersey on the night of December 9. He had appeared at the Boston Golf Writer's dinner the night before.

He also made trips to Los Angeles, where with the help of Danny Arnold, he was attempting to launch an acting career. He filmed the episode of *Hazel*, and while there, signed a contract with Screen Gems to star in a proposed golf show.

As the New Year approached, he went to Palm Springs for the taping of the *CBS Golf Classic*. Held at the La Quinta Country Club, outside of Palm Springs, the *CBS Golf Classic* was a series of two-man best-ball matches that featured a purse of $166,000 with the winning team sharing a $50,000 first prize. Although filmed in black and white, at a time when other shows, specifically *Shell's Wonderful World of Golf*, were switching to color, the CBS series exhibited exciting technological innovations.

These included cameras mounted on cranes and players wired for sound making their discussions and banter available to viewers. Frank Chirkinian, the CBS director of *The CBS Golf Classic* had to keep reminding Tony that he was wearing a microphone. Tony's language oftentimes got quite colorful on the golf course and the microphones were picking up his curses. Taped in December and broadcast in the depths of winter, the show offered sports fans action during a lax time for televised sports.

Tony paired with Bobby Nichols in the 16-team field while Venturi teamed with Souchak.

The PGA, along with *Golf Magazine* released, in their year-end review issue, the inaugural "PGA All-American" team. The team featured a selection of pros that played the different clubs in the bag the best. Tony won a place on the team for his play with the wedge—the one club that he did not use much during the British Open at St. Andrews.

Others selected for the team were Jack Nicklaus for the driver, Gary Player for fairway woods, Arnold Palmer for long irons, Bobby Nichols for mid-irons, Ken Venturi for short irons, Julius Boros for the sand wedge, and Billy Casper for the putter.

On December 17, a banquet in New York honored the eight players with Gene Sarazen, Lloyd Mangrum and Byron Nelson in attendance.

Tony's stardom made him a hot commodity and the Christmas season saw "Tony Lema" balls hit stores. Made by Kroydon, a company that specialized in value-class golf equipment, the balls came packaged with a picture of Tony on the box, while each ball featured his reproduced signature.

J.C. Penney offered a "baker's dozen" of the balls, in a gift box, for $6.88, while other retailers, including Walgreen's, sold a regular dozen for $7.77.

As the year wound down, the Hilton Hotel in Puerto Rico announced a contest with a grand prize of a 30-day round-the-world trip. The trip promised to be special as the Hilton announced Tony, and his wife, would accompany the winner.

It had been quite a year for the man from the wrong side of the tracks in San Leandro. He definitely arrived as a top-echelon player and the proof was in his schedule. With so many endorsements, personal appearances and exhibitions on his plate, it was a wonder he fit in any tournaments. He also had to be careful not to let these extracurricular activities get in the way of his performance on the golf course. He would have to continue his fine play in 1965 to enjoy these fruits of stardom.

30 COLD TURKEY
1965

As the New Year kicked off, Tony went through his usual evaluation of the year just completed and set goals for 1965. He had a magical year in 1964 establishing him as a major star on tour. He had won a major championship, earning comparisons to Arnold Palmer and Jack Nicklaus as the best in the game. His time off the course was in high demand with requests for exhibitions, interviews, personal appearances, and endorsement activities. He filmed television commercials and sat for both advertising and feature story photo shoots. Because of his star status, the Fernquist and Johnson golf clubs that carried his name were selling beyond the company's wildest dreams, as were the clubs endorsed by Ken Venturi.

Tony thought about how best to build on his momentum in 1965 as he began formulating his goals for the new season. For him, winning major titles were what mattered; winning money was nice, but golf history remembers the players with multiple major championships.

His overarching goal for the year was winning the Masters or U.S. Open. He loved everything about the Masters, coveted a green jacket, and he craved the prestige that a U.S. Open victory would garner.

The tour prepared to kick off the new season in Los Angeles at the L.A. Open. Palmer celebrated the New Year as Grand Marshal of the Rose Parade in Pasadena. He rode in a white convertible along with his wife Winnie and their two daughters, Peggy and Amy. Palmer was the first athlete, still active in his profession, to serve as the Grand Marshal for the event. More proof that golf was a major sport in the United States.

Tony played with Danny Arnold as his partner in the pro-am preceding the L.A. Open. No doubt, Mr. Arnold had provided some help in arranging Tony's recently signed contract with Screen Gems. As usual, Betty and Tony stayed with the Arnolds during the week.

Tony enjoyed the relaxed atmosphere at the Arnolds, and he sought to replicate that feeling at the other stops on the tour. With his success of 1964, he could afford to add a personal touch to his peripatetic lifestyle. Instead of staying in hotels and motels, he and Betty rented furnished apartments near the courses used for tournaments. A furnished apartment felt more like a home than a hotel did.

In the apartments, he could enjoy Betty's home cooking while they spent private time together. His new stardom exposed him to the occasional annoying aspects of celebrity, such as unending autograph requests. The couple could no longer go out for a quiet dinner without fans intruding. The apartment allowed the couple some private time away from the public eye.

The Surgeon General released a 387-page report in 1964, titled "Smoking and Health," noting that the average smoker is nine to ten times more likely to get lung cancer than a non-smoker is. The report was widely read and frightened many people into kicking their cigarette habit.

Palmer took Tony aside to have a personal talk with him about his smoking habit. Palmer felt he was finally successful in kicking the habit and wanted Tony to do the same. Tony read the report and it scared him enough to give up his cigarettes. However, as anybody who has tried it knows, overcoming a tobacco addiction is not easy.

Tony found time before the first round of the L.A. Open to speak with Jerry Wynn, a southern California sports writer, about a number of things.

"Do you really enjoy your champagne sessions with the press?" Wynn began the interview.

"Yes," Tony replied, "But it's not the champagne. I love to be interviewed. It gives me a chance to communicate with people. It's a privilege."

"Ken Venturi has challenged Palmer and Nicklaus to a match against you and Venturi. Which team would win?" asked Wynn.

"I certainly think we would. What else can I say? It would be a very good match. The purse and course would be unimportant. I think it's a good challenge," Tony responded.

"If you could trade places with any other athlete, who would it be?" Wynn asked wrapping up the interview.

In typical Tony fashion, he answered, "I'm very happy to be me."

Tony played solidly tying for fourth place earning a check for $3,300 in Los Angeles.

The circuit next headed down to San Diego, and while there, Tony appeared at a banquet promoting the *CBS Golf Classic*.

At the banquet, Frank Chirkinian presented reels of film to each player featuring their matches. He saved Tony's for last finally presenting Tony with a strip of film about two-feet long.

"That's all I could get after I cut all the foul language out," he said as he presented the strip to Tony. Everyone laughed, including Tony who threw his head back and guffawed.

In the San Diego Open, Tony finished at 276, nine-strokes back of Wes Ellis and Casper, who faced each other in a sudden-death playoff won by Ellis.

Tony and the tour next headed to Monterey where he would defend his Crosby title. Tony revealed in *The Oakland Tribune* he planned to move to Dallas immediately following the Lucky International Open the week after the Crosby. He told reporters he would still register on tour from San Leandro as it would make it easier for his mother to forward mail to him.

"I am going to live in Dallas for a year," Tony informed the paper. "But I am a native Oaklander, and believe me, you can't take Oakland out of Tony Lema."

Tony cited business reasons, unrelated to golf, for the move, indicating he planned to invest in oil.

"I'm not going to try to strike oil digging big divots with my wedge," Tony joked. "I have some close friends in Dallas in the oil business I plan to become associated with."

Even though Betty was happy in the Bay Area, she was in favor of the move to Dallas, which she knew so well having lived there when she was a flight attendant. Travel for the couple would be much easier from the centrally located city and that had as much to do with the decision as business reasons did.

"This won't be permanent," Tony assured Ed Schoenfeld. "I'm coming back to Oakland."

It did not matter where Tony set up his home base because the road was his real home.

He turned his attention to the state of his game going into his defense of the Crosby.

"I am hitting the ball almost as well as I was last year at this time. You've got to drive the ball real good to win here. If I do the same this year, I think I will have a good chance to win."

In the first round, on the Cypress Point course, Tony had a 71.

"I'm playing good, especially from tee to green," Tony insisted while recounting his round for reporters. "I didn't feel I putted too good. That's where I think I laid down the most."

He caught fire in the second round. Playing the new Shore Course at the Monterey Country Club, used for the first time in the Crosby, Tony got his hot round off to a fast start. His four-wood approach to the first hole resulted in a two-foot tap-in for birdie and he then birdied five more holes on the front nine. He offset his one bogey on the back nine with a birdie. His 65 was a new course record, and his 136 after two rounds was leading. Don Massangale tied his course record less than two hours later.

"Boys," Tony said to the press, "if this were only Sunday I'd buy you twice the champagne you got last year."

He understood, better than most, a lead in the Crosby does not count for much, especially if you have yet to play Pebble Beach, the most difficult of the three courses. Moreover, the weather could turn nasty without notice on the coast at Monterey.

"There is no way to play it safe," Tony declared about Pebble Beach. "I'll just play it the way I always do—which ain't so good sometimes," he chuckled.

Tony, again paired with Father Durkin, could not help but poke some fun at his amateur partner.

"If Father Durkin doesn't start putting better, he'll have to get a new altar boy," Tony joked.

Tony was attempting to become the first player to defend the Crosby since Dr. Cary Middlecoff did it in 1955-56. The famous Crosby weather returned for the third round as rain and strong winds buffeted the courses. The weather blew Tony off his game.

Things went downhill in a hurry as he shot a 41 on the front nine. He began to make up ground with birdies on the eleventh and thirteenth holes, but it all went to hell on the sixteenth hole.

His second shot on the 375-yard par 4 hole hit a tree and the ball ricocheted into a ditch. He eventually wound up with a nasty double-bogey. On the seventeenth hole, a 218-yard par 3, he missed the green and then pitched into a bunker—another double-bogey.

On the famous finishing hole at Pebble Beach, Tony managed to coax in a six-foot putt for birdie. When the putt dropped, he playfully threw his arms over his head in a mock celebration for breaking 80.

After his round, Tony again met with the press and was in a jovial mood considering the round he had just endured.

"I'm three shots off the lead. That's kind of unusual for someone who has just shot a 79," Tony observed. "Has anyone ever won a tournament after shooting a 79?"

He admitted he was grinding on the final hole.

"I was really sweating out that eighteenth hole. It was a personal thing with me because I haven't shot an 80 in a long time."

The last time Tony failed to break 80 was back in May of 1964 in the first round of the Tournament of Champions.

Somebody commented that Tony appeared to be laughing coming down the eighteenth fairway.

"I wasn't laughing," Tony corrected, "I was crying."

However, he was laughing—he was joking with the gallery as he made his way through the wind and rain.

"This was the worst weather I've played in since St. Andrews," Tony said. "You don't mind if I get a plug in for the British Open, do you—after shooting a 79?"

When he was through with the reporters, he went to the practice tee to try to recapture the swing that had resulted in a course record the day before. Tony did not often go to the practice tee after a round, but he felt he needed work as he was still in contention, despite his 79.

Rocky Thompson, a tour rookie, held the lead after shooting a 68 on the Monterey course for a three round 212 while Tony was at 215. Thompson completed his round before the worst of the winds started to blow.

The weather conditions wrecked havoc on the third round scores; Bobby Nichols posted a 90, while Walter Burkemo shot an embarrassing 92. The wind, clocked at 50 miles an hour, blew so hard that sand blown out of the bunkers covered the eighteenth green.

Tony stood in the rain after his practice session and happily signed autographs.

"You've got to be an idiot to smile after nearly shooting an 80," he wryly observed.

As usual, on Sunday, before his final round, Tony attended Mass and he again served as Father Durkin's altar boy (Father Durkin's putting must have improved).

Bruce Crampton received help from Jack Nicklaus on the practice tee prior to the start of the tournament, and utilized what he learned to shoot a blistering final round of 69. Tony shot a final round 72 and finished in second-place, three-strokes behind Crampton.

The turning point in the round, in Tony's mind, came at the fourteenth hole where he faced a four-foot uphill putt.

"I had one big opportunity on the fourteenth and didn't make it," Tony recalled. "Bruce had bogeyed the hole and if I had made my putt I would have been just one shot back. Then I had real good birdie putts on the sixteenth, seventeenth and eighteenth and didn't make a one. All of a sudden, my putting got awfully cold. I'll tell you, if I had made one or two of those putts it would have been a real ball game."

His second place finish was worth $4,000 in unofficial money and this was his eighth finish of ninth or better in the last 12 tournaments he played.

After his round, he found time to dash off a hand-written letter to Sister Mary Martin Bush at St. Elizabeth High School. An inveterate letter writer, he kept up a correspondence with Sister Bush who had informed him, in a previous letter, about the death of another Sister at St. Elizabeth.

I was very sorry to hear about Sister Mary, he wrote. *I sometimes believe that death is the best thing that can happen to people, if they are at peace with God.*
I didn't fare too well the last day of the Crosby tournament, but that is the way it goes. Please keep your fingers crossed for me this week in the Lucky International here in San Francisco.

Before the Lucky, Murray Olderman featured Tony in his syndicated column "Between You 'n' Me."

"I'm a goof off, I'm not really a serious person," Tony informed Olderman and his readers.

Olderman was interviewing Tony while he was receiving a massage at the Executive Suite in La Cienga. Olderman noted that Tony had a tattoo on his left calf, another, a Marine Corps slogan, on his left arm and another one, "Tony," on his right bicep.

"We're fortunate enough to be in a profession where the winners make a lot of money," Tony remarked. "You know, I could have been a long-haired musician who doesn't make a whole lot of money. I really enjoy what I'm doing."

Bill Hunter in his "Highlightin' Sports" column in the Burlington, North Carolina *Daily Times-News* wrote, "Jack Nicklaus and Arnold Palmer make the money, but Tony Lema has the devil-may-care attitude that is going to make him the galleries' choice of the nation."

At the Lucky, Tony was involved in a bizarre incident on the twelfth hole during the first round. He sliced his drive into the trees that lined the right side of the par 5 hole and the ball remained stuck up in a tree. After searching in vain from the ground for the ball, in order to identify it, Tony was about to return to the tee and take a stroke-and-distance penalty for a lost ball.

However, John Dugan, a supervisor of production at a San Leandro breakfast food plant, came to the rescue. He climbed the tree, up about 30-feet, under the direction of Tony and his caddy from the ground. He finally located the ball and dropped it down to Tony. Tony could now take an unplayable lie and thereby save a stroke, but wound up taking a double-bogey on the hole and finished his round with a 73, tied with defending champion Chi-Chi Rodriguez.

"The only other one who could have got up there would have had to be Tarzan," observed Tony after his round referring to Dugan.

Dugan's tree climbing act drew a great deal of attention from the press. The incident made Dugan a celebrity, of sorts, at least for a day or two. He was asked why he would take such a risk for a man he had to pay $3 to watch play.

"We in San Leandro believe in working together," he simply stated.

Tony gave Dugan a sleeve of new balls for his troubles and Dugan posed for newspaper photographers displaying the gift.

Usually hatless, Tony wore an Oakland Raiders ball cap at the Lucky. He was becoming a rabid fan of the Raiders and considered many of the players as friends. In fact, his circle of friends was starting to include many of the rich and famous; he gave golf lessons to Ted Williams, befriended actor Phil Harris and hung out with Archie Matsos, a linebacker for the Raiders.

Tony had a miserable second round shooting a 77 and missed the cut. He turned the front nine in 37 and came home in 40—with a missed eight-inch putt. He carelessly backhanded a short putt on the eleventh hole and ended up with a double-bogey.

Discouraged, he changed his moving plans to Dallas after he missed the cut. He intended to make the move immediately following the tournament, but after his poor play, he decided to move on to Palm Springs and work on his game. He badly needed a dose of Danny Arnold's wisdom, and he wanted to be ready for the next tournament, the Bob Hope Desert Classic. He planned to return to Oakland following the Hope to make the move to Dallas.

Things did not go much better for him in the Hope as he finished in a tie for 40th. His game had suddenly deserted him. He wanted to get his swing, and his confidence, back before the Masters.

Golf fans were already getting excited about the Masters, still two months away. Oscar Fraley wrote a syndicated article that centered on Tony's strategy for playing in the Masters.

"Putting is the key at Augusta," Tony informed Fraley. "Sure, you have to play your irons with finesse and the five-par holes can make or break you. But, putting is the determining factor."

Tony underscored the need for accurate iron play at Augusta National.

"You can't be too erratic with your irons because those greens are monsters. There are places you can put it on the green where you easily can three, or even, four-putt. You have to get it near the hole with your approach because the greens are so large and undulating. They are also smooth and fast. At Augusta, you can hit every green in regulation and still shoot yourself an 82 without any trouble."

His lackluster play continued the next week at the Phoenix Open. His rounds of 73-71-70-70 put him into a tie for 15th and a check of $660.

The next week at the Tucson Open, he caught fire in the pro-am before the tournament shooting a course record 64. He ran off a string of six straight birdies in his record round as his putter came alive. He carded a 29 on the back nine.

"They had the pins in easy places today. The course will play a lot more difficult tomorrow," Tony assured reporters. "I really can't understand what happened. My putter's been pretty cold up until now. I just hope I can keep it warm."

In the first round of the tournament, his putter did remain warm—until the last two holes. He put on a charge going six-under in the first sixteen holes, but then threw it away with three-putts on both the seventeenth and eighteenth holes. Still though, he was able to post a 68 that was three-strokes off the leader Bob Charles.

He finished the tournament with mediocre rounds of 72-71-73 to finish well down the leader board in a tie for 21st and a check for $575. To add insult to injury, Don January shot a 63 in the final round to eclipse Tony's short-lived course record.

After Tucson, he took a break from the tour to complete the move to Dallas. However, he did find time to visit New York City celebrating, with Betty, his 31st birthday at a midtown Manhattan hotel. The couple, joined by a small gathering of friends, and an Associated Press photographer, celebrated with cake, and of course, champagne. He also sent his mother 31 roses, a birthday tradition he started when he first went out on tour. He sent her the same number of roses as his age every birthday.

While in New York, he sat down with Will Grimsley of the Associated Press to talk about his game. He blamed his current slump on the effects he was feeling from giving up cigarettes.

"I quit cigarettes about two months ago, at the insistence of Arnold Palmer," Tony said. "And I'm having one heck of a time. I've put on about ten pounds, most of it around my waist. I can't sleep. I'm nasty to myself on the course. Until I can get adjusted to the change, my golf is bound to suffer, but I expect to have it whipped in another month. I should be okay for the Masters."

Grimsley inquired about his thoughts concerning the 1965 tour to date. The reporter pointed out that lesser-known players won all the tournaments while the stars of the tour, Palmer, Nicklaus and Tony, had yet to notch a victory.

"We've got a lot of youngsters on the tour who are going to be tough," Tony stated. "I regard Casper as the most underrated player in the game. He's always in there, scoring well and making money, but getting little attention."

Tony then made a prediction for the remainder of the year.

"By June the money list will be jumping around like a rock 'n' roll dancer."

Tony revealed that he was going to take it easy, only playing in the Greater Greensboro Open prior to the Masters. He also said he would defend his titles from the previous summer, including the Thunderbird Classic.

"I want to work on my game, and I want to kick this smoking habit," he said. "I don't see any point in going around buying lung cancer. I'm going to let young athletes know how lousy cigarettes are. I think everybody in sports ought to do the same," he said exhibiting the born-again conviction of a reformed smoker.

The topic of conversation turned to the U.S.G.A and the announcement that they would be abandoning the traditional 36-hole final day of the U.S. Open. Perhaps Venturi's near physical collapse in the 1964 U.S. Open at Congressional influenced their decision. More likely, the lure of the additional television revenues that a Sunday finish would provide made the move irresistible.

"I think the U.S.G.A. made a mistake in cutting out the double round on the final day of the U.S. Open," Tony stated. "The 36-holes on Saturday was the one feature that distinguished the Open from other tournaments."

Grimsley then asked Tony if he wished Palmer would not play in the Masters.

"It wouldn't be as much fun winning it," he answered.

The move to Dallas, completed in early March, had Tony and Betty settling into a suburban Dallas apartment. He would grow to love the Dallas area, Betty's hometown, and the two were very happy there. In Dallas, she was close to friends, many of whom were flight attendants and she enjoyed the shopping at the department stores she knew so well. This made it easier for her on those few occasions when she stayed at home while Tony traveled.

"Dallas is booming and it's going to keep growing," Tony told the Associated Press. "I want to be a part of it. Besides, my wife lived here for two years and she likes the place."

Newspaper ads for department stores were frequently displaying Tony Lema clothing for sale. Levy Brothers, with three locations in Burlingame, San Mateo, and Redwood City in the Bay Area, ran a display ad with drawings that advertised a "Tony Lema Gaucho" shirt. The ad copy details the shirt as being for "on or off course wear. Combed cotton knit that is machine washable. Tapered cut with extra long rear tail. Embroidered champagne glass on the pocket is the Tony Lema signature."

Ironically, one of the drawings shows the model smoking a cigarette.

Another ad, for a different store, advertised "Tony Lema Slacks by Palm Beach" selling for $12.95. These slacks featured a color coordinated cloth belt.

With all the interviews that Tony was doing, as well as the frequent advertisements he was in, it was clear that Corcoran was doing a good job representing him. At about this same time Fred Corcoran added Bobby Nichols to his stable of clients. Nichols was a frequent partner of Tony's practice round matches, as well as the television matches that featured two-man teams. The two first became friends when Tony met Nichols at a Mass at church when the younger Nichols first came out on tour.

After spending time with Nichols, Tony called his sister Bernice and told her about a conversation he and Nichols had. Tony related to Nichols how he used to get out of washing dishes when he was a kid because he needed to protect his hands for golf.

"Oh, that worked for you, too?" Nichols replied.

Both Tony and Bernice laughed about the story. Once out on tour, Tony purchased a dishwasher for his mother to compensate for ducking out on the dishwashing duties as a kid.

After completing the move to Dallas, Tony returned to Oakland for the baptism of a new nephew, his brother Harry and wife Judi's son, Roger, who was born on February 3. Ed Schoenfeld caught up with Tony for an interview that ran in *The Oakland Tribune*. Tony predicted to Schoenfeld that Casper would have a great year.

"Casper is playing like heck," Tony stated. "He is off to a flying start."

Schoenfeld asked him to make a prediction about his year but Tony demurred saying, "I like to do something before I talk about it."

He then elaborated, "I think my game will be all right. But I'm not playing real good now. I'm still not putting good enough. I am still not smoking and I feel good. I've gained about 12 pounds and am up to 190. I think it will be a good playing weight for me."

From Oakland he went to Las Vegas to appear at a meeting of executives of the Kaiser Aluminum and Chemicals Company. He also kept a full schedule of exhibitions. As one can see by this schedule, Tony's idea of "taking it easy" still kept him busy.

Moreover, he would get busier. He informed Schoenfeld that he had three trips abroad planned; a match for *Shell's Wonderful World of Golf*, another for the defense of his British Open title, and the around-the-world tour in November for the Hilton Hotel contest.

He rejoined the tour for the Greater Greensboro Open. He started with a 71 and followed up with a mediocre 74 in the second round. Sam Snead, just shy of his 53rd birthday, held the halfway lead as he attempted to win his eighth Greater Greensboro Open title.

Tony made a comeback in the third round shooting a 68, a score matched by Snead who continued to lead the tournament. In the fourth round, Tony again played well shooting a 67 and after he signed his scorecard, he stood by the large leader board near the eighteenth green signing autographs. He glanced up at the scoreboard and just shook his head in amazement.

"If Snead goes on to win this thing, he isn't a golfer anymore—he's a legend," Tony stated. "This is simply fantastic."

Snead was on the fourteenth hole at the time clinging to his lead while Tony continued to talk with a few reporters. Snead then rallied with a barrage of birdies coming down the stretch to win by five strokes.

Tony, along with the other fortunate invitees, now focused on the year's first major, the Masters at Augusta National. Tony arrived in Augusta for the enchanted week the Masters always promised, yet he did not feel as if he had the magic touch.

"I'm playing so bad I almost wish I wasn't here," Tony informed Milton Richman of the United Press International. "I remember my first time here very well. I was so awed by this place that I was nervous as a cat. Now I'm not nervous at all, but I wouldn't give a nickel for my chances. My game is simply terrible. Which part? Only from tee to green."

He laughed hollowly after he said this but his true feelings became apparent.

"My spirits are so low that I don't even think you could place a ball marker under them," he went on. "I haven't won a tournament since last August and I'm starting to wonder whether I'll ever win another one again."

He did not want to fall into the trap of pressing too hard for a tournament victory. He knew he had to remain patient, but the state of his game made that difficult. Patience was never his strong suit.

He played a practice round with Gary Player and then another one with Arnold Palmer. As he and Palmer finished the first nine, Palmer headed over to the tenth tee. Tony suddenly announced he was quitting and would not finish the round.

"What's the matter, you sick?" asked Palmer.

Tony took a deep breath and said, "If you were driving the way I've been, you'd be sick, too."

Instead of playing the back nine, he spent a lengthy time on the practice tee attempting to discover what was wrong with his swing. He did not find a magic cure and left the practice tee discouraged, lacking confidence as the start of the tournament loomed.

He was asked who he thought would win. As usual, the press named Palmer and Nicklaus as the favorites, but Tony disagreed. He thought Billy Casper had a good chance to win.

"He's playing, by far, the best golf," Tony said about his fellow Californian. "Everybody's talking about Nicklaus and Palmer, but they'd better leave some room for Casper. He'd be my choice in this thing."

He did not feel confident about his own chances.

"My timing is way off," Tony complained. "I really can't put my finger on it but I just don't feel as good and solid as I should. I get a laugh when people ask me what I think of my chances in this one. Not much. Not much at all. Unless maybe lightning strikes and I suddenly come around. I'm not kidding myself, though. I'm way off my game and I'd be the most surprised individual in the state of Georgia if I did well here."

Queue the lightning. The playing conditions were excellent for the first round with temperatures in the 80s, and the course was dry. The scores during the first day reflected the perfect conditions as 33 players broke par—a Masters record. The previous record, set in 1958, was 11. Tony bogeyed the eighteenth hole but was still able to post a fine 67. His round included a run of birdies from the eighth hole to the eleventh hole before he bogeyed the treacherous par 3, twelfth hole. He bounced right back with an eagle on the par 5 thirteenth, where his drive left him with just a 175-yard second shot. His bogey on the finishing hole was the result of a three-putt.

Tony met with the press and said, with tongue in cheek, "Well, it was a very uneventful day."

In the pressroom Tony laughed, "I was disgusted when I went to bed last night, disgusted when I woke up, and disgusted when I teed off. After I got those first couple of birdies I forgot all about my troubles."

One of the reporters asked Tony how he now felt, to which he quickly snapped, "Disgusted!" but his grin gave him away.

"Well, you can't feel too happy finishing a round with a bogey, can you?" he asked. "I'll admit I got a little antsy there on eighteen, I wanted a birdie, or at least a par, to finish six-under-par, and I three-putted from 30-feet."

A reporter asked him if he was still using the putter that Palmer had given him.

"Well, for the 9,999th time, the answer is yes and he's not going to get it back," Tony answered.

Player, who rejoined the tour after a lengthy period spent with his family, shot a first round 65, the second lowest opening round in Masters history. Nicklaus, with a 67, and Palmer with a 70 rounded out "The Big Three's" representation near the top of the leader board.

The old guard of the PGA Tour was doing well, also; Ben Hogan shot a 71, as did Jimmy Demaret and 53-year-old Byron Nelson trumped them both with a 70.

Gusty winds, up to 30 miles an hour, arrived in the second round turning the greens slick. The lords of Augusta also exacted revenge for the low first round scores by placing the flagsticks in much tougher locations. Only four players broke par in the second round while eight others managed to match it.

Player slumped to a 73 for a 36-hole 138 but still retained a stake to the lead, tied with both Nicklaus and Palmer. Palmer shot a 68 in the second round while Nicklaus came in with a 71.

Tony got his second round off to a hot start by chipping in on the first hole for a birdie and followed up with nine straight pars. He actually worked himself into a tie for the lead as he approached the thirteenth tee. He hit a big drive and then a good two-iron short of Rae's Creek that guards the front of the green. The hole played into the wind making this par

5 unreachable in two shots and Tony faced a little pitch over the creek.

George Lake, the head pro at the Long Beach Recreation Park golf course was watching the action and later wrote an account for the *Long Beach Independent Press-Telegram* newspaper.

"Lema had a chance to take the lead, but made what I thought was a foolish gamble which cost him a double bogey on the par 5 thirteenth. Tony tried to hit it stiff and it went into the creek."

He wound up shooting a disappointing 73, but with the scores soaring in the second round, he was still in the thick of the battle, just two off the lead.

The elder statesmen in the tournament also struggled in the windy conditions. Hogan shot a 75 and was at 146, as was Demaret who shot a 75 while Nelson was hanging tough at 144 after a second round 74.

In the third round, Nicklaus grabbed the tournament by the throat shooting a fantastic 64. On a windless, 72-degree day, he negotiated Augusta National without any bogeys and his 202 total for 54-holes was the lowest in the tournament's history. He enjoyed a five-stroke cushion over Player, who shot a 69, while Palmer faced a whopping eight-stroke deficit to make up in order to catch the Golden Bear.

Tony's game completely collapsed under the weight of a faulty putter and he soared to a 77. His rash of bogeys included three in a row at one point.

After Nicklaus labeled the round, "the finest I ever shot," Reporters informed Nicklaus he had a chance to break Ben Hogan's tournament record of 274.

"I only want to win," he responded. "I'm not interested in records or wide margins. I'll be happy to win by a shot."

Even so, he coasted to victory the next day, and set a new scoring record of 271 in the process. His margin of victory was nine-strokes over both Palmer and Player who finished at 280. Tony shot a 74 in the final round finishing in a tie for 21st, good for a check of $1,200. However, the money did not assuage his feeling of disappointment in his performance at his favorite tournament.

Palmer slipped the green jacket over Nicklaus's massive shoulders at the traditional ceremony on the putting green at Augusta. He declared Nicklaus's performance as, "the greatest tournament performance in all golfing history."

All of the televised golf that Sunday suffered the same fate as the Masters, as far as drama was concerned. Just as Nicklaus had tucked away the title, for all practical purposes, before the cameras focused in on the fourth round action at Augusta, the same occurred in the filmed *CBS Golf Classic*. Tony and his partner Bobby Nichols were seven down to Bruce Devlin and Bob Charles as they teed off for the final 18 holes of the 36-

hole final.

"We played well," Nichols recently recalled. "We just ran into a buzz saw. Devlin and Charles just played fantastic."

The players wore microphones and it was easy to pick up Tony's quips to Nichols.

"This will go down as the day that they showed every shot on every hole, get in every commercial, and still had to stretch to fill the hour's time," Tony laughed.

Tony and Nichols went down in defeat in a lopsided final match, but still won $10,000 each while Charles and Devlin took home $25,000 apiece.

After the Masters, Tony returned to San Leandro to visit Cleo who was recuperating at Doctor's Hospital after a successful operation to remove a tumor from her neck. While in town, Tony signed a contract to become a business partner of Jack Vincent in his San Leandro Travel Bureau.

"Tony has been my most loyal customer," Vincent informed Phil Smith, the reporter for the *Daily Review*.

The paper ran a picture in its edition the next day showing Tony about to pop the cork on a bottle of Moet champagne to celebrate the signing.

Whenever he was in San Leandro, he held court at either Vincent's travel agency or at Augie Benitas's clothing store. He would usually gather his long-time friends, including Leo Moschetti, Chet Smith and Bill Craig, and he would invite a local reporter along, as well.

While Tony was at the agency, Vincent's secretary was busy making his travel arrangements. His schedule for the next ten days was extremely full. After departing San Leandro, his stops included Dallas, New York, Washington D.C., North Carolina, Miami, Puerto Rico and Las Vegas. Also on his itinerary, but not arranged through Vincent's travel service, was a trip to Greece for a *Shell's Wonderful World of Golf* match against Roberto DeVincenzo. Shell handled the travel arrangements to Greece for Tony and a companion.

Smith asked Tony if his busy schedule and fast pace was "getting him down."

"No, I've come to really love it," Tony answered. "The faster I go, the better I like it."

It was true that he liked the constant traveling. He never liked to be in one place for too long a stretch. Nevertheless, Smith noted in his article that, "Lines are beginning to show on Tony's tanned face and flecks of gray are noticeable in his hair."

The conversation turned to his game and he noted, "I'm practicing more than ever."

He then pantomimed a golf backswing.

"It's somewhere between here and here," he said as he made his downswing. "And whatever I'm doing wrong, it's making me come out wrong here," he pointed out as he completed his follow through

"But don't worry;" he said reassuringly, "I'm getting it straightened out."

Moschetti, visiting with his friend at the agency, felt that Tony was the one doing the worrying.

"The TV cameras stayed on you for quite a while Saturday in the Masters," Moschetti said. "And never once did I see you smile. You shouldn't look so serious; people expect you to be smiling and carefree."

Tony quickly retorted, "How can you be anything else but serious when you're in the process of shooting a 77?"

Smith asked Tony about the around-the-world trip in November and wondered if it was a vacation.

"No, it's no vacation; it's work all the way," Tony said.

The around-the-world trip was a new promotion conducted by the Dorado Hilton in Puerto Rico. Each week of the winter season, amateurs staying at the hotel for seven nights or more could compete in a 54-hole tournament, using their full handicap. The winners of the weekly tournament would be flown back to play the Dorado Hilton Hotel and Country Club course in late April for a "Grand Tourney," the winner awarded the globetrotting trip.

Accompanying the winner as travel companions would be Tony and Betty. Stops would include stays at Hilton hotels in London, Paris, Rotterdam, Berlin, Rome, Istanbul, Athens, Tel Aviv, Teheran, Hong Kong, Tokyo and Honolulu. The runner-up in the "Grand Tourney" would receive a ten-day vacation for two at the Kahala Hilton in Hawaii.

When Corcoran first approached Tony with the idea of the promotion, it did not appeal to him.

"What do I want to do that for?" he asked. "I already spend all my time on an airplane, the last thing I need is to spend more time flying around the world."

Corcoran then informed Tony how much the Hilton was going to pay to which Tony quickly said, "I'll do it."

While in the Bay Area, Tony also found time to talk with George Roos of the *Oakland Tribune*.

He succinctly summed up his Masters performance by saying, "The tournament was finished on Sunday. I was finished on Friday."

Near the end of April Corcoran informed the press that Tony might soon appear in movies, possibly playing himself in a film story of his life. Roos asked him about his future in films.

"If they ask me to play Tarzan," Tony laughed, "they'd have to paste on some shoulder muscles and use a taped yell, but I'd try."

After his busy schedule of exhibitions and personal appearances, he finally got back to tournament golf with the Tournament of Champions in Las Vegas. He was never a threat and a fourth round 77, during 35 mile an hour winds, was a disappointment. He finished in fifteenth place, good for a check of $1,500, but his game was still not up to his expectations.

He prepared for the trip to Greece to play in the *Shell's Wonderful World of Golf* match. His companion for the trip would be Archie Matsos, the center linebacker and defensive captain of the Oakland Raiders. Matsos would serve as "caddy and interpreter" as he spoke Greek. Tony would actually use a local caddy during the match but would need his friend to interpret the caddy's advice.

Before he left for Greece, he admitted to reporters that he was smoking again.

"I'll soon be back smoking a half-pack before breakfast," Tony told Tommy Hart, a writer for *The Daily Herald* in Big Spring, Texas. "The first thing I do when I open my eyes is to light one, and the last thing I do before I turn off the light is extinguish one."

31 DEFENDING TITLES
1965

In Late April, Tony met Roberto De Vincenzo at the Glyfada Golf Club in Athens, Greece in a *Shell's Wonderful World of Golf* match. It was apropos for these two to face off on the show as they both possessed undefeated Shell records. This was Tony's third appearance on the show while De Vincenzo was playing his fourth.

De Vincenzo made more appearances on the show than any other player. The reason was twofold: He was a perfect player for the international matches providing a foreign presence as an adversary against the usually American pro, and he exhibited a fantastic sense of humor delivered in broken English with a Latin accent.

The course was located next to the main airport in Athens and featured tight fairways lined with trees and grainy greens. The fairways featured grass imported from Canada. A church, located in the middle of the course, added a quant touch to the layout.

The imported grass was not doing well in the heat of the Grecian summer. It turned brown and with the match filmed in color, the producers of the show were concerned about its appearance. Eventually, they decided to dress up Mother Nature. The producers rented a crop-duster, filled the tanks with green paint, and sprayed the course. In the end, it looked great on camera, however, the players contended with some less than perfect lies.

Gene Sarazen and George Rogers again hosted the show, and introduced the players. Tony then called, and lost the coin flip to determine who would tee off first.

"I'm already one down," he joked.

The two players traded the lead back-and-forth before Tony grasped control of the match. They made the turn with Tony shooting a two-under 34 and De Vincenzo shooting an even par 36. However, Tony started to struggle on the greens. He was hitting good putts but they lipped out or stopped just shy of the hole. After a 25-foot putt on the sixteenth caught the lip, and stayed out of the cup, Tony walked over to Rogers and Sarazen. Sarazen commented on how close he came to making the putt.

"Aw, it wasn't even close, Gene," he said sarcastically.

Everybody laughed, including Tony even though he was frustrated.

The players arrived at the seventeenth hole all even.

On the seventeenth, his luck on the greens took a turn for the better. After De Vincenzo made an impossible recovery shot onto the green from the trees, Tony holed a 45-foot putt across the green. After the ball disappeared into the hole, he threw his hands up into the air and broke out into a wide smile. He took a one-stroke lead in the match into the final hole.

De Vincenzo lashed a powerful drive, approximately 300-yards, right down the middle of the fairway. He was out driving Tony, who was a long hitter, all day, because he was using the small British ball. Tony hit his drive into the rough on the right side and then dug his ball out of a bad lie onto the back of the green.

De Vincenzo hit a six-iron to 35-feet and two putted for his 68. Tony lagged his putt to two-feet from the hole and then he tapped-in for a 67 and the victory. He earned $7,000 for the win.

After the match was completed, a filmed tip from Tony showed amateurs how to maintain a firm left side during the swing.

Upon his return to the states, Archie Matsos of the Oakland Raiders, Tony's travelling companion, spoke about the trip with Jack Smith of the *Hayward Daily Review*.

"People don't realize that when Tony is not actually competing in a tournament, he's flying to or from an exhibition appearance—it's part of the life," he explained. "The filming itself took the entire day. We left New York on Monday and Tony flew back that Friday, so it didn't leave him much time."

Matsos, serving as Tony's interpreter, proved his worth acting as a go-between with Tony's local caddy. After the two were well into their trip, however, Tony asked him what kind of press they were getting in the local papers.

"How should I know?" said Matsos, who could speak the language but was unable to read it. "It's all Greek to me."

After returning from Greece, Tony returned to the tour at the Colonial National Invitational where he finished in a tie for third. He won a check for $5,100 and jumped into the 16th place on the money list. The next week, in the Greater New Orleans Open, he withdrew after rounds of 73 and 69 when back pain caused him to quit after nine holes of the third round.

"This is just my luck," Tony lamented to reporters. "If there ever was a course I thought I could play, this is it."

"I don't think it's anything serious," he speculated. "I believe it was caused mainly by sleeping on soft beds. I'll let a doctor look at it. I'll get a hard bed and I think I'll be all right in a couple of days. I definitely will be ready for the Open."

At the end of the month, in the 500 Festival tournament he overcame a first round 75, finishing with a pair of 69s on the weekend, to finish in a tie for twelfth place.

As the calendar turned to June, Tony prepared for the defense of the titles he had won the summer before. First up was the Buick Open at Warwick Hills near Detroit. Betty remained at the apartment in Dallas while Tony played in the Buick. This tournament offered twice the prize purse for the 1965 event than was offered in 1964. The winner would also receive, for their personal use, two brand-new cars every year for the next five years. Tony won the use of a single car the year before as the 1964 winner. The champion would also win an opal for his wife. Television revenues helped fuel the increase in prize money that was now up for grabs.

With the arrival of summer, the tour again reverted to the use of local boys as caddies replacing the regular tour caddies. Max Winters, who caddied for Tony for the first time at the 1962 Western Open at Medinah in Chicago, made his annual pilgrimage to the summer tour to work for Tony.

They usually finagled with the caddy master to assure that Winters carried Tony's bag, but they were not always successful. At the Buick, they were unable to make the connection, so Tony provided the teenager with an inside-the-ropes pass. He walked all four rounds with Tony providing moral support whenever he could.

An unknown pro from Indianola, Iowa, Steve Spray, captured the first round lead with a four-under-par 68. Then, a few hours after he sank his last putt, Spray received his college diploma in absentia. Boros was one back and Nicklaus was two off the lead. Only 11 players managed to break par, Tony among them with a 71.

In the second round, Boros, with the aid of a holed-out bunker shot on the eighth hole, propelled himself into the lead at 139 after a second round 70. He enjoyed a two-stroke cushion over Tony, Nicklaus, Player, Bert Weaver, Doug Sanders and the first round leader, Spray.

In the third round, Tony found himself in trouble all day but used razor-sharp putting to recover. He managed to scramble to a 69 and took over the lead, by one, over Boros, Nicklaus and Pott. In Tony's view, Nicklaus was the biggest threat.

Huge crowds, estimated at over 20,000, paid their $1 admission fee that included free parking. Independent television stations broadcast the last two rounds. Calling the action were John Derr, Jimmy Demaret, Jim McArthur, Bob Toski, and Ken Coleman.

Tony spoke to the assembled press about the pressure of leading.

"I looked at the scoreboard a couple of times on the back nine but it was more out of curiosity than anything else," He asserted. "I wasn't pressing. I save that for Sunday."

Spray found out about the pressure of leading firsthand as he finally succumbed to the pressure with a 78 in the third round. At the end of the afternoon, storm clouds stacked up over Warwick Hills, threatening rain for the fourth round. Certainly, it would rain during the night softening the greens and setting up ideal scoring conditions, provided the rain dissipated by the start of play.

The rain did stop before the leaders teed off. As Tony thought it would, the tournament boiled down to a head-to-head battle between him and Nicklaus. He continued his scrambling, from the day before, making a birdie on the fourth hole with a holed bunker shot. He had already posted birdies on the first two holes and would add birdies at the seventh and tenth holes. He built his lead to four-strokes by the time he approached the tee at the fifteenth hole. He then promptly bogeyed the hole.

Nicklaus, playing with Tony, mounted a charge. He made a long putt for birdie on sixteen and sank another good putt on the seventeenth to save par. After a par on sixteen, Tony bunkered his approach on the seventeenth. He faced a terrible lie behind a rock that forced him to play out sideways. The resulting bogey left him with only a one-stroke cushion as the players walked through the crowd and onto the eighteenth tee. The scene was both electric and tense. Winters proved his worth to Tony who needed help on the tee.

"I'm shaking, man," Tony admitted to Winters.

"Well, say a Hail Mary," Winters advised Tony.

Winters could then see Tony fingering a relic of St. Martin medal he recently received as a gift from Sister Mary Martin of St. Elizabeth. He mouthed the Hail Mary, a traditional Catholic prayer that asks for the intercession of the Virgin Mary. Tony said his prayer as Nicklaus, who had the honors, prepared to hit his tee shot.

What happened next stunned the crowd around the tee and lining the fairway. Nicklaus hit a wild, high hook heading out-of-bounds; he whipped his head around in disgust, not wanting to watch the flight of the errant ball.

The players were not sure if the shot was out-of-bounds or not, so Tony decided to play his shot safe. He hit his tee shot well off to the right into an adjacent fairway.

Nicklaus's ball was, indeed, out-of-bounds. Upon learning of this, Tony took his time, walking up the fairway to the green to inspect the scoreboard to discern exactly where he stood. He saw that Pott was in the clubhouse with a 282 and a bogey or better would win the tournament.

He returned to his ball and hit his second shot onto the green. He lagged his first putt close and tapped in to defend the title. His final round score was a 70 for a four round 280.

After holing the winning putt, Tony did a little victory dance and then heaved his ball far into the gallery. Nicklaus looked on with a grim smile; he wound up with a triple bogey seven on the hole and dropped all the way down to fourth place. Pott secured a solo second place finish, two-strokes behind Tony.

"It's been a long time since I've heard that sound," Tony chuckled as stewards popped the corks on a number of Moet bottles. He took a big drink from the glass of bubbly savoring his victory.

"I've forgotten what that stuff tasted like," he commented.

Meanwhile, Nicklaus spoke to the press about his tee shot on the final hole. He said that as he approached the eighteenth tee he realized that he was one-stroke behind and decided to gamble for a birdie on the final hole.

"I usually play this hole on the right," the calculating Nicklaus stated, "but I tried the left side this time hoping I would get the roll. But something went wrong on my backswing and I hit it a little fat. I'll no doubt do it again," he shrugged.

Asked about Nicklaus's tee shot Tony said, "I never saw him hit a drive like that before."

"Let me say this about Nicklaus," Tony went on. "Things were really tight when he and I came to the eighteenth. He had just made some good putts on the sixteenth and seventeenth and his adrenalin was up. He was putting the pressure on me, as if I didn't have enough already."

Tony went on, "When he hit his shot, I didn't know whether it was out-of-bounds or not. I was stunned, honestly. I didn't know what to think, so I just put my own tee shot down the safety slot and played it nice and cozy with a four-iron to the green."

Tony added, "Jack is a real gentleman. He's not a crybaby. I've played with him a number of times and he never lets a good shot of mine go without some kind of nice comment. You feel like you're in a pressure cooker playing against him. Walking side by side with him makes you feel queasy. But I have only one fault to find with him; he has too much talent."

The reporters laughed as Tony reached for another bottle of Moet. He showed no concern as the contents spilled onto his olive green pants. Then he told the reporters about a conversation he had with his wife before the tournament.

"She said to me, 'Honey, you're not that good.' She set me straight on all my outside activities. You know what I mean. Taking care of business commitments, making TV appearances and neglecting my real bread and butter—golf. She said, 'you're not that good. You can't go running around the country all the time and show up at tournaments the first day and expect to do well.'"

Tony had heeded Betty's advice and showed up for the Buick two days early.

He took another sip of champagne and then said, "My only regret is that she isn't here to share this victory with me. I have a great wife, really."

At the award presentation Tony accepted the large silver cup, a check for $20,000, the opal and the keys to a couple of brand-new Buicks; one for himself and the other for Betty. His winnings propelled him up into the number four spot on the money list, a jump of 17 places.

Tony and Betty reunited in Cleveland as he prepared to defend his Cleveland Open title. Both Player and Nicklaus withdrew from the Cleveland Open, going instead to St. Louis to get in extra practice on the Bellerive course, the site of the U.S. Open the following week.

Palmer, suffering from a bad cold, announced he was flying home to consult with his personal physician. He assured tournament organizers and the press, however that he would return to Cleveland in time for his opening round tee time. Stationed in Cleveland while in the Coast Guard, and working as a paint sales representative in the city before he turned pro, he was a crowd favorite in Cleveland.

In the first round, Tony, also suffering from a cold, found the elusive cure—five birdies. His only bogey came at the 446-yard ninth hole when he three-putted. His 67 put him into a tie for the lead with Casper. Pott was right behind the pair with a 68, tied with rookie Bob Reith, Jr., of Minneapolis, Tommy Aaron, Bill Martindale and Dan Sikes. Palmer turned in a 71 on the Highland Park course he knew so well.

Casper and Tony required only 29 putts in their rounds, Tony having eight one-putt greens.

"A few more birdies and I would have forgotten I had a cold," Tony joked to the press.

Casper shot his good round despite having minor surgery on Wednesday night for the removal of a hemorrhoid.

"It's a good thing I had a late starting time," Casper admitted. "If I had been scheduled to go out early, I don't think I could have made it."

While the players battled it out in Cleveland, previews of the U.S. Open were starting to run in the papers. The articles quoted players who speculated whom they thought the favorites should be.

"You have to like Lema," Former champion Julius Boros stated. "He's playing real well now."

Before the crowning of a new Open champion could occur, though, the Cleveland Open needed to be decided. In the second round, Tommy Aaron wrestled the lead away from Casper and Tony with a second round 67. Tony made a 12-foot birdie putt on the eighteenth hole for a 70 leaving him two behind Aaron and tied with Gordon Jones of Orlando, Florida. Jones had the best round of the day, a 66.

Casper had trouble with his alarm clock and arrived at the course a mere ten minutes before his scheduled tee time. He never recovered from having his routine disrupted and skied to a 73.

Tony and Aaron played in the same group in the third round. After birdies on three of the first six holes, he caught Aaron. His 66 put him into the lead with a two-stroke cushion over Aaron, Dan Sikes and Jones.

Tony claimed he was recovering from his cold saying, "My voice is still a little husky, but I'm feeling a lot better. I played pretty good today. Come in here tomorrow and we'll have champagne."

The fans that came out to Highland Park, or watched on television on Sunday, witnessed a very exciting day of golf. Bruce Devlin came out of nowhere shooting a 65, just one-stroke off the course record and leapt into contention. Dan Sikes, who started the day three-strokes behind Tony, mounted a charge shooting a 33 on the front nine to share the lead. The battle between Sikes and Tony went back and forth all day. Sikes caught Tony on the fifth hole, but just as quickly fell one behind with a bogey on the sixth hole. Tony gained a stroke on the tenth hole, but gave it right back by bogeying the eleventh hole. He regained his lead with a birdie on the par 4, 421-yard fourteenth and then quickly handed it right back with a bogey on the fifteenth.

The two arrived at the eighteenth hole still tied. Tony was off-line with his approach shot landing in the lap of a spectator while Sikes managed to put his approach shot on the green, albeit a long distance, about 35-feet, from the hole.

Tony knew that he had to make a four to have any chance of tying Sikes or beating Devlin. His chip left him a reasonable chance at securing the par he needed. He marked his ball and stepped aside to watch Sikes attempt his winning putt. Sikes amazingly drained his long putt denying Tony the victory. Although disappointed, Tony focused on his short putt, made it and secured second place.

"I had to make that putt...who wants to playoff with Tony Lema?" Sikes asked reporters rhetorically.

Tony's winnings moved him up the money list to the second position, trailing Nicklaus by only $2,000.

The pros headed to St. Louis and Bellerive Country Club for the U.S. Open—the first scheduled four-day Open in history. The U.S.G.A. did not have to resort to its usual tricks to toughen up the course. The Robert Trent Jones design was tough enough already.

The 7,191-yard course, the longest in U.S. Open history, is on the banks of the Mississippi River with occasional strong winds blowing off the river from the west and southwest. Of course, the rough penalized an errant shot, but the length of the course, along with the wind, would provide enough of a challenge for the 150-man field.

As the players arrived in St. Louis, the press began to refer to the tournament as the "Nicklaus Open." It was widely accepted that Nicklaus's length would provide him with an almost unbeatable advantage over the field on the long course.

Tony was not buying that line of thought.

"There's no one man to beat on a layout like this," Tony asserted.

Asked about his chances he said, "When you play like that (the last two weeks), back to back, you haven't any complaints. I'm just hoping I can keep it up, at least for another week."

Kel Nagle, a 44-year-old Australian pro, proved that a short hitter could compete on the long course shooting a first round 68. He admitted to hitting a number of fairway woods for his approach shots. He enjoyed a one-stroke advantage over amateur Deane Beaman and Mason Rudolph.

Gary Player lurked just two off the lead while Tony's 72 placed him four back. Nicklaus shocked everyone by shooting a horrendous 78. He double-bogeyed the very first hole and added another at fifteen. Arnold Palmer did not fare much better shooting a 76.

Venturi opened up his title defense with a miserable 81, but Dick DeMane, a club pro from Roslyn, New York, who shot an unbelievable 93, posted the worst score.

He found trouble and bad luck all the way around the course. He pleaded with reporters to omit his score from their reports and turned down requests for photos lest he embarrass his membership back in Roslyn.

"I'm going out and get loaded," DeMane informed reporters as he departed.

The second round started out with two straight bogeys for Tony, but he managed to make the turn in 35. Then, disaster struck, with three bogeys and a double bogey in the next five holes. It all added up to a 74 and a two round total of 146.

Gary Player fired his second straight 70 to capture the lead, one-stroke ahead of Nagle and Mason Rudolph. Deane Beaman, trying to become the first amateur to win the Open since Johnny Goodman in 1933, was hanging tough. His 73 put him just two-strokes back. Nicklaus rallied to a 72, and barely made the cut, while both Palmer and Venturi would not be around for the weekend.

Player continued to lead at the end of Saturday's round; in fact, he increased his cushion to two-strokes after shooting a 71 for a 211 total. Nagle persisted in applying pressure and remained in second place, tied with Frank Beard who shot a fine 70. Player was on a quest to become the first foreign player to win the Open since Ted Ray in 1920.

Golf purists were disappointed as it was becoming apparent that an amateur would not win this Open. Beaman soared to a 76 and shot himself out of contention. Tony managed a 73 and he faced an almost insurmountable eight-stroke deficit.

During the first nine holes on Sunday, it seemed that Gary Player had the championship wrapped up, but things got interesting on the back nine.

Julius Boros seemed to be a threat after he went three-under in the first eleven holes, but his charge fizzled coming down the stretch. Nagle managed to draw even with Player on the twelfth hole and then quickly backtracked with a double-bogey on the fourteenth. A short time later, Player birdied the same hole sinking a 12-foot putt.

Nagle rallied again, from three back, on the finishing three holes while Player double-bogeyed the par 3 sixteenth and the pair was once again even. With pars on the final hole, the two were deadlocked requiring a Monday 18-hole playoff.

Tony finished with a 70 for a 289 total, a solid final round that earned him a tie for eighth place and a check for $2,500. The winnings kept him solidly in the second spot on the official money list, and with Nicklaus's poor showing, he was within a mere $786 of the top money spot.

Player prevailed in the playoff shooting a 71 to Nagle's 74 and then at the presentation ceremony refused the winner's check of $25,000. He turned the check back over to Joseph Dey, the executive director of the U.S.G.A., asking only for a donation of $5,000 to the Cancer Fund.

"The money is immaterial—the honor is the thing," Player explained. "I feel I owe this country a great deal. I feel it is my duty to do something for this country and for golf."

He also paid his caddy the exorbitant sum of $2,000.

The tour moved on to the St. Paul Open, which had increased its purse for 1965 and moved up on the schedule to the week after the Open. Both changes helped secure a much stronger field than the tournament featured in past years.

Tony posted rounds of 70-70-72-71 for a disappointing tie for 23rd and a check for $875.

At the Western Open the next week, Tony was the biggest name in the field as the "The Big Three" elected to travel to Britain in preparation for the British Open. Tony would fly over after the Western and again would have a very limited time to practice and get familiar with the Royal Birkdale course in Southport, England. That the defending champion chose to attempt his defense with so little preparation intrigued the press, who questioned the strategy.

Tony found time for a telephone interview with Ed Schoenfeld of *The Oakland Tribune*. The topic of his late arrival for the British Open arose.

"I wouldn't go over there if I didn't think I could win it," Tony stated. "I feel good about the British Open. My game is in pretty fair shape. My putting is not as good as I would like it to be. I might be moving my head or something, but I will be working on it this week."

Schoenfeld informed Tony that the experts picked Nicklaus as the favorite to win The Open.

"That's OK, Nicklaus is picked every week to win a tournament," Tony replied.

Whereas there were only eight Americans in the field for the British Open the year prior, U.S. players flocked to the event in 1965. Tony's victory the year before was responsible for an increase in interest in playing in The Open Championship amongst U.S. players.

When Tony arrived in Chicago for the Western Open, he spoke with the press. There would be a dispute later over what he told them about his delayed arrival for the British Open. Whether he was misquoted, or reporters quoted him out of context, the remarks did not make a good impression when read on the other side of the Atlantic.

"I'm not too crazy about playing golf in England," was the quote.

It seems dubious that Tony said this, seeing how much he enjoyed his time at St. Andrews, and how much he valued his major championship victory from the year before. More likely, he was trying to explain why he chose to participate in the Western Open rather than prepare on the grounds of Royal Birkdale. After all, he had captured the Claret Jug with very little preparation time the year before and felt he could defend it the same way. He had a special affinity for the British golf fans, and the last thing he wanted to do was to offend them.

"They (the Western Golf Association) weren't getting too many of the top money-winners and I'm one—even if I'm not a big draw," Tony humbly explained. "I also don't think I can afford to pass up a tournament like this one to practice all week for another."

In reality, he was simply preparing for this major championship the same way he always did; by playing the tournament the week before.

A day later in England, Open officials expressed annoyance over Tony's remarks.

"He was happy enough to play at St. Andrews last year, win the Open and go on to win the World Series of Golf," one official stated.

At the Western Open, Rex Baxter, a Texan, fired a first round 66 to take the lead by one stroke over Chi-Chi Rodriguez. Par took a beating as 32 players bettered it. Tony was among 13 players who shot a first round 69, and he drew the largest gallery of fans.

Baxter continued to occupy the top spot with a second round 67 for a 36-hole 133. Al Geiberger added a 65 to go with his first round 70 and trailed the leader by two. Casper was in third place at 137 and Tony was at 138, after his second straight 69.

"I'm tired golf-wise," Tony admitted. "I'm going to sleep out there on the course."

Not a good omen considering he was facing a trans-Atlantic flight before his most important title defense.

In the third round, Geiberger shot a 69 tying for the lead with Jack

McGowan who had a 65, the best round of the day, at 204. Tony sat tied for second at 206 with six other players. His round featured nine one-putt greens, including a 50-foot birdie putt, but he also had three three-putt greens. At one point in the round, two-strokes separated the 12 players at the top of the leader board.

In the fourth round, Casper put on a charge, blazing to a 64, and won the championship, his second tour title of the year. Geiberger had a disappointing 73 and finished third. Tony's final round 69 placed him in fourth place and won him a check for $3,067.

Sunday night he boarded a jetliner for the flight to Southport, England and defense of his British Open title at Royal Birkdale.

32 CHAMPAGNE IN A BEER WORLD
1965

Tony arrived at Royal Birkdale with the Claret Jug trophy in tow for his biggest title defense to date. Once again, he made the trip without Betty who stayed back in Dallas. He immediately sought out Brigadier General Eric Brickman, secretary of the Royal and Ancient Club, and relinquished the trophy.

"Please keep it in safe keeping for me for four days," he instructed lightheartedly.

His confidence oozed as he spoke with reporters.

"I don't want to push my luck, but I'm playing well," he stated. "I understand Birkdale requires you to be straight. I'll try to learn the course quickly."

The remarks, added to those attributed to him from the Western Open that found their way into the U.K. papers, offended some local fans and reporters. This Lema chap seems to have swelled too large for his knickers, they thought. He did not waste any time winning them back, however.

Asked about his denigrating remarks about British courses and the British Open made at the Western Open, Tony attempted to administer some damage control.

"I never said that," he protested. "You fellows know me and you know how I enjoyed playing the last Open."

Reporters asked how he felt physically.

"I quit smoking for a while and my weight ballooned to 195 pounds," he explained. "So I started again and now I'm back to 175 pounds which is my fighting weight."

Palmer, too, had succumbed to the evil weed and was seen puffing away during practice rounds.

Tony headed out to the golf course, accompanied only by his caddy, and played a practice round. He studied the course playing balls from different areas while not keeping a score.

The course measured 7,073 yards and played to a par of 73. Peter Thomson, the Australian, won the Open when played at Birkdale in 1954, one of four British Open titles he owned. Arnold Palmer won his first of two British Open crowns at Birkdale in 1961. Thick rough lined the fairways right up to the edge of some of the greens. Combined with winds hard off the Irish Sea, the narrow fairways place a premium on accurate drives. Great undulating sand dunes cut into fairways making accurate drives all the more important.

Tony played a second practice round, again alone until he caught up with the group in front of him. He joined the group of English players for the last seven holes and played them in four-under.

He informed reporters after his round that he put his driver away because the tee shots must be, "absolutely straight, and placed just so." He saw no reason why he could not retain his title. He went to bed on Tuesday night full of confidence and eager to get his title defense underway.

In the first round on Wednesday, he came out and displayed just how serious he was about defending his title. He shot a 68 placing his name in the top spot on the large yellow scoreboard at the final green. Because Royal Birkdale had recently undergone a redesign, his round established a new competitive course record, bettering Ireland's Christy O'Connor's 69 posted earlier in the day. Another Irishman, Joe Carr was another stroke back in third place.

Tony's round included six birdies, including the first and last holes. On the eighteenth hole, he narrowly missed an eagle leaving himself a tap in birdie. On three of the par 5 holes, he two putted for birdies. In addition, he drained putts of thirty, twenty-one and eight feet for birdies, although he missed a five-foot putt for another on the fifteenth hole.

He was striking his irons crisply, with the exception of the second hole where his approach shot wound up in the rough resulting in his only bogey. He had seven one-putt greens and no three-putts for the day.

"My driving wasn't as good as I'd like it to be," he said after his round. "I only had two real practice rounds here so I guess I feel good about it all today. But I figure I can look at a course in two days and tell you where all the trouble spots are—not that it means I can avoid them."

Palmer, despite a sore throat, managed to post a 70. Nicklaus missed numerous short putts and his long iron play was not sharp as he posted a disappointing 73. Bruce Devlin shot a 71, Peter Alliss a 73, and Peter Thomson a 74. The players enjoyed excellent weather conditions, a rarity for the British Open.

Tony experienced driving difficulties in the second round and his putter did not save him as it had in the first round. However, he managed a one-under-par 72. His 140 gave him an early one-stroke lead over his closest pursuer, Arnold Palmer, but Bruce Devlin, playing later, came in with a 69 to tie for the lead. Brian Huggett, a Ryder Cup member from Wales, matched Tony's course record 68 and was in with a 141 total.

Tony carded three birdies in his round, including one on the first hole by striking a brilliant 3-wood second shot from the rough onto the par 5.

He left a seven-foot birdie putt on the second hole just short and narrowly missed birdie putts on the next three holes. He was frustrated and bogeyed the ninth, tenth, and twelfth holes, but got his game and emotions back under control with birdies on the thirteenth, fifteenth and seventeenth holes.

"My driving was poor," Tony complained after his round, "and I got nothing at all from my putter. Today was a hard playing day. You make a mistake here and you sure pay."

As disappointing as his driving was, his putting was the reason for his higher second round score. He needed 34 putts as opposed to just 29 on Wednesday.

For the second year in a row, Tony heaped praise on his caddy.

"Last year Arnold Palmer's caddy Tip Anderson helped me tremendously at St. Andrews," he recalled. "This year I am lucky to have another Scot, Willie Aitchison. He was sure good to me out there."

Palmer thrilled the crowd with an assortment of daring recovery shots including one from a shrub on the fifteenth hole.

Nicklaus bounced back with a 71 for a 144 total, while Peter Thomson made a move up the leader board with a 68 for 142, tied with Christy O'Connor.

While Nicklaus remained in the running, he had his work cut out for him. Even so, he still felt confident he could make up the four strokes that separated him from Tony and Devlin. However, it was Tony he had in his sights.

"Lema had better watch out," he told reporters.

In the 36 hole final round, high winds and heavy rain buffeted the course during the morning round. Tony shot a 75 as he fumbled off the tee and found "places I should have never seen."

Tony stayed in contention thanks to his putter. He holed one putt after another to keep his defense of the title alive.

Peter Thomson shot a 72 in the morning round, for a 215, wrestling the lead from Tony and Devlin by one stroke. Palmer used 38 putts, shot a 75 in the morning round, and was at 216. He did not exhibit the demeanor of a man about to mount a charge.

"It's ridiculous for me to be in the picture after this round," Palmer said at lunch.

Nicklaus also had trouble in the weather shooting a 77 and fell from contention.

The rain and blustery winds continued in the afternoon. Palmer was the first player to drop from contention in the afternoon's final eighteen holes. He blew any chance to win with a 41 on the front nine. This was after a good start with a birdie on the first hole; however, three straight bogeys followed, and on the fifth hole disaster struck when he carded a double-bogey after driving into a high willow scrub. He staggered home with a 79 as most of his gallery deserted him.

"I'm sick," is all he could say after his round.

Devlin, also soon fell from the fray, as he piled one bogey on top of another. The tournament boiled down to a head-to-head battle between Tony, saving strokes with his putter, and Peter Thomson, playing the better golf.

Tony kept pace with Thomson, matching him shot-for-shot at the start of the afternoon round, but it was not long before his tee shots got him into trouble. On five, he drove into a bunker and took a bogey. Thomson increased his lead with a birdie at eight and took a three-stroke advantage into the back nine.

Thomson began to feel the strain when he missed a six-foot putt on the eleventh hole that would have closed the door on Tony. Tony birdied thirteen, whittling Thomson's lead to just a single stroke. The players both were able to par the next three holes. Tony's birdie putt on the sixteenth violently lipped-out.

An enormous crowd of 10,000, a television crew, the press and a cadre of police officers accompanied the two players to the seventeenth. Tony hit an errant tee shot winding up in the rough. He was unable to reach the par 5 in two and had to settle for par. Thomson easily reached in two and two putted for the clinching birdie.

Dejected, Tony played a sloppy eighteenth hole bunkering his approach shot and three putting for a six and a final round score of 74. Thomson added a birdie on the last hole for a 71 securing his fifth British Open title. He was two strokes better than Brian Huggett and Christy O'Connor who tied for second place.

All alone in fourth was De Vincenzo while Tony's poor finish put him in a tie for fifth place with Bernard Hunt and Kel Nagle. Tony won $1,330 for the week, although it would not count towards the PGA official money winnings list.

"This is the greatest of my five Open wins because I was against the toughest field this time—a field with great golfers," Thomson said afterwards.

For his part, Tony said, "I don't mind losing, but what a terrible finish. I hated that. I know the shot went the wrong way on the seventeenth, but I felt the sixteenth was my end. My putt went in-and-out there."

Disappointed, he departed England for Canada to play in the Canadian Open. Upon arrival at the Mississaugua Country Club in Mississaugua, Ontario, Tony admitted to reporters that he was both mentally and physically tired and that he was planning a break after the Canadian Open.

He opened with a 70 and trailed the first round leader, Joe Campbell, by four-strokes. During the second round, he walked in after playing the eighth hole complaining of a pain in his back. He was three-over-par for the tournament at the time of his withdrawal.

"My back was paining me so much that I couldn't swing," Tony told reporters. "I knew it wouldn't get any better so I decided not to continue. I hated to make the decision after my first round 70 put me in a fine spot for a run at the leaders."

He went on to explain that the trouble was with his sacroiliac, joints located at the bottom of the back, a recurring condition that flared up from time to time.

He blamed his back flare-up on playing too much golf and spending too much time on airplanes. Even though he blamed airplane travel, he immediately flew to Dallas and had plans to fly on to Oakland to visit family and friends. While in Dallas, he found time to talk with Ed Schoenfeld of *The Oakland Tribune* by phone.

"I had a good night's sleep on a hard mattress in my own bed here in Dallas," Tony informed Schoenfeld. "I feel much better. I will take a few treatments on my back here this week, fly out to Oakland the first of next week for a few days visit and then go back on the tour."

A week later, his back condition fed a rumor that he was not going to defend his Thunderbird Classic title. He quickly sent word to the tournament organizers informing them he would be at the tournament.

"I definitely will defend," Tony said.

Schoenfeld wrote in an article a day later that Tony would no longer register at tour events as being from San Leandro. He had just signed a deal, where he would represent Marco Island, a new 10,000-acre yacht club and golf course development on the southern tip of Florida's west coast.

"I'm not deserting San Leandro or Oakland," he informed Schoenfeld. "This is strictly a business opportunity in a beautiful spot."

He planned to register for the Thunderbird as playing out of Marco Island.

While in San Leandro to visit with family, and friends, he commented to Schoenfeld about his trim figure crediting his return to smoking for his 172-pound weight.

"I move faster and feel freer when I swing. I had got kind of heavy and it was hard for me to move around after I gave up smoking. Smoking is a lousy habit, but I'd rather be skinny and smoke than fat and not smoke," he rationalized.

He analyzed his title defense at the British Open for Schoenfeld and his readers.

"Two things killed me in England—I wasn't driving too well, and my putting wasn't too sharp. I still thought I had a chance, however, up to the 71st hole," he said.

He looked forward to the last major of the year, the PGA Championship at Laurel Canyon.

"I have not yet played the course, but I hear it is a great one," Tony said. "I feel good about the PGA, and will be giving it a big try."

He also looked forward to returning to Royal Birkdale for the Ryder Cup and hoped for an invite back to the Piccadilly World Match Play Championship.

Tony flew to New York, again staying at Fred Corcoran's house in Mamaroneck. While there, he discussed business matters with his manager and visited with Corcoran's two daughters. Judy, Corcoran's 12-year-old, challenged Tony to a fly swatting contest.

Tony accepted the challenge but wanted to make it interesting so he proposed a modest wager and Judy quickly agreed. The two started in, neither having much luck, until finally Tony declared the contest over and himself the winner, by the score of 2 - 0.

Judy disappeared before returning with two shiny dimes to pay off her gambling debt. Tony would not accept the coins.

"You only owe me 16 cents," Tony said. "Don't you remember that your father gets 20 per cent of anything I win?"

He spoke with reporters about defending his Thunderbird title, "I've always liked this course, it suits me fine."

In the first round, he recorded a 70, four-strokes off the lead posted by a Monday qualifier, Pat Schwab. He followed up with rounds of 73, 71 and 71 to finish in a tie for 36th. The tour packed up and moved on to Philadelphia.

Tony opened with a 72 and followed up with a second round 69 that put him five strokes back of the leader, R.H. Sikes. His third round 67 moved him into sole possession of the lead one in front of Sikes. A disappointing fourth round 74 left him four shots back of the winner, Nicklaus who charged up the leader board with a 68.

Throughout Tony's second round, he swallowed pills to alleviate pain in his sore back as well as a new pain; his elbow was starting to bother him.

The pros moved to the hills of Pennsylvania for the year's final major, the PGA Championship. Played on the Laurel Valley Country Club course in Arnold Palmer's backyard, Ligonier, it was Tony's last chance at a major for the year.

Tony fired four caddies in his Tuesday practice round before he found one that was acceptable.

He informed the press that he was rooting for Nicklaus or Player to win—if he did not, that is. The reason was simple: those two players had already won a major championship, and if either captured the PGA, the fourth spot in the World Series of Golf would go to the defending champion, Tony.

"I'd be foolish not to like Jack or Gary here," Tony declared. "That's a lot of money, $50,000. But even though the present set-up favors me, I don't think it is right. The World Series is a wonderful tournament, a real test—and it should be for champions only. If three men win four titles, it should be limited to those three."

The course was in fantastic shape after a week of rain that gave way to warm sunshine on Wednesday. In the first round, Tommy Aaron shot a blistering 66 to lead Gardner Dickinson and Mason Rudolph by one, and Sam Snead, Raymond Floyd and Bruce Devlin by two. Nicklaus trailed by three while Tony was five off the pace.

Palmer shot a 72, despite a two-stroke penalty on the very first hole, assessed after he had a railing on a bridge that interfered with his swing removed. He should have taken a free lift from the immovable object.

Venturi, was working for ABC-TV as a commentator and Tony spotted him near the tenth tee. Tony wandered over to talk with his friend, and inquired how his hands were recovering from an operation he recently underwent at the Mayo Clinic. Venturi stretched out his arms to exhibit the scars on the undersides of his wrist.

"They're coming along fine now," Venturi said.

Tony wished him well, hoping for his speedy return to the tour, and resumed his round.

Tommy Aaron extended his lead in the second round, shooting a 71 for a 137 total, with Nicklaus and Dave Marr at 139. Palmer encountered another penalty mess when he drove into a drainage ditch that played as a hazard. In preparing to take his shot, he dislodged a rock and called the two-stroke penalty on himself.

He took a nine on the hole, shot a 75 and fell down the leader board to 147—the same total as Tony after his dismal 76.

In the third round, both Nicklaus and Casper made a run at the lead before fading under the hot sun. Dave Marr shot a 70 and shared the lead with Aaron who was in and out of trouble all day. Hogan put together one of the finest rounds of the day, a 70 and was eight-strokes off the lead. Tony continued to struggle on his way to a 75, for 227, totally out of contention.

In the fourth round, Dave Marr fought off Nicklaus to capture his first major championship with a 71 for a 280. Nicklaus and Casper tied for second at 282.

Tony blew up to a nice, big, fat 80 in the final round for a 302 and finished in a tie for 61st place. His winnings of $300 dropped him into the fifth position on the money list. He left Pennsylvania disgusted with his game and in a foul mood.

His mood did not improve upon arrival at the Carling World Open in Sutton, Massachusetts. In fact, the course he found during his practice round made his mood darker. He did not like the size of the greens at the Pleasant Valley Country Club.

"When I get through playing I'm going to become a golf course designer," he said sarcastically. "I'll not make any more mistakes than some guys now operating. How can I go wrong when you find guys making greens a mile long and a half mile wide?"

"What are you complaining about?" asked a reporter. "Haven't you got a bigger target to shoot at?"

"I'm not complaining," Tony said, as reporters looked up in disbelief. "I just can't understand the theory behind such large greens. Here, a guy shooting for the pin can miss the target by 80 or 90 feet and still be on the green. What kind of a game is that? If I was designing a course, I'd have the greens vary in size in proportion to the length of the hole. If it was a short hole, I'd have a small green."

A reporter asked Tony how he was feeling physically.

Tony replied glumly, "I've probably never been at a lower point. I've done nothing but play golf since last April and my nerves are shot. My mental attitude is no good. I haven't been sleeping well of late and my temper is horrid. Outside of that, I guess I'm in good shape."

Tony closed by saying, "I'm really not complaining about this tournament. For $20,000 I'd play on Lake Michigan when it was completely frozen over and with the 'thin ice' sign staring me in the face."

Tony had a much better frame of mind while playing his second practice round. He posed for pictures with fans, joked, and laughed. Suddenly he whirled around.

"Miles, how about a pair of my Tony Lema golf shoes?" he yelled out.

Photographers waited while Tony put on a pair of white shoes, which Miles Baker, sales manager for the E.E. Taylor Corporation of Freeport, Maine, the new company he represented, handed to him. He then posed, clowned, and smirked for the crowd.

One member of the crowd turned to a friend and remarked, "His next step is the legitimate theater."

Rain washed out the entire first round, even though more than 125 players had completed their rounds before the worst of the weather hit.

Tony's nice 70 fell victim to the rainout, as did George Archer's 67. In the restart the next day, Mike Souchak shot a 68 and enjoyed a one-stroke lead over an unknown Japanese pro, Hideyo Sugimoto, and Arnold Palmer. Tony tied Ben Hogan and Gary Player at 71, while Nicklaus sat at 74. George Archer, unfortunately, traded-in a 67 for a 73.

In the second round, Homero Blancas, a rookie, added a 67 to his first round 71 to take over the lead at 138. Tony's old friend Jim Ferree shot a

70 to go with his first round 69 and sat alone in second place.

Ferree sank a putt he termed the longest, "I've ever made, or seen or even heard of."

The putt measured 95-feet, affirming Tony's comment of the large greens.

At 140 was the quartet of Sam Snead, Gary Player, Joe Campbell and Mike Souchak. Tony shot his second straight 71 placing him nicely on the leader board at 142, tied with newly crowned PGA champion Dave Marr and Arnold Palmer.

Before Sunday's third round, Tony attended Mass, held in the main dining room of the clubhouse. He then went out and through a steady drizzle shot a four-under 67 to tie Blancas for the lead at 209. The rookie Blancas ran into trouble on the back nine as Tony applied pressure.

After he "seriously considered" passing up the Carling because of his poor play, Tony's game had come around considerably. He described his third round as "my best round in a month. I started out putting well and that gave me a lift. I also felt a little looser, which may explain partly my good round."

Before the fourth round began, Tony voiced concerns about winning a tournament sponsored by a beer company. He was Champagne Tony, after all.

Preceding the round, Dr. Paul V. Shannon of Worchester, Massachusetts, a member of the tournament medical staff, treated Blancas. Blancas suffered from a 99.6 temperature that the doctor described as a virus, but there was never any doubt he would play. He had won nearly $20,000, in just four months since joining the tour after his discharge from the army, and he would not pass up this chance to add more.

Blancas, battling both Tony and his virus, got off to a shaky start by bogeying the second hole, while Tony birdied it. Tony added birdies at the 425-yard fourth, and the 362-yard fifth, enjoying a three-stroke advantage over Blancas and playing one group in front of him. Palmer, playing with Blancas, started birdie - bogey while Souchak, playing in the same group, double-bogeyed the second and bogeyed the fourth dropping out of contention.

As the players made the turn, Palmer put on one of his patented charges and finally caught Tony on the fifteenth hole. But his charge fizzled when he bogeyed both the sixteenth and seventeenth holes. When Tony heard that Palmer bogeyed seventeen, giving him a two shot lead, he gave himself a little lecture, "You're a fool if you blow this now."

He found some good fortune on the seventeenth when he hit his approach, from the rough, too long. The ball bounced off a person in the gallery and ended up on the green. Not one to look a gift horse in the mouth, he two-putted for par. The gallery had saved his ball from going into thick rough where he would have faced an almost impossible up-and-down for his par.

He tapped in a short putt on the eighteenth hole for the victory and hurled his ball up into the gallery in celebration. His margin of victory was two strokes over Palmer who finished in second place.

After his round, Tony, interviewed by George Rodgers of CBS television said, "George, I'm just going to slip some of that Moet champagne into a Carling cup and mix it up."

His victory, with the $35,000 first place check, shot him back up into the second spot on the official money list.

"If anyone had ever told me ten years ago that I'd make $98,000 in one year playing golf, I'd have told him he was crazy," Tony said as he popped the cork on a bottle of champagne at his victory party with the press.

"Hell, I've never had it so good," Tony went on. "Golf has been good to me and I'm the first guy to admit it. I love the game and this win has got to be one of the biggest thrills of my life."

Frank Sargent writing in *The Lowell Sun* in Lowell, Massachusetts, described Tony at his victory celebration. "His enthusiasm was more bubbly than the champagne he was pouring and he made no effort to hide his joy."

Somebody from the Carling brewery, the sponsors of this rich event, slapped a Carling beer label on Tony's bottle of champagne. Tony gave out a big laugh.

"Well I guess this is one time that beer and champagne can live together. It sure seems funny for a guy who loves champagne to be winning a beer tournament, but after all, this is an age of non-segregation and I believe that beer and champagne can live together," he said with a big smile on his face.

Tony also accounted for the thrashing he gave the course after his practice round in regards to the large greens.

He said, "Gentlemen, I'll have to admit that this is probably one of the most underestimated courses we've played on the circuit. When I first came in here I felt sure there would be a lot of 67s and maybe a few 66s, but I was wrong."

When asked about the size of the check, Tony pointed out it was not the largest single check he had won.

"I picked up a little piece of paper worth $50,000 last year but there were only four golfers in that competition," he pointed out. "I honestly love to win. I'm not taking anything away from the size of the check because we love money, but I'd rather win a $2,000 tournament than come in second in a $20,000 event."

Betty shot Tony a look that said, *"Are you crazy?"*

He recalled his days working at a golf course for $200 a month.

"I didn't mind it a bit because I was able to be at a golf course all the time. Yet, I'd do it all over again starting out. As I said before, golf has been good to me and I'll never forget the fact."

Photographers asked for a picture of Betty and Tony.

"She's a little shy here, but she won't be shy when she asks for the check," he joked.

Palmer entered the pressroom and saw the bottles of champagne sitting up on the front table.

"I'm not sitting up here with that stuff. Give me a beer," he joked. As usual, he was most gracious to the victor.

The two men were very good friends, and Paul Hahn, the trick shot artist, liked to tell the story of when he was master of ceremonies at a dinner with Palmer and Tony as the featured guests. Palmer had just signed a deal forming the Arnold Palmer Laundry, Dry Cleaners, Maid and Valet Services, and when introduced, Tony pulled out a pile of dirty shirts.

"Have them back in the morning, Arnie—no starch, please," he said as he plopped the pile down on the table in front of Palmer.

The PGA announced the Ryder Cup team for the upcoming matches in England. Casper garnered the most points with 1,065.22 and Palmer was next with 797.30. Tony had 513.66 points while Venturi had 369.83. Rounding out the team was Dave Marr (331.50), Tommy Jacobs (312.57), Gene Littler (293.32), Johnny Pott (292.10), Julius Boros (272.94) and Don January (243.97). Jack Nicklaus was not yet eligible for the team because he needed to complete the requisite five years of tournament play before becoming a full-fledged member of the PGA.

Bill Bosshard, a young Akron, Ohio executive won the Hilton 30-day trip around-the-world contest with Tony and Betty. Visits to the Eiffel Tower, the Acropolis, elephant rides on the grounds of a Rajah's palace in India, and a ceremonial luau in Honolulu were on the itinerary. Included on the trip, of particular note to Tony, was an audience with the pope, Pope Paul VI.

33 WORLD TRAVELER
1965

The pros prepared for one of the sternest tests they faced each year—the Firestone Country Club and the American Golf Classic. The sore elbow that Tony first noticed upon his return from Greece continued to be a concern. The pain actually was getting worse. He popped aspirin in an attempt to relieve the ache.

In Akron, Arnold Palmer finished second, behind winner Al Geiberger, and on the strength of his two consecutive second-place finishes, clawed his way into the top ten on the official money list. Nicklaus made the cut, but finished out of the money, yet he continued to sit in the top position on the money list with $127,445. Tony finished the tournament tied for fifth earning $3,800 and comfortably retained the second spot on the money list. With his yearly earnings of $101,816, he became only the third person, after Palmer and Nicklaus, in PGA history to earn more than $100,000 in official prize money in one year.

The PGA announced Nicklaus and Tony as the team to represent the United States in the Canada Cup, Fred Corcoran's tournament matching two-man teams from countries around the world. The team looked forward to contending for the cup at the Club de Campo in Madrid, Spain, September 30 through October 3. Spain, as the host country, selected the American team from a list of six leading players submitted by the PGA.

Tony also received an invitation, based on his lofty status on the money list, to the Piccadilly World Match Play Championship in England.

After the American Golf Classic, he returned to the Bay Area to visit his family. Ed Schoenfeld of *The Oakland Tribune* caught up with him there, and they discussed his busy travel schedule, with stops in Marco Island, Spain and England.

He also weighed in on the debate currently waging among the players on whether the tour should break away from the PGA. Some players felt that it had outgrown the PGA organization and wanted more player control over the revenues generated by television. Tony was not so eager for a split.

"The home pro is our real link to the game," Tony stated.

At the end of the interview, Tony asked Schoenfeld, "Do me a favor? I'm going to buy a batch of season tickets for Oakland Raiders games and

I'd appreciate it if you would pass them out to the poor kids around town. I was in their shoes once. I know how it feels. Now that I can do something, I'd like to help them out. I not only want them to see a football game, I want them to go in style and sit in the best seats."

He was not seeking publicity in connection with this project.

"Don't mention my name," he requested. "This is strictly between you and me. Just tell the kids that the tickets came from a friend."

He purchased the tickets and Schoenfeld distributed them to Boys Clubs, Boy Scout troops and underprivileged kids. Schoenfeld abided by Tony's request for anonymity.

While Tony rested, Player captured the World Series of Golf, with Nicklaus in second, Peter Thomson third and Dave Marr fourth. Following the World Series, the Tour moved to the Pacific Northwest where with his win at the Portland Open, Nicklaus set a new yearly earnings record with $134,045.

Despite taking a break from the tour, Tony, remained firmly entrenched in the number two spot on the money list at $108,869.

Arriving in Madrid, Spain, for the Canada Cup, Tony took in his first look of the Club de Campo. Tony found the heavily wooded, topsy-turvy course difficult.

His continued to experience pain in his elbow and it threw him off his game as the team of Nicklaus and Lema struggled. He opened up with two rounds of 76 before seeking the services of Dr. Gaillard, a physician provided by the PGA for the American team. Dr. Gaillard administered a pain killing shot to Tony's arm and his game rebounded with a third round 71. He backpedaled in the fourth round with a 75 and the Americans finished a distant third place behind the winners South Africa and the host country Spain.

Discouraged with his play, he headed for England and the Ryder Cup matches followed by the Piccadilly World Match Play Championship. The seeding for the Piccadilly pitted Tony against Bruce Devlin in the first round match.

Tony was the last member of the United States Ryder Cup team to arrive at Royal Birkdale. He and his captain for the matches, Byron Nelson, were very familiar with each other. They first met when Tony was an assistant pro at San Francisco Golf Club, and Nelson visited to give lessons to Venturi. Since then, they had become close friends.

Tony and Betty used Nelson as a reference when they applied for their apartment at Turtle Creek, an upscale complex north of Dallas. Tony often traveled to Nelson's ranch, bringing along his mother Cleo when she came to town to visit. Cleo visited with Nelson's wife Louise, while the men talked golf and ranching.

Nelson admired Tony's game and noted, "Of all the golfers out there,

Tony uses his feet and legs more like I did than anyone else."

Nelson also looked forward to the return of his student, Venturi, in the matches. Returning to competitive golf after the operation on his wrists, Venturi hit the ball well recording a two-under 71 in one practice round.

"I'll use him in every match I possibly can," Nelson vowed.

Tony was not the only Ryder Cup team member to be hurting; Johnny Pott quit his practice round because of a pulled back muscle. The injury forced him to the sidelines unable to compete in any of the matches.

The British captain, Harry Weetman, exuded confidence.

"I would say our team is definitely playing better than the Americans on the balance of play so far," he declared.

Although it was still only practice rounds, the Brits were shooting some fine scores. Lionel Platts went low with a 32 over the front nine.

Tony and Palmer spent a great deal of time counseling the other members of the American squad on the intricacies and eccentricities of Royal Birkdale. Having played the course in The Open a few weeks earlier, they passed on what they learned to the other members of the U.S. squad. Yet, Tony lacked his usual confidence in his game.

"I didn't play particularly well," he admitted after a practice round. "I have been fiddling with my putting."

The first day matches featured the two-ball foursomes, or alternate shot, format. The weather dawned bright and sunny and helped attract immense crowds who witnessed outstanding golf in the benign conditions.

Tony paired up with Julius Boros against the British team of Lionel Platts and Peter Butler. The Americans held off a spirited comeback mounted by the Brits to win the match 1-up on the final green. Tony and Boros combined to shoot a round of three-under. As he played the match, Tony could feel his game returning along with his confidence.

After the morning matches were complete, the teams wound up knotted with two points apiece.

In the warm afternoon sunshine, the teams again battled and produced some of the greatest golf in Ryder Cup history. There were 48 birdies and three eagles during the first day of competition and an immense gallery of 12,000 took it all in from their perches atop the dunes that line the fairways at Royal Birkdale.

In their second match, Tony and his partner, Boros, soundly defeated the British duo Jimmy Martin and Jimmy Hitchcock, 5 and 4. In the other afternoon matches Palmer and Marr administered a sound thrashing to Dave Thomas and George Will, 6 and 5 after shooting a 30 on the front nine. The British team of Bernard Hunt and Neil Coles handled Venturi and January 3 and 2, while O'Conner and Alliss defeated Casper and Littler, 2 and 1.

"I've never seen anything like it," Byron Nelson said after the dust finally settled with the two teams deadlocked at four points apiece. "It was an unbelievable day of golf."

The weather continued in a most uncharacteristic fashion with warm temperatures and sunny skies for the second day matches. The matches, under the four-ball format, or as Americans know it, best-ball, featured fantastic comebacks. Don January and Tommy Jacobs defeated Dave Thomas and George Will, 1-up after being four holes down at the turn, while Billy Casper and Gene Littler won the last four holes of their match with Lionel Platts and Peter Butler earning a halve.

Palmer and Marr continued to rip up the course, this time shooting a 33 on the front nine, and easily handled the team of O'Connor and Alliss, 6 and 4.

Tony and Boros, shot a 67 against the British team of Bernard Hunt and Neil Coles—and still lost. The scoreboard at the end of the second day's morning matches had the Americans in possession of the lead, 6 ½ to 5 ½.

Harry Weetman needed his team to mount a comeback in the afternoon four-ball matches. It was widely believed that the Americans held the advantage once play reached the singles matches on the final day and if the U.K. team harbored any hopes of a victory, they would have to build up a lead in the four-ball matches and then hang on in the single matches. The galleries swelled to 14,000 in the afternoon and they enjoyed warm, sunny weather with just the slightest of breeze.

Don January and Tommy Jacobs defeated Dave Thomas and George Will 1-up to gain the American squad another point. Tony, this time teamed with his good friend Ken Venturi, won another hard-fought point as they defeated Bernard Hunt and Neil Coles 1-up.

Casper and Littler halved their match with Lionel Platts and Peter Butler, however Littler had to finish birdie – birdie to earn the resulting half point. Palmer and Marr finally came back down to earth losing to O'Connor and Alliss, 2-up. The U.S. finished the day with a two-point lead, 9 to 7.

The fine weather continued for the singles matches on the third day and in the morning, Tony added another point defeating Peter Butler, 1-up.

The British team earned their points of the morning session when Peter Alliss defeated Billy Casper, 1-up, Bernard Hunt beat Gene Littler, 2-up and Don January and George Will halved their match, each earning a half point.

It was clear that Byron Nelson's team had a great desire to win.

"If we played this hard in the tournaments back home," one of his team members informed him, "we'd all be millionaires."

Tony led the American team off in the first match of the afternoon and easily handled Christy O'Conner by the score of 6 and 4. His win gave the Americans 15 ½ points with only 16 needed for an outright victory. A short time later, Palmer produced the winning point when he beat Peter Butler 2-up.

The crowd of 15,000, including the Prime Minister of England, Harold Wilson, saw some great golf. It was the thirteenth win in sixteen matches for the Yanks and Tony and Palmer played the starring roles.

Tony hit fantastic iron shots all week. In the afternoon singles match he put together a string of seven birdies, including two deuces, and was six-under par for the fourteen holes played before he closed out the match. The shot he received in Spain to relieve the pain in his elbow seemed to have done the job. He and Palmer accounted for over half the points of the American team's total.

The American team retired to their locker room to await the official award ceremony and Tony broke out a case of Moet champagne. Nelson allowed Tony to pour everybody on the team a single glass to celebrate the victory before he put the bubbly away until after the award ceremony.

"I wanted to be sure we'd behave all right during the ceremony, with Prime Minister Wilson there and all," Nelson wrote in his autobiography.

The players, on their best behavior, accepted the cup, posed for pictures and quickly got back to the business of celebrating, with many of the Brits joining them. The celebration was a fitting end to a very well played, and despite the lopsided final score, a hard-fought Ryder Cup match.

Tony and Palmer traveled east from Royal Birkdale, on the coast of England, near Liverpool, to Wentworth Golf Club in Surrey, just northwest of London. They were among the eight players invited to play in the Piccadilly World Match Play Championship, the brainchild of Mark McCormick, manager for Palmer, Nicklaus, Player, Sanders, and many others.

Because of an operation for varicose veins, Bruce Devlin withdrew, opening the door for the first alternate, Peter Alliss, to play. He would battle Tony in the first round match.

Tony played his first practice round with Palmer and British legend Henry Cotton, winner of the British Open in 1934, 1937 and 1948. Cotton enjoyed the high life in his retirement and was fond of champagne, so of course, he and Tony got along quite well.

In addition to the Lema versus Alliss match, other first round matches were; Palmer versus Kel Nagle, Player against Neil Coles and Christy O'Connor would take on Peter Thomson. The tree-lined course was a stiff test during the 36-hole matches, even for the world's best golfers.

Palmer advanced to the semifinal round by throwing ten birdies at Nagle finishing him off 3 and 2. He waited to meet the winner of the

O'Conner/Thomson match that ended deadlocked at the end of 36-holes with a sudden death playoff scheduled for the next morning.

Tony also advanced to the semifinals by beating Alliss 5 and 4 and he would meet the red-hot Gary Player who handled Coles by the same 5 and 4 score.

Friday morning Thomson came out, finished off O'Conner in sudden death, and then took on the mighty Palmer. He built up a lead in the first 18 holes of the match and then withstood one of Palmer's patented charges to hold on and win by the score of 1-up.

In his 36-hole match against Gary Player, Tony caught fire in the morning shooting a 67 that included one stretch of five straight birdies. While Tony was lighting up the course, Player was fighting his driver.

At the lunch break, Tony held a seemingly comfortable lead of six holes. After lunch, Player was able to reduce Tony's lead by one at the turn, and then the fireworks began.

With a five hole deficit to make up with only nine holes to play, Player went to work. He won the twenty-eighth and twenty-ninth holes with birdies and then added another birdie on the thirty-first hole to reduce Tony's lead to just two. Tony made a mess of the thirty-fourth hole, conceded it to Player, and now led by only one hole with two holes to play. Player birdied the thirty-sixth hole while Tony could only manage a par and the two headed for a sudden-death playoff.

Losing such a large lead in heads-up play makes a golfer feel shell-shocked. Tony felt stunned as he headed to the playoff. The caliber of golf that the two players exhibited over the grueling 36-hole match and the ferocity of the battle left both players exhausted.

Tony pulled his drive into the rough on the first playoff hole and struggled on the hole winding up with a par. Playing the hole solidly, Player faced a birdie putt to cap off his fine comeback. He drained the putt for his birdie and advanced into the championship match against Thomson. Riding the momentum of his exciting victory over Tony, Player handled Thomson in the championship match, winning 3 and 2.

Tony returned to Dallas after the Piccadilly and spoke by phone with Ed Schoenfeld of the *Oakland Tribune*.

Tony informed Schoenfeld that he was taking the remainder of the year off. He would not play in any of the remaining PGA events because of his sore right elbow. The elbow had bothered him since the Philadelphia Golf Classic back in early August and he felt the pain must be the result of a bone chip or calcium deposits.

The pain came and went, but when it hurt, it hurt to swing the club. He was taking drugs to ease the pain and told Schoenfeld that the injury would not prevent him from making the round-the-world trip for the Hilton Hotel contest, the first week of November.

He traveled to London where he would meet up with the Hilton group. While there, he posed for photographers outside his London hotel decked out in a snappy tailor-made business suit, felt derby hat with an umbrella and newspaper tucked under his arm. He met with representatives of Slazenger, Ltd., makers of the Dunlop line of golf equipment. The Associated Press reported that Tony signed an endorsement deal with the company to use their equipment on tour in 1966. Still, the pain in his elbow concerned him about his prospects for the next year.

Tony talked about the injury with a reporter from the United Press International wire service while in London.

"I can't play at present because of my elbow which I think may be chipped. I am taking pills to deaden the pain and it depends on these and my condition in the next six weeks whether or not I shall have to undergo an operation."

An operation on the problematic elbow could put him off the tour for two to three months. To give the elbow rest, he cancelled all the exhibitions arranged as part of the world tour.

Tony, Betty, Bosshard, the winner of the contest, and a group of eight others made their way through the stops on the Hilton world tour. They took in the sights of London, Paris, Rome, India, and Hawaii.

During the trip, Tony excitedly phoned Corcoran and told him of his biggest thrill of the excursion—an audience with Pope Paul VI in Rome. Both he and Betty met the Pope after attending a Mass in the Vatican. Following custom, Tony knelt on one knee and kissed the Pope's ring.

While away from the PGA Tour, his number two spot on the official money list remained safe, as Casper was unable to overtake him by the time the season concluded. Casper finished the year with $99,931.

Tony gave notice to the Fernquist and Johnson Company that he was changing his equipment endorsement. The oral agreement with F & J allowed for termination by either party with notification. Tony informed the company he desired to end the agreement and asked for a final accounting on royalties owed to him.

Golf Magazine and the PGA announced the All-American team for 1965 again naming Tony a member, this time for his short iron play. Other members of the team were; Jack Nicklaus for the driver; Gary Player, fairway woods; Arnold Palmer for his long iron play; Gene Littler, mid-irons; Dave Marr for his mastery of the pitching wedge; Sam Snead for the sand wedge; and for handling the putter with expertise, Billy Casper.

Tony attended the All-American press conference in New York City at the Sheraton East Hotel on Park Avenue. While in town, he met boxer Sugar Ray Robinson at Billy Reed's Little Club. A big fan of Robinson's and boxing, he got a huge thrill from the meeting.

While in New York, Fred Corcoran put Tony in touch with Bud

Harvey, the writer who co-authored Corcoran's book, *Unplayable Lies*. Tony and Harvey planned to collaborate on an instructional book to provide tips to the exploding recreational golf population. The planned book would feature photographs of Tony showing the correct form used for different shots and different situations a player encounters on the golf course.

Returning from New York to spend a quiet holiday season with Betty at his mother's house in San Leandro, he reviewed his year and laid down goals for 1966. Disappointed with his showings in the major tournaments in 1965, he resolved to perform better in them in 1966—if his troublesome elbow allowed him to play at all.

The amount of prize money he won during the past year was a source of pride. However, he desperately wanted to add more majors to his British Open championship and the one he set his sights on was the 1966 U. S. Open in San Francisco, at the Olympic Club.

Nevertheless, everything in 1966 depended on his annoying elbow. The rest during the world tour helped, as did the rest during December, but his worry consumed him. He fretted the injury would force him to undergo surgery causing him to miss two to three months of tournaments. Unsure if the surgery would correct the problem he worried about recapturing his form.

While back in the Bay Area for the holidays, he visited Dick Fry at Lake Chabot in December to begin preparation for the opening tournaments of the 1966 schedule. The two sat in Fry's teaching booth located on the practice tee of the driving range and talked, for about an hour, about his plans and how he was preparing for the future, financially. For the last few years, he had put $15,000 a year into a trust fund for when his playing days were through. In addition, his myriad of business endeavors would provide income once he hung up his clubs.

He also bought property in the mountains east of the Bay Area where he and Betty could relax. He began construction of a cabin across the street from Brentwood Lake near Twain Harte close to where his sister Bernice and her husband, Art, had a cabin. Augie Benitas also owned a cabin nearby.

On the home front, Tony and Betty began to make plans to have children. Tony loved kids and looked forward to children of his own to raise, spoil, and play with. Betty also wanted children, although the thought of caring for a young baby filled her with a certain amount of fear.

34 PILLS AND NEEDLES
1966

The traditional kick-off of the tour, the Los Angeles Open, got underway in early January at the Rancho Mirage course. The day before the opening round, in *The Oakland Tribune,* Ed Schoenfeld reported that Tony and Billy Casper had agreed to make a visit to Viet Nam in late February. The two pros planned to stage a number of exhibitions to entertain the troops fighting there.

The State Department and the Department of Defense requested the two golfers, who jumped at the chance to give something back to their country. Both President Johnson and Secretary Robert McNamara expressed their delight in the planned trip and the fact that the two pros had agreed to volunteer their services.

Tony arrived on the practice tee with his brand new Dunlop equipment. With his new endorsement deal, he switched clubs, playing Dunlop blade irons and using Maxfli balls. Equipment changes are often tricky, especially if a pro signs the endorsement deal for the money and later finds the equipment does not fit his game. Even though Tony had spent time practicing with the new clubs and ball, it was another uncertainty, along with his elbow, as he entered the 1966 campaign.

With one of the largest galleries of the day, Tony shot a first round 71 and trailed the first round leader, Dave Ragan by five-strokes. His disappointing 73 in the second round put him at 145. He followed up with a 70 and then shot the low round of the final day, a 66, that moved him up to a tie for 13th place. Arnold Palmer held off a courageous charge mounted by defending champion Paul Harney to capture the title.

The pros headed south, following the routine that Tony had grown so familiar with, for the next stop on the tour, the San Diego Open. Here, he opened up with a very disappointing 76, and after adding a 73 in the second round missed the cut by one stroke. He headed back up to the Bay Area to work on his game in preparation for the Crosby.

Tony went out to catch some of the action in the Hayward City Golf Championship played at the Hayward Golf Course. Dressed stylishly in slacks and a sports coat, he watched Ron Cerrudo, a 20-year-old Castro

Valley player play a few holes. While at the course, he spoke with Sid Hoos, the sports editor of *The Hayward Daily Review*, about the upcoming tour events in the Bay Area.

"There's nothing I'd like better than to win the Lucky," Tony disclosed. "So many of my friends are there pulling for me but I never seem to do well. I remember two years ago when I won the Crosby, came up to San Francisco and took the first round lead, and then had nothing go right after that."

Tony shrugged off any suggestion that his elbow was hindering his play. "There's nothing wrong with the elbow—it's fine now and I don't pay any attention to it."

Upset that the Raiders dealt his friend Archie Matsos to Denver he called Ed Levitt at *The Oakland Tribune* to vent.

"The Raiders just lost a fan," Tony declared. "Here they're trying to build a championship club and sell tickets, yet they trade off a guy the Oakland Raiders themselves voted the most valuable man on the team."

The year before the announced trade, Matsos had become a partner with Tony and Jack Vincent in the San Leandro travel agency. He was seriously considering retiring from football to remain in the Oakland area.

In another interview, Tony made a prediction saying, "Watch out for Venturi. He's going to win one pretty soon."

The tour arrived on the Monterey Peninsula to find warm sunny weather, a rarity for the Bing Crosby National Pro-Am. Playing alongside Father Durkin as his pro-am partner, Tony opened with a 70 on the tough Cypress Point course. A double-bogey on the final hole led to a second round 72 leaving him five strokes off the lead.

On Saturday, before its national broadcast of the Crosby began, NBC ran a special produced for the 25th anniversary of the tournament. The special featured Ray Bolger, who played the scarecrow in the *Wizard of Oz*, as the host. One of the featured stories was of Tony and a friend sneaking into the tournament as teens and marshals kicking them out.

In Saturday's round, Geiberger shot a 67 on Cypress to take the lead at 209. He enjoyed a nice lead over Billy Martendale, who, after a 69 was at 212. Massengale, skied to a 76 and was another shot back, tied with Palmer. Tony added a 72 at Pebble and was one stroke further back at 214.

In the fourth round, Tony could not do anything right and ballooned to a 79. Don Massengale, in the thick of the battle for the title once Geiberger and Martendale fell from contention, played in the same pairing with Tony who lent his support as they came down the stretch. Tony and Massengale had spent time together as young bachelors on the tour.

"We made a trip together to Mexico City and used to mess around together," Massengale explained to reporters after holding off a Palmer challenge to capture the victory.

"Tony was extremely helpful as the pressure built up," Massengale explained. "He helped calm me down and a couple of times told me, 'you have everything under control...let them chase you.'"

Massengale's final round 70 beat Palmer, who started his round with a double-bogey, by one shot.

The next week, at the Lucky International, Tony drew Paul Horning of the Green Bay Packers as his pro-am partner.

After a disappointing 76 in the first round, Tony informed tournament officials, before departing Harding Park for the day, he might withdraw because of pain in his elbow. A few hours later, he phoned the course and made his withdrawal official.

He spoke with Ed Schoenfeld about his injury and subsequent withdrawal informing the reporter that he was flying back to Dallas to see an orthopedic specialist, Dr. Charles Gregory.

"There's a good chance of surgery," Tony told him.

"The last couple of days I've been hitting the ball off the hard ground at Harding Park and it hurt like hell."

Deeply concerned, Tony felt a glimmer of hope when Dr. Gregory advised him to test the elbow with "very light practice" for a week before considering surgery.

"If it is still sore after a week, I probably will have to have my elbow operated on," Tony pessimistically told Schoenfeld by telephone. "If not, the doctor says I could continue playing for a while."

He was not optimistic about the prognosis and seemed resigned to the fact that he would have to go under the knife.

Meanwhile, back in San Francisco, Venturi proved Tony an excellent forecaster as he won the Lucky International with a fantastic 66 in the final round. It was a most satisfying win on the course he had played so often as a youth. It would be his last victory on tour.

After his short time in Dallas, Tony was off to Marco Island where on February 5 he headlined the "dedication foursome" for the official opening of the golf course he represented on tour. He had also convinced his boyhood friend, Chet Smith, to turn pro and operate his pro shop at the development. Tony thought that working the shop in Marco Island would benefit Smith, who suffered from health problems.

From there, he went to New York City to appear on the Ed Sullivan Show on Sunday, February 6. The show featured the music group The Animals performing "We Gotta Get Outta This Place," Rosemary Clooney singing and Alan King telling jokes. In his segment, Tony gave Sullivan golf tips, hitting shots off a mat into a net off screen. As usual, Tony appeared totally at ease in front of the camera as he demonstrated shots.

Then, he returned to Dallas for a follow-up examination of his elbow.

After consulting with Dr. Gregory, he decided to rejoin the tour for the Phoenix Open the second week of February. However, in Phoenix, the pain returned, forcing him to withdraw. Upon departing the golf course for the airport, he informed reporters his destination was Dallas where he would finally undergo surgery on the elbow. He vowed he would be ready to play in the Masters in April.

"I'll be there if I have to go in a wheelchair," Tony said. "I just wish I'd had it done some time ago. Now, I'm going to have to miss all those big money tournaments in Florida including the $100,000 events in Miami and Orlando."

When he got to the airport, though, he changed his plans. At the airport, he decided to fly to Los Angeles instead of Dallas. Dr. Robert Kerlan, the same doctor who administered to a similar injury in Sandy Koufax's elbow, practiced in Los Angeles and agreed to see Tony. Fred Corcoran and Danny Arnold may have been instrumental in Dr. Kerlan agreeing to see Tony.

Dr. Kerlan was the team doctor for the Dodgers and the Lakers where he treated Wilt Chamberlain. He also served as a doctor at the horse tracks around Los Angeles and treated Willie Shoemaker, the famous jockey.

"Dr. Kerlan consulted with my doctor (Dr. Gregory) here, and they've advised I try a new drug," Tony told Ed Schoenfeld of *The Oakland Tribune* from Dallas after returning from Los Angeles.

This new drug was most likely ibuprofen, a drug first patented in 1961 and not generally available in the United States until 1971. If he suffered from arthritis, the drug would alleviate the pain and allow him to keep playing. However, if he suffered from tendonitis, it would be more painful and would require rest to heal.

"They hope the drug will reduce the pain and allow me to play throughout the year," Tony explained to Schoenfeld. "I'm going to start on the drug later this week and do some practicing to see its affect. I have no idea when I'll be back on the tour. All I do know at this point is that this is my last go before I go to the hospital."

The elbow drove him nuts and played havoc with his schedule. He canceled his planned exhibition trip to Viet Nam and the Philippine Open, although Casper would still make the trip.

He had an air of resignation about the elbow and figured he would need surgery. He sent a typewritten note to Sister Mary Martin dated March 1.

> *Thank you for your very kind note,* the letter began. *I am afraid surgery on my elbow is definite. I am just hoping that with the use of some new drugs I will be able to put it off until August or September. If this is possible, it will be a miracle.*

*I am afraid that just about the time the big tournaments are to
start, this will be the time I have to go to the hospital. But,
I have had an awful lot of good fortune, and the Good Lord has
been very good to me, so I have no kicks coming.*

While he was off the tour, tending to his elbow, Tony celebrated his
32nd birthday on February 25. As was his custom, he sent Cleo 32 yellow
roses to mark the occasion. Cleo, who exhibited a talent for gardening,
rooted one of the stems and planted it between her driveway and a fence.

"She had quite the 'green thumb,' " her daughter Bernice recalled.

The rose took root, began growing and matured into an attractive
flowering bush that Cleo enjoyed for many years.

Tony started on the drug that Dr. Kerlan prescribed for him and the
pills helped ease the soreness in his elbow. In fact, his arm felt so good
when he tested it in practice that he entered the Doral Open getting
underway March 11.

"I've been taking pills and getting injections and I no longer have any
pain," Tony informed Will Grimsley of the Associated Press upon arrival at
Doral, a suburb of Miami. "I feel so good I plan to play in every
tournament leading up to the Masters."

He barely survived the cut after a pair of 74s, eventually finishing in a
tie for 59th, which was out of the money. Next was the Citrus Open where
he finished in a tie for 28th and a check for $756. He sat in the lowly 68th
position on the money list, but his elbow felt good enough to keep playing.
For the first time all year, he felt optimistic about his chances to continue
his year, uninterrupted by surgery, or forced rest.

The Masters was just around the corner and reporters began asking the
players who should be favored.

"When a guy plays the game like Casper does, every course in the
world is suited to him," Tony said.

A writer remarked that the only thing Casper could do was putt.

"Well, I guess he's been sinking a lot of 400-yard putts, then," Tony
quickly said, "as he has won quite a few tournaments lately."

He turned his attention to the state of his game heading into the year's
first major.

"I'm not playing very well yet," he admitted. "But I am in fine physical
condition now and I hope my game comes around in time."

He finally notched a top ten finish at the Jacksonville Open. After
opening with a mediocre first round 74, he came back with two 68s and a
69, tying for sixth and a nice check of $3,250.

The next week, at the Greater Greensboro Open he finished in a tie
for fifteenth place, with his two close friends Johnny Pott and Phil Rodgers.

He earned $1,550 for the week, jumping up to the 34th place on the money list.

After the Greensboro, it was the annual trek to Augusta for the Masters. He played a practice round with Gene Sarazen, who he had gotten to know quite well from his travels with *Shell's Wonderful World of Golf* and at Marco Island where Sarazen owned a lot. The press asked him about the condition of his elbow.

"It's okay now," Tony answered. "My arm is in perfect shape and I'm ready to go nine innings."

Tony's near miss of a green jacket in 1963 had whetted his appetite for a Masters victory and he pointed to the second week of April on his calendar each year.

"This is my fourth trip to the Masters and frankly I always feel a certain amount of anxiety each time I play here. I'm certain Arnold Palmer feels it, too," Tony told Milton Richman of the United Press International. "What I wouldn't give to win this one? The prestige is the big thing, of course, but with endorsements and everything else it would be worth at least a quarter of a million bucks to me."

Strong winds had turned the course hard and fast. The weather dawned clear for the first round, but rain started falling and continued intermittently throughout the day. Jack Nicklaus shot a 68 to take a three-stroke lead, despite receiving news the night before, of the death of his boyhood friend Bob Barton, and his wife, in an airplane crash.

The Bartons were flying down to Augusta to watch Nicklaus play, and the news hit Jack and his wife very hard. He thought of withdrawing from the tournament but instead vowed to dedicate the tournament to Barton's memory.

Trailing Nicklaus were the quartet of Don January, Mike Souchak, Billy Casper, and amateur Charles Coe, all at 71. Tony's 74 tied him with the impressive group of Palmer, Sanders, Brewer, Player and Hogan.

The next day, Nicklaus lost his focus on the greens with five three-putt greens, struggled to a 76 and now trailed Paul Harney and Peter Butler by one.

Palmer mounted a charge vaulting into contention with a 70 and trailed the leaders by one. He had birdied four of the first eight holes mobilizing his vast army of fans and only a bogey on the last hole kept him from tying the leaders.

Tony's second straight 74 left him five back needing a couple of sub-70 rounds on the weekend to get him back into the fray. Unfortunately, he could only manage a third consecutive 74.

Meanwhile, Tommy Jacobs came from out of the pack with a 70 in the third round that tied Nicklaus, who shot a third round 72, for the lead at

216.

Some of the largest roars around Augusta that day resulted from the round that Ben Hogan constructed as he worked some of his old magic shooting a 73. Both he and Arnold Palmer, who shot a 74, were at 218.

The crowds were enormous, estimated at between 40,000 and 50,000 (the Masters never releases official attendance figures).

Sunday's final round featured a wild finish. Nicklaus came from three strokes off the lead at the turn and mounted a comeback on the back nine. He birdied fourteen and fifteen and barely missed his birdie at the final hole to post a 72 for a four round 288. Brewer, playing with Palmer, three-putted the eighteenth hole, from 75-feet, posted a 70 and tied Nicklaus at 288. Jacobs played a very steady round of even par 72 and finished at 288, as well.

The green jacket would remain in the closet until the three players met the next day for an 18-hole playoff. Their 288 score was the second highest to win, or get in a playoff, in Masters history.

Tony finished with a disappointing 76, for a 298 total, far down the leader board.

CBS television carried the concluding holes of Monday's playoff as Nicklaus cruised to victory on the strength of five birdies and three bogeys for a 70.

The players had no time to rest after the Masters — they headed straight to the American desert for the Tournament of Champions in Las Vegas. Bo Wininger modified the Desert Inn course with the intent to test the touring pros. He had allowed the rough to grow, lengthened seven holes and rebuilt three greens with added undulations. The course would prove to be a stern test for the touring pros, a much different course than they had played in prior years.

35 FAVORITE SON-IN-LAW
1966

Upon arrival in Las Vegas, Tony informed reporters he still took the pain medication prescribed by Dr. Kerlan and his elbow was not bothering his game. In fact, he was hitting the ball well. Bo Wininger was successful in his quest of making the Desert Inn course tougher for the pros. Tony did not enjoy a good week and finished well down the leader board. The next week, he withdrew from the Dallas Open after three rounds with a sprained ankle.

After his withdrawal, Tony found time to dash off another letter to Sister Mary Martin. His elbow continued to be the main topic of his correspondence.

> *Dear Sister;*
> *So far, my elbow is in pretty good shape, without surgery. I just take a few*
> *pills every day, and it seems to hold it under control. I am completely positive*
> *that it is not the pills alone but prayer that has brought this about.*
> *I am afraid that eventually I will have to have the surgery, but*
> *just the fact that I will be able to probably get by most of this*
> *golf season is really a miracle. I thank God for this.*

He pushed his concerns about his elbow aside as he prepared for a trip to his father's birthplace, the Bahamas, for a match against Peter Alliss on *Shell's Wonderful World of Golf*. Tony arranged for his whole family to make the trip and they planned to visit relatives they rarely saw. The family also planned to celebrate his and Betty's third wedding anniversary.

Cleo, brothers Walter, and Harry, and sister Bernice, as well as their spouses, enjoyed the warm sunny weather and white sandy beaches of the Bahamas. It was a wonderful family vacation and he was extremely pleased he could provide this getaway.

However, he also had some work to do on the trip. His match against Alliss, a friend from their Ryder Cup competitions, on the Mid-Ocean Golf Club would not be easy. The seaside course features hilly terrain, blind tee shots, and of course, Bermuda grass greens.

He dressed for the show, now filmed in color. He wore a pale yellow polo-style golf shirt, with his trademark champagne glass logo embroidered on the left chest, green-brown slacks with matching yellow stripe cloth belt, a white glove and two-tone yellow and dark green shoes with kiltie flaps over the laces. The green portions of the shoes were suede. As usual, he played hatless. His caddy carried his new red and black Dunlap tour staff bag and he played a Maxfli ball.

Alliss also dressed colorfully and both men looked young and vibrant, at the height of their respective careers.

Sarazen wore his trademark plus-four suit, in a dark shade of brown, a white shirt, tie and a white straw fedora-style hat. Sarazen's new sidekick, Jimmy Demeret, always a sharp dresser, wore pale blue slacks very high on his waist, and a bright reddish, almost orange, horizontally striped mock-turtleneck golf shirt.

As the two commentators were talking at the side of the first green, Sarazen predicted that the outcome of the match hinged on who could handle the tricky Bermuda grass greens. "It'll all come down to one thing," said Sarazen, "three-foot putts."

Both players were able to par the first hole and scored birdies on the second hole. After holing out on the second hole, Demeret asked Tony about his strategy of switching between the American ball and the smaller British ball. The Bermudas, being a commonwealth of the British Empire, meant the rules of the Royal and Ancient Golf club were in effect. The players could use either ball, even alternating balls, as long as they made the change between holes.

Tony explained he planned to use the smaller ball when he was playing into the wind, as it was easier to control, or when he needed extra distance because the smaller ball traveled further. Demeret asked Sarazen if he had ever used this strategy of switching back-and-forth between the smaller and larger balls. Sarazen shook his head, about to answer in the negative, when Tony leaned into the microphone.

"He only had big balls in his day," he cracked.

Everybody laughed and the comment somehow made it by the usually diligent Shell editors.

Both players were having their difficulties on the greens. Alliss exhibited a unique putting grip whereas he used a conventional interlocking grip on long putts and switched to a cross-handed grip on shorter putts.

At the end of nine holes the match was all square. The two players joined Sarazen and Demeret at the edge of the ninth green and the four men laughed as barbs flew back and forth. They headed to the tenth tee, where Alliss hit first. Tony then took a practice swing and dug up a huge divot. The crowd murmured and Alliss broke up in laughter, while Tony gave a slightly embarrassed chuckle.

"I think that practice swing registered at Cal Tech," commented

Demeret.

After hitting his approach over the green and flubbing his recovery chip shot, Tony made a sloppy par on the par 5 eleventh hole while Alliss made a birdie to take a one shot lead. Tony evened the match with a birdie on the fifteenth.

After making a very long putt for birdie on the seventeenth hole, Tony broke into a huge smile as he walked across the green. Leading by one, he faced a long putt on the eighteenth hole needing only to two-putt to win the match and the $7,000 first prize. The loser of the match got $3,000 and in the case of a tie, the players split the $10,000 purse.

Sarazen's prediction came true; after Tony lagged his first putt to three-feet, he then missed the putt, resulting in a tied match. Although unhappy with his three-putt, he was still very gracious as he joined Alliss, Demeret and Sarazen for a few comments about the match. Sarazen then asked the players to show the viewers a few tips on how to play shots into the wind.

Tony jokingly said, "I'll show them how to make a three-foot putt."

On May 10, *The San Mateo Times* reported that Fernquest and Johnson Golf Company of Colma, California, had filed a damage suit against Tony in Superior Court in Redwood City. The company charged that Tony breached his equipment endorsement contract under which they manufactured the Tony Lema clubs from 1961 to 1965.

The company also named Fred Corcoran as a co-defendant, as well as the Dunlap Tire and Rubber Company, the company Tony now represented on tour. The suit asked for $35,000 in actual damages and $150,000 exemplary damages. Fernquest and Johnson charged that Corcoran, as Tony's agent, persuaded him to forsake F & J and sign with Dunlop. The company also asked the court to enjoin Dunlop from continuing to manufacture Lema clubs.

Tony answered by filing a counter-suit, filed by San Francisco attorney George Liberman, contending that the company owed him more than $20,000 in royalties. He contended that he had notified the company in October of 1965 intending to cancel the oral agreement and had offered F & J the necessary time to dispose of their existing stock. He had asked for a full accounting from the firm, which to date had not been provided. His understanding was that he could terminate the agreement with F & J at any time.

Fernquest and Johnson seemed to agree that the contract was an oral agreement. They claimed a written agreement to back up the oral agreement would have occurred in 1964 "but for the interference of Corcoran." They also admitted that they owed Tony $12,000 in royalties.

Convinced that the facts were on his side, Tony viewed the case as nothing more than an annoyance. He left the matter in the hands of his lawyer and turned his attention back to golf.

The Greater New Orleans Open, the second week of May, was his next competition. With a very nice 68 in the first round, he tied for the lead with Frank Beard, Bob Goalby, Charles Coody and Jack Nicklaus. Tony and Betty had introduced Beard to their neighbor in Dallas, Pat Roberts. It had turned out to be a successful match, with them getting married, and now expecting their first child.

After the round, Tony said, "I missed some good birdie chances but this is probably the best round I've played in six months." He brushed aside questions about his elbow saying, "I'm sick and tired of talking about it...hearing about it. I just swing it."

In the second round, Bob Goalby broke away from the pack with a 69 to take a one-stroke lead over Nicklaus. Tony was another stroke back tied with Beard. Kel Nagle, Harold Henning and Coody were four back.

In the third round, Tony and Nicklaus staged a furious head-to-head battle finishing tied for the lead at 208. Tony posted a 69 to the 70 recorded by Nicklaus. Bob Goalby fell back after a front nine 39, but rejoined the fray with a 33 on the back and sat at 209. Frank Beard kept himself nicely positioned with a third round 71, two off the lead. Gardner Dickinson, with a blazing 66, moved into a tie at 210 with Casper.

Forecasts predicted rain for the final round and although the skies were threatening, it was dry as the leaders teed off. Tony, in the next to last group, prepared for a battle with Nicklaus, who was in the final grouping.

Tony birdied the fourth hole to regain a share of the lead with Nicklaus, who birdied the first hole. As predicted, the rain arrived, in force, causing a delay in the round. Tony and Nicklaus sought refuge in a house near the fourth green where they relaxed and chatted while waiting out the downpour. Eventually, the players received word of the postponement of the round until the next day.

In the restarted fourth round, all eyes were on Tony and Nicklaus, fans expecting the two to wage a duel for the trophy and first place check. They both faded coming down the stretch, shooting 71. Tony, playing the front nine in even par, stumbled with a bogey on the eleventh, then recovered with two birdies. Nicklaus fell out of contention with bogeys on the eleventh and twelfth holes.

It was Frank Beard and Gardner Dickinson who waged the real battle in the fourth round. With a ferocious stretch drive, Beard finished with a 67 and won by two over Dickinson who shot a 68. He earned a $20,000 check, the largest of his career up to that point, while Nicklaus and Tony tied for third and made $5,150. Tony moved up into the 24th place on the official money list.

Tony's game had jelled nicely and thanks to the pills and an occasional cortisone injection, his elbow was not bothering him as it had earlier in the year. Once again, his confidence was soaring. At the Colonial the next week he finished in a tie for third, earning a check for $6,765 and moved up another six places on the money list into the top 20, at 18th place.

Feeling good about his game, Tony looked forward to the next stop, at Oklahoma City, Betty's childhood hometown. Quail Creek Golf and Country Club, a course that measured 7,000 yards with a par of 72 hosted the Oklahoma City Open. Ernie Vossler, a pal of Tony's dating back to the Caribbean tour, was the head pro at Quail Creek.

Johnny Pott opened the tournament with a sizzling 64 to jump out to a four-stroke lead. Tony had a 69, as the pros found Quail Creek straightforward with 41 players matching or breaking par.

Tony received bad news before the second round when he learned that Chet Smith died at Marco Island. His long-time friend lost his lengthy battle with colon cancer. He turned pro three months earlier and was working the pro shop for Tony at Marco Island. Although he knew the prognosis was not good for Smith, the news of his death nevertheless upset Tony. He had to force himself to focus on his second round.

Pott continued his fine play, adding a 69 in the second round, for a 133, retaining his four-stroke lead. With a very steady 68, Tony was four back, tied with Tom Weiskopf.

Tony's birdie on the fifteenth hole morphed into a bogey, after taking a penalty for an illegal drop. He felt fortunate, however, that his mental lapse did not cost him more. Wanting to see how the pros played his course, Vossler wandered out to a vantage point on a hill overlooking the fairway on fifteen. While there, he noticed Tony taking a free drop from ground under repair. He saw that Tony did not take his drop at the nearest point of relief as stipulated by the rules. Once Tony finished his round, but before he could sign his card, Vossler informed him about his error. Tony added the penalty strokes, for an incorrect drop, before he signed his scorecard. If he had signed an incorrect scorecard, for a score lower than he had actually shot, the consequence would have been disqualification. The fifteenth was his only bogey in the first two rounds.

"I should have known better," Tony admitted to reporters. "But I was playing so good I just didn't think. I'd have been a little upset if I'd been disqualified. It's a lot better to be at 137 than on the way to Dallas."

Young Tom Weiskopf took the lead in the third round shooting 68 for a 205. Tony was one stroke back after shooting a 69 without a single bogey on his card.

The leader board now read:

Weiskopf 205
Lema 206
Pott 207
Dill 208
Nicklaus 208

The weather for the fourth round continued as it had for the whole week—clear, sunny and lacking the usual Oklahoma City wind. Tony took advantage of the conditions and came out blazing shooting a 65 to coast to a six-stroke victory. Weiskopf finished second while Nicklaus, playing with Tony, finished third, eight strokes off Tony's pace. The only bogey that Tony recorded during the entire week was the bogey that resulted from his penalty at the fifteenth hole during the second round.

"I don't care what anybody says about that two-stroke penalty, I played 72 holes without a bogey, as far as I'm concerned," he said arriving in the press tent.

He grabbed a bottle of Moet champagne, popped the cork and poured Betty and himself a glass.

"I haven't had any of this since last August," he gleefully said sipping the bubbly. "Make sure everybody in the working press gets some of this," he instructed waving his extended forefinger around the room.

He made a point of telling reporters Vossler "showed a lot of class" pointing out the improper drop in the second round, prior to Tony signing his card.

He explained he had focused on Nicklaus as his main threat in the final round and that "the eighth hole was probably the turning point in the whole match, really."

He had made birdie and Nicklaus drove into a water hazard, then hit a three-wood to the front of the green, but failed to convert the four-foot putt for par falling two back of Tony's lead. Tony's 271 set a tournament record and his six-stroke margin of victory was the largest of the 1966 tour.

"I'm never coming back to Oklahoma," he joked. "Because I want to remember it this way—windless."

News photographers asked Tony to pose with Betty. Using his scorecard as a prop, he acted as if he were explaining his strategy to her.

"Get down the fairway," Tony began with an impish smile, "on the green and in the hole as fast as you can."

He and Betty giggled while the reporters joined in the laughter.

"I was hoping for a 64 or 63, since I haven't had a round that low in some time," Tony said. "I didn't play conservatively until the sixteenth, a par 3, where I hit an iron to the fat of the green. The pin was behind a trap and I didn't want to risk a bogey."

Telling reporters he intended "to play a lot of golf" the rest of the year, he said his elbow was feeling fine. Still, he admitted he would probably be required to undergo an operation "sometime in the future."

In the last four tournaments, Tony shot 14 straight rounds of 71 or better and his winner's check of $8,500 moved him up into the top ten on the official money list.

He and Betty left the champagne party with the press and rushed to the airport so that they could fly to Indianapolis to take in the Indy 500 race. From there, the two headed to Memphis for the Memphis Open at the Colonial Country Club. He felt that his game jelled at just the right time, focused as he was on the U.S. Open in his hometown, now just two weeks away.

In Memphis, he opened with a 69 and matched it in the final round to finish in a tie for ninth and a check for $2,175. Even though he cashed a nice check, he slipped one place on the money list to the tenth spot.

The next tournament, in Flint, Michigan was the Buick Open, the last tournament before the U.S. Open. Tony made a quick trip to Dallas before going to Flint. While waiting for his flight to Flint, he ran into Mickey Mantle, waiting for the same flight.

Mantle was heading back to join the Yankees after a break at home. The two stars shook hands and exchanged pleasantries before they boarded the plane where they sat next to each other. Mantle peppered Tony with golf questions while Tony wanted to talk nothing but baseball.

With the Open approaching, the media got busy handicapping the field. Byron Nelson told the Associated Press that Tony posed a strong threat to win at the Olympic Club.

"Tony is playing marvelously," Nelson told Fred Corcoran after seeing Tony's performance in Oklahoma City. "It's been a long time since I have seen such an exhibition of iron play. I can only remember playing one tournament without a bogey and that was the Canadian Open in 1945. Lema played marvelously."

Tony flew into Detroit and shared a car ride to Flint with Leo Peterson and Milton Richman, sports writers for the United Press International. The two writers were planning an in-depth piece on the rigors of travel that a star of the PGA Tour must go through.

"I better do well this week and next," Tony allowed, "because if I don't win a total of $15,000 here and in the U.S. Open next week, I'll have to borrow some money. My annuity payments are coming due."

The two writers could sense the mirth in Tony's voice. He also spoke about settling down with Betty to start a family. What he did not tell the reporters was that there were problems with the couple's ability to conceive children.

Betty had visited a doctor who assured her there was no reason why she could not get pregnant, but when Tony went to a doctor for a check-up, he did not receive the same good news. He learned he was sterile, leaving adoption as the only option for the couple to have children.

He was deeply disappointed—and angry. Angry with the mother he was paying child support to, feeling the woman had duped him. He contacted his lawyer to remove the boy, David Lema, from his will, although he continued to pay child support. In the days before DNA testing, there was no way of knowing, for sure, if he was the father.

Upon arrival at the Warwick Hills course in Flint, Tony could not help but think ahead a week to the U.S. Open.

"That's the one every golfer wants to win," he told a UPI reporter. "But what's wrong with trying to pick up $20,000 along the way? I don't like to take a week off before the really big one. If I do, I get too charged up thinking about it. This way I concentrate on the job at hand and let next week take care of itself. Of course, I'm thinking about the Open—all golfers do. But I honestly feel I'll have a better chance to win it by playing here."

After a pause Tony added, "I notice that Arnie is here, too."

Palmer was returning to action in the Buick after a four-week layoff to rehabilitate his sore back. Warwick Hills played tougher this year with 33 new bunkers added and 37 new trees planted.

The changes did not affect Tony's view of the course where he notched two of his tour titles. He was attempting to win the Buick for the third year in a row.

A rain washout of the first round caused a lot of consternation amongst the pros scheduled to play in the Open. Tournament organizers, fully cognizant of the fact these pros wanted to get to the Olympic Club, scrambled to get the tournament completed on schedule. They planned to play 18 holes on Friday and Saturday with a 36-hole finish on Sunday. If rain caused the cancellation of another round, then the tournament's conclusion included 18-holes on Saturday, 36-holes on Sunday and a final 18 on Monday.

"That's crowding it for most of us who want to get a chance to size up the Olympic course," Tony said.

A reporter asked Tony his views on the USGA's intent to have the players play in no more than four hours.

"Out of the question," Tony unequivocally stated. "How can they direct the men who make their living at the game to speed up play to such an extent that it could affect their game? When you are shooting for a big one like the Open, there should be no time limit imposed."

Once the Buick finally got underway, Tony opened up with a 78 and thought he had blown his week. However, he bounced back from this horrendous start to shoot a fantastic 66 in the second round. He played the back nine first and stuck his irons close as he birdied five of the first 12 holes. His longest birdie putt was 18 feet and the four others were all six-feet, or less.

"I have to do two things right away," Tony, informed the press after his round. "Cancel my airplane reservations and unpack four suitcases."

Fully expecting to miss the cut after his opening round of 78, he had prepared for his early departure to San Francisco.

"I was embarrassed and ashamed of that 78," he admitted with a smile. "My short game was terrible. I just couldn't concentrate. But that 66 was a wonderful thing to happen. I just wanted to make the cut. I didn't want to watch the finals on television from a hotel room in San Francisco Sunday."

He finished with a 70 and a 73 in the Sunday 36-hole finale to finish in a tie for fourth. His check for $4,650 moved him to the ninth spot on the official money list for the year.

"Naturally, I wanted to win here," he told reporters, "but the way I came back gave me a big lift for the Open. I ought to do all right in San Francisco."

Tony actually fought his way into the lead in the afternoon round but Phil Rodgers birdied the eighth hole to catch him, then added another birdie on the ninth to take the lead, and never relinquished it thereafter.

"Phil deserved to win," Tony conceded. "He played well. I gave it a try but it just wasn't good enough."

Although disappointed with finishing in a tie for fourth at the Buick, Tony was confident in his game and eagerly looked forward to the Open in San Francisco. He felt he held an advantage playing a course he was familiar with and playing in front of friends and family. If ever there was an Open with his name on it, this was it.

36 OLYMPIC OPEN
1966

All eyes of the golf world focused on the beautiful Olympic Club in San Francisco. The club features two courses, the Ocean Course and the Lakeside Course, the latter hosting the U.S. Open.

A headline in *The Oakland Tribune* read; CHAMPAGNE TONY IS PLAYING IT COOL. A LITTLE PRACTICE IS ENOUGH.

Tony quit his practice round and walked off the course after only eight holes on Tuesday, explaining to reporters that he would come back to play the other ten holes on Wednesday.

"This way I can conserve my energy for the Open by staying out of the heat," Tony explained. He then went to Candlestick Park to take in a Giants baseball game.

After playing ten holes on Wednesday, he again met with the press, many of whom questioned his preparation.

"No, I don't think it will hurt my chances, or I wouldn't have done it this way," he defiantly stated.

He felt good about his chances in this Open, despite his short preparation time. He admitted that his eighteen holes of practice was his only look at the course in the last five years; however, he played it plenty of times during his time as assistant pro at San Francisco Golf Club. His game was sharp, evidenced by the $28,500 he had collected in the last five weeks on tour. He was definitely in one of those hot streaks that he got into around this time every year. His fellow touring pros agreed, and most thought he belonged in the top five favorites to capture the U.S. Open.

Another player considered a favorite was Billy Casper. Tony felt that Casper's overall game was vastly underrated and he felt Casper had all the tools to win the Open at Olympic.

A reporter asked Tony if Olympic had any particularly tough holes.

"Well, seventeen is tough," he began. "There's a tough string on two through six and eleven through fifteen. I guess they're all tough. There's no place to gamble here."

Tony predicted 284 should win the Open. Once through with the press, he departed the grounds, off to catch another Giants game.

In the first round, Al Mengert, an unknown from Tacoma,

Washington took the first round lead by shooting a 67. He enjoyed a one-stroke lead over Don Massengale and Gene Littler while Casper lurked just one stroke further back after a first round 69. They were the only players to break par on the par-70 Lakeside course while four others managed to match it. Nineteen-year-old Johnny Miller, who had signed up to be a caddy before qualifying for the Open, played his home course in even par. Miller was a student of John Geertsen and showed a calm demeanor for such a young competitor in his first national open.

In front of a large gallery including family and friends, Tony shot a 71 and sat tied with a group of players including Palmer and Nicklaus.

Mengert, almost predictably for a relatively unknown first round Open leader, skied to a 77 in the second round. Another young, anonymous pro, Rives McBee, set a new course record, and tied the U.S. Open single round record of 64, to post a 140 early in the day. Later in the day, Palmer charged to a 66 and posted a 137. Casper scrambled to a 68 for a 137 tying Palmer for the halfway lead.

Tony finished poorly, scoring three straight fives for a 74 and sat at 145, tied with Ben Hogan, but still well within sight of the leaders. He needed a good third round.

Palmer not only wanted to win the Open, he wanted to set a scoring record, breaking Hogan's 276 set in 1948. The weather for the third round was a picture perfect day for golf—sunny, temperatures in the 70s and negligible winds. Nicklaus played with the young amateur, Johnny Miller, who seemed unfazed by his exceptional play in the tournament, or the specter of playing with Nicklaus in front of huge crowds.

Palmer scrambled and charged his way to a 70 that put him one off Tommy Jacobs's 54-hole record score of 206. He ran into problems on the back nine when he lost three strokes to par on the twelfth and thirteenth holes, but made up ground when he sank a five-foot birdie putt on the fourteenth and a 23-foot birdie putt on the sixteenth. Yet, he cautioned against over-confidence.

"I went into the final round of the Masters one year four shots ahead and had to win it in a playoff," he reminded the press.

The leader board now read:
Palmer 207
Casper 210
Nicklaus 211
Marr 213
Rodgers 213
McBee 214
Lema 215

Johnny Miller accounted for himself quite nicely shooting a 74 in front of enormous galleries. His score of 216 gave him the inside track for the Low Amateur medal.

For his part, Tony was disappointed.

"I played thirteen holes like a pro," Tony explained to the press after his round, "and five holes like a jerk. I'm pretty far back. I don't know if it's because I've been playing so much golf lately, but my concentration seems to come and go."

Tony, paired with Ben Hogan, thoroughly enjoyed watching the aging master at work even though Hogan could do no better than a 76. He approached Hogan after the round in the player's locker room.

"I don't want to sound corny, but that was something I've been looking forward to for a long time," he said.

In the final round, it looked as if the only suspense would be over whether or not Palmer could break Hogan's scoring record. He started his round with two birdies and made the turn with a seven-stroke lead over his closest pursuer, Casper.

"I thought he was sure to do it and my only concern at that time was to stay ahead of Nicklaus and Lema for the second money," Casper admitted. "I figured there was no way I could catch Arnie." Tony had mounted a charge early in his round that landed him on Casper's radar.

On the back nine, Palmer began to drive erratically as he focused all his attention on Hogan's record instead of on winning the tournament. He bogeyed the tenth hole and Casper birdied the twelfth. Casper got his par on the 191-yard par 3 thirteenth hole while Palmer could only manage a bogey and the lead suddenly shrank down to five strokes.

Both players managed pars on fourteen. However, Palmer missed the green on the par 3 fifteenth winding up in a bunker resulting in another bogey. Casper birdied the same hole whittling the lead down to just three strokes. Palmer found himself in real trouble at the sixteenth hole.

"The sixteenth was the turning point," he said. "I had been driving into the right rough on that hole so I decided to hit it left. I did, far too much left. The drive went only about 180-yards in deep rough and on the second shot, I moved the ball less than 70-yards and left it in the rough."

It added up to another bogey on the par 5 hole while Casper carded a birdie pulling to a single stroke of Palmer's lead. Palmer again hooked his drive on eighteen and missed the green with his approach shot resulting in yet another bogey.

Casper secured his par on the last hole capping off an amazing comeback to tie Palmer. He and Palmer would meet the next day in an 18-hole playoff. Palmer ended up with a 71 in the final round and Casper, a solid 68. Nicklaus finished in a distant third place after a final round 74 for a 285, seven behind Palmer and Casper.

Coming down the stretch, Tony pressed for birdies to secure a high finish. He finished with a devastating three-putt on the final hole for a disastrous double-bogey that dropped him from third place down to a tie for fourth. His 71 tied him with Dave Marr, earning a check for $6,500 that moved him up to the eighth spot on the money list.

Unnoticed by most observers was a pro from Dallas playing in his first U.S. Open. Lee Trevino qualified, first through local, then sectional qualifying, and managed to make the 36-hole cut. He scored an unimpressive 78 in each of the closing rounds to finish well down the leader board. The next year, Trevino exploded onto the golf scene when he finished in an impressive fifth place at the Open held at Baltusrol.

Palmer completed his historic collapse the next day during the playoff, again having difficulties on the back nine. He blew to a 40 on the inward nine for a 73 while Casper put together a 69. Palmer actually held a two-stroke lead at the turn. As he struggled through the back nine, he appeared shaken and glassy eyed. Casper drew even with Palmer after sinking a 25-foot putt on the eleventh hole and then took over the lead with a 35-foot putt on the twelfth.

"It's unbelievable, but I never gave up," declared an ecstatic Casper.

A despondent Palmer could only say to reporters, "I haven't got much to say. I had trouble on the back nine all week. I've kind of been fighting it, particularly the last two days. I got that bogey on eleven, and Bill made that long birdie putt and that kind of changed things. I guess I just wrapped up my business too soon."

The tour moved on to Medinah Country Club, near Chicago for the historic Western Open, considered a major in the time of Sarazen and Hagen.

On the practice tee, Jack Brown, a Buick dealer in Michigan, approached Tony about a benefit golf tournament, the Lincolnshire Open at the Lansing Sportsman Golf Course in Lansing, Illinois near the Indiana border. Brown asked Tony to participate, offering to pay him $1,000 in addition to what he won in prize money. Tony felt a certain obligation to participate, because the Buick dealers treated him so well, and happily agreed to play in the 36-hole tournament, held the day after the upcoming PGA Championship.

"Sounds good," Tony said, committing to the event and then turned to Max Winters, his caddy.

"Whaddya say, Jerry?" he asked using the name Winters went by at that time. "Can you work the bag for me?"

Winters agreed to caddy, so Tony asked him to go to the course early to scout it. Winters assured him he would, although it would require him to forsake working the PGA championship and hitchhike to Lansing.

Tony and Winters had grown quite close since first matched up at the 1962 Western Open at Medinah. The two kept in regular contact exchanging letters. Tony told Winters "not to worry about it, I'll handle it," when it came to college expenses after Winters expressed concerns about affording college. Tony felt a real affinity for the 19-year-old.

Casper, riding the high of his U.S. Open victory, won the Western Open shooting a 283—the only sub-par score for the week. Palmer, suffering from his U.S. Open hangover, shot a third round 75 and finished at 289.

Tony opened up with two straight rounds of 71 before blowing up to a 75 in the third round. He came back with a 71 in the fourth round securing a tie for fifth place and a check for $3,650. Since his withdrawal in Dallas, he had recorded two ties for third, a win, a tie for ninth, two straight ties for fourth and a tie for fifth. He won $37,390 in that two-month stretch.

After an exhibition at the Shawnee Inn Golf Course in Stroudsburg, Pennsylvania, he flew to Scotland for the British Open held at Muirfield. He made a stop in New York to meet up with Fred Corcoran for the trip to Scotland while Betty again remained stateside.

37 CHAMPAGNE ON THE GREEN
1966

Tony caught a terrible cold on the long flight to Edinburgh for the British Open. He checked into the house he used for the week and his housekeeper, "Ma Ferguson" whipped him up a local concoction to fight his illness. Tony drank the healing elixir consisting of liberal quantities of lemon juice, honey, and scotch.

"It helped me forget my cold," Tony said crediting the homemade medication for being able to play in the first round.

But the cold hampered his play all week at the Muirfield Golf Course.

"I'd just as soon go home now," he said after the first round.

Jack Nicklaus captured his first British Open title, nipping Doug Sanders by a stroke while Tony finished well down the leader board, in a tie for 30th.

After The Open, Tony remained in Great Britain to play an exhibition with Peter Alliss at Kingswood in London. Tony defeated his friend 2 and 1 shooting a blazing seven-under 64 that equaled the course record. Tony won $1,700 in the challenge match put on by the Variety Club of Britain Golfing Society with proceeds donated to the society's Fund for Handicapped Children. Tony donated his winnings, after expenses, to the fund.

He had increased his philanthropic activity since becoming successful on tour. In addition to raising money through exhibitions for many varied causes, he also quietly donated money to children causes and sent regular donations to other organizations such as the Poor Claire's in Oakland, the cloistered order of nuns near St. Elizabeth High School. He remembered how he had visited the nuns while he was in high school, and the spiritual guidance that they had provided.

After arriving back in New York City from England, Tony sat down with Howard Cosell for an extended filmed interview at the Westchester Country Club in Rye, New York. Tony stayed with Cosell and his wife, Emmy, and their two daughters at their lodge-style house on eleven acres of woodland outside New York City.

The interview, filmed in grainy black-and-white, started in a three-wheel golf cart with white fringe dangling from the roof, on the grounds of Westchester. Cosell, dressed in a suit and tie, posed his questions while perched on the front of the cart. Tony, dressed in a white polo golf shirt, sat behind the cart's tubular, triangle steering mechanism provided thoughtful answers.

Cosell commented on the pressures that a pro golfer faced.

"I'm thirty-two now," Tony mused, "and I must have the nerves of about an eighty-year-old; they're shot."

Tony spoke to what it took to be a winning golfer on the PGA Tour.

"I think the thing that makes a winner in golf is the guy that is not only the best player, but also the one that can keep control of his nerves better than the next guy," he explained.

"How do you do it?" Cosell asked.

"Talk to myself, concentration, prayer—many things," Tony answered.

He then informed Cosell the true key to his success after five years out on tour was love.

"I fell in love just prior to the fall of 1962, when I won my first two or three tournaments. And I think that falling in love with my wife gave me just the edge that I needed to settle myself down. I think it has made a tremendous amount of difference. Just goes to show you—love can do anything."

Cosell rattles off his official money winnings for the last three years while Tony's eyebrows shoot up and he looks over his shoulder with a grin.

"I hope there's no tax man around," he sheepishly jokes.

"They say now," Cosell, comments, "golfers are spoiled, the money is too much, they're getting their hands on it too easily. What do you think?"

Tony narrows his eyes, points his finger at Cosell and says with a grin, "I'll tell you something right here, Howard. I can't agree with you more, but it's wonderful." Cosell chuckles at the response.

Cosell said, "Tony, in perfect candor, you saw the emerging in this country of the so called 'Big Three.' Palmer, Player and Nicklaus…"

Tony cuts him off while pantomiming the removal of an imaginary hat from his head.

"If I had a hat, I'd take it off and place it over my heart," he jokes. He then leans back and folds his arms with his head tilted back defiantly as he continued, "They're three wonderful guys, and they're the great names in the game of golf, but too many times players like Bobby Nichols, Billy Casper and some great young players are really not getting a fair shake."

Cosell points out Tony has the personal glamour that two of the big three do not.

Tony modestly said, "Well, I don't know. I really don't follow you there. I love to play golf and I'm an emotional kind of a character. If things are going badly, I'm liable to frown, but then at the same time, I like to laugh at myself. I am fortunate enough I can do that. And, if I'm happy, well, laugh a little and live it up."

Cosell then invites Tony to go over to the first tee and hit a few shots.

"I'd love to," Tony says and with a grin, "Hope I don't shank too many."

"Let's go," Cosell says.

"Come on," Tony responds adjusting his position in the seat of the cart, "Hop in—I'll give you the ride of your life."

Cosell climbs in on the passenger side of the bench seat while Tony takes control of the steering bar and the duo wheels away. On the first tee, Tony hits an iron shot before resuming the interview as the conversation turns to his victory in the British Open.

"The British Open," Tony begins, "is one of the four prestige championships in the world. Contrary to what you probably believe, when I won it, it was the most humbling experience I've ever had in golf. When I won it, I was taken into the room where they make all the rules of golf and saw the old golf balls and the old clubs and all these pictures of the old players. It made me realize how it started and what it's all about. I really felt quite humble about being fortunate enough to win it."

Cosell wonders how the pros get along, on a personal level, out on tour.

"Well, I'll tell you," Tony began. "I think you'd be very surprised. I've never seen any fights and very few times, have there been any harsh words. With all the pressure that we're under constantly, everybody's on edge. I think everybody respects everybody else's feelings. We're living with each other, practically, you know, every day. There's a comradeship there that is second to none. I think it's a great bunch of guys."

Cosell asked him who his best friends out on the tour are.

"Phil Rodgers, Bobby Nichols, quite a few of 'em," Tony responds. "I'd say they're all good friends of mine."

Cosell asks Tony to come up with the perfect fantasy golf team taking various aspects of any of the player's game out on tour, except for his. Tony says he would like to play Nicklaus's second shots naming him as his driver on the team. For iron play, Tony selects Billy Casper, Tom Weiskopf, Frank Beard and Phil Rodgers.

"On the green, I'll take two California boys and you can pick anybody else you want," Tony says. "I'll take Phil Rodgers and Billy Casper, and, uh, I'll go with my team."

"You running a Billy Casper hour these days?" Cosell asks Tony.

"It sounds like it," Tony admits, "but I'll tell you…the guy is a very underrated player and as far as mechanics of the game, I don't think there's too many people much better."

The pair moved to the veranda of the clubhouse with Tony adding a stylish dark sports jacket. He and Cosell, seated at a small round table, have a bottle of champagne situated in a silver stand, on ice, between them.

"Tony," Cosell begins, "a lot of people figure this is the life. A plush country club veranda, soft breeze, beautiful surroundings. This is the way you fellows are generally figured to live. But tell the people how many weeks out of a year you're at home."

"Howard," Tony responds, "I'm lucky if I get home six weeks a year, and I'm darn lucky if I get to sit on the veranda at a country club. We keep a pretty hectic schedule."

"What does it do to your marriage?" Cosell asked.

"Well, I take my wife with me so I don't have that problem," Tony answers. "But I don't see how the guys with kids going to school and their wives at home really make it. I think it'd be a lousy life."

"You want children and you and Betty will have children," Cosell states.

"I hope so," Tony responds with the thought of his recent discovery that he is sterile surely in the back of his mind. "What I'm going to do, Howard, you know, I'm no spring chicken. When the kids get up to the age where they have to stay at home and go to school, that's the day I'm going to quit playing. I hope it won't be much over five or ten years from now."

"How would you like people to remember you, how would you like them to characterize you?" Cosell asks.

"Well, I really hadn't thought of that, Howard," Tony responds. "I'd just like to play good golf, successful golf as long as I can and if I'm remembered, that's fine."

"Do you want to be remembered as a great golfer?" Cosell presses.

"Oh, I don't know," Tony says. "I'd rather be remembered as a decent sort of person than an athlete, as far as greatness."

"So," Cosell says, "that will be enough for you to be thought of as one of the glamour boys in the golden age of golf?"

"In the right way, glamour, yes," Tony responds.

"And that glamour includes champagne?" Cosell inquires.

Tony glances down at the bottle resting on ice in the silver stand, raises his eyes with a little twinkle in them and puts on his impish grin.

"Would you like some?" He asks Cosell.

"Love some," says the sportscaster.

"Why, not," Tony says and Cosell instructs him to pour.

Tony removes the foil and cage from the bottle of Moet.

"We ought to have a little pop here, too, Howard," he warns. "Hang onto your hat."

He releases the cage and gives the cork a little push ejecting it from the bottle and it flies away off-camera. Tony fills the two champagne glasses and hands one to Cosell.

"There's nothing like ending a nice day," Tony states, "or a good game of golf, with a little taste of the bubbly. Cheers."

The network scheduled the half hour taped interview for broadcast after the upcoming PGA Championship.

38 N538B
1966

After the Cosell interview, Tony departed New York for the 50th anniversary of the PGA Championship played on the tough Firestone Country Club in Akron, Ohio. The AFL-CIO International Association of Machinists, involved in a strike against Trans World Airlines, Eastern Airlines, National Airlines, Northwest Airlines and United Airlines, the nation's five leading carriers in the country, made air travel difficult.

The machinists went out on strike on July 8, looking for higher wages, and the strike disrupted travel plans across the U.S. Despite the efforts of small regional airlines, and airlines not affected by the strike, it was very difficult to book reservations on a long-distance flight. The pros scrambled to find seats on the regional airlines to fly into Akron, and Tony managed to find a flight into Akron for both he and Betty. His scheduled exhibition tournament for Buick in Illinois at the conclusion of the PGA proved more problematic, as far as travel plans were concerned. He was unsure whether he would drive or charter a small plane to make the short trip.

Pre-tournament forecasters listed Palmer as a favorite ahead of Nicklaus, Sanders, Brewer, Player and Tony. Again, forecasters underrated Casper.

The ageless wonder, Sam Snead, shocked and delighted tournament observers by posting a first round 68, to tie for the lead with Al Geiberger. Sanders, Boros and January were one back. Tony opened with a 78 virtually eliminating him from a chance at the championship. Once again, it looked to be a year of major tournament disappointments.

Snead grabbed the solo lead after a second round 71 gave him 139. Geiberger had an up-and-down round with five birdies, five bogeys and a double-bogey for a 72 and sat at 140. January had a 71, salvaging the score with eight one-putt greens. Tony bounced back with a 71, tying Venturi at 149, safely within the cut line. No golfer beat par during Friday's round.

In the first round, Tony told Miller Barber and Gary Player, his playing companions, how tired he was.

"I'm worn out," Tony complained. "I'm going home to rest for three weeks after this thing in Chicago."

The Lincolnshire Open Pro-Am, the one-day 36-hole benefit

tournament in Lansing, Illinois, was "this thing in Chicago."

On Saturday, Tony approached Butch Baird on the practice tee who was also scheduled to play in the Lincolnshire Open.

"Monday we have to go over to Chicago to play," Tony said to Baird. "Why don't we rent a plane?"

"Okay," Baird replied.

Renting a plane would be the easiest way to avoid the hassles caused by the airline strike.

"I'll get the rental plane," Tony proposed.

Baird was quick to agree, "Okay, I'll leave the details to you."

Jack Brown, the Buick dealer who organized the Lincolnshire Open, phoned Tony with concerns about his travel plans.

"Listen Tony," he began. "With this airline strike going on, let us send down a car and a driver for you. It's not that long a drive and it would be safer than flying up here in one of those small planes."

Tony informed Brown that he had already chartered a plane and not to worry, he had been on hundreds of flights in small planes. He thought back to all those quick hops in Cliff Whittle's small plane.

Back at the hotel, Betty called her friend Pat Beard, wife of fellow pro Frank Beard, who was home in Louisville, expecting the couples' first child. The two women talked for close to a half an hour and Betty told Beard how happy she was and how well she and Tony were getting along.

Tony and Betty were very much in love.

"I've never been so happy in my life and if I met Betty five years before, I would have married her then," Tony recently told a friend.

Al Geiberger took control of the PGA Championship with a 68 in the third round resulting in a four-stroke lead at 208. Sam Snead, finally showing his 54 years, shot a 75 and dropped to fifth at 214. With a 72, Tony was well down the leader board at 221. Only six golfers broke par in the third round on the ferocious Firestone course.

Tony woke up early on Sunday so that he could attend Mass at St. Bernard's Catholic Church. He walked to the church by himself, passing Max Elbin, president of the PGA, as he walked up the hill toward the church's entrance.

"These hills are getting steeper and steeper," Tony said to Elbin as they greeted each other. He joined his friend, Johnny Pott at the service.

After Mass, Tony met Leo Peterson and Milton Richman for breakfast. The two sportswriters, still working on their in-depth article of his life on tour, sat at a table in the restaurant at the hotel where Tony was staying. They watched as he arrived and slid into a chair at the table. He asked the server to bring his check with his order of juice, bacon and eggs.

"Betty has eaten and I told her I would be only 15 minutes," Tony explained as he signed the check with one hand and shoveled food into his mouth with the other.

He then talked with the reporters about the rigors of being on the road.

"A couple of years from now, Betty and I are going to settle down and start raising a family," he said.

He admitted he was getting tired of the traveling and living out of a suitcase.

"Just give us a couple of more years and that's what I'm going to do," he went on. "Golf is great and it has given me everything. Everything I have I owe to the game."

The conversation turned to his efforts in the PGA Championship.

"I never tee up without thinking of one thing; winning," Tony assured the writers. "It sure doesn't look good, but I'll be out there trying."

The server came back to the table picking up Tony's check, including a generous tip.

"Now don't spend this tip all in one place," Tony instructed her.

The two writers shook Tony's hand and wished him luck in the final round.

"Thanks. I'll need it," Tony replied.

Back in San Leandro, Cleo made a trip to place flowers on Tone's grave on her late husband's birthday. She returned to the house on Hays street and spent time in the yard and garden with her son-in-law Art's father and his second wife, who were houseguests.

In the final round, Al Geiberger negotiated Firestone with an even-par score of 70 and captured his first major title. Tony finished well down the list at 295 winning a meager $775 after finishing with a 74.

After his round, Tony made his way out to the eighteenth hole where Butch Baird was just finishing his round. Tony explained to Baird that the charter company sent a four-passenger plane instead of the requested six-passenger plane for the flight to the Lincolnshire Open.

"I'd like to take my wife with me," Tony explained. "If it's alright with you, I have a United friend who has a reservation to Chicago you can get on."

Baird, as a pilot himself, knew the chaos the airline strike caused. He understood the small charter companies had to scramble to supply the necessary aircraft needed to satisfy the demand.

"That's fine," he told Tony. "Go ahead."

Tony quickly returned to the locker room in the clubhouse to clean his locker, impatient to get to the airport for the flight to Hammond, Indiana. From Hammond he planned to drive to Crete, Illinois for the one-day event at the Lincoln Oaks Golf Course the next day. His caddy, Max Winters, had already arrived at the course a day earlier.

Tony rushed into the locker room and showered quickly pausing only to discuss a putt he missed during his final round.

"How could I possibly have missed it?" he lamented. "If I only could have sunk it, it would have made a big difference in how I did the rest of my round."

Ken Venturi delayed him further when he confronted him in the locker room. The two friends were soon embroiled in an intense argument. Venturi was dismayed that Tony was not going to attend a local American-Italian dinner honoring Tony along with other players.

"What are you doing?" Venturi asked. "You promised these people that you would be there."

Tony tried to explain he committed to the benefit outing weeks before and felt that he owed Buick something in return for all they had done for him. Venturi ignored Tony's explanation; he was truly angry with him. He thought the trip to Chicago was simply for the money. Venturi wrote in his autobiography, *Getting Up and Down*, that Tony was paid $2,000 for participating in the Lincolnshire event, while newspaper accounts put the figure at $250. Winters, present when Tony agreed to play in the event, remembers the figure being $1,000, and whatever prize money he could win. Tony and Venturi parted with angry words.

Tony quickly cleaned out his locker, number 333 located between the lockers of Raymond Floyd and Miller Barber. In all, he spent about 15 minutes in the locker room. In his haste to leave, he neglected to pack a pair of black and white wing-tip shoes leaving them behind in his locker.

Many of the other players in the field at the PGA, at Nicklaus's invitation, were off to Columbus to participate in the Columbus Pro-Am, a one-day event. The event, played at Scioto Country Club, the course that Nicklaus grew up on as a teenager, raised funds for local charities.

Tony finally met up with Betty for the ride to the airport. After arriving at the Akron airport, they learned that their plane was at the Akron-Canton Airport 20 minutes away. The mix-up was due to the charter company scrambling to supply planes during the strike.

"I think Tony had a premonition after that," Pott told *Sports Illustrated* in 1995.

At the Akron airport, they encountered Fred Corcoran. Tony told Corcoran the original plane he rented had been double-booked forcing him to charter another. The two men bade farewell to each other and Tony and Betty quickly drove to the Akron-Canton airport. When he walked out on the tarmac where their substitute charter plane, a Beechcraft Bonanza 35 with the tail identification number N538B sat, he discovered his pilot was a woman, Mrs. Doris Mullen.

"Tony often said there were a lot of things he enjoyed doing with women," Pott told *Sports Illustrated*. "But flying was not one of them."

In the pre-feminist days of 1966, male chauvinism still reigned. At first, he refused to board the flight. After assurances that Miller was a qualified pilot, he boarded the small plane unenthusiastically.

"Wish us luck," he yelled back to friends.

Dr. George Bard, co-piloted the flight to log flight time. Mrs. Mullen was an attractive blonde mother of five children with approximately 2,000 hours of commercial flight time.

Tony struggled to get his tall frame comfortable on the bench seat as he and Betty fastened their seat belts and prepared for take-off.

Mrs. Mullen started the engine and the plane taxied down the runway before taking off and heading north by northwest towards the Chicago Hammond Airport near Lansing, Illinois along the Indiana state line.

Winters, hitchhiked to Crete, arriving the day before and was at the Holiday Inn, attending a reception for the tournament. In attendance at the reception were the celebrities of the pro-am tournament including Vince Lombardi, Illinois football Coach Pete Elliott, and retired boxer Joe Louis. In addition to Tony, other PGA players in the field included Butch Baird, Chi-Chi Rodriguez, Dean Refram, and Charlie Sifford.

Fred Corcoran was a passenger on another private plane heading in the opposite direction. After talking with Tony at the Akron airport, Corcoran had just enough time to talk with a reporter and expressed concerns about the pace the golf pros traveled.

"It's a wonder we don't get a lot of them killed," Corcoran observed. "That Palmer flies around in his own jet, and he told me the other day it didn't go fast enough for him anymore."

As the Beechcraft made its approach to the Hammond airport, Mrs. Mullen's husband, Dr. Mullen, who was waiting, spotted the plane. The plane made a swing around the airfield and then he watched in horror as the engines cut out while the plane was over the Lansing Sportsmen's golf course that abutted the airport.

Small plane pilots learn in training to switch from the gas tank used for the flight to a second reserve tank for landing. Mrs. Mullen became confused as to which tank she was using and failed to make the switch to the full reserve tank. She then began to panic and radioed the tower.

"I'm being forced down," she frantically relayed.

She gave no reason for the emergency landing.

The engines sputtered to life shortly before again falling silent. The engines, starved of gas, cut out completely. Mrs. Mullen surveyed the ground below assessing her options for putting the plane down in an emergency landing. A few eyewitness accounts maintained she swerved to avoid a group of people standing near the clubhouse while others claimed she went into evasive actions to avoid an angler on a small lake. Tony and Betty, both very much accustomed to plane travel, albeit on large jetliners, grew concerned as they watched the situation develop. Tony may even have started to finger his religious medal while saying a Hail Mary.

Mrs. Mullen attempted to put the plane down on the golf course with her intended landing spot the seventh fairway and green just short of a lake separating the golf course from the airport. As she came in for the emergency landing she caught a wingtip on the ground, and the plane dug a furrow in the fairway, near the green. The distressed plane hit a mound between the golf course and the lake, flipping the plane so that it entered the lake nose first.

The impact caused the highly explosive gas to ignite much to the horror of the many onlookers at the golf course. Some rushed from the clubhouse towards the flaming wreckage to see if they could be of some assistance. It was obvious there was nothing anybody could do as flames fully engulfed the plane.

Firefighters from the Lansing, Illinois, fire department arrived and went to work extinguishing the fire. For reasons unknown, the four bodies remained in the wreckage for hours.

Around 7 p.m., a person approached Max Winters, eating in the coffee shop at the Holiday Inn. The person claimed something had happened to Tony's plane, that there had been an accident. Winters quickly returned to the reception and found Jack Brown of Buick.

"Son, there's been an accident," Brown slowly said to the young man. "Tony and his wife were killed."

Winters felt his whole body begin to shake and tremble. He dashed from the reception, sobbing, out into the motel parking lot. Hysterically he threw himself over the hood of a parked car. Shortly, Pete Elliott, the coach of the University of Illinois football team, came out and found Winters. He helped Winters up from where he had collapsed and helped him to somewhat compose himself.

The two walked back into the now subdued reception filled with shocked people. Winters made a few phone calls attempting to find out details of the crash before going to the open bar where he grabbed a full bottle of scotch and began drinking heavily in an attempt to drown his sorrows.

The news of the crash, and Tony and Betty's death, reached many of the players who had already arrived in Columbus for the Nicklaus pro-am.

"Oh, my God!" exclaimed Nicklaus, who had to deal with the shocking news of a death of a friend in a small airplane crash for the second time in 1966. His friend Bob Barton and his wife Linda perished in a plane crash on the way to watch Nicklaus in the Masters.

"What a terrible thing. Tony was one of the real great guys on the tour," he said.

"I'm just extremely shocked and upset about the whole thing," Arnold

Palmer said. "I knew Tony when he was just starting to play. We traveled a great deal together. He was a great guy and this is a great loss to the game."

Sam Snead said, "It's a shame. He was in the prime of his life. Tony was very popular with the players."

Back in Akron, Venturi returned from dinner to his hotel and went to the front desk to pick up his room key.

"It's too bad about that golfer who got killed today," said the woman behind the counter.

Venturi did not have to ask her who had died; he somehow knew it was Tony.

Max Elbin, president of the PGA, and Lee Frasher, secretary, released a statement to the press.

"The PGA has lost one of its most glamorous stars," the statement began. "He was a great inspiration to the younger tournament players and was a great attraction to the galleries. He stimulated interest in the game among players and non-players alike."

Butch Baird made it into Chicago, on the ticket Tony arranged for him, very late and caught a cab into town to a hotel. He went to bed preparing for his early morning tee time in the Lincolnshire Open the next day. Unaware of the accident or that Refram received information there was a "Bard" on-board and misheard it as "Baird," he fell asleep. Refram retired for the night believing he had lost two friends in the accident.

In San Leandro, Harry Lema and his wife, Judi, put their 18-month-old son Roger down to bed and settled in to watch television around 7:30 p.m. With her newest born child, six-month-old Ryan in her arms, Judi sat in a rocking chair as the couple tuned in "Voyage to the Bottom of the Sea." A news bulletin soon interrupted the program.

"We are interrupting our broadcast to bring you a bulletin from our West Coast newsroom," the report began. "Professional golfer, Tony Lema and his wife were killed in a small plane crash."

Harry and Judi sat stunned before Judi rose from the rocker and put Ryan in his crib, instructing Harry he had to go right then to his mother. Neither Harry nor Judi wanted Cleo to hear the news on television as they just did. Harry did not want to leave Judi alone.

Judi told him, "Just GO!"

Harry made the two-block drive to Cleo's house.

Shortly after Harry left the house, the phone rang with Danny Arnold from Los Angeles on the other end. He was not sure if Judi had heard the news, or not, so he treaded lightly as the conversation began. Judi informed Arnold they had just seen the news on television. She also told Arnold that she did not know anything other than what she heard on the news bulletin.

Arnold promised her he would call a friend on the Associated Press desk to see if he could find any more details, but called back a few minutes later to say he could not find any further information. Judi arranged for a relative to come over and watch the two children so that she could go over to Cleo's house.

Meanwhile, Cleo and her houseguests were spending time in the garden. She heard the phone ring and rushed into the house to answer it. Her hairdresser was on the other end of the line.

"Are you alone?" her hairdresser asked her.

Cleo told her that no, she had company.

"Okay," the hairdresser began, "Sit down, I have something to tell you."

The hairdresser then gave her the heartbreaking news that her youngest son and his wife perished in a plane crash.

Later, Judi told Harry she was sorry that he was not the one to tell Cleo about the accident.

"How was I supposed to tell her that her Tony was gone?" Harry could only say.

Bernice, Tony's sister, had gone with her son Marc on some errands. They returned home and her husband Art, told the two the news, which he heard on the television. Tony's other brother, Walt, heard the news on the radio in his car.

Jimmy Cline, Betty's brother found out about the accident the same way as the rest of Betty's family—from news reports on television and radio.

The next day, the Lema family gathered at Cleo's house to comfort one another. The press descended on the house in hopes of getting pictures and quotes from the grieving family. It became a chaotic scene as reporters and photographers jostled with each other for position with little regard for the family. The family hunkered down in Cleo's house, grief-stricken, while the press kept a vigil on the sidewalk outside.

The family made funeral arrangements over the next few hectic days while the transfer of the bodies from Indiana to California was completed.

At the crash site the wreckage, hauled out of the lake, was loaded on a truck from the Red Top Trucking Company. The company transported it to their lot in Hammond, Indiana where Civil Aeronautics Board investigator Noel Lawson planned a scrap-by-scrap analysis as part of his investigation on the cause of the accident.

On Monday, the Lincolnshire Open went on as planned. Tony's name remained on the scoreboard as a tribute to him. Harry Field, manager of the tournament felt that Tony would have wanted them to continue with the event.

"We were having a meeting of some of the tournament players when the news came in," Field said. "It was a tremendous shock. But, we decided to go ahead with plans to hold the tourney and dedicate it to Tony. We left Tony's name on the scoreboard. We didn't even print in that he did not start. Just his name among the others and a blank after it."

Winters switched to Chi Chi Rodriguez's bag and suffered through the 36-holes in sweltering 95-degree heat attempting to deal with his sorrow and the aftereffects of his scotch binge the night before. Rodriquez finished second in the event and talked with the press.

"I loved that man," Rodriguez said about Tony. "I cried like a baby Sunday night. Nothing has hit me like this since my father died. He'd have been flying a big, commercial plane if it wasn't for the airline strike."

Rodriguez actually identified the bodies for the authorities using Tony's personal possessions including his golf bag and a briefcase. Lake County, Indiana, officials the next day revealed they found in the briefcase over $19,000 in traveler's checks, a 50 Pound Scotland note, and 1,000 Pounds in English and Irish notes.

Earlier that day, Refram had arrived at the course and was making his way to the practice tee when he stopped dead in his tracks. There stood Baird whom he believed went down in the accident the day before. Baird found out about the accident when he saw the headlines in his hotel lobby that morning.

"All I knew is I saw a ghost out there," Refram told Baird once the shock of seeing his friend alive had worn off.

The one-day event in Columbus went on as scheduled on Monday at Scioto.

"I'm sure Tony would have wanted it to go on," Nicklaus said.

The players observed a moment of silence in honor of Tony before play began. After the tournament, Arnold Palmer flew his private jet to Oshkosh, Wisconsin, to attend a banquet for a group of golf course maintenance products representatives. Palmer flew his plane over the exact spot where Tony's plane attempted to crash land.

"Tony was my great friend," Palmer told the dinner attendees. "His death Sunday night was among pro golf's most tragic incidents. I am extremely sad."

At dawn on Tuesday, Harry and Walter, along with their brother-in-law Art, waited at a cargo air terminal at the San Francisco International Airport as a jetliner delivered the bodies of Tony and Betty. They oversaw the transfer of the coffins to the Santos-Robinson Mortuary in San Leandro. The San Leandro City Council ordered flags to fly at half-mast until the entombment of Tony and Betty's bodies.

Funeral arrangements, hurriedly made, called for a Rosary at St. Leander's Church, the same church where Tony and Betty exchanged marriage vows, on Wednesday night at 8 p.m. The following day, at 10 a.m. the funeral, a Requiem Mass of Concelebration, would be at the St. Elizabeth Church next door to Tony's high school. The family asked that in lieu of flowers, they would rather have condolences expressed in contributions to the Hanna Boys Center in Sonoma, California.

PGA president Max Elbins named Tommy Jacobs, chair of the PGA tournament committee, the representative of the PGA at the funeral. The family also named Jacobs as one of the pallbearers at the funeral. Other pallbearers included Ken Venturi, Fred Corcoran, and John Fry. Bob McCaffery who played golf with Tony as a youth and was now a pro at an indoor driving range in San Francisco and Augie Bentes, owner of a clothing store in San Leandro and a close friend of Tony's also served as pallbearers. Bill Craig, a friend since the two were schoolboys, and who served with Tony in the Marines, Jack Vincent and Dr. Francis Rasche, associates of Tony's in the San Leandro travel agency, Ed Schoenfeld, the sportswriter for *The Oakland Tribune* and Danny Arnold rounded out the list of pallbearers.

Eight priests, all who knew and loved Tony, many having played golf with him, would share in the offering of the Mass at the funeral. They included Monsignor John Silva, Reverend Harold Pearce, Reverend Roch Fitzgerald, Reverend George Monaghan, Reverend Campion Welsh, Reverend Ken Hunt, Reverent James Keely and Reverend Joseph Ferreira. Every effort made to locate Father Durkin to deliver the eulogy fell short. Reverend Monaghan, at St. Elizabeth during Tony's student days, would deliver the eulogy.

Wednesday's papers were full of the reminiscences of Tony's many friends. Everybody had a Tony Lema story to pass on that illustrated his extraordinary life.

"This wasn't one of the graduates who became very successful and came back to his old school puffed up about it," Father Campion Welsh, a priest and golf coach at St. Elizabeth, related. "Tony Lema was a sincere friend who came by whenever he was off the tour. He not only gave the boys a lesson, but left several dozen golf balls, golf shirts, a shag bag and passes to see the Lucky Open."

"It's very tough," Venturi said. "Like brothers, we'd fight and make up. Tony was 100 percent on my side when I was down. He was the only one who went around before the 1964 Open and told writers that I would win it. In fact, the first call I had when I got back to my room after winning the Open was from Tony. In my entire life, one of the few men I would give the key to my front door would be Tony."

Those who knew Tony in Elko spoke about his days there as the head pro at Ruby View Golf Course.

"I knew him as a kid," Peter Marich, manager of the Washoe County

Golf Course in Reno said. "Then as a player in the mountain tournaments, and later when he became a great star. He was one of the few big-time stars who never forgot his old friends. He had a cheerful greeting whenever he saw you during the tour. He always invited me to play a friendly game."

Nearly every paper in the country ran tributes to Tony, and not only on the sports pages, but on the editorial pages, as well.

Omer Crane in the Fresno Bee wrote; "For Anthony (Tony) Lema we cannot recall of an unkind word or a critical paragraph while he played the game. Tony Lema was the Walter Hagen of this era."

On the editorial page of *The Oakland Tribune* a tribute ran that read, "Champagne Tony made thousands of friends in his all-too-brief career. But he was a special friend of the sports writers who wrote about him. He was never too busy for an interview and his flamboyant personality made him a sentimental favorite with many of the writers who cover the golf tour.

"Success never spoiled him. He never forgot those friends who helped him early in his career and his many private charities for under-privileged youth were his way of acknowledging his own humble background."

In Gastonia, North Carolina, a town that fell in love with Tony after he gave an exhibition, the local paper, *The Gastonia Gazette*, wrote a tribute on its editorial page.

"On some people, the cloak of fame looks like it's two sizes too large. Not so for Champagne Tony, he wore it like it is supposed to be worn— with not much pomposity and a whole lot of winking of the eye."

The church at St. Elizabeth, just four blocks from Cleo's house, crammed to overflowing on Thursday morning as the Requiem High Mass began. The flower-covered coffins were positioned at the foot of the alter. Over 1,000 mourners, dressed in everything from mourning suits to work clothes, filled the church while hundreds of others stood in the vestibule, on the steps of the church and on both sides of the street outside the church.

The highly structured Mass was sung by the high priests as they began with the line *et lux perpetua luceat eis* (eternal rest grant unto them, O Lord, and let light perpetual shine upon them.)

Father George Monaghan said the golfer was a man with all the beautiful qualities of a boy who had an open heart for all.

"That is not unusual for a boy," the Father said, "But what is remarkable is that he carried this open heart into adulthood. He was always the same Tony. He married a girl with the same qualities—humble, simple in the good sense, and unassuming."

The Father said that Betty once told a priest, "Wherever Tony goes, I go."

"She went with him wherever he went, and they never parted, even in death."

Winters attended the funeral, although he had to scramble to find a flight to Los Angeles during the airline strike. He then rode a bus to Oakland. John Fry rode in the same limousine with Danny Arnold from the church in the long procession to the Holy Sepulchre Cemetery for the entombment.

"What a terrible waste," Arnold said. Nearly everyone at the service said, or thought, the same words at one time or another during the day. It was a waste of talent, of an effervescent life, of a loving couple.

The procession made its way slowly to the cemetery where Tony and Betty were entombed side-by-side in the mausoleum. A few friends and relatives of the Lema family went to Cleo's house after the ceremony.

Tony's interview with Howard Cosell was broadcast a week after the accident. Ken Venturi provided the introduction for the broadcast and touched on his relationship before informing viewers about Tony's tragic plane crash. After Venturi's introduction, the camera switched to a shot of Cosell and Dave Marr sitting at an outdoor table. They talked about Tony's career and the circumstances surrounding the interview. The interview then runs in its entirety.

Sister Mary Martin wrote a eulogy in the Catholic Monitor, which was subsequently reprinted in *The Oakland Tribune* on July, 29.

"Most of the fine qualities of Tony's character can be traced to his religious background. Tony had great faith. It came from the heart, and he was not afraid to tell others about his faith. In a letter to Father Monaghan he wrote, 'God has been very good to me and I am a firm believer in the power of prayer. It has always been the 15th club in my bag. I am deeply grateful for my Catholic background. Without it, I would never have stayed out of jail.

"It seems like 200 years since you gave me that talking to at St. Louis Bertrand when I was still in grade school," Tony went on. "An awful lot of things have happened, both good and bad. I only wish on the final day the good will offset the bad and I can go to where the fairways are lush and the greens very smooth."

Father Joseph A. Ferreira, assistant at San Leander's Church once invited Tony to be the guest of honor at a teen club Communion and breakfast. Tony went to Mass and Communion with the youngsters, and spoke to them later at breakfast.

"Kids, if I am what I am today, it is because of my faith. Fame and money will never give you peace and happiness, but faith in God will. Love and respect your priests and your parents. Mom and dad come next to God. Yes, I play golf, but the bigger game is the faith. You have to fight for it.'"

Tony fought for the faith that, along with the love of Betty, saved him and inspired him to be one of the greatest, and most colorful, players of the game. His family, friends and golf fans around the world, both present and future, lost one of the brightest lights of his era on tour. His premature death deprived his fans the joy and exuberance that he brought to the game, and to life. His easy flamboyance and style could never be replaced, nor could his humor, generosity and kindness.

EPILOGUE

While doing color commentary for ABC Television at the Western Open in Chicago in the early 1990s, a fan approached Bob Rosburg.

"Do you remember that sudden-death playoff you had with Tony Lema at the Orange County Open in 1962?" the fan asked.

"Oh, I remember it like it was yesterday," Rosburg answered.

"Well, I was a marine at Camp Pendleton and I was at the tournament with a few of my buddies. We were walking around, having a few beers, and we were pulling for Tony because he was an ex-marine. That drive on the first hole was out-of-bounds; we kicked it back in."

The pain of losing the tournament long since worn off, Rosburg simply chuckled at the story. As he later recounted, he was able to laugh it off since the difference between first and second-place amounted to only $500.

"It would have been nice to win that tournament, though," he admitted more than 40 years later.

One has to wonder, though, if it was not for those marines if there would have ever been a Champagne Tony Lema.

Rosburg approached the matter from a different direction. He felt he had to say something to the fan. Therefore, he related what Tony told him before the final round at the Orange County. At that time, Tony informed Rosburg that if he did not win the tournament, which he was leading, he was going to give up the tour and take a head pro job at a club.

"You know," Rosburg continued to the fan. "If you had not kicked his ball back in, he would probably still be alive."

He then walked away from the stunned fan.

Tony and Betty were entombed, side-by-side as they were in life, in the mausoleum at the Holy Sepulchre Cemetery in Hayward. As one enters the mausoleum, brightly lit from stained-glass skylights, they find the markers a little more than halfway down the center aisle, at eye level. There, chiseled in the marble, reads; "Anthony D. Lema" on the lightly colored stone next to the stone bearing the inscription, "Betty Lema".

Below their names are the dates of their birth separated by a dash from July 26, 1966, the date of their deaths. However, their lives were not about their birthdates, or July 26, 1966, but all about the dash between the two dates. The dash contained all the wonders of the life they led.

Against all odds, Tony navigated through the rough waters of growing up without a father and the inevitable drifting that incurred. His youth was wild and troubled, yet under the exterior of a rough and tumble boy beat a good and kind heart. Golf literally saved him, the game giving him a tangible task at hand while providing various father figures and mentors to help him.

These father figures included Lucius Bateman, a black man who, despite the racial inequities of the times, found the time and love to pass on valuable lessons about the game to Tony at an impressionable age.

Dick Fry, with his own son to nurture, still found the time to teach Tony. He also kept Tony busy as a caddy, making it possible to meet such men as Lou Moschetti, Bob Doten, and Frank McCaffery. Later, he provided Tony with odd jobs to do around the course and pro shop, keeping him out of the kind of trouble he found all too easily.

John Geerston, by giving him his first assistant pro job at San Francisco Golf Club, a club with an exclusive, and well-to-do membership, gave Tony the polish that helped make him a star on the PGA Tour. Tony learned that elusive thing we call style during his time at the San Francisco Golf Club.

The friends that Tony made so easily, especially upon his departure from San Francisco to Elko, would never forget him. A more loyal friend would be impossible to find. Don Bilboa, the owner of the Stockman's Hotel and Casino in Elko considered him a friend and allowed Tony to head off to the tour with his gambling debts covered by an I.O.U. Tony faithfully paid off the I.O.U. with his first earnings from the PGA Tour.

Cliff Whittle, a fellow golf pro who played on the intermountain circuit with him during his Elko days, as did Jim Chenoweth, another fellow pro considered themselves friends. These two men introduced Tony to Jim Malarkey, his benefactor who allocated the financial means for him to play on the pro golf tour.

The other players on the PGA Tour did not know just how to take Tony at first, but it was not long before he made friendships that lasted the rest of his life.

"Most of us didn't understand Tony when he first joined the tour," his friend Tommy Jacobs said. "But we learned we were just taking him the wrong way. We found he was a great guy."

His travels on the tour spanned the car caravan days to the jet age. The tour invaded cities for a week and, in many cases, provided the only major league sporting event available to the local fans. The explosion in prize money, due to corporate sponsorship and television money occurred during Tony's time on tour. Tony was at the forefront of the colorful players fans flocked to see play.

He truly felt a friend of every player on tour. In his era, the players traveled, dined, and drank together, sans the entourages that accompany today's pros. Comfortable with the superstars such as Arnold Palmer, Jack Nicklaus, Gary Player and Billy Casper, he was equally at ease with lesser-known pros such as Butch Baird, Frank Beard, and Chi Chi Rodriguez.

Palmer especially befriended Tony soon after he came out on tour and offered help in many ways, as the two men grew quite close.

Marc Matoza, Tony's nephew remembers that, "Arnie had a soft spot in his heart for Tony."

Friendships he forged during his two stints on the Caribbean Tour with the likes of Ernie Vossler and Don Whitt would last him the rest of his life.

For Tony, corporate and tournament sponsors quickly transitioned from business acquaintances into close person friends. Caddies who worked for him, none more so than Max "Jerry" Winters, became members of the family.

Tony was forever indebted to tour caddy Wally Heron who helped him over the hump to his first official victory in Orange County. Tip Anderson, pivotal in his victory in the British Open, always received full credit from Tony for contributing to his winning the Claret Jug.

Tony met and befriended very important people, including Danny Arnold, the Hollywood producer that became a member of the extended Lema family. He provided love and assistance to not only Tony, but also the rest of the Lema clan.

Fred Corcoran, became his business manager, but grew to be so much more, providing Tony with business advice, friendship and love. Corcoran instilled in Tony the kind of confidence he required to break through into superstardom and achieve the kind of year he had in 1964 when he captured his one and only major championship.

Tony could comfortably hobnob with celebrities from Hollywood all the way up to royalty. The time spent with the Duke of Windsor, his audience with the Pope and meeting the prime minister of England during the Ryder Cup came easily to Tony. His friendships with James Garner, Danny Kaye, Phil Harris, Bing Crosby, and Howard Cosell proved he could hang with the Hollywood types as well.

The press surely loved him and it was not just because of the occasional free champagne he provided them. He was a colorful personality that always provided great copy and even better quotes. He always had time for reporters even meeting them in steam rooms as he did with Murray Olderman. He would share car rides, or breakfast as he did with the United Press International reporters Milton Richman and Leo Peterson. He thought nothing of picking up the telephone to talk with favorite reporters such as Ed Schoenfeld of *The Oakland Tribune*.

Even the acerbic Howard Cosell was not immune to his charm and he considered Tony a close friend inviting him into his home to stay and spend time with his family. The press corps in the United Kingdom fell in love with the "Jolly Yank."

However, he was just as happy to spend time alone with Betty. Leaving behind the hectic lifestyle of hotels and restaurants, he and Betty preferred to rent an apartment near the tournament site where they spent quiet evenings. Betty prepared dinner and they passed their time in the evenings playing dominoes and gin. For Tony, home was on the road.

It was finding true love with Betty that really turned his life around fulfilling it in ways he probably never imagined. It was no coincident that his career took off into the stratosphere at the same time the two fell in love. Moreover, it was a love that continued to grow as they jumped around the country, and the world, pursuing his career.

As with any person, he was not perfect. He could be quiet, dark, and moody. If he was in one of his dark moods, he could be gruff with an answer to a question. Once asked by a reporter if "Lema" was a Portuguese name he gave a brusque answer.

"It's an American name," Tony growled in response.

Money was never far from his mind, but to be fair, in an occupation where money is the means of keeping score, it consumed him to the same degree as any of his fellow players, especially the superstars.

He was a master of the art of manipulation when it came to his image in the press. His Champagne Tony image was the epitome of this image control. Champagne was not his drink of choice during an evening out; he actually preferred scotch and soda with a twist of lemon. But the wine provided him a unique niche that he capitalized on. He became quite knowledgeable about champagne after visiting Moet and observing up close the méthode champenoise process that creates a secondary fermentation in the bottle providing the bubbles. He became a respected spokesperson for the champagne industry even winning the "Salesman of the Year" industry award in 1964.

Sportswriters ignored his youthful indulgences while watching him mature into a graceful superstar. In an era when the press and players enjoyed close relationships, less intrusive and combative than today's press and athletes, this image control was recognized and condoned. Tony and reporters shared actual friendships spending time socially over the occasional cocktail. No other golfer, except possibly Arnold Palmer, enjoyed as great a relationship with the press.

A couple of weeks after his death, his first wife, now remarried, Shirley

Kozy, announced plans to dispute his will that excluded David Lema, the son that she alleged was Tony's. Tony had taken the step of removing David from the will once he learned that he had become sterile. Attorney William G. Webb of Dallas, executer of the will, informed the press that the only heirs were Cleo and Betty's mother.

Since the divorce from Kozy in 1962, Tony had paid child support payments of $75 per month, which shortly before his death increased to $250. Kozy told the press that he never missed a child support payment. She also told *The San Francisco Examiner* Tony was very proud of his son and visited often, although she may have been saying this to bolster her claims on his will.

In 2018 the Lema family conducted DNA testing to determine if David was, in fact, Tony's son. David's DNA was compared with Tony's sister, Bernice, and brother Walter. The test on Walter's DNA showed less than a 6% family match while the test done on Bernice showed less than a 3% family match proving, once and for all, that Tony was not David's father.

Tony and Betty executed mutual wills naming each other as beneficiaries of their estate. Assets included a trust fund established by Tony that he funded with $15,000 a year, and the property in Twain Harte, his mountain retreat. The 7.45-acre parcel was valued at $11,000, and Tony did not live to see the completion of the cabin constructed on the land.

The Lema estate filed a $3 million damage suit against the Joliet Air Charter Service and Mainline Aviation, Inc. The suit charged negligence in the accident and an out-of-court settlement awarded the estate $65,000 including $250 a month to David Lema.

For the most part, despite a few mistakes, Tony lived his life along the lines of his goal stated to Howard Cosell in their lengthy television interview. All he desired in the way of posterity was the recognition that he was a "decent guy" and those who came to know him all agree that is exactly what he achieved.

He exhibited vast generosity to his family, friends and the underprivileged. He sent Cleo an allowance that more than covered her living expenses. Even so, she continued to work up into her eighties, continuing on in the industrious and strong willed life she had led, and which was so instrumental in Tony's upbringing and character.

The tributes continued to appear in the weeks and months following his death. In August, the San Leandro City Council proposed naming a new golf course in the planning in his honor.

"Tony Lema always played out of San Leandro, so it seems only natural that we should name our course in his honor," said Mayor Jack D. Maltester.

The Tony Lema course at Monarch Bay, along the water in San

Leandro, plays host to thousands of recreational golfers to this day.

The Variety Club of Britain Golfing Society announced that it would award a perpetual trophy in Tony's name. He played an exhibition with Peter Alliss benefiting the society's fund for handicapped children in Kingswood in 1966. One of the balls Tony used while winning his British Open in 1964 at St. Andrews adorned the new trophy awarded to the winners of the Society's annual pro-am tournament.

On July 30, ABC's Wide World of Sports show paid tribute to Tony. At the end of August, American flags flew at half-staff over the clubhouse at Royal Birkdale during the play of the Carling World Open in his memory. In October, the Bermuda Open Golf Championship announced the awarding of the Tony Lema Memorial Trophy to the winner of the tournament.

In January of 1967, Shell Oil aired the match between Tony and Peter Alliss, played at the Mid-Ocean Golf Club in Bermuda. Before deciding to air the match, Shell had consulted Cleo.

"Naturally," Cleo told the Shell people in a letter "use Tony's match. Tony wouldn't want it any other way."

In February of 1968, the unveiling of a bust of Tony occurred at the first Tony Lema Memorial Tournament at Marco Island, the course where he served as head pro at the time of his death. The tournament field included many of his friends including Gene Sarazen, Sam Snead, Ken Venturi, Chick Harbert, Ray Floyd, and amateurs John Brodie and Mickey Mantle. Proceeds from the tournament benefited the Hanna Boys Center in Sonoma, California, one of his pet charities.

Monsignor William O'Conner, director of the boy's center unveiled the bust during a brief ceremony. After removing the cloth covering the bust, the Monsignor looked at Tony's likeness for a lengthy time and swallowed hard.

"This is a sad occasion for me," he began. "But at least the boys at the center will profit from this day and I know that would make Tony happy. His father died when he was quite young and he often told me he could have easily wound up in a place like ours if it hadn't been for his fine mother."

Frank Mackle, Jr., who ran Marco Island, spoke about his employee.

"He told me he planned to put in only a few more years on the golf tour and that he'd quit as soon as he and Betty had children. He had even picked out a lot here where he was going to build his house."

Tony had been extremely happy with his arrangement at Marco Island, and was eager to extend the contract at the end of its term.

"Put whatever number of years you want in the contract," he told Mackle. "As far as I'm concerned it's for life."

The pros also played a one-day fund raising event in his honor following the Tournament of Champions. Proceeds from this event funded a scholarship fund that in November of 1967 awarded three, four-year scholarships.

The California Golf Hall of Fame voted Tony for induction in April of 1967. Honored at a dinner at the Los Altos Golf and Country Club, put on by the California golf writers, E. Harvie Ward accepted Tony's enshrinement "on behalf of Tony, Betty and the entire family."

In the fall of 1968, Lee Trevino, the new U.S. Open champion, dedicated the Tony Lema Champagne Room at the Mesa Verde Golf Course. Tony scored his first official PGA tour victory there in 1962 and his champagne celebration with the press ushered in the Champagne Tony era.

Tony's accident, like all accidents, was avoidable. A plane running out of gas is simply a tragic human error.

The Civil Aeronautics Board team investigating the crash divulged that, "It's very unusual for both engines of a twin-engine aircraft to quit together; we suspect a fuel shortage."

The Beechcraft Bonanza 35 has a fuel capacity of 44-gallons and a range of 779 miles. The roundtrip flight from Joliet to Akron, approximately 640 miles, was well within the range of the aircraft, if the tank was full.

So how did the plane run out of fuel? Most likely, Mrs. Mullen made an error in changing from one fuel tank to another. When switching from the empty fuel tank to the full reserve, she may have become confused and then panicked.

The fact that the plane ran out of gas so close to the airport where they intended to land makes the accident all the more heartbreaking. For the want of a couple pints of gas, Tony Lema would have made a routine landing and gone on living his charmed life.

"He had it all," his friend Bobby Nichols recalled recently. "He drove the ball long and straight, hit his irons well and he could putt. If he had lived, he would have gone on to win many more tournaments."

Still, he had stated shortly before his death that he only wanted to play on the tour for a few more years. He intended to retire from the tour and start a family with Betty.

He and Betty loved kids and deeply desired to have a family. Whether he would have found a solution to his sterility problem, or the couple would pursue adoption, no one will ever know. It is certain that they would have found a way to start, and raise a family.

He also had a great desire to add another major championship to his resume. He wanted to win the Masters and the U.S. Open and he definitely had the game to win either one. He came tantalizing close to capturing both championships, first the 1963 Masters, finishing one stroke back of the winner Jack Nicklaus and then in the 1963 U.S. Open when two pars on the finishing holes would have gotten him into the playoff, eventually won by Julius Boros.

What would have become of him after his playing days were through? It is hard to imagine Tony completely settling down at some club pro job, he had to keep moving, had to keep busy. A job as a pro at a club more than likely would have grown old quickly for him.

A much more likely scenario would have him working for a television network doing the color commentary at tour golf events, as his friends Ken Venturi, Byron Nelson, and Dave Marr did. The schedule would be light enough for him to be at home with Betty, while still providing enough travel and interaction with the players to keep him busy. He already did some work for ABC and was quite comfortable behind a microphone and in front of a camera. His quick wit would have added a great deal of flavor to the broadcasts, and he would have been an asset to a broadcast either in the tower or as an on-course commentator like Bob Rosburg became.

Of course, his business interests would have kept him busy after retirement, as well. The trouble with the "what ifs" that follow a tragic accident is that we will never know the answers.

Arnold Palmer never captured another major championship after his collapse at the 1966 U.S. Open at the Olympic Club in San Francisco, though he did contend in a few. However, his well-documented career ranks with the finest in the sport and he remains one of the most loved athletes of all time.

Palmer passed away on September 25, 2016 in Pittsburg, PA at the age of 87, five days before the start of the 2016 Ryder Cup. His bag from the 1975 Ryder Cup where he was the captain stood in a prominent position at the back of the first tee in his memory.

Jack Nicklaus went on to become the finest golfer of his era, if not the finest golfer of all time. He went on to add 12 major victories after Tony's death including an amazing win in the 1986 Masters at the age of 46. He battled against Lee Trevino, and later, Tom Watson amassing his record eighteen major championships victories.

After leaving the PGA Tour, Nicklaus went on to play the Champions Tour from 1990 to 1996 where he won ten times. He has designed and built courses all around the world and owns a golf equipment manufacturing company in Florida, where he resides.

Gary Player continues to travel the world as an ambassador for golf to this day. His penchant for physical fitness served him well as he continues to play competitively into his 70s. He played in the 2009 Masters for a record 52 appearances in the celebrated tournament, even breaking 80, at

72 years of age, in the first round. He is the only player from the 20th century to have won the British Open title in three different decades.

He currently designs courses and keeps up a hectic travel schedule from his ranch in South Africa.

Billy Casper went on to add the Masters to his major championship record in 1970. He finished his regular tour career with 51 PGA tour victories before moving onto the Champions Tour where he logged another nine wins including the U.S. Senior Open in 1983 and the Mazda Senior Tournament Players Championship in 1988. He played on eight Ryder Cup teams and captained another. In 2000, *Golf Digest* ranked Casper as the 15th greatest golfer of all time.

Casper designed courses and was actively involved with the Mormon Church doing charitable work and hosting fundraisers before passing away in 2015.

Ken Venturi retired from CBS after a 35-year career as a color commentator in 2002. He finished his career with 14 victories on the tour with his last victory coming at the Lucky International in 1966. He never recovered from his hand condition, eventually diagnosed as carpal tunnel syndrome. The condition, finally alleviated after a number of surgeries, kept him from competing at a high level and he retired from the tour in 1967. He went to work for CBS upon his retirement. He passed away on May 17, 2013 in Rancho Mirage, California.

Doug Sanders never managed to win a major championship, although he came very close. Needing just two putts at the finishing hole at St. Andrews to win the 1970 British Open, he lagged his first putt up to 30-inches from the cup. He assumed his stance over the short putt, stepped with his left foot to pick up a piece of dirt from his line and then returned his foot to his stance. He then came up and out of his putt missing it to the right. He reached out his putter as if to rake the ball back and stroke the putt again, much like the hacker who wants a "do over." He lost the 18-hole playoff to Nicklaus the next day by a stroke.

He won 20 PGA titles with the last one coming at the 1972 Kemper Open. He added the 1983 World Senior Invitational as his sole Champions Tour victory. Sanders was one of the few players who was even more colorful than Tony as he enjoyed his pastel color outfits complete with custom made matching shoes, the women and his liquor. Today he runs a golf corporate entertainment company.

Johnny Pott won his last PGA tour event at the 1968 Bing Crosby National Pro-Am. His career total of PGA tour victories is five and he was a member of three Ryder Cup teams. He retired from the PGA tour in 1972. Today, he is the executive vice president of Landmark Golf, a real estate company in Indian Wells, California that specializes in golf course real estate development. Pott is in charge of design and development for the number of excellent courses the firm has designed and built.

Tommy Jacobs last won on the PGA Tour at the 1964 Palm Springs Golf Classic and has four wins on tour in his career. After retiring from the tour, he became the head pro at La Costa Hotel Spa and The Farms Golf Club in Rancho Santa Fe, California. He played the Champions Tour from 1985 to 2003. In 1995, he formed a company that bought the Bel Air Greens golf course in Palm Springs, California and changed the name to Tommy Jacob's Bel Air Greens, a nine-hole, par-32 course. He went on to form a company that specializes in corporate golf outings.

Jim Ferree retired from the PGA Tour, played on the Champions tour, and now spends his time teaching the game on the lesson tee. He counts Rocco Mediate as a former student.

Phil Rodgers won the last of his five PGA Tour tournaments at the Buick Open in 1966. Diagnosed with chronic myelogenous leukemia in 2003, he controls the condition with medication. Rodgers became a much-respected teacher after retiring from the tour. He also played on the Champions Tour. He currently resides in La Jolla, California with his wife, Karen, in a bungalow full of memorabilia from his playing days.

Bobby Nichols went on to enjoy a lengthy career on the PGA Tour with his best year, as far as money won, in 1974 when he cashed checks that totaled $124,747. His only major title was the 1964 PGA Championship in Columbus, Ohio where his tournament record low score of 271 stood for 30 years. He totaled 11 PGA Tour wins with the last one coming in the 1974 Canadian Open.

Nichols played on the Champions Tour notching one victory in the 1989 Southwestern Bell Classic. He splits his time today between his hometown, Louisville, Kentucky, and Florida.

Fred Corcoran passed away in 1977 after induction into the World Golf Hall of Fame in 1975. Danny Arnold passed away in 1995. He was a double Emmy award winner with his most popular television show being "Barney Miller." Bob Rosburg passed away in 2009 after a lengthy battle with cancer. He worked for three decades for ABC television as the first on-course reporter making the term "he's got no chance" his trademark. Jim Malarkey passed away, date unknown.

Lucius Bateman died April 21, 1972 of a stroke and heart attack. His grave in Mountain View cemetery faces the Claremont Country Club.

Harry Lema passed away in July 2013, while Judi still resides in San Leandro, California not far from Tony's sister, Bernice and her husband Art. Walter resides in the Napa Valley of Northern California. Tony's nephew Marc Matoza resides in Florida. Jerry Winters resides in Illinois and is currently working on a book about his time spent with Tony.

Cleo passed away on the day of her wedding anniversary, in 2000, at the age of 90.

"It was almost like my father said, 'it is time to join me,' " Bernice says about her mother's death.

She continued to work well into her eighties. The beautiful, large yellow rose bush along her fence started from one of the roses that Tony sent her on his 32nd birthday, mysteriously died shortly after her death.

Fellow players from his era remember Tony as popular a player as he was, as do family and friends. But even the most devout golf fan under the age of forty knows little of his impact and history on the PGA Tour. This is due, in large part, to the failure to induct him into the World Golf Hall of Fame.

Tony qualifies for induction into the hall on three different levels—the Lifetime Achievement category, the International category and the Veteran's category. The Lifetime Achievement category recognizes individuals who have made major contributions to the game, the International ballot uses a point system for performance and the Veteran's category honors professionals or amateurs whose careers concluded at least 30 years prior to induction.

The only reason Tony does not qualify on the PGA Tour ballot is the requirement of 10 years of PGA Tour membership. The plane crash that killed him denied him the opportunity to fulfill this requirement. He fulfills every other requirement for placement on the PGA ballot. Payne Stewart's induction into the hall required an exemption from this 10-year requirement, and in Tony's case, the same route should be taken.

Tony's name appears on the ballot each year for induction into the World Golf Hall of Fame, but to date, he has not garnered enough votes for induction. Yet he has not received so few votes to result in his removal from the ballot. It takes at least 5% of the votes for a player to remain on the ballot.

As one of the most popular and colorful players on the PGA Tour during a time that the tour went through an explosive growth, much of the credit can be attributed to Tony and his style. His record during his all too brief career is exemplarily and more than enough to qualify him for the Hall of Fame. However, it was the style, flair and excitement he brought to fans that will make his induction seemingly inevitable.

ABOUT THE AUTHOR

Larry Baush has written extensively about craft beer in *The Pint Post, The Celebrator Beer News* and *All About Beer* and he was inducted into the inaugural class of The Beer Writers Hall of Fame at Portland Brewing Company. He has also written about golf equipment and golf course reviews for the PuetzGolf.com blog. He caddied professionally at the SAFECO Classic Championship on the LPGA Tour. Larry lives in Seattle, Washington with his wife Carol and their Cocker Spaniel, Arnie Pawmer. Larry carries a single digit handicap at Rainier Golf and Country Club.